THE REAL DOPE: SOCIAL, LEGAL, AND HISTORICAL PERSPECTIVES ON THE REGULATION OF DRUGS IN CANADA

Recent debate around the potential decriminalization of marijuana, along with a growing perception that illicit drug use is on the rise, has brought the role of the state in controlling intoxication to the forefront of public discussion. Until now, however, there has been little scholarly consideration of the legal and social regulation of drug use in Canada. In *The Real Dope*, Edgar-André Montigny brings together leading scholars from a diverse range of fields – including history, law, political science, criminology, and psychology – to examine the relationship between moral judgment and legal regulation.

Highlights of this collection include rare glimpses into how LSD, cocaine, and Ecstasy have historically been treated by authority figures. Other topics explored range from anti-smoking campaigns and addiction treatment to the relationship between ethnicity and liquor control. Readers will find intriguing links across arguments and disciplines, providing a much-needed foundation for meaningful discussion.

EDGAR-ANDRÉ MONTIGNY is an independent scholar and lawyer living in Toronto.

EDITED BY
EDGAR-ANDRÉ MONTIGNY

The Real Dope

Social, Legal, and Historical Perspectives on the Regulation of Drugs in Canada

UNIVERSITY OF TORONTO PRESS
Toronto Buffalo London

© University of Toronto Press Incorporated 2011
Toronto Buffalo London
www.utppublishing.com
Printed in Canada

ISBN 978-0-8020-9942-6 (cloth)
ISBN 978-0-8020-9655-5 (paper)

Printed on acid-free, 100% post-consumer recycled paper with
vegetable-based inks.

Library and Archives Canada Cataloguing in Publication

The real dope : social, legal, and historical perspectives on the regulation of drugs
in Canada / edited by Edgar-André Montigny.

Includes bibliographical references and index.
ISBN 978-0-8020-9942-6 (bound). – ISBN 978-0-8020-9655-5 (pbk.)

1. Drug control – Canada – History.   2. Drug abuse – Social aspects – Canada –
History.   3. Drug control – Social aspects – Canada – History.   4. Drugs – Law
and legislation – Canada – History.   5. Liquor laws – Canada – History.
6. Tobacco – Law and legislation – Canada – History.   I. Montigny, Edgar-André

HV5840.C3R42 2011   363.450971   C2011-900925-0

Greg Marquis, 'From Beverage to Drug: Alcohol and Other Drugs in 1960s–70s
Canada,' *Journal of Canadian Studies*, 39, no. 2 (2005): 57–79, copyright © 2005 *Journal
of Canadian Studies*, is reproduced with permission.

Jarrett Rudy, 'Unmasking Manly Smokes: Church, State, Governance, and the First
Anti-Smoking Campaigns in Montreal,' *Journal of the Canadian Historical Association*,
12 (spring 2001), copyright © 2001 Canadian Historical Association, is reproduced
with permission.

This book has been published with the help of a grant from the Canadian Federation
for the Humanities and Social Sciences, through the Aid to Scholarly Publications
Program, using funds provided by the Social Sciences and Humanities Research
Council of Canada.

University of Toronto Press acknowledges the financial assistance to its publishing
program of the Canada Council for the Arts and the Ontario Arts Council.

 Canada Council
for the Arts
Conseil des Arts
du Canada

 ONTARIO ARTS COUNCIL
CONSEIL DES ARTS DE L'ONTARIO

University of Toronto Press acknowledges the financial support of the Government
of Canada through the Canada Book Fund for its publishing activities.

In memory of
Edgar Joseph Montigny
(1927–2007)

Contents

Acknowledgments

This collection began as a fourth-year honours research paper for the University of Toronto, Faculty of Law, under the direction of Professor Lorraine Weinrib. In that paper, I explored something I had noticed earlier while teaching issues of race and immigration: a purely historical link, or so it seemed to me then, between a particular intoxicating substance and a particular unpopular new immigrant group and the subsequent criminalization of that substance. At the same time, as a teaching assistant for Professor Alan Young (Osgoode Hall Law School), I encountered Professor Young's ample legal scholarship on constitutional arguments against the criminalization of marijuana. I also worked with Professor Ed Morgan (University of Toronto, Law), assisting with test-case litigation. The case I worked on dealt with the recent criminalization of khat. I was struck by how hard it was to ignore the association of this relatively unknown drug with a new immigrant group and its rather hasty criminalization. It became obvious to me that the link between race and the criminalization of drugs may not be the purely 'historical artifact' I thought it was.

In exploring the issue further, I was exposed to numerous other provocative and interesting works on various aspects of the regulation of drugs in Canada. It also became increasingly clear that the public debate over the (de)criminalization of marijuana was making the use and regulation of drugs a hot current topic. I realized that there were relatively limited resources available to people who wished to explore these issues within a Canadian framework. Sources that offered both historical and modern perspectives on the issues were even more rare. While there were adequate materials dealing with Canadian responses to marijuana, tobacco, and alcohol, sources dealing with drugs such as heroin, cocaine, LSD, or modern 'club drugs' were few and far between. Certainly, it was nearly impossible to find material on more than one or two of these drugs in any one location. I was inspired to produce this collection to bring together a broad range of recent writing on as wide as range of drugs as possible. I wanted to explore the use and regulation of drugs in Canada from a variety of perspectives, offering in one location a healthy taste of the breadth and scope of Canadian writing on the topic and, in so doing, encouraging a more rational and informed debate on what has been a frequent topic of public discussion for several decades now.

I was encouraged and supported in this endeavour by a number of people. The contributors, of course, made a massive donation of time, talent, and energy. They had enough faith in the project (and me) to remain loyal and supportive throughout a long and sometimes frustrating process of funding applications and peer reviews. I appreciate their commitment. Without them there would be no collection.

Marcel Martel and Catherine Carstairs gave me the initial moral support I required to get started and played a crucial role in helping me turn my idea into an actual project, identifying potential contributors and defining the nature and scope of the collection. Marcel made possible a key step in the process when he organized and hosted a one-day conference at York University where the contributors were able to meet, present their work, and offer useful comments and advice to one another. Bringing together authors from across the country, who might otherwise have known each other only as e-mail addresses, was invaluable in helping to create bonds and a sense of belonging that made working together that much more rewarding.

Len Husband of the University of Toronto Press took on this project and patiently and efficiently helped to guide it through the various stages, making the process as smooth as possible, even when the occasional roadblock reared its head. I greatly appreciate the work of Len and the team at the University of Toronto Press. Anonymous reviewers offered their time and expertise, providing insightful critiques and suggestions, and editor Curtis Fahey added polish to the final product. The collection is stronger for their efforts. Despite the many obstacles and frustrations involved in producing a collection of this size, it was a worthwhile and enriching experience.

I dedicate this book to my father, who died just as I started work on it. He had spent over twenty years of his life as a policeman, much of that time in narcotics control. Although it did not manifest itself until much later, it is quite likely that the seed of my interest in the subject of drug regulation was planted in my childhood as my father proudly displayed newspaper articles about major drug busts he was involved in and I listened to his comments about what type of deviant and dangerous person would use illicit drugs. His views softened with time. When I began working on this book, I doubted very much that he would be impressed with the arguments presented here. Yet, during my last visit with him, when I mentioned that I was putting together a collection of articles on the regulation of drugs, he surprised me by saying: 'I hope some of them recommend a better way to deal with things – the way we did it before didn't work.' So perhaps he would have been impressed with this collection after all.

THE REAL DOPE: SOCIAL, LEGAL, AND HISTORICAL
PERSPECTIVES ON THE REGULATION OF DRUGS IN CANADA

Introduction

EDGAR-ANDRÉ MONTIGNY

The legal and social regulation of the consumption of drugs in Canada is a controversial topic with a complex history. Various versions of the Narcotic Control Act and, since 1996, the Controlled Drug and Substances Act[1] have dictated which narcotic and other substances are licit or illicit in Canada. Possessing, seeking, or obtaining a substance declared illicit by the act can result in severe penalties. Punishment for simple possession of marijuana can range from a fine of $1,000 and/or up to six months in prison to as long as seven years in prison. Trafficking in marijuana or opium can result in a potential life sentence.[2] It is clear that the law treats illicit drugs as serious threats to the health, welfare, and safety of Canadians, strictly prohibiting their use and potentially providing punishments more severe than those offered for a number of serious violent crimes. Assault, for instance, carries a maximum sentence of only five years. Even 'sexual assault with a weapon' or 'assault causing bodily harm' carry maximum sentences of fourteen and ten years respectively. There are in fact very few crimes that carry the potential for life imprisonment applicable to trafficking in opium or marijuana. If sentencing provisions are any indication of the potential threat that crimes are supposed to represent to the nation, simply possessing a drug such as marijuana is considered a substantial threat and trafficking in illicit drugs is assumed to represent a danger equal to murder, kidnapping, or high treason.

The penalties associated with illicit drugs would suggest that there is a clear and obvious distinction, visible to all, between the threats posed by illicit and licit drugs. However, this distinction is often difficult to see. A simple comparison between tobacco and marijuana makes this clear.

Throughout decades of debate over the use and regulation of drugs in Canada, tobacco has remained a legal substance. Aside from a few early attempts to regulate tobacco use,[3] and despite recent successes in that regard, there has never been any serious initiative to criminalize tobacco or impose upon users of the substance the type of punishments allotted to persons who use substances such as marijuana. This has been the case despite mounting evidence of the serious health risks tobacco poses to not only those who use the substance but non-users as well. On the contrary, many have fought against attempts to limit or regulate tobacco use in any way, claiming they have a 'right' to smoke.

If the dangers posed to the health of society have any impact on the decision to declare a substance illegal, tobacco should have been criminalized decades ago. It has been clear for some time that tobacco use is North America's leading cause of preventable death.[4] Smoking tobacco has been conclusively linked to heart disease, strokes, brain aneurisms, bronchitis, emphysema, and a variety of cancers. There are approximately 40,000 deaths a year from tobacco, or 100 deaths a day by some calculations.[5] Tobacco, because of its nicotine content, has been proven to create a potent addiction, very similar to that created by heroin or cocaine, substances banned by the Criminal Code on the basis of the danger their addictive properties represent to society.[6] Tobacco-related health-care costs amounted to $9.5 billion in Canada in 1992 alone. Yet the Supreme Court of Canada concluded in *RJR-Macdonald* that, even though 'the detrimental health effects of tobacco consumption are both dramatic and substantial, the government was justified in not criminalizing tobacco consumption.'[7] So, despite obvious health risks and costs, there is no obligation on Parliament to criminalize a drug such as tobacco on that basis.

Even if health risks justify the criminalization of a substance, there is ample evidence that at least some substances, such as marijuana, remain illegal in Canada despite the fact that they pose little or no obvious health risks, and certainly nowhere near the risks associated with tobacco. The most detailed examination of the medical evidence relating to marijuana on file with the Canadian court system was prepared for the Supreme Court of Canada's review of *Clay v. R.*, *Malmo-Levine v. R.*, and *Caine v. R.* The judges in *Clay* and *Caine* heard expert-opinion evidence from more than ten expert witnesses and five civilian witnesses on issues relating to the botanical, pharmacological, and medical aspects of cannabis. The trial judge in *Clay* found that the consumption of cannabis is relatively harmless compared to the so-called hard drugs including tobacco and alcohol, that cannabis is not an addictive substance, that there is no evidence of a casual relationship between cannabis use and criminality, and that cannabis does not make people more aggressive or violent. The British Columbia Court of Appeal concluded that there was no conclusive evidence demonstrating any risk to the users of marijuana.[8]

The more research is conducted on marijuana, the more evidence emerges that cannabis, rather than being harmful, may in fact have positive medical properties. A growing body of modern medical research confirms that cannabis has significant medical value in the treatment of glaucoma and as an anti-emetic to reduce nausea and vomiting from chemotherapy related to cancer treatments. Cannabis also has beneficial effects on patients with certain chronic neurological diseases such as multiple sclerosis, cerebral palsy, and spinal-cord injury. Moreover, cannabis has been found to slow the process of brain decay, suggesting that it may have a meaningful role to play in combating degenerative diseases such as Alzheimer's, Parkinson's, and Huntington's and motor-neurone diseases.[9]

Clearly, the criminal sanctions related to cannabis use or possession are entirely out of proportion to any threat the drug poses to most Canadians. This was recognized as early as 1972 by the federal commission of inquiry into the Non-Medical Use of Drugs (otherwise known as the Le Dain Commission). The Le Dain Commission concluded that the known, probable, and possible side effects of cannabis use did not justify the enforcement policies that were then, and are essentially still, in place. Internationally, at least nine government-sponsored reports have come to the same conclusion, namely that cannabis does not cause sufficient harm to the individual or society to justify resort to criminal sanctions.[10]

At the very least, the comparison between the treatment of tobacco and the treatment of marijuana suggests that the distinction between licit and illicit drugs has little to do with the actual harm or threat they represent to society, since at least some illegal substances pose little threat while some legal ones pose an obvious and significant threat. Laws that criminalize a rather harmless substance on the basis of the health or medical risk involved but leave citizens free to consume a particularly dangerous substance would seem to lack rationality.

It is the apparent irrationality of many aspects of the legal and social regulation of drug use in Canada that has stimulated scholars to explore the subject. Much of the writing in the area has sought to explain or at

least point out contradictions and irrationalities inherent in the regulation of drug use in this nation both in the informal, social sense and in
the legal context. Many authors have taken the stand that if, the 'threat'
posed to society by certain substances cannot be explained in medical terms, then it must be that other, perhaps 'unspoken,' fears have
constituted the justification for treating drugs like tobacco and marijuana so differently. Much of the controversy related to the regulation of
drug use stems from conflict between various ideals of the relationship
between the state and citizen and the extent to which the state can or
should curtail certain activities in the interests of promoting a particular
set of moral values. For this reason, the history of the regulation of drug
use provides an excellent arena in which to study how social values
become translated into policy, which groups in society have the greatest
influence over social values and policy, and the role of the media and
public opinion in the process. The essays in this collection touch on all
of these issues, offering but a sample of the scope of the subject. To put
the essays in context, it is best to provide a general overview of some of
the key themes dealt with in the historical literature on the regulation
of drug use in Canada.

Race, Ethnicity, and Drug Laws

Numerous authors have argued that early drug laws were essentially
racist in nature, targeting the use of certain substances for criminal sanction not because of the threat posed by the substance itself but because
of the perceived threat posed to society by the use of the substance by a
particular minority group. A number of authors have pointed out that
a full understanding of the origins of Canadian drug laws requires that
drug laws be placed within the context of the overall moral-reform campaign that was in progress at the time the first such laws were passed.[11]

Most of the work in this area has linked the development of drug
laws to the fears of the Canadian white Anglo-Saxon middle class during the latter decades of the nineteenth century and the early decades of
the twentieth century, when industrialization and immigration stimulated widespread concern over rapidly changing social conditions. A
varied group of religious, medical, and social reformers, often referred
to as moral reformers, campaigned on several fronts to put in place a
wide range of laws, by-laws, and regulations to curb what they saw as a
moral decline caused largely by the increasing numbers of non-Anglo-
Saxon immigrants in their midst.

The basic problem, as the moral reformers saw it, was that non-Anglo-Saxon immigrants were of a lower overall genetic quality and, therefore, less intelligent and less able to control or regulate their desires and passions. This meant that they would be inclined towards immorality. At the very least, it was argued that Anglo-Saxons had a basic understanding of right and wrong and were able generally to contain their behaviour within accepted limits. Immigrants from different cultures could not be expected to have the same understanding of Canadian 'rules of conduct' or the same ability to regulate their behaviour accordingly. It was thus necessary for Parliament, legislatures, and municipalities to create laws that made the basic moral rules explicit and that would allow the various levels of the state to monitor, regulate, and, when warranted, punish the activities of those people, mainly immigrants, who might not abide by the rules. Immigrants would be forced to conform to Anglo-Saxon behavioural and moral standards 'for their own good.'[12]

Demands for legal regulation were generally most successful when the activity in question could be depicted as a moral threat because of its association with a non-Anglo-Saxon immigrant group. It is no coincidence that what became the basic outline and form of Canada's drug laws was put in place between 1908 and 1929, when the largely anti-immigrant 'moral law' movement was at its height. Opium became the first drug targeted by the moral-reform movement and the legal treatment of this substance helped lay the groundwork for the treatment of various other substances.

As with many of the activities prohibited during the moral-reform era, the use of various drugs had gone on in Canada for several decades before it was identified as problematic. In the nineteenth century, opiates were freely prescribed by Canadian physicians and they could also be obtained without prescriptions. There was no customs duty on opium imported into Canada before 1879 and after this date only minimal fees applied. In 1907 alone, forty-four tons of opium were legally imported into Canada.[13]

Cocaine and opium were widely used in most patent medicines and physicians employed them to treat a wide range of problems from diarrhea to pain.[14] Heroin was used to relieve coughs. The majority of users were white middle-class Protestants, members of the dominant class in Canada.[15] There was no pressure to control the use or importation of any of these drugs. None was seen as dangerous.[16] In fact, it appears that no Western nation used the criminal law to prohibit the distribution of narcotics for recreational or other purposes until Canada pioneered the practice in 1908.[17]

Despite periodic concern over the use of opiates and narcotics, these drugs were not identified as worthy of legislative concern, perhaps because most known addicts were from the respectable classes.[18] It was only once opium became identified with an unpopular social group of the day, namely the Chinese, that use of the drug suddenly became an issue of public significance and parliamentary action. The fact that addiction had been identified as a medical problem at least thirty years earlier only makes it all the more apparent that drug use was tolerated as long as it was not associated with what were assumed to be socially 'dangerous' groups.

Pressure to limit the importation and use of opiates developed shortly after 1900, the point by which the Chinese had become the largest non-Anglo-Saxon immigrant group in British Columbia and, as a consequence, anti-Chinese sentiment had reached a fever pitch. As long as labour shortages made the Chinese necessary, they were tolerated. An economic downturn in the early twentieth century, however, created frustration and anger among the province's white population and soon this anger was directed toward the Asian minority. Groups such as the Asiatic Exclusion League grew in popularity and the attitude of the white population became increasingly hostile. In 1907 this anger boiled over into a full-scale riot as a crowd of white protesters in Vancouver went on a rampage through the Chinese section of the city, pitching rocks, bottles, and bricks at every business or home in Chinatown. It was in this period of high anxiety and racial tension that the Chinese population of British Columbia was declared a potential danger, seemingly because of its use of opium.[19]

Once the Chinese were linked to opium, banning the drug became seen as a way to control the unpopular minority group. Suddenly, opium smoking was identified as one of several traits exemplifying the alien and inferior character of the Chinese immigrants in British Columbia. Consequently, by 20 July 1908, with little discussion or debate in either the House of Commons or the Senate, the federal government passed what is commonly known as the Opium Act, which made the importation, manufacture, and sale of the drug for other than medical use a criminal offence, with a penalty of up to three years in prison and fines of between $50 and $1,000.[20] Possession and personal use were not affected.

The act focused on specific forms of drug use favoured by a vulnerable minority.[21] The much wider use of opium by mainly middle-class white Canadians in patent medicines remained legal. It was clear, even at the time, that the properties of the drug itself had little to do with the criminalization of opium. Instead, long-standing fears about the potential danger that unassimilable Chinese supposedly represented to the moral fibre of the nation motivated the government to limit access to a drug that was thought to increase that danger.[22]

At the same time, a private member's bill to ban the manufacture and importation of cigarettes in 1908 failed because tobacco was not felt to be as physically or morally debilitating as narcotic drugs.[23] The arguments made in favour of tobacco regulation were called 'alarmist.'[24] It seems more likely that the reason tobacco was not added to the list of addictive and dangerous drugs was that it was popular among respectable white middle-class Anglo-Saxon Canadians. Whatever the properties of the drug itself, it was not considered a threat largely because the people using it were not considered socially or politically dangerous. The distinction made by legislators between the tobacco used by the Anglo-Saxon middle class and the drugs employed by other social groups offers evidence that the true motives behind early drug laws were racist. Tobacco use, rather than threatening the morals of white Anglo-Saxons, actually was seen as a means to prove or reinforce the moral superiority of the group.

Moral Panic

The link between drug use, criminality, and supposedly dangerous subcultures has also helped fuel what has been called moral panic over the use of particular substances. Moral panic refers to the sudden rise of an issue, often out of proportion with reality. Frequently, groups of 'moral entrepreneurs' disturbed by conditions and/or behaviours they feel affect the moral order, seize the issue to try to regain control of the public agenda or to (re)impose or maintain their values and code of conduct. This theory holds that any time society discusses illegal drugs it is easy for the media, law enforcement, or interest groups to create a moral panic or climate of fear to help gain support for the creation or maintenance of a regime of regulation or repression. Early-twentieth-century fears that an increase in the population of immigrants from other 'races' posed a threat to the genetic superiority of the dominant white Anglo-Saxon Protestant population set the stage for a 'moral panic' over the use of certain drugs.

Not long after fears of opium use among Chinese immigrants led to the criminalization of that drug, a second 'moral panic' emerged with wider-reaching consequences. The 'White Slavery Panic' refers to the widespread belief that non-Anglo-Saxon immigrants, particularly the Chinese but also blacks and Italians, were using businesses such as laundries and restaurants to employ young white women and then kidnap them, drug them, and sell them into a life of sexual slavery to serve the physical needs of 'depraved brown-skinned men.' This moral panic over drug-induced miscegenation fuelled the creation of specific laws, such as Saskatchewan's Female Employment Act of 1912, which prohibited Chinese immigrants from employing white women in businesses they owned or operated.

Similarly, the 1923 criminalization of marijuana owes a great deal to the moral panic created by the publication in *Maclean's* of several articles by Emily Murphy. In her articles, which were published collectively in a book, *The Black Candle*, in 1922, Murphy set out to provide the public with the kind of information that was certain to generate public pressure for expanded drug laws and increased penalties. She openly exploited the general racist sentiments among her readers, helping to create a clear link between immigrants, drug use, immorality, and imminent danger to white society and particularly white women. Her most startling claim was that the Chinese and other 'blackamoors' were consciously attempting to bring about the demise of the white race through the introduction of opium.[25]

The drug problem was defined by Murphy as a moral threat. Drug use degraded the morals, enfeebled the will, and caused people to become thieves and liars with no more idea of responsibility or of what was right and wrong than animals.[26] For her, drug traffickers were the true villains. They destroyed youth, innocence, and virtue. These villains were almost always foreign, usually Asian, or 'gentlemen of colour.'[27] The victims of drug addiction were almost always young white women from respectable families. Although the drug addict began as an innocent victim, it did not take long for the evil trafficker to turn these young women into dope fiends, living lives of debauchery and prostitution and eventually suffering from the ravages of venereal disease and mental decay.[28]

It seems no coincidence that, at the same time as Emily Murphy was creating images of evil immigrants leading innocent white girls into lives of immorality, drug use became one of the most widely discussed social issues of the day. Indeed, drug use became linked to every social evil imaginable, from prostitution to eugenic decline, from miscegenation to deficient manhood and bad mothers.[29] In this same period, the most concerted campaign to limit the immigration into Canada of a particular race, the Chinese, was under way. By 1923, this effort had succeeded with the passage by the federal government of the Chinese Immigration Act, which virtually stopped all immigration from China.[30]

Eliminating drug use was seen as the solution to all that troubled a society feeling the full effects of industrialization, urbanization, and ethnic diversity. Consequently, public pressure for harsh drug laws mounted. The unfavourable set of beliefs generated about drug use and drug users legitimatized the employment of increasingly repressive criminal sanctions to control the problem.[31] Throughout the 1920s, Parliament passed five amendments to the Opium and Narcotic Drug Act, each one broadening the scope of the law, increasing penalties, and expanding police powers of search and seizure while reducing the legal rights of the accused, usually with almost no debate, discussion, or meaningful investigation. Imprisonment became mandatory for most offences. The maximum sentences for traffickers were increased from one to seven years in prison. Those found selling to children could be lashed. New laws allowed for the deportation of immigrants convicted of narcotics offences.[32] The onus of proving innocence was placed on the accused in 1921. In 1923 limitations were imposed on the right of appeal for those convicted of drug offences.[33] All this culminated with the Opium and Narcotic Drug Act of 1929, which established the framework of Canadian drug law for decades to come.[34] The only evidence used to support the changes to drug laws during the 1920s was usually popular, usually totally fictional, narratives such as those created by Emily Murphy.[35]

The drug scare Emily Murphy helped fuel certainly played a role in the criminalization of marijuana or *Cannabis sativa*, or hashesh as it was often called at the time. In 1923 marijuana was added to the schedule of illegal drugs in Canada, although few Canadians, including parliamentarians, had any knowledge of the drug or its properties. It was certainly not considered a social problem in Canada. There is no real evidence of why marijuana was criminalized at this time. It was not a major policy decision and no explanation was given or asked for in the House of Commons. No scientific evidence of any harm posed by the drug was presented.[36] The first actual parliamentary debate on marijuana did not occur until 1938 during discussion of a bill to make the cultivation of marijuana an offence. Then, the drug was described as a 'weed with far reaching, poisoning and demoralizing effects.'[37]

Most Canadians had first heard of the drug through one of Emily Murphy's articles, where she described cannabis as a drug that drove its users completely insane, turning them into raving maniacs liable to kill or indulge in any form of violence.[38] The lack of knowledge about marijuana was made clear when the Canadian Medical Association began to lobby for its regulation in 1928, five years after it had already been added to the schedule. Certainly, many in the medical community were not aware that cannabis and marijuana were the same thing. The first actual seizure of a marijuana cigarette in Canada did not occur until 1932, almost a decade after the drug was declared a threat.

Emily Murphy's articles were able to fuel a moral panic largely because Canadian society of the day was ready and willing to see the combination of racial minorities and drugs as creating a particularly potent threat to social stability and to the position of Anglo-Saxons. In a climate of panic, the unknown is easily portrayed as dangerous and Emily Murphy's linking of drugs with non-Anglo-Saxon immigrants and foreign cultures made the threat seem tangible.[39]

The threat was all the worse once the link was made between drugs and the increasingly troubling youth culture that was emerging during the 1920s – a youth culture seemingly based upon the rejection of older social norms and morals.[40] The only possible explanation for such behaviour among youth had to be the evil influence of drugs. Along with marijuana, which was linked to East Indians, cocaine, often associated with black immigration,[41] was assumed to be popular among adolescents, further emphasizing the idea that drugs were related to youth rebellion and threatened the future of the respectable classes.[42] The greater the threat, the greater the justification for employing harsh measures to protect society.

It was easier to pass laws that infringed upon civil liberties when it was assumed the victims would be 'socially devalued persons.' The laws were never seen as being anything that would worry most 'real' Canadians.[43] The conviction statistics for the period seem to confirm this assumption. Of the 1,864 persons convicted of drug-law offences by 1921, 1,211, or 65 per cent of the total, were Chinese.[44] Chinese and blacks made up two-thirds of the total number of people convicted of drug offences in Canada during the 1920s.[45] This was at a time when the Chinese represented an almost negligible portion of the total

Canadian population.[46] By 1921, the probability of a Chinese person being convicted of a drug offence was 1 in 33, while the probability of a non-Chinese person being convicted of the same type of offence was 1 in 13,500.[47] The conclusion that the increasingly severe nature of Canadian narcotic laws was politically facilitated by the assumption that their impact would fall mainly upon the Asiatic population, rather than middle-class white Anglo-Saxons, appears impossible to avoid.[48]

The constant linkage in the media of drugs with immorality, criminality, and depravity created a strong image in the mind of the public. By responding with ever increasing criminal sanctions against drug use, Parliament helped confirm the impression that not only drugs but drug users themselves were dangerous.[49] Public perceptions and government action were mutually reinforcing – the panic over drugs motivating the government to act and the government's actions against drug use increasing the panic.[50] What was earlier thought of as a minor private indulgence became recast as a serious public evil.[51] Once drugs were so defined, it became increasingly difficult for society to think of drug use in any other way.

It did not matter that, over twenty years after marijuana had been added to the list of 'dangerous' drugs by Parliament, it was still largely unknown in Canada. Convictions for all drug offences fell dramatically after the initial drug panic of the 1920s.[52] While there were almost 2,000 drug convictions in 1921–2, almost all related to opium, there were only 230 in 1932–3. It certainly had not become a social problem. In 1955 a House of Commons committee was able to declare that there was 'no problem' with marijuana in Canada. Only a few charges were laid every year and most of these involved 'visitors from outside the country.'[53] As late as 1960, a grand total of fifteen ounces of marijuana were seized by police. Nevertheless, it was still asserted by most commentators that drug use was innately linked to promiscuity and prostitution in women and criminality in men.[54] This became all the more significant once the use of marijuana and other drugs began to increase dramatically after 1965.

While the new users of marijuana and other drugs such as LSD did not necessarily belong to a particular unpopular ethnic group, they were assumed to be part of a new youth subculture based upon a rejection of conventional social norms and moral rules. This made the 'hippie' generation, as it came to be called, disturbing. Just as the youth culture of the 1920s was thought to pose a threat to the established order, so too did the hippie counterculture. As in the 1920s, the association of drugs and youth rebellion created powerful images of a threatening moral and social crisis. Once again drugs became identified as a threat, largely because the people seen to be using them were viewed as a threat.[55] The actual properties of marijuana and drugs such as LSD certainly had little to do with the degree of threat that such drugs was deemed to pose. Even in the midst of this second wave moral panic over drugs, the Le Dain Commission was still able to conclude that marijuana itself was not a dangerous or harmful substance. As mentioned earlier, however, this finding did nothing to alter the criminal sanctions against marijuana, largely because the finding failed to alter the image of threat associated with the drug. This helps support the claim that the real 'harms' which prohibitions against marijuana are protecting against are not to be found in the properties of the drug itself but rather in the types of people who might employ the drug and what they are believed to represent to society.

Although it could be argued that the racist and invalid purposes behind drug laws are merely unfortunate historical artifacts, the recent addition of Cathinone and *Catha edulis Forsk* (commonly known as khat) to the Controlled Drugs and Substances Act should dispel this assumption.[56] Khat is a product that is almost unknown outside a particular region of the world, namely eastern Africa and parts of the Arabian peninsula. Most Canadians are completely unaware of its existence. Within Canada it is overwhelmingly immigrants from east Africa, mainly Somalis, who desire to import and use khat. On 14 May 1997 the drug was criminalized with little or no evidence of the harm that use of the substance represented to individual users or Canadians in general. As Justice Ian B. Cowan stated in *Philpot*, 'I have not received any evidence before me in terms of the dangers of Khat ... only that Parliament has decreed it a dangerous substance.'[57]

One has to wonder what motivated Parliament to criminalize khat in the absence of evidence that the drug has any harmful properties. Making the criminalization of the substance still more problematic is the fact that khat is associated with a visible racial and cultural minority in Canada. In essence, as the only group likely to use the drug, Somali immigrants in Canada are inordinately affected by this law, which targets a substance that has been a crucial and significant element of Somali culture for thousands of years. Just as the criminalization of opium almost 100 years ago targeted a drug mainly because of its association with a visible 'foreign' racial community, the impact of the prohibition against khat falls almost exclusively upon one racial group, singling them out for criminal sanctions in a manner that is directly related to their distinctive cultural practices. Since Parliament has not produced strong evidence that khat is dangerous by virtue of its properties, it seems inescapable that the drug's designation as dangerous is largely the result of its association with a particular racial minority. At the very least, the criminalization of khat provides disturbing evidence that the prohibition of drugs based upon concerns about who uses them may not be as much of an irrelevant historical artifact as we think. Therefore, there is more than mere historical interest at stake when discussing policies related to the regulation of drug use in Canada.

Decisions regarding which drugs are licit and which are illicit and how the state deals with those individuals who employ illicit drugs are closely linked to, and have a significant impact on, the ideals our society holds concerning what activities are the proper subject of state regulation and how society identifies 'threats' to its well-being. Both these questions are intimately tied to our conception of equality and equality rights, and the extent to which dominant groups in society have a right to impose their beliefs and preferences upon minority groups. The essays in this collection certainly do not and cannot provide answers to these questions. They do, however, offer a number of intriguing insights which can help readers come to their own conclusions. The essays build on previous research, apply existing arguments to new issues and new periods, and test older theories within new contexts, adding nuance and complexity to our understanding of how drugs and drug users have been treated in the nation, and what the development of our current regulatory regime says about the interaction of drug policy, public opinion, and equality rights.

Outline of the Book

Line Beauchesne's contribution, 'Setting Public Policy on Drugs: A Choice of Social Values,' provides a starting point for the collection. Using the report of the Le Dain Commission as her focal point, Beauchesne examines how the political options suggested by the commission reflected differing social values. As she points out, although the commissioners unanimously believed that cannabis has few harmful effects, they could not agree on a public policy regarding its use. The dissension stemmed primarily from a conflict over the social values that should shape relations between the state and its citizens. Beauchesne outlines the three different approaches recommended and the social values underpinning them. She then goes on to analyse current Quebec policies on alcohol and illegal drugs to illustrate how these approaches and values are still influencing government thinking today.

In the first minority report of the Le Dain Commission, its author, Ian Campbell, asserted that existing prohibitions against cannabis should be maintained and the repression of users increased. Beauchesne identifies this as the 'legal moralism' approach to policy, which holds that the state as the guardian of public order has the responsibility to use public policy to maintain a common morality within society. The loss of a common morality is seen as promoting the disintegration of society. The state may wage a battle against any threat to the common values and even target specific groups as long as these groups are considered to be outside the common morality. This approach, which was clearly dominant during the creation of Canada's drug-law regime, justifies drug prohibitions on the basis of morality rather than public health.

The main approach identified in the Le Dain Commission report is 'legal paternalism.' More flexible than legal moralism, this approach argues for the de-criminalization of cannabis on the grounds that it is relatively harmless, but not for its legalization, since the law should not encourage the use of products harmful to the young. The state can limit individual liberties in the exercise of its paternalistic function, using certain forms of legal constraint to prevent non-autonomous persons from harming themselves.

Finally, Beauchesne identifies the 'legal liberalism' approach to policy outlined in the second minority report of the Le Dain Commission. That approach, as Beauchesne puts it, calls for the legalization of cannabis on the grounds that 'the state as guardian of public order, must restrict its action to those areas that disturb the public peace in general, such as road safety, and limit its actions so as to preserve civil rights to the greatest extent possible.' Penal repression and mandatory treatment of cannabis users are an abuse of the state's power. Even if a large portion of the population finds certain types of drug use morally suspect, that does not make it legitimate for the state to regulate such activity if such use does not in itself constitute a threat to others.

To a large extent, competition between these three approaches – legal moralism, legal paternalism, and legal liberalism – has fuelled debates over the regulation of drug use in Canada. Beauchesne's outline offers a means for readers to categorize historical trends in drug policy according to particular social values espoused and the conception of the relationship between state and citizen inherent in the various policy trends.

Clearly, much of the writing on early drug-law policy, either implicitly or explicitly, situates this policy within a social context of legal moralism, particularly the concept that the state can target the behaviour of certain groups on the basis that the group exists outside the common morality which the state has an obligation to defend. The behaviour of those accepted as being within the 'common morality' is less often targeted for regulation.

Jarrett Rudy's article, '"Unmaking Manly Smokes": Church, State, Governance, and the First Anti-Smoking Campaigns in Montreal, 1892–1914,' supports this contention. His examination of campaigns for the passage of anti-tobacco laws between 1890 and 1914 demonstrates that, during the very same period that Parliament was legislating against the use of opium, there was little interest in, and even hostility towards, any attempt to treat tobacco in a similar manner. As Rudy outlines, tobacco was simply not seen as threat, largely because it was popular among the 'respectable' middle class. Even if it was technically addictive, addiction was not an issue for those white Anglo-Saxons who used it, since their superior moral control would allow them to use a 'dangerous' substance without any ill effects. It was only the drugs popular among less 'respectable' immigrant groups which were seen to pose any threat to the social order, whatever the health risks of those substances might be.

Greg Marquis's article, 'From Beverage to Drug: Alcohol and Other Drugs in 1960s and 1970s Canada,' reinforces the point that drugs popular with the dominant social group were perceived and treated differently than substances employed by minority groups, regardless of their medical or other properties. He outlines the 'alcohol and other drugs' movement of the 1960s and 1970s which promoted the concept that alcohol was a harmful drug from the point of view of public health. As Marquis explains, despite the apparent risks involved in alcohol use, alcohol, unlike narcotics or marijuana, could not be fully demonized. From the 1930s onward, any problems associated with alcohol consumption, such as alcoholism, were blamed on the man, not the 'bottle.' Alcohol, because of its cultural acceptability and despite its psychoactive properties, was seen as a 'non-drug' drug. Attempts to treat alcohol in a fashion similar to the treatment of illicit drugs received little support.

Dan Malleck's contribution, '"Their Medley of Tongues and Eternal

Jangle": Liquor Control and Ethnicity in Ontario, 1927–44,' illustrates some of the complexity inherent in the merging of racial assumptions and the regulation of drugs in Canada. Malleck documents the widespread belief that it would not be wise to offer licences to immigrant or 'ethnic' social clubs, thereby confirming that older theories regarding the inability of certain 'ethnic' groups to control their consumption or behaviour adequately remained intact. However, Malleck also shows that official policy resisted calls to restrict liquor licences among ethnic populations. Not all drug use by minority groups was considered a threat to the status quo; or at least, once a drug was considered legal for use by the general population, the state did not feel it was possible to limit its use by minority groups on the basis of their ethnicity alone.

Malleck's article also reveals the social nature of some drug use. One of the main sites for 'ethnic' drinking was the ethnic social club. The Liquor Control Act carved out a special place for these clubs. While ethnic clubs may have received more scrutiny than their more mainstream counterparts, often because certain ethnic groups were considered radical, overall there was a general acceptance that drinking was part of forming and maintaining a sense of community.

Articles that examine drug use from the perspective of the user rather than that of those attempting to prohibit or restrict their use tend to highlight social and community-building aspects of drug use. These articles illustrate that activities that some members of the dominant majority might see as threatening, such as the use of illicit drugs, while perhaps flouting social norms, may be viewed by drug users themselves not as a means of attacking the social order but as a form of building community and identity among the marginalized.

Catherine Carstairs's study of heroin users in Vancouver in the 1940s and 1950s, 'Becoming a "Hype": Drug Laws, Subculture Formation, and Resistance in Canada, 1945–61,' illustrates that the use of illicit drugs by subcultures or minority groups could have elements of defiance or rejection of dominant social norms. However, rather than being a threat to the social order, as most social commentators and lawmakers feared, the use of illicit drugs such as heroin by the socially marginalized was often more about creating a sense of community and belonging among populations of people who were otherwise among the abandoned and abused. Drug use was not an activity that isolated the user; on the contrary, joining the ranks of users could provide a form of social support and a sense of belonging to people who were otherwise socially outcast.

Sharon Cook's 'From Flapper to Sophisticate: Canadian Women University Students as Smokers, 1920–60,' offers a useful point of comparison in her study of tobacco use by women. Although focusing on a rather privileged group – university-educated women – rather than a social subculture, Cook demonstrates that women often smoked cigarettes for some of the same reasons that the poor and marginalized of Vancouver used heroin, although with far less dramatically negative consequences. Cook outlines how women came to see certain advantages to smoking. The fact that for much of the twentieth century women smokers embodied a daring lifestyle of rebellion against dominant social norms allowed them to fashion a certain identity for themselves. This was certainly part of the attraction of smoking, as was the sense of bonding and community that the act of smoking created. Of course, the women who dared to challenge convention by smoking were often seen as heroines – while the poor and marginalized Vancouverites who used heroin for some of the same reasons were considered dangerous outcasts.

The assumption that drug use and drug users were inherently dangerous is evidenced in Dawn Moore's contribution, 'Considering the Revolving Door: The Inevitability of Addiction Treatment in the Criminal Justice System.' Moore demonstrates how assumptions developed during the early years of drug regulation have continued to influence policy and the treatment of drug users. She discusses how the assumed inherent link between crime and drug use, which fuelled earlier moral panics over the issue, has led penal authorities to assume that all use of illicit drugs creates addiction and that addiction leads to crime. She explores how the image of the criminal addict has been employed at various times for political purposes. Finally, she argues that the very flexibility of the image of the criminal addict has allowed it to survive, despite changing concepts of both drug use and the nature and causes of addiction.

Similarly, the tendency to criminalize substances based upon who used them rather than the particular properties of the drug continued well beyond the initial moral panics of the early twentieth century. Erika Dyck's article, '"Just Say Know": Criminalizing LSD and the Politics of Psychedelic Expertise, 1961–8,' recounts the process by which LSD became identified and criminalized as a dangerous substance although it was initially considered to be a promising treatment for a variety of ailments, including migraines, mental illnesses, and addiction. Scientists testing the drug's properties often did so by ingesting the drug themselves. Once LSD entered the underground marketplace and became popular among the emerging youth subcultures of the 1960s, official attitudes towards it changed. By the 1960s, there was widespread concern about the rebellious youth culture and the potential for social disorder that this population posed. As with opium use by the supposedly 'dangerous' population of Chinese immigrants over half a century earlier, it was the association of LSD with a supposedly dangerous subgroup that transformed it from a promising medical treatment into a dangerous vehicle of social degeneration. By the mid-1960s, various jurisdictions had begun to criminalize the substance.

Marcel Martel's 'Setting Boundaries: LSD Use and Glue Sniffing in Ontario in the 1960s,' offers a more optimistic picture of the development of drug law and policy. Comparing two media campaigns of the late 1960s, one focusing on LSD and the other on glue sniffing, Martel questions the impact of moral panic. He outlines how media and public-pressure groups attempted to convince authorities to respond to the perceived threat these substances posed with repression or strict regulation. Media accounts exaggerated the treat posed by LSD by reporting the same incidents several times over, suggesting that there were far more drug-related 'tragedies' than was actually the case. While the federal government did make the possession of LSD a criminal offence, the penalties, being less severe than those related to the possession of marijuana, were not what many had hoped for. In the case of glue sniffing, an episode of moral panic, followed by an active lobby by parents, the city of Toronto, and the Toronto School Board, did not lead to repressive measures being adopted. In both cases, despite serious public pressure for stringent regulation, the government chose to emphasize education rather than repression. This raises the possibility that the legal-liberalism approach identified by Beauchesne may have had more influence over drug-law policy than is usually assumed.

However, Kyle Grayson's study of the political reaction to recent 'club' drugs, 'Biopolitics, Geopolitics, and the Regulation of (Club) Drugs in Canada,' highlights the fact that the basic assumptions underlying the regulation of drug use have changed little since the early decades of this century. Grayson demonstrates that even today substances are deemed dangerous less because of their medical properties than because the drug is used by a particular 'subgroup' in particular locations considered threatening by the dominant elements in society. Just as the Chinese were considered a threat in the early decades of the last century, their use of a particular drug only increasing the inherent threat they posed, modern youth subcultures are also seen as socially dangerous, the threat being enhanced by the group's use of newer 'club' drugs, such as Ecstasy or GHB. It is the very social aspect of this drug use – which tends to bring large groups of potentially radical youth together – that adds to the potential danger represented by these new drugs.

Overall, the essays in this collection offer new and useful insights into a wide spectrum of issues related to the regulation of drug use, assumptions about illicit substances, and the treatment of drug users in Canada. The subject does not lend itself to easy answers; indeed, most new work simply adds to the complexity of the subject matter. It is this complexity and nuance that makes the study of the legal and social regulation of drugs and drug use in Canada a vital and vibrant area of study with relevance and meaning that extends to some of the most basic questions a democracy must deal with, such as the relationship between the individual and the state and the extent to which the state can control and regulate activities that are not directly harmful to others. Drug law and policy force people to ask where the line should be drawn between individual liberties and the freedom to choose, on the one hand, and the power of the state to control citizens' activities, on the other. This collection, it is to be hoped, will stimulate further work in this exciting area.

NOTES

1 Controlled Drugs and Substances Act, S.C. 1996 (hereafter CDSA).
2 CDSA s. 4(3) and s. 5(2).
3 Jarrett Rudy, 'Unmaking Manly Smokes: Church, State Governance, and the First Anti-Smoking Campaigns in Montreal, 1892–1914,' *Journal of Canadian Historical Association*, 12 (2001): 95–107.
4 Stephen E. Smith, '"Counterblasts" to Tobacco: Five Decades of North American Tobacco Litigation,' *Windsor Review of Legal and Social Issues*, 14, no. 1 (2002): 1.
5 See Jake Epp, Minister of National Health and Welfare, Canada, House of Commons *Debates*, vol. 9, 2nd session, 33rd Parliament, 23 November 1987,

p. 11042; cited in *RJR-Macdonald Inc. v. Canada (Attorney General)* [1995] 3 S.C.R. 199.

6 See Smith, '"Counterblasts" to Tobacco,' 2.

7 *RJR-Macdonald Inc. v. Canada.*

8 *R. v. Malmo-Levine* (2000) B.C.J. no. 1095 (BCCA).

9 Jeremy Laurance, 'Marijauna May Slow Effects of Aging,' *Hamilton Spectator*, 19 April 2003, A1, A16.

10 See Joint Statement of Legislative Facts, prepared for *Clay v. R.*, *Malmo-Levine v. R.*, and *Caine v. R.*

11 Terry Chapman, 'The Anti-Drug Crusade in Western Canada, 1885–1925,' in D. Bercuson and L. Knafla, eds., *Law and Society in Canada: Historical Perspectives* (Calgary: University of Calgary Press 1979), 89–116; Melvyn Green, 'A History of Canadian Narcotics Control: The Formative Years,' *University of Toronto Faculty of Law Review*, 37 (1979): 42–80; Robert Solomon and Melvyn Green, 'The First Century: The History of Non-Medical Opiate Use and Control Policies in Canada, 1870–1970,' *University of Western Ontario Law Review*, 20, no. 2 (1982): 307–36; Neil Boyd, 'The Origins of Canadian Narcotics Legislation: The Process of Criminalization in Historical Context,' *Dalhousie Law Journal*, 8, no. 1 (1984): 102–37; P.J. Giffen, S. Endicott, and S. Lambert, *Panic and Indifference: The Politics of Canada's Drug Laws* (Ottawa: Canadian Centre on Substance Abuse 1991); Dan Mallack, '"Its Baneful Influences Are Too Well Known": Debates over Drug Use in Canada, 1867–1908,' *Canadian Bulletin of Medical History*, 14 (1997): 278–82; Catherine Carstairs, 'Innocent Addicts, Dope Fiends and Nefarious Traffickers: Illegal Drug Use in 1920s English Canada,' *Journal of Canadian Studies*, 33, no. 3 (fall 1998): 145-62.

12 Giffen, Endicott, and Lambert, *Panic and Indifference*, 47.

13 Chapman, 'The Anti-Drug Crusade in Western Canada,' 91–2.

14 Jacalyn Duffin, *Langstaff: A Nineteenth-Century Medical Life* (Toronto: University of Toronto Press 1993), 75–6.

15 Cheryl Warsh, *Moments of Unreason* (Montreal and Kingston: McGill-Queen's University Press 1989), 155–69.

16 James Walker, *'Race,' Rights, and the Law in the Supreme Court of Canada* (Toronto: Osgoode Society for Canadian Legal History / University of Toronto Press 1997), 83.

17 Green, 'A History of Canadian Narcotics Control,' 42.

18 Malleck, '"Its Baneful Influences Are Too Well Known,"' 278–82.

19 Madge Pon, 'Like a Chinese Puzzle: The Construction of Chinese Masculinity in Jack Canuck,' in Joy Parr and Mark Rosenfeld, eds., *Gender and History in Canada* (Toronto: Copp Clark 1996), 90.

20 The formal name of the act reflected its purposes: Act to Prohibit the Importation, Manufacture and Sale of Opium for Other Than Medical Purposes. See Chapman, 'The Anti-Drug Crusade in Western Canada.'

21 Tina Loo and Carolyn Strange, *Making Good: Law and Moral Regulation in Canada 1867–1939* (Toronto: University of Toronto Press 1997), 77.

22 Ibid., 76.

23 Giffen, Endicott, and Lambert, *Panic and Indifference*, 49.

24 Green, 'A History of Canadian Narcotics Control,' 46.

25 Chapman, 'The Anti-Drug Crusade in Western Canada,' 103.

26 Giffen, Endicott, and Lambert, *Panic and Indifference*, 151–2.

27 Walker, *'Race,' Rights, and the Law*, 111.

28 Carstairs, 'Innocent Addicts, Dope Fiends and Nefarious Traffickers,' 146.

29 Ibid., 141.

30 Donald Avery, *Dangerous Foreigners: European Immigrant Workers and Labour Radicalism in Canada, 1896–1932* (Toronto: McClelland and Stewart 1979), 87.

31 Giffen, Endicott, and Lambert, *Panic and Indifference*, 149.

32 Carstairs, 'Innocent Addicts, Dope Fiends and Nefarious Traffickers,' 157. Also see Giffen, Endicott, and Lambert, *Panic and Indifference*, 155.

33 Giffen, Endicott, and Lambert, *Panic and Indifference*, 257.

34 Green, 'A History of Canadian Narcotics Control,' 42.

35 Carstairs, 'Innocent Addicts, Dope Fiends and Nefarious Traffickers,' 146.

36 Giffen, Endicott, and Lambert, *Panic and Indifference*, 493.

37 Ibid., 185.

38 Ibid., 179.

39 Carstairs, 'Innocent Addicts, Dope Fiends and Nefarious Traffickers,' 157.

40 Cynthia Commachio, *The Infinite Bonds of Family: Domesticity in Canada, 1850–1940* (Toronto: University of Toronto Press 1999), 99–101.

41 Loo and Strange, *Making Good*, 90.

42 Boyd, 'The Origins of Canadian Narcotics Legislation,' 122.

43 Giffen, Endicott, and Lambert, *Panic and Indifference*, 245.

44 Chapman, 'The Anti-Drug Crusade in Western Canada,' 103.

45 Loo and Strange, *Making Good*, 90.

46 Pon, 'Like a Chinese Puzzle,' 88–100.

47 Giffen, Endicott, and Lambert, *Panic and Indifference*,' 97.

48 Green, 'A History of Canadian Narcotics Control,' 58.

49 Ibid., 62–3, 79.

50 Ibid., 62.

51 Boyd, 'The Origins of Canadian Narcotics Legislation,' 104.

52 Carstairs, 'Innocent Addicts, Dope Fiends and Nefarious Traffickers,' 158.

53 Doug Owram, *Born at the Right Time: A History of the Baby Boom Generation* (Toronto: University of Toronto Press 1996), 199.

54 Ibid., 197.

55 Giffen, Endicott, and Lambert, *Panic and Indifference*, 491.

56 See s. 6(1) of the Controlled Drugs and Substances Act, Schedule III (Cathinone) and Schedule IV (*Catha edulis Forsk*); what follows has been taken from a *Notice of Constitutional Validity of s. 6(1) of the Controlled Drugs and Substances Act, Schedule III (Cathinone) and Schedule IV (Catha edulis Forsk), Provincial Court Criminal Division, between Her Majesty the Queen and Mohamed Abdirahman Abdi (2003)*, for which the research was prepared by the author.

57 *R. v. Philpot* [1998], O.J. no. 5084.

1 Setting Public Policy on Drugs: A Choice of Social Values

LINE BEAUCHESNE

> To feed someone and not love them is the same as dealing with swine.
> To love someone but not respect them is like raising pets.
> – Mencius, Chinese philosopher, 300 B.C.

A public policy is the articulation by the state or its institutions of the directing principles for guiding its actions in a particular area. The establishment of these principles and the direction of the ensuing actions can be brought about through force and through violence. In such a case, we have dictatorship. Alternatively, the establishment of these principles can be the result of debates which are structured in such a way as to garner the greatest public credibility, and which allow for the implementation of administrative, economic, social, and legal strategies that are then seen as more legitimate and coherent and, importantly, that use the criminal law and state force only as a last resort. In this case, we have democracy.

Of course, in most matters of public policy, the lines are not so clearly drawn. One of the jobs of criminology is to study criminal law in order to determine whether its utilization in particular areas is as a last resort. The premise in this essay is that criminal law represents a serious act of institutional violence whose use must be limited to situations where social order is threatened and which cannot otherwise be managed in the short term. Criminal law is first and foremost a mechanism of social exclusion and stigmatization.[1] The recurrent use of the criminal law by the state to maintain a policy can be seen as an important indicator of the failure of that policy's content, of the absence of a consensus among those affected by the policy, or of a lack of sufficient state support to ensure its implementation. To view the criminal law as an essential component of a policy and not as an exceptional measure is equivalent to accepting the legitimacy of violence as a fundamental aspect of the state's role and as an appropriate means of forcing the public to comply with its decisions.

But how can we determine whether criminal law is being used to enforce a policy as a method of last resort? To answer that question, we must examine the social values that we wish to promote as citizens. This is the exercise we shall conduct on drug policies.

Social Values and Public Policies

The report of the Le Dain Commission[2] was the product of a detailed study of the use of drugs for non-medical purposes where, for the first time, experts from different disciplines came together in a royal commission of inquiry in order to advise the government on public policy relating to drugs. Little effort has been made to analyse the report's various political options as reflective of the varying social values at the basis of its conclusions and recommendations, as compared to the attention devoted to the issue of drugs. In this regard, the first volume of the report on cannabis is particularly interesting: the commissioners all recognize that cannabis has few harmful effects but fail to agree on a public policy with regard to this drug. As we shall see, the dissension stems primarily from differing visions of the social values that should underlie relations between the state and its citizens.

Legal Moralism: Imposing the Values of Selected Groups through the Force of Law

The first minority report submitted to the Le Dain Commission was written by Ian Campbell. Taking his cue from the political philosophy of Lord Devlin,[3] Campbell argues that not only should the current prohibition against cannabis be maintained, but repression of its users should be increased through police raids, compulsory medical treatment, long-term monitoring with urine tests, control of associations, and so forth. It is essential, argues Campbell, to stop crime-inducing elements from 'contaminating'[4] young people from good families, whose parents may lose all hope of a productive future for their offspring on account of drugs, including cannabis.

Campbell explains that the state has not only the responsibility to use its public policies to act as a guardian of public order and a protector of non-autonomous persons, *but also the responsibility to maintain a common morality within society*. The state may therefore use the criminal law in response to behaviour that threatens the 'established morality,' regardless of the dangers such behaviour poses for the individual or for society. The goal is to prevent the disintegration of our existing society through the loss of a 'common morality,' which Campbell sees as an essential element of social cohesion and economic prosperity.

Although Campbell recognizes that cannabis has few harmful effects, he says that the criminal prohibition of its use should be maintained as an embodiment of the moral prohibition:

> It seems to me to be an unassailable proposition that the majority may properly prohibit through the law conduct that is manifestly offensive or disturbing to them whether or not that conduct inflicts an injury on any particular person beyond the actor. This principle is recognized in our laws against public nudity. There is every reason to think that the public use of cannabis is offensive and disturbing to the vast majority of Canadians. There is even more reason to think that public use by young people is particularly offensive. Hence, it appears not inappropriate that such behaviour should be forbidden by law.
>
> ... To whatever extent youthful experience of intoxication predisposes one to chronic adult intoxication or acts to limit the full and healthy development of human potential it lessens the capacity of the individual for a full, rich and creative life and lessens his potential contribution to his society
>
> ... But it seems to me that recently we have been far too little concerned with the consequences of placing too many rights and freedoms on the shoulders of the young.[5]

From the perspective of legal moralism, the state intervenes in drug use in the name of its responsibility to preserve 'common values' that are vital for the well-being of society. This makes it legitimate to wage a battle, by force if necessary, against the 'contaminants' attacking our society; the state may apply drug controls and prohibitions, and even target specific groups, without raising an outcry from other segments of the population if the latter consider those groups to be outside the 'common morality.' Moreover, legal policies and practices are both coloured by this moralistic vision since users, whether or not they are capable of handling their consumption, may be condemned for their choice of 'vice' over 'virtue.' *This approach justifies drug prohibitions on the basis of morality rather than public health.*

Legal moralism dominates the current discourse supporting the maintenance of prohibitions against drugs. It is deeply rooted in the history of the Protestant culture as it developed in North America,[6] and so it is not surprising that the United States originated the 'war on drugs' and is the principal advocate of the argument that perpetuates this war.

The assumption that underlies this position is that there exists a common morality which must be protected by the powers of the state. Yet the study of morality has been seeking common denominators on which to base a universal morality for centuries:

> When it comes to universal standards, although almost all philosophical doctrines claim the same objective – the happiness of humanity – there is great disparity as to how to achieve that goal and what values to uphold: their relative importance varies from one doctrine to another, from one culture to another, from one individual to another and often, in one individual, from one moment to another as circumstances dictate ... In other words, our morality ebbs and flows in accordance with our personal ethics, where our ethics are the ideal and morality is the means by which we approach that ideal.
>
> Morality and ethics are rooted, therefore, in a relativism of situations, sentiments and values.[7]

In fact, there is no common morality other than the refusal to respect the very real pluralism of values held by individuals and groups in society.

The reasoning behind legal moralism is valid: when everyone thinks the same way, social management is simpler, in the same way that a dictatorship is a simpler method of political management than the democratic search for consensus. Anyone who has had the experience of repeated meetings knows this. Democracy is a long and sometimes arduous process. But would we, as citizens, prefer to remain uninformed and to allow political authorities to decide which social values to promote and impose upon us, by force if necessary?

If we choose the search for consensus, the process of constructing our drug policy is necessarily going to involve an encounter with the pluralism of values. And to arrive at a policy that respects that pluralism, *we must take the time to inform the public properly* of the foundations of the policies we advocate. To impose a drug policy in the name of a common morality is to impose the morality of selected groups in society.[8]

This leads us to the first question concerning social values: To what extent does the prohibition of drugs under the current public policy represent an imposition of the values of certain groups in society? We will answer some aspects of this question later in this essay. For now, let us proceed to examine the other positions on cannabis policy found in the Le Dain report.

Legal Paternalism: Mandatory Protection under Threat of Criminal Sanctions

The majority report of the Le Dain Commission, which is based on the political philosophy of H.L.A. Hart,[9] presents a varied stance, combining both treatment and punishment. It calls for the decriminalization of cannabis because of its relative harmlessness, but not for its legalization, stating that the law should not encourage the use of products harmful to the health of our young people. The commissioners explain that they understand the need to preserve individual liberties at any price, but they take the view that the state, in addition to being the guardian of public order, has a *paternalistic function that allows it to use certain forms of legal constraint to prevent non-autonomous persons from harming themselves.* The state therefore has a responsibility to use criminal law to restrict the availability of cannabis, particularly for young people.

This position, common in countries where a Catholic culture dominates, opened the door to medical control over drug use in the name of public-health protection, and assumed that the experts had the necessary knowledge to protect individuals who do not know better.[10] It is more complex than the legal-moralism approach. First, there is the larger question of non-autonomous persons. Who designates these individuals? Second, there is the significance of the term 'protection,' a key issue when it comes to drugs. Does it include protecting individuals against their will, and by force, if need be? And protecting them from what?

Let us look at the first question. Historically, it was long maintained that the working class was incapable of handling alcohol, in contrast to the ability of the upper class to do so. Today, aboriginal people are considered inferior to whites in this regard, somewhat in the same way that, in the United States, blacks are believed to be less able than whites to handle illicit drugs. This form of discrimination may also be seen in regard to homosexuals, who, supposedly, are less able than heterosexuals to handle their sexuality, and to women, who are allegedly less capable than men of handling their emotions. Such preconceived notions avoid not only the whole issue of the living conditions of certain populations relative to other, dominant ones, but also any discussion of the values that are promoted in order to maintain such dominance. Of course, there are more fragile populations in a society with which the state must concern itself. Must this, however, take the form of prohibitions and punishments to ensure their welfare? This leads to the question of 'protection.'

It is possible to protect people by making them more independent and better able to make choices, and by improving their living conditions and their access to services and information. It is also possible to decide that, if these people make choices that do not conform to 'our' values, it is because they are unfit to do so, and we must impose choices on them by force.

Every parent can see the difficulty here. There are emergency situations in which, in the short term, a prohibition is most appropriate: 'Do not cross the road without Mommy!' Nevertheless, a child must eventually be taught how to cross the road without Mommy, to be aware of the dangers and to take the necessary precautions. A parent will not always be there to hold the child's hand. So we prepare our children by giving them information and by teaching them how to judge when it is safe to cross the road; we do this for their own sake and for that of others. However, should an accident occur, we would hope that it is not fatal and that the hospital will provide the best possible care.

Now imagine the following scenario: parents forbid their children to cross the road until they are adults because they are not independent; as adults, if they cross the road, the authorities imprison them for breaking the prohibition – whether or not they have crossed the road successfully – or, if they are involved in an accident, treatment is provided only on condition that they promise never to cross the road again. In legal terms, the argument in favour of prohibition as a way of protecting young people does not make much sense. It is not possible to justify a prohibition that includes adults on the pretext that we wish to protect the health of children, just as we would not prohibit adults from drinking wine on the premise that it is dangerous for children. Protection would be better accomplished by regulating the quality and marketing of a product, and by prohibiting its consumption by minors.

The basis for legal paternalism, which combines punishment and conditional treatment in the name of paternalism[11] and protection of the weak, is the refusal to consider that *the role of the state is to maximize the opportunity for each individual to become a full-fledged, independent citizen*. If we accept that this is the state's role, it must be proven, on the legal level, that criminal law is the only way of preventing non-autonomous persons from harming themselves.

Has this been proven with respect to drugs?[12] It has not; in fact, the opposite is true. The war on drugs has not only failed to meet the public-health objectives of preventing addiction, intoxication, and abuse, and of prompting an overall decrease in drug use, it has actually aggravated the situation by fostering a black market for drugs and by depriving thousands of medical treatment. This situation prevails in Canada as well as elsewhere.[13]

New trends in and attitudes towards certain illicit drugs over the past thirty years indicate that, despite having been prohibited since the early twentieth century (when reasons for their consumption changed), new groups have begun to try them. The most detailed report on the use of legal and illegal drugs in Canada, that of the Canadian Centre on Substance Abuse (CCSA) and the Centre for Addiction and Mental Health,[14] reports that in 1994 one out of four Canadians admitted to having used illegal drugs at least once in their lives and 7.7 per cent used illegal drugs in the year preceding the survey, with cannabis being the most commonly used drug. The following table[15] reveals some of these data on drug use:

Table 1

Lifetime use of illegal drugs by persons aged fifteen years and over, by province (in percentages)

Province	Cannabis	Cocaine	LSD, speed, heroine	Total Use[1]
British Columbia	35.4	8.1	10.4	36.6
Alberta	29.4	5.2	7.9	30.1
Ontario	16.6	2.0	4.1	17.5
Manitoba	25.2	2.5	5.6	25.8
Newfoundland	16.3	1.0	1.9	16.3
Prince Edward Island	18.6	2.0	3.0	18.6
Nova Scotia	25.1	1.8	4.1	25.5
Quebec	24.7	4.9	6.0	25.3
Saskatchewan	22.0	2.6	5.6	22.2
New Brunswick	21.7	1.9	6.5	22.3
Canada	**23.1**	**3.8**	**5.9**	**23.9**

[1] Note that this total represents people who have used at least one of the five drugs listed, while some have used more than one.
Source: Canada's Alcohol and Other Drugs Survey, 1994. Statistics Canada. www.statcan.ca.

These data cannot be explained solely by a lack of information on the potential harmfulness of the drugs in question, by the deviant personalities of the users, or by the new availability of the products. Of course, the drugs must be available. But availability is not sufficient to explain their consumption. By way of illustration, let us also look at some data on alcohol consumption in Canada.

Quebec has always had a more liberal policy than the other Canadian provinces on the drinking age and on sales outlets for alcohol. Nonetheless, Quebec's per capita rate of alcohol consumption has been lower than the national average for as long as we have had reliable data, that is, since the early 1970s.[16] The most recent data are as follows:

Table 2
Sales of alcoholic beverages and volume of absolute alcohol per person[1] (litres), by persons aged fifteen years and over, 1996–7

Province/Territory	Beer	Wine	Spirits	Total
Yukon	7.61	2.28	4.50	14.39
British Columbia	4.28	1.74	2.63	8.65
Alberta	4.31	1.23	2.95	8.49
Northwest Territories	4.15	0.66	3.66	8.47
Ontario	4.29	1.21	2.22	7.71
Manitoba	3.83	0.80	3.01	7.64
Newfoundland	4.56	0.44	2.61	7.61
Prince Edward Island	4.00	0.66	2.46	7.12
Nova Scotia	3.75	0.74	2.56	7.05
Quebec	4.48	1.57	0.95	7.01
Saskatchewan	3.53	0.53	2.88	6.94
New Brunswick	3.77	0.69	1.75	6.22
Canada	**4.27**	**1.29**	**2.08**	**7.64**

[1] These data represent litres of pure alcohol consumed, based on the percentage of alcohol in each drink, rather than litres of the actual beverages. A litre of beer and a litre of whisky represent very different quantities of alcohol. Statistics on alcohol consumption that neglect this distinction would considerably falsify the perception of consumption rates in Quebec compared with the other provinces.This oversight has the benefit, however, of supporting those who wish to suggest that Quebec's more liberal policies have increased alcohol consumption and that it is higher in that province than in other parts of Canada. *Source*: Canadian Centre on Substance Abuse, Centre for Addiction and Mental Health, Ottawa: CCSA 1999: 36. www.ccsa.ca.

Because there are more liquor outlets in Quebec, people assume that alcohol consumption is greater. In fact, the number of outlets in Quebec did increase from 350 to over 12,500 with the passage of Bill 21 in 1978, a bill that permitted the sale of beer and wine in small grocery stores and allowed for considerably longer hours of business (an additional forty hours). Yet alcohol consumption before and after passage of the bill was measured: despite the much greater availability of this drug in Quebec under the new law, there was no significant change in its consumption, and the percentage of drinkers in Quebec remained below .the national average.[17] This example shows that drug consumption is not motivated solely by availability, while at the same time restricting availability does not automatically lead to a drop in consumption.

Furthermore, fear of the law has little influence on a person's decision to reduce or stop the use of illicit drugs. According to studies conducted by the Addiction Research Foundation, health concerns are more likely to be the determining factor in this decision:

> The use of marijuana, for example, is the most studied crime available for comparison. Conclusions from a number of studies consistently indicate that the perceived certainty and severity of punishment are insignificant factors in deterring use. Similarly, cocaine users have been found to view the legal threat as remote. What apparently has been much more important in reversing the trend of increasing illicit drug use that marked the 1970s has been the growth in perceived harmfulness of the activity, which has in turn likely augmented social disapproval of drug use behaviour. In any weighing of legal and health risks of drug use, concerns about health predominate.
>
> ... As a primary preventive tool, criminal law is particularly ineffective against juveniles at the ages when much drug initiation occurs. Thus, declining illicit drug use has likely been independent of existing criminal law, and is unlikely to be affected by the easing of criminalization.[18]

In short, studies to determine how effective the law is at decreasing public-health problems related to drug use show that the criminal law has little effect; at most, the law may decrease the consumption of specific drugs by limiting their availability. There is no proof, however, that the use of one drug is not simply replaced by the use of other, sometimes more dangerous, drugs.[19] This is what happens with the black market fostered by the war on drugs. In the absence of a legal market, the black market meets the demand for illicit drugs. Drug-trafficking networks have developed that do not allow for the regulation of product quality or distribution:

> Illegal street-drugs have a set of risks all their own. Users of street-drugs

can never know exactly what they are taking. Dealers may not know (or reveal) exactly what they are selling. Some drugs are laced with other drugs or chemicals which can be harmful. Often one drug is sold in place of another.

In 1988 nearly two-thirds of all street-drug samples tested by the Addiction Research Foundation of Ontario were found to be different from what they were alleged to be by the seller. That means that about two out of every three times a drug was bought on the street, it was not what the buyer thought it was.

Many bad drug reactions, including fatal overdoses, are caused by the users' ignorance of exactly what drug and how much of it they are taking.[20]

Sellers of illicit drugs are found everywhere – schools, clubs, the streets, workplaces, and so on, usually offering either adulterated products to increase their profits or highly concentrated ones to encourage sales and even dependence, and, in the case of some drugs, promoting such 'hard' methods as injection. This harks back to the days of alcohol prohibition, from which we seem to have learned little.[21]

In fact, the current drug laws present a much greater danger than Prohibition. Because these laws are found internationally, the black market operates in more than sixty countries, and its size has attracted major players with substantial means; prohibitions have transformed the illicit drug trade into a flourishing international market.

Dealers in this market have the same objectives as in any lawful market: identifying a potential clientele, ensuring its ongoing custom, and creating new clienteles. However, since the trade, concentration, and quality of products are not regulated, any effort to expand the market is permissible, whether it be the sale of drugs to children or the sale of highly toxic products. Some dealers even attempt to create lifetime customers, by encouraging methods of consumption that can more easily create dependence than other, safer ones. In addition, dealers vary their products from time to time in order to keep their clients' interest, and create fads with the regular introduction of new products, such as crack, ice, Ecstasy, and so on. Dealers also try to reach a broad market by offering drugs at various prices; depending on the locale, cocaine, amphetamines, or crack will dominate. Dealers similarly seek to extend their markets geographically by dumping drugs in previously unexplored areas so as to attract new clients. None of this should be surprising. Right now the drug trade is a highly profitable one that operates worldwide. It is worthwhile for traffickers to use the best possible techniques for distributing and promoting their products. The result is that the black market is much more effective than a lawful, regulated market would be in promoting the use of drugs, with hundreds of thousands of dealers actively penetrating all segments of society.[22] We have had an example of this kind of situation with the black market for tobacco, which saw highly active dealers in all locales, dealers who in many cases were young people in school. There was also violence associated with this market, not because of the nicotine, but because of the operating rules of the black market.

Not only have prohibitive drug laws failed to lower the consumption of illicit drugs, then, they have also prompted the development of a black market in which the lack of control over drug quality, concentration, and places of distribution promotes intoxication and makes it extremely difficult for users to learn how to handle drugs. Moreover, they deprive thousands of sick people of drugs that could ease their suffering, as demonstrated by many studies on the therapeutic use of illicit drugs. Finally, the war on drugs deprives illicit drug users of appropriate medical treatment for problem habits. Such users, especially young people, are often reluctant to seek medical assistance for fear of encountering repression, lack of understanding, and discrimination. The result is that many users come to treatment with very serious problems because no intervention occurred earlier, a result of the government's decision to spend funds on repression rather than on assistance, education, and social programs.

In short, who does prohibition protect if it leads to a higher incidence of public- health problems? At present, there can be no doubt not only that the cure is ineffective against the disease but that, to use a familiar metaphor, its effects are worse than the disease itself.

> Simply stated, drugs are more dangerous because they are illegal. Just as tens of thousands of people died or were blinded or poisoned by bad bootleg liquor 60 years ago, perhaps the majority of overdose deaths today are the result of drug prohibition.
>
> Ordinarily, heroin does not kill. It addicts people and makes them constipated. But people overdose because they don't know what they are getting; they don't know if the heroin is 4 percent or 40 percent, or if it is cut with bad stuff, or if it is heroin at all – it may be a synthetic opiate or an amphetamine-type substance.
>
> Just imagine if every time you picked up a bottle of wine, you didn't

know whether it was 8 percent alcohol or 80 percent alcohol, or whether it was ethyl alcohol or methyl alcohol. Imagine if every time you took an aspirin, you didn't know if it was 5 milligrams or 500 milligrams ... Fewer people might take those drugs, but more would get sick and die. That is exactly what is happening today with the illicit drug market.[23]

Furthermore, a war on drugs implies the use of violence to achieve its goals. The violence will be even worse if the adversaries have been encouraged to assume a 'warrior mentality' because of a lack of public information and the consequent fear generated. Those deemed 'non-autonomous,' on whose behalf this prohibition has been justified, are likely to pay dearly: 'War mentality cleaves the world into noble allies and despicable enemies; justifies any measures necessary to prevail, including violence to innocent bystanders; and disdains accommodation, compromise, or any questioning of authority until total victory is achieved. In essence, war mentality suspends normal human compassion and intelligence. This mentality pervades current Canadian drug-control efforts.'[24]

What social values underlie the legal paternalism inherent in maintaining a prohibition that has created a context of violence, more serious public-health problems, and a black market that actively recruits young people? Clearly, they are not values that promote the best interests of society.

Legal Liberalism: Humanism, Social Responsibility, and Respect for Citizens

A second minority report to the Le Dain Commission, that of Marie-Andrée Bertrand, uses the political philosophy of J.S. Mill[25] to support its call for the legalization of cannabis. This report takes the position that *the state, as a guardian of public order, must restrict its actions to those areas that disturb the public peace in general*, such as road safety, and limit its actions so as to preserve civil rights to the greatest extent possible. Penal repression and mandatory treatment of cannabis users represent an abuse of the power of the state and its institutions because this relatively harmless drug could be handled properly by consumers if the state regulated its quality and its marketing. From this standpoint, the fact that many people find certain methods of drug use morally suspect does not make it legitimate for the state to regulate them by means of prohibition, unless such use constitutes in itself a threat to others.

Does this mean that, in a context of legal liberalism, the state has no responsibilities with respect to drugs unless such a threat exists? Quite the contrary. Prohibition is not the only form of intervention. For a better understanding of the role of state within a context of legal liberalism, some terms must be clarified.

First, we must distinguish legal liberalism from economic liberalism. Economic liberalism implies a withdrawal by the state to let market forces play themselves out; this ultimately results in rampant capitalism in which the strongest get stronger while the weakest are left to fend for themselves, with no means of changing their condition or achieving a satisfactory quality of life. In legal liberalism, the state maintains its responsibility for management of public order by providing the safest possible environment for all its citizens, as well as ensuring the social conditions most conducive to each individual's development. However, its preferred style of management preserves individual rights and liberties to the maximum extent possible. In other words, when it comes to drugs, the state is responsible for ensuring the safest possible environment for drug use and for establishing the conditions needed to minimize any harmful effects arising from such use.

Does this mean that the state promotes drug use or abandons its capacity to intervene in order to prevent abuse? Absolutely not. This is confusing legal liberalism with libertarianism,[26] which does not grant the state any social or political responsibility nor any legitimate authority to limit individual freedoms in any way whatsoever. This philosophy, which has its supporters in relation to drug use, is quite distinct from legal liberalism.

In fact, in the area of drugs, defining precisely what is meant by legal liberalism and the social values that underlie this philosophy requires an explanation and a discussion of the harm-reduction approach.

Harm Reduction and Drugs: A Different Approach and Different Practices

The harm-reduction approach to drugs has two components: reducing high-risk use and reducing the negative consequences associated with problem use. Reducing high-risk use may involve efforts to decrease demand for the product itself if any use of that product is high risk (as in the case of tobacco), or it may involve discouraging either high-risk use or methods of use that are risky (such as drinking and driving).[27] With respect to reducing the negative consequences of problem use, intervention may involve decreasing the problems associated with such use (for example, teaching abstinence or controlled drinking) or decreasing the environmental conditions that increase problem use (for example, through public policies that ensure a safe market).[28]

This approach is characterized by two principles: pragmatism and humanism. P. Brisson[29] defines this pragmatism by the following maxim: 'Since drugs are here to stay, let's limit the problems they cause for users and their family and friends'; and humanism by the motto: 'The drug user is a whole person, *worthy of respect*, with the same rights and power to act as any other citizen.'

If the 'cultural' roots of the harm-reduction approach are connected with drug use itself, through the transmission of the knowledge and know-how that will enable users to benefit from the positive effects of drugs while minimizing the harmful effects, the political roots of this approach, which led the state to give it some support, are essentially health-related, associated with the advent of AIDS in the 1980s. Since the middle of that decade, however, the concept of harm reduction has broadened in scope and has led to profound changes in intervention philosophies, as one major rehabilitation centre, the Centre Dollard Cormier in Montreal, attests: 'It is no longer the act of using (or overusing) drugs that is the client's problem, it is the development of a significant problem in the client's life that signals abuse. In other words, the drug problem in itself does not have consequences, it is the consequences that signify a drug problem ... From this perspective, the primary target for intervention is not the drug use itself but rather the negative consequences – the harm – stemming from the client's drug use.'[30]

This change of philosophy has also led a growing number of workers in the field to reject the contradictory discourse of the law and to call for drug users to receive the same treatment as any other citizen. According to Dr A. Mino, then chief physician of the Division pour toxicodépendants de la psychiatrie publique (Psychiatric Division for People with Chemical Dependencies) in Geneva: 'Paradoxically, we thought that drugs annihilated any capacity for choice and, at the same time, that using drugs was essentially a free choice. Our patients had freely chosen their lives of poverty, delinquency and physical degradation. AIDS was only one particularly horrible consequence of that choice. We could, using this reasoning, evade our responsibility for perpetuating the epidemic.'[31]

The claim that drug users should be treated the same as any other citizen means that the function of doctors is to keep them alive and in the best possible health. According to a pioneer of this approach in Great Britain, Dr John Marks,[32] when doctors cure ulcers or perform bypass surgery, they do not make their patients' treatment conditional on their changing their habits, eating better, avoiding stress, or exercising more, even though they may encourage such changes. A doctor offers care and advice and accepts that it is up to the individual to modify his or her lifestyle. For many professionals, this role implies, in the case of drug addiction, first, that addicts have their own opinions regarding their needs, and second, that they can be prescribed any drug, including heroin, that can aid them and preserve their lives. This is now an accepted practice in certain clinics in Switzerland, England, and the Netherlands. We are also beginning to consider the same approach in Canada.

This new philosophy, both among health practitioners and the community, has led to a call for the harm-reduction approach to be expanded from a situational strategy linked with the advent of AIDS to strategies legitimized by public-health policy. What does this mean in terms of social values? To answer this question, we must first identify the difference between an emergency strategy and a public policy.

Harm Reduction and Drugs: From an Emergency Strategy to a Public Policy

The harm-reduction approach has united players with very different motivations. Some are still essentially fighting against AIDS, and if a vaccine were available, their involvement would most likely be limited to an HIV vaccination program. Others have seen the problem of AIDS as an opportunity to help a neglected and often misunderstood clientele that has been difficult to reach. Although AIDS has brought together people with varying motivations and with many different approaches to drug users, it is still the case that traditional morality dominates public policy, and harm-reduction strategies essentially represent an emergency response to AIDs rather than a change in social values. Actually, these emergency strategies have brought about a change from an uncompromising legal moralism to a greater willingness to provide medical treatment for some clients, within a context of legal paternalism. The status of some addicts has therefore changed from that of 'offender' to that of a potentially contagious patient, from whom all 'upstanding' citizens must be protected. By assigning the status of medical patient to the IDU (injection drug user), public policy has maintained the illusion that the user's lifestyle has essentially been caused by the drug and has no relation to the conditions of use caused by prohibition.[33]

The status of medical patient also perpetuates the public perception that AIDS programs for IDUs will be needed only until these individuals make the 'right' choice to solve their problems, namely abstinence.[34] In this regard, these programs are perceived as a social-defence strategy – protecting 'good' citizens from being contaminated by drug users – rather than a social-protection strategy – reducing the harmful effects of drug use by people who are considered full-fledged citizens.[35] As IDU groups have pointed out,[36] people dependent on tobacco are not viewed as drug-addicted patients because the black market does not oblige them to adopt a lifestyle based upon their addiction; in the case of dependence on an illegal drug, the lifestyle, with the risks and difficulties that it implies, is tied to the black market and not to the drug per se. By viewing the user as sick, this issue can be ignored, along with all the normal other desires and needs felt by the addict (and by all other individuals): 'We, like other drug users, have a life besides drug use, and, given the choice, we certainly wouldn't want our drug use to circumscribe our lives. Unfortunately, in the current hostile environment within which drug users live, our drug use is considered the most important issue by those who have power over our lives ... We don't want this to happen, it is imposed on us – even when we do everything necessary to survive.'[37]

In short, although the harm-reduction approach can legitimately translate into multiple forms of intervention in response to emergencies in the field, while at the same time keeping silent about the law and its effects, it cannot be called a public policy on drugs nor can it become one unless its underlying social values allow us to consider drug users full-fledged citizens and, as a result, create obligations for the state. In fact, this approach cannot become a true public policy on drugs unless it is associated with a philosophy of legal liberalism based on humanism, social responsibility, and respect for all citizens, including drug users.

These values create obligations for the state. What are these obligations? First, just as the state is responsible for ensuring that the consumption of food and other products is as safe as possible for the public, it is also responsible for ensuring a safe environment for drug consumption. To do so, certain tools designed to *reduce high-risk use* are essential:

- regulations to control product quality. These regulations, if necessary, may lead to the modification of some of the components and of the growing or manufacturing conditions of a drug to reduce its toxicity;
- regulations to ensure that the marketing of a drug is accompanied by proper consumer information, including precise labelling;
- regulations on the distribution of a drug, such that, if necessary, its availability can be restricted to certain locations or clienteles; and
- the availability of the funds needed to establish prevention programs designed to inform the public about the benefits and risks of use for each product, method of use, context, and so forth.

Further, efforts to *reduce the negative consequences associated with problem use* must also be made by means of the following:

- availability of the funds needed to set up a varied range of treatments;
- availability of the funds needed to train workers in the field so that they can provide the best possible treatment; and
- availability of the funds needed to pursue research in this area in order to improve our understanding of the products, the risks associated with different forms of use, the methods of use by different populations, and the best treatments for the differing needs.

These elements, essential to the realization of a public policy on harm reduction, represent state obligations in the context of a legal liberalism that seeks increased autonomy for each citizen in relation to the choices offered.[38] Bearing in mind this social responsibility on the part of the state and the need for humanism and respect for the drug user as a citizen, we will now proceed to analyse some of our current public policies.

Analysis of Our Current Policies

Public Policies on Legal Drugs: The Case of Alcohol

Recent studies on alcohol clearly demonstrate that a public policy aimed at decreasing consumption, regardless of its method of management, can result in failure to reach the ultimate objective of the reduction of problems. In other words, an average decline in alcohol consumption does not necessarily translate into a decrease in drinking problems, as is shown by studies done in Australia, England, Ontario, and Quebec. In an interview in this regard, Louise Nadeau gave an excellent explanation of this phenomenon:

> There are two categories of drinkers that should not be confused.
>
> A typical example of the first category, Mr or Mrs X, always drinks two glasses of wine at dinner. His or her physician approves: alcohol, taken regularly in moderate doses – that is, no more than two glasses a day – reduces the risk of heart disease. Numerous studies indicate that moderate drinkers are healthier than abstainers, even after excluding the influence of such variables as age and physical activity. In short, for Mr or Mrs X, alcohol is a source of pleasure and health, not problems.
>
> It is a different story for Mr or Mrs Y, who drinks the same amount of alcohol in a week, but all on one or two occasions. The physician disapproves, and the social worker is starting to take an interest. Why? A significant portion of those who drink too much alcohol drink because they have problems ... and they have problems because, among other things, they drink ...
>
> This is where we discover a flaw in the statistics published by Santé Québec. The number of moderate drinkers has shrunk while the number of abstainers has grown. Returning to our example, Mr or Mrs X has replaced wine with mineral water. If drinking was not politically incorrect, his or her doctor might be somewhat critical of this. Therefore, the drop in consumption has a perverse effect.
>
> But it gets worse. The same data show that the heavy drinkers, the ones who get drunk, are not drinking any less. [39]

In Quebec, the drinkers who continue to drink excessively form a hard core. To reach them, according to Louise Nadeau, we must change the message. But first we must change our objective: 'Given what we now know, if we wanted to make sensible recommendations to the department, we would no longer set the objective in terms of overall volume [demand reduction], says the researcher. We would try to decrease the incidence of excessive drinking [harm reduction].' [40]

In 1997 a similar observation led Quebec's Comité permanent de lutte à la toxicomanie (CPLT) (Standing Committee on Addictions) to recommend that the Department of Health and Social Services change the objective of Quebec's 1992 policy on alcohol – 'reduce alcohol consumption in Quebec by 15 per cent within ten years' – to the following:

'reduce the number of people who engage in high-risk alcohol consumption and reduce the harm associated with that consumption, for the users, their family and friends, and society as a whole.'[41]

In fact, from the standpoint of legal liberalism, it is an abuse of power for the state to seek to regulate alcohol-related behaviour on a moral basis or to decrease alcohol consumption regardless of its management. However, the state does have a duty to provide not only a safe environment but also the institutional mechanisms required to implement programs to reduce both heavy use of this drug and the harmful consequences that result. As for any drug, light and heavy use present different levels of risk. This distinction between light and heavy use has been very slow to make an impact in the political sphere: the issue of alcohol use is still strongly associated with the idea of abstinence as a moral ideal for all citizens. These are the social values revealed in the strident debate on controlled-drinking programs,[42] and in the recent debate on the criminalization of drinking and driving which sees the recourse to criminal law gaining in popularity.[43] This last statement merits more detailed discussion.

Educational campaigns intended to change the behaviour of people who drive motor vehicles while their faculties are impaired focus primarily on alcohol consumption. Similarly, criminal infractions for impaired driving apply almost exclusively to drunk driving. The Criminal Code contains a specific charge for those who drive with more than 80 mg of alcohol per 100 ml of blood. Defining the penalty in terms of alcohol level means that no preventive effort is focused on other factors: 'Alcohol consumption is not the only possible factor in an automobile accident; there are many others, including road and weather conditions, speed limits, mechanical failure, sudden health problems, and so on. In the case of young people, we must remember that they are usually very inexperienced drivers. They may not be skilful enough because they have not had enough opportunities to drive. In addition, they may not be as aware of how alcohol affects them and their ability to drive as an older driver with more experience.'[44]

The focus on drinking and driving allows the state to avoid costly measures related to road safety (for example, economical and convenient public transit, road repairs, improved signalling, and safety standards for automobile manufacturing, and so on), and fails to teach drivers the importance of not driving while impaired, regardless of the cause (such as fatigue, cold medications that reduce attentiveness, strong emotions following an argument, and so on). Instead of teaching members of the public to assess whether they can drive well enough to ensure the safety of themselves and others, they are taught to be afraid of the police, since 'drinking and driving is criminal!'

Emphasis on the danger of getting caught drinking and driving rather than a more comprehensive attempt to prevent driving while impaired creates perverse effects. For example, a person has had a few drinks; for fear of police roadblocks, he or she takes an alternative route or waits a few hours, without drinking, before leaving. Finally, the person drives, without necessarily being sober, but practically falling asleep at the wheel. Where is the prevention of impaired driving in this situation? This person has made a choice based not on his or her ability to drive but solely on the possibility of getting caught. Statistics may indicate a decline in drunk driving, but would road safety have increased as much if social values regarding the responsibility to drive unimpaired had not changed? Not necessarily.

If the true objective of the law is to prevent driving while impaired in order to decrease the presence on the roads of drivers who represent a potential danger to themselves or others, then someone who is very tired, has taken cold medication, has just quarrelled with his wife, has worked overtime, or is too elderly may have impaired faculties and constitute a potential danger to himself and others. Why isolate one of the causes of impairment and give the state the right to use the criminal law in that case only? Is there driving with 'good' impaired faculties and driving with 'bad' impaired faculties?[45] The reflex tests used in the past and perhaps some additional skill tests are excellent instruments for measuring a person's ability to drive. In terms of road safety, the issue is to determine whether a person is in a proper or improper state to drive, regardless of the reasons, not whether he or she has consumed alcohol. From this standpoint, would we be as quick to resort to criminal law as a way of 'correcting' all impaired drivers? Probably not.

What makes the use of criminal law so easy a solution to the problem is the perception that it is 'immoral' to drink and drive, an argument that is difficult to uphold if the definition of impaired faculties no longer focuses solely on alcohol consumption before driving but rather on better road safety in general. It is particularly important to rethink how to reduce the problems caused by impaired driving now that new tests, such as urine and blood tests, have been developed to detect drivers who have consumed other drugs.[46] These tests could represent a major abuse of power, especially since the drug-testing industry is seeking to expand its market.[47]

As for the state's responsibilities with regard to road safety, it is just as important to ensure that the criminal law is used as a last resort and not as compensation for the state's failure to assume its responsibilities in this area (through, for example, a road-safety network, the adequate regulation of car manufacture, the availability of public transportation, and a comprehensive prevention program).

In short, this first case study reveals two major difficulties hampering the implementation of a true public policy on drugs based on legal liberalism: first, the moral ideal of abstinence that still impregnates our culture, even when it comes to legal drugs; and second, the state's interest in translating this moral ideal into legal standards – punishing an immoral individual, the root of all evil – and avoiding an examination of its obligation to protect its citizens. In fact, legal moralism remains well entrenched in public policies on alcohol.

Public Policies on Illegal Drugs

In Quebec, the Comité permanent de lutte à la toxicomanie called for a public policy of harm reduction for illegal drugs in 1997.[48] In its advisory report to the Department of Health and Social Services, the committee explains that the objectives of the Quebec policy on illegal drugs are still based on the moralistic goal of reducing drug use, regardless of the risks involved. It clearly calls for the government to abandon the federal strategy of zero tolerance that is supported by the law, and for recognition of the fact that repression is the main source of harm for users of these drugs. It recommends a complete turnaround in policy towards a harm-reduction approach that would involve recognizing, both for alcohol and for a number of illegal drugs, that most users do not have problems and that the department's money and energy would be better spent on preventing high-risk use and on reducing the negative consequences of problem use. The CPLT suggests changing the 1992 objective, 'Increase the number of people who never use illegal drugs,' to the following: 'Reduce the number of people who make excessive or inappropriate use of illegal drugs and reduce the harm associated with the use of these drugs, for the users, their family and friends and all of Quebec society.'

These recommendations by the CPLT are echoed in the *Plan d'action en toxicomanie 1999–2001* released by the Department of Health and Social Services.[49] However, in contrast to the CPLT's recommendations, this document does not discuss the harmful effects of the law, with the result that the actual public policy does not represent a harm-reduction approach based on legal liberalism, but rather a form of 'wartime medicine' based on moralism and legal paternalism. This type of medical intervention is actually needed in the current context, but to give it the status of public policy is to legitimize the harmful effects of this war as 'normal,' without questioning the basis of the war itself. It is akin to establishing a public environmental policy involving the distribution of gas masks to people living in the vicinity of industries that are major polluters. This would send a message that such industrial pollution is a normal situation to which the public must adapt, and that the government is graciously supplying gas masks to those segments of the population who cannot afford to live elsewhere.

In his 1994 report, Chief Coroner J.V. Cain of British Columbia[50] emphasizes that repression is extremely expensive, in terms both of implementation and of outcome. He is referring, of course, to the staggering costs of police intervention and the involvement of the criminal justice system, particularly in the case of simple possession (through the cost of arrests, court appearances, and, in some cases, prison sentences). In addition, there are those who are introduced to injection drugs and high-risk use in prison, who go into debt for drugs and who must pay the costs physically, socially, and financially upon release.[51] To these direct costs of repression Cain adds the indirect costs that fall upon the health system and social-services agencies in general. There are, for example, the injection drug users who, fearing this repression, delay treatment, with the tragic result that much more serious intervention is needed; there is also the rise in the number of cases of HIV and hepatitis, as well as the much more serious deterioration in living conditions caused by the black market itself.

Finally, the increase in the harmful effects of repression for addicts is not limited to the individual but extends to his or her family (particularly children) and society in general (criminality,[52] deterioration of the neighbourhood, growing numbers of dealers on the street trying to support their habits, and so on). Moreover, addicts who are HIV-positive or who have Hepatitis A or B have sexual contact with non-addicts, thus increasing the incidence of these diseases in the rest of the population. Prostitutes engage in thousands of unprotected contacts, at the client's request,[53] but sexual contact also occurs in all the ordinary settings because, contrary to the mythical image of injection drug users, they are not necessarily on their last legs, suffering from AIDS and easily identifiable. On the contrary, many are occasional users who can be found at work, at school, in clubs and bars, and so on.

Cain refers to all these costs[54] and openly questions our repressive approach to drugs, as well as the laws that embody this approach. His report is one of the few in Canada that have explicitly stated that the legalization of drugs is essential to a true public policy of harm reduction. Even if there is increasingly open recognition in some public documents that repression, or enforcement of the law, is the main source of harm for drug users, it is less clearly stated in those documents that prohibition and the laws themselves are the main source of the black market and the resulting repression. Cain states in his report:

> I am recommending the establishment of a commission to examine and challenge those legal aspects of the problem, amongst so many other things. The problem must be looked at with regard to not only the aspect of deaths from heroin and cocaine, but rather the entire smorgasbord of available illicit narcotics, so-called 'soft' and 'hard' drugs.[55]

> Legalization should not be considered the panacea or solution to substance abuse problems plaguing British Columbia and the rest of the country. It would not solve all the anti-social and criminal acts committed by confirmed addicts. Nor do I believe legalization would increase the incidence of those acts. On the contrary, what it would do is create that necessary 'window of opportunity' for the addicts who have lost hope and freedom of choice.[56]

In Canada and Australia, as well as several European countries,[57] the traditional repressive approach has been maintained in response to U.S. pressure through international conventions, as well as pressure from certain industries and bureaucracies that benefit from the current prohibition against some drugs.[58] In Canada, for example, this recently resulted in a new Controlled Drugs and Substances Act (May 1997), a statute that expands the government's power of repression.[59] The supporters of this statute justified the expansion of power by the need for more effective weapons against clandestine laboratories manufacturing synthetic drugs. But, as the Canadian Bar Association and the Ontario Criminal Lawyers' Association noted during the hearings preceding its passage, and as legal statistics on drugs show, the clientele targeted by drug laws are more likely to be users or small dealers in disadvantaged neighbourhoods than major traffickers.[60]

There are still 65,000 drug-related criminal charges in Canada each year, and Canada is second, after the United States, in terms of its rate of incarceration of drug users. This must not be forgotten.[61] Moreover, it has been noted that the more cannabis is seen as a harmless drug with no addictive power and therefore no longer a priority for repression, the statistics in regard to charges reveal something very different, both in Canada and elsewhere.[62] In Canada, 45,000 of the drug-related charges relate to cannabis, and 30,000 represent cases of simple possession. While it is true that police priorities have changed so that at the investigation level private consumption is disregarded, and that the judicial system gives few prison sentences for simple possession, cannabis charges have actually increased since 1990 while cocaine and heroin charges have dropped.[63] Furthermore, these thousands of people now have criminal records. To date, more than 600,000 Canadians have criminal records because of cannabis.[64]

Groups lobbying in support of the new statute also justified its increased powers of repression by stating that Canada had to conform to the relevant international conventions[65] and had little flexibility as a result. This is misleading. The conventions oblige us to have certain prohibitions but leave significant flexibility in how to apply them.[66]

The recent decisions in favour of repression convey to the public the idea not only that intervention to counter the harmful effects of this war is normal, but also that drug users have the primary responsibility in this regard and are themselves responsible for the hostility shown towards them. These decisions also perpetuate the host of contradictions surrounding the development of harm-reduction strategies because of the official priority given to health budgets for HIV prevention. In fact, without any explicit challenge to prohibition, we are left with the legal moralism and legal paternalism that so thoroughly permeate the issue of legal and illegal drugs, preventing the state from assuming its proper responsibilities in this area: to normalize use, recognize the benefits as well as the harmful effects of drugs, treat users as full-fledged citizens, and conduct prevention and intervention activities in a safe context where criminal law is used as the method of last resort.[67]

We must no longer consider it normal for public-health activities to correct the actions of our justice system. We must refuse to restrict the harm-reduction approach to that of a 'wartime medicine.' We must examine the social values we wish to promote in our drug policies in order to better define the state's responsibilities in this regard.

Conclusion

Drug policies are currently being developed amid tremendous confusion because there has been no debate over the objectives and underlying social values of such policies. As a result, initiatives are being taken today to stop people from using drugs, while at the same time safe places are being established in which people can use intravenous drugs. Similarly, some drug users are being locked up at the same time that sterile needles are being handed out in prisons. This state of affairs means that counsellors who want to help integrate drug users into society have to work surrounded by the damaging effects of prohibition and the ensuing efforts to stop people from using drugs, and have to constantly justify themselves to a public that is hostile towards their clients. Workers in the field are growing more and more uncomfortable, because it is difficult in the circumstances to clarify the priorities and ethical boundaries of their intervention, to overcome operational problems, and to set adequate criteria for evaluating program results. This explains why many people are beginning to conclude that the argument that drug-use prevention fights AIDS exacts a heavy toll in dealing with drug addicts, and drug addicts, as stated earlier, are starting either to claim to be something other than a possible source of contamination or to challenge the political status of the requirement that they be labelled 'sick' in order to receive assistance and support.

In the course of considering Canada's drug policy, everyone ought to take another look at the options for the role of state set out at the beginning of this essay in order to make a final determination as to which social values are important. This will not bring about change overnight, but it will provide some direction and help in choosing more consistent and more credible actions.

Legal Moralism

Taking the view that one of the state's legitimate roles is to preserve a common morality, independent of the imperatives of public order, amounts to taking the view that the state can legitimately keep the upper hand by imposing values that meet its needs. This line of thinking leads to drug users being blamed for their own economic, health, and criminal problems. And the solution is to deal with their moral failings through the criminal justice system without exploring the state's responsibilities in that regard.

Legal Paternalism

Taking the view that one of the state's roles is to protect non-auton-

omous persons, without questioning what constitutes a non-autonomous person or the meaning of the word protection, amounts to letting
the state not only designate as non-autonomous people those who have
been unable to adapt to current living conditions, but also disregard the
harmful effects of measures to eliminate drug use and the black market.
Drug users who do not know what they are doing and find themselves
caught up in legal, economic, and health problems thus come to bear
sole responsibility for their plight. If they fail to see that their problems
arose because drugs rendered them unable to manage their lives, and if
they refuse to be declared 'sick' so that they can get help, the solution is
to punish them as criminals, without exploring the state's responsibilities in this regard.[68]

Legal Liberalism

Taking the view that one of the state's responsibilities is to create a safe
environment in managing public order while at the same time preserving civil rights as much as possible amounts to taking the view that
the state cannot legitimately keep the upper hand other than by maxi-
mizing opportunities for everyone to become a full-fledged citizen. The
state must be accountable for the opportunities it gives people to use
drugs safely by compiling and providing access to information on soft-
and hard-drug use, by setting up adequate high-risk drug-use prevention programs, and by offering the most appropriate services and care
for people who have developed drug problems. In terms of principles,
this means two things: pragmatism – drugs are here to stay, and are
something we have to deal with; and humanism – drug users are full-
fledged citizens. These same principles underlie the harm-reduction
approach. But, if civil rights are to be given maximum respect, this also
means that criminal proceedings should be a method of last resort for
handling any problems encountered in the course of harm reduction.

What Values Should Underlie Canadian Drug Policy?

Opting for legal liberalism in dealing with drugs, as in any other area
of public policy, is a necessary ideal in a democratic society. Everyone,
from the lowest of the low to the highest of the high, has a duty to use
whatever forum he or she is afforded to state how drugs should be
addressed. And one thing is certain: in today's prohibitionist world, it
takes a great deal of courage and imagination to articulate the steps in

that process. But only if we pay that price will we be able to say that we have implemented a Canadian drug policy which is based on humanism, social responsibility, and respect for drug users as full citizens. In short, that is the price of democracy and the way to reduce the public-health problems caused by drugs.

NOTES

1 A.P. Pires, 'Quelques obstacles à une mutation du droit pénal,' *Revue générale de droit*, 26 (1995): 133–54.
2 Le Dain Commission of Inquiry into the Non-Medical Use of Drugs, *Rapport Le cannabis* (Ottawa: Information Canada 1972) (hereafter Le Dain, *Rapport*).
3 P. Devlin, *The Enforcement of Morals* (London, New York: Oxford University Press 1965, 1968).
4 Use of this terminology in connection with drugs came back in force with the advent of AIDS.
5 Le Dain, *Rapport*, 313–14. Of course, Campbell's paper was written in 1972, before the Charter of Rights, when indecency was not defined in the same way it is today. The Supreme Court considerably restricted the notion of indecency after the advent of the Charter (see, for example, the 1992 *Butler* case). However, for our purposes, the interest of Campbell's position lies in its justification of prohibitions in the name of morality.
6 Protestant culture also produced legal liberalism, discussed later, which is the approach taken by the Protestant cantons of Switzerland and the Netherlands, for example. See L. Beauchesne, 'La politique de tolérance néerlandaise: 20 ans plus tard,' *L'Écho-toxico*, 8, no. 2 (1997): 7–8; Y. Boggio, 'De l'indifférence à l'acceptation de la complexité, la trajectoire suisse en matière de drogues,' *GRD Psychotropes, politique, société* (2000); M. Lap, 'About Netherweed and coffeeshops,' in L. Bollinger, ed., *De-Americanizing Drug Policy* (Frankfurt, Germany: Peter Lang 1994), 137–50. To understand how Protestantism led to the development of legal moralism in North America, see L. Beauchesne, 'La culture protestante américaine: influence sur les politiques en matière de drogues,' *Histoire sociale/Social History*, 33, no. 66 (2000). This moralism is still very much alive: D. Wagner, *The New Temperance: The American Obsession with Sin and Vice* (Boulder, Colo.: Westview Press 1997).
7 M. Rosenzweig, 'Pour une éthique de la clinique des assuétudes et des addictions Conférence prononcée au Colloque Quelle prise en charge des

patients toxicomanes ... aujourd'hui ... demain ?' *Société Belge d'Éthique et de Morale Médicale*, 23 April 1999, 3–4. Translation.

8 The State of Kansas in the United States offers an example of this kind of imposition of values. On 1 September 1999 the government of that state prohibited the teaching of Darwin's theories in schools because those theories run counter to the dominant religious values.

9 H.L.A. Hart, *Law, Liberty and Morality* (Stanford, Calif.: Stanford University Press (1963, 1969).

10 What Foucault describes as bio-power; see M. Foucault, *La volonté de savoir* (Paris: Gallimard 1976). This type of medical control appears in other contexts as well. In Quebec, for example, not so long ago, the decision to have an abortion was made not by a woman but by a medical body (the therapeutic committee), which decided on the validity of her request. The criteria used to make such decisions, while rendered in medical terms and accompanied by therapeutic justifications, went far beyond medical considerations.

11 The impact of paternalism becomes clear when we study the status of women. In the name of paternalism, women were long considered non-autonomous and were not even viewed by the law as 'persons.'

12 E. Van Ree, 'Drugs, the Democratic Civilising Process and the Consumer Society,' *International Journal of Drug Policy*, 13, no. 5 (1991): 349–53.

13 L. Beauchesne, *Les drogues: Les coûts cachés de la prohibition* (Montreal: Bayard Canada Livres 2006).

14 CCLAT (Centre canadien de lutte contre l'alcoolisme et les toxicomanies/ CTSM (Centre de toxicomanie et des sante mentale), *Profil canadien: l'alcool, le tabac et les autres drogues* (Montreal : CCLAT/CTSM 1999), 136.

15 Ibid., 143.

16 R.G. Smart and A.C. Ogborne, *Northern Spirits Drinking in Canada Then and Now* (Toronto: ARF 1986).

17 P. Lamarche, *The Impact of Increasing the Number of Off-Premise Outlets of Alcohol on Per Capita Consumption: The Quebec Experience* (Montreal: GRAP 1987).

18 P.G. Erickson, 'A Public Health Approach to Demand Reduction,' *Journal of Drug Issues*, 20, no. 4 (1990): 565–6.

19 Examples often found in the literature include the prohibition of tobacco in China, which encouraged (there is no automatic cause and effect) the use of opium; the American prohibition of opium smoking in the United States and elsewhere, which led to the use of morphine and heroin; the prohibition of alcohol, which encouraged the use of ether among the Irish; and the use of opium by American women because of the (moral and social) pro-

hibition against drinking alcohol. C. Bachmann and A. Coppel, *Le dragon domestique* (Paris: Albin Michel 1989; published in 1992 under the title *La drogue dans le monde, hier et aujourd'hui*). It should also be remembered that 'forced abstinence' can create stress and compensatory habits, such as eating habits, that actually harm a person's health rather than improving it. All too often, studies on the effectiveness of programs are limited to measuring abstinence or the rate at which drug use is resumed, and not the possibly harmful compensatory habits that may develop when abstinence is forced on someone: 'Studies of forced abstinence have shown that the effect on a person's social and personal life is not all positive. Researchers see various emotional problems: anxiety, nervous behaviour, hostility, depression – all of which may lead to violence, physical symptoms, regular use of psychoactive medications and dependence on social groups, in other words, a shift to behaviour that is not much healthier for these people and those around them.' D. Cormier, S. Brochu, and J.P. Bergevin, *Prévention primaire et secondaire de la toxicomanie* (Montreal: Le Méridien 1991), 196–7. Translation.

20 Health and Social Welfare Canada, *Les drogues, faits et méfaits* (Ottawa: Ministry of Supply and Services 1990), 7. Translation.

21 L. Nadeau, 'L'amérique en guerre des dépendances,' *Autrement*, 106 (1989): 123–30.

22 C.H. de Choiseul-Praslin, *La drogue, une économie dynamisée par la répression* (Paris: CNRS 1991).

23 E. Nadelmann, 'The Solution Becomes the Problem,' in *Drug Prohibition and the Conscience of Nations* (Washington, D.C.: Drug Policy Foundation 1990), 27.

24 B.K. Alexander, *Peaceful Measures: Canada's Way out of the "War on Drugs"* (Toronto: University of Toronto Press 1990), 3.

25 J.S. Mill *On Liberty* (1859; New York: Norton 1974).

26 Libertarianism dates from the late nineteenth century and stems from the political ideas of Pierre-Joseph Proudhon and Michel Bakounine, who claimed that only anarchy was legitimate and that the government had no power to restrict individual freedoms.

27 We will have an opportunity to discuss these two examples later.

28 Harm reduction and abstinence, as well as the harm-reduction approach and legalization of drugs, are often presented as parallel issues; see L. Nadeau, 'Toxicomanie et réduction des méfaits,' *Conférence d'ouverture présentée au XXVIe colloque de l'AITQ*, 26 October 1998. Excluding abstinence from harm reduction confuses the end with the means. Harm reduction is an overall objective in relation to drugs and abstinence may legitimately constitute

one of the means, among others, of reducing the harmful effects for some users. We must avoid limiting harm reduction to the initial movement which brought this approach into the realm of public policy, namely reducing the incidence of HIV and hepatitis by distributing syringes, sterile equipment, and substitute drugs. In fact, such actions represent harm-reduction strategies that are extremely limited, whereas the harm-reduction philosophy encompasses all harm related to drug use, including harmful effects whose sources cannot be analysed in the same way for legal and illegal drugs.
See P. Brisson, *La réduction des méfaits: sources, situation, pratiques* (Quebec: Government of Quebec / CPLT 1997). The rest of this essay will discuss the consequences of this statement, namely the inevitable link between a public harm-reduction policy and legalization of drugs.

29 Brisson, *La réduction des méfaits*, 43–5.

30 J. Boilard, 'La réadaptation à Domrémy-Montréal La réduction des méfaits,' *L'Écho-toxico*, 6, no. 2 (1995): 5. Translation.

31 A. Mino and S. Arever, *J'accuse, les mensonges qui tuent les drogués* (Paris: Calmann-Lévy 1996), 34.

32 A. Henman, *Drogues légales. L'expérience de Liverpool* (Paris: Éditions du Lézard (1995).

33 P. Mary, *Délinquant, délinquance et insécurité. Un demi-siècle de traitement en Belgique (1944–1997)* (Brussels: Bruylant 1998).

34 Similarly, efforts to prevent HIV infection among prostitutes have not changed perceptions nor led to a debate on the possible legalization of prostitution. This does not mean that workers in the field are not trying to circumvent these restrictive policies. For example, the Stella program in Montreal does more than HIV prevention, even though its funding originates from HIV-prevention programs.

35 J.-F. Cauchie, 'Effets des contrats de sécurité sur le secteur de l'intervention médico-psycho-sociale en toxicomanie,' in L. Van Campenhoudt et al., eds., *Réponses à l'insécurité. Des discours aux pratiques* (Bruxelles: Labor 2000), 99–27; F.-X, Colle, 'Prohibition, propagande, prévention,' *La revue THS*, 2 (1999): 43–4; F.-X. Colle, *Toxicomanies, systèmes et familles où les drogues rencontrent les émotions* (Paris: Éditions Érès 1996); C. Perron, 'Le regroupement d'usagers,' in *Recueil des présentations lors de la quinzième rencontre provinciale des intervenant(e)s en prévention de la transmission du VIH chez les UDI* (Quebec: CQCS 1999).

36 With respect to user groups and their demands, see C. Perron, 'Le regroupement d'usagers,' and www.actup.org.

37 R. Balian and C. White, 'Defining the Drug User,' *International Journal of Drug Policy*, 9 (1998): 392.

38 With regard to the significance of this autonomy with respect to drugs, see P. Cohen, 'Shifting the Main Purposes of Drug Control: From Suppression to Regulation of Use, Reduction of Risks as the New Focus for Drug Policy,' *International Journal of Drug Policy*, 10, no. 3 (1999): 223–34; and P.G. Erickson et Y.W. Cheung, 'Harm Reduction among Cocaine Users: Reflections on Individual Intervention and Community Social Capital,' *International Journal of Drug Policy*, 10, no. 3 (1999): 244.

39 E. Denis, 'La modération a bien meilleur goût, mais ... ,' *Interface*, 17, no. 1 (1996): 53–5. Translation.

40 Ibid., 53–4.

41 Comité permanent de lutte à la toxicomamie (CPLT), *Avis sur l'objectif de la politique de la santé et du bien-être de 1992 qui porte sur l'alcoolisme et l'usage abusif de psychotropes au Québec* (Quebec: Government of Quebec 1997). Translation.

42 J.A. Tucker, D.M. Donavan, and G.A. Marlatt, eds., *Changing Addictive Behavior* (New York: Guilford Press 1999).

43 To follow the debate on this question in the House of Commons, see the Canadian Drug Policy Foundation website: www.cfdp.ca.

44 D. Cormier, S. Brochu, and J.P. Bergevin, *Prévention primaire et secondaire de la toxicomanie* (Montreal: Le Méridien 1991). Translation.

45 Just as there seem to be good and bad reasons for contracting HIV. The responsibilities of the government and public support are not the same in both cases.

46 In this connection, see the CPLT's recommendations in 1999 on the decriminalization of cannabis in *Avis sur La déjudiciarisation de la possession simple de cannabis*: 'develop methods of reducing the harm associated with cannabis consumption, such as impaired driving, as was done for alcohol' (10; translation). See also D. Notte, 'Fumer ou conduire, il faut choisir ...' *Les Cahiers de Prospective Jeunesse*, 4, no. 2 (1999): 3–6.

47 A. Hanson, 'Le dépistage des drogues: contrôle des drogues ou des esprits?' *Psychotropes*, 7, no. 3 (1992): 71–87.

48 CPLT, *Avis*.

49 Quebec, Ministry of Health and Social Services, *Plan d'action en toxicomanie, 1999–2001* (Quebec: Government of Quebec / Directorate of Communications 1998).

50 J.V. Cain, *Report of the Task Force into Illicit Narcotic Overdose Deaths in British Columbia* (Government of British Columbia / Office of the Chief Coroner / Ministry of Attorney General, 1994).

51 The rapid rise in the incidence of HIV in prison demonstrates the presence of injection drugs there. See R. Jurgen et D. Riley, 'Responding to Aids and

Drug Use in Prisons in Canada,' *International Journal of Drug Policy*, 8, no. 1 (1997): 31–9.

52 Think of the recent debate concerning threats to the physical safety of farmers and their families in the Montérégie region of Quebec, because their lands have been taken over by drug traffickers for growing their crops. This recalls the violence generated by the trafficking that occurred when tobacco prices were prohibitive.

53 G. Bibeau and M. Perrault, *Dérives montréalaises. À travers des itinéraires de toxicomanies dans le quartier Hochelaga-Maisonneuve* (Quebec: Boréal 1995).

54 To which he could have added, on the macro level, 'criminalization of the politician,' i.e., the various alliances between criminal structures and banks, industries, and governments. In this regard, see the recent report of the L'Observatoire géopolitique des drogues (1999), found at www.ogd. org. And on the micro level, there is the difficulty of giving the right information to warn about the harmful effects of certain methods of using illicit drugs when many users have lost all faith in official sources of information. See B. Lebeau, 'Neurotoxicité de l' "ecstasy," la science, la prévention et les jeunes,' *La revue THS*, 2 (1999): 22–5.

55 Cain, *Report*, vi.

56 Ibid., 88.

57 'Debat: politiques (criminelles) et problème de drogue: évolution et tendance en Europe,' *Déviance et société*, 22, no. 1 (1998); 'Politiques publiques et usage de drogues illicites,' *Déviance et société*, 23, no. 2 (1999); F. Caballero, ed., *Drogues et droits de l'homme* (Paris: Les empêcheurs de tourner en rond 1992); P.G. Erickson, D.M. Riley, Y.W. Cheung, and P.A. O'Hare, *Harm Reduction: A New Direction for Drug Policies and Programs* (Toronto: University of Toronto Press 1997).

58 The Netherlands, as well as Switzerland, is currently debating prohibition at the political level, as the contradictions inherent in the current development of harm- reduction strategies become increasingly apparent. See Boggio, 'De l'indifférence à l'acceptation.'

59 L. Beauchesne, 'Un sujet d'actualité: la loi C-8,' *L'Écho-toxico*, 8, no. 1 (1997): 710. Some changes with respect to cannabis penalties may suggest an easing of these sanctions. However, the new sentences for less than thirty grams and provision for summary conviction have not resulted in much change in current judicial practice (the average prison sentence is between fifteen and twenty days in Quebec in the case of simple possession for adults), and have not reduced the stigmatization and harmful consequences associated with a criminal record in any way. Moreover, the

streamlining of legal procedures seems to have allowed for an increase in cannabis-related offences rather than a decrease because of the fact that they are now less costly for the system. See G.A. Dion, *Les pratiques policières et judiciaires dans les affaires de possession de cannabis et autres drogues, de 1995 à 1998: portrait statistique* (Montreal: CPLT 1999). Nevertheless, the Canadian Association of Chiefs of Police has given its support to a marijuana decriminalization policy (but remains opposed to its legalization) and holds the view that individuals found guilty of certain offences related to possession of small quantities of this drug should not be burdened with a criminal record. Stay tuned.

60 www.cfdp.ca.

61 Even the Supreme Court denounced the excessive rate of imprisonment in Canada on 23 April 1999 (*R v. Gladu*, no. 26300), stating: 'Canada is a world leader in many fields, particularly in the areas of progressive social policy and human rights. Unfortunately, our country is also distinguished as being a world leader in putting people in prison. Although the United States has by far the highest rate of incarceration among industrialized democracies, at over 600 inmates per 100,000 population, Canada's rate of approximately 130 inmates per 100,000 population places it second or third highest ... This record of incarceration rates obviously cannot instil a sense of pride.' This is the first time that the Supreme Court has made such a statement and it is significant for our purpose, since we know that many of those incarcerated in provincial and federal penitentiaries are there for 'drug crimes.'

62 Among others, in the United States, there were more arrests – a total of 695,201 in 1997 for offences related to marijuana than in any other year. And 87 per cent of these cases involved simple possession. See Federal Bureau of Investigation (FBI): www.fbi.gov. For an analysis of the U.S. data on repressive drug practices and trends in health policies, see E. Drucker, 'Drug Prohibition and Public Health: 25 Years of Evidence,' *Drug Policy Letter*, 40 (1999): 4–18.

63 In 1997 cannabis charges in Canada accounted for 72 per cent of offences compared with 58 per cent in 1991. Statistics Canada, Canadian Centre for Justice Statistics.

64 N. Boyd, 'Rethinking our Policy on Cannabis,' *Options politiques*, October 1998, 31–3.

65 I am referring here to the 1988 Convention on Prohibition against Trafficking and the Single Convention on Narcotic Drugs of 1961, amended by the 1971 Convention on Psychotropic Substances.

66 Beauchesne, *Les drogues.*
67 M. Roelandt, 'Justice et thérapie ou l'impossible alliance,' *Cahiers de Pro-spective Jeunesse,* 1, nos. 1–2 (1996).
68 These examples were not pulled out of thin air. There is a large body of lit-erature in criminology and law dealing with government policies on pub-lic management in which the purpose of sentencing is not to reintegrate offenders into society but to supervise and monitor them. Making reinte-gration the very clear objective entails developing resources and re-exam-ining some of the social conditions that give rise to this delinquency. See M. Feeley et J. Simon, 'The New Penology: Notes on the Emerging Strategy of Corrections and Its Implications,' *Criminology,* 30 (1992): 449–74; M. Feeley et J. Simon, 'Actuarial Justice: The Emerging New Criminal Law,' in D. Nelken, ed., *The Future of Criminology* (London: Sage Publications 1994), 173–201.

2 'Unmaking Manly Smokes': Church, State, Governance, and the First Anti-Smoking Campaigns in Montreal, 1892–1914[1]

JARRETT RUDY

This essay examines the anti-smoking campaigns of the Montreal Woman's Christian Temperance Union (WCTU) from 1892 until the First World War. During the period, the Montreal WCTU were part of local, provincial, and federal campaigns for age restrictions on smoking and cigarette prohibition. The Montreal campaigns, both on the provincial level and as part of the Dominion WCTU's federal campaign, stand out as being particularly unsuccessful when compared to those undertaken in other provinces. The essay argues that, while women's exclusion from formal politics and the particularly masculine symbolism of smoking were important factors in accounting for the weakness of the Montreal WCTU's campaigns, the specificity of the Montreal case is found in the religious demography of the city. Thus, the essay uncovers the social gospel beliefs of the Montreal WCTU and the theological roots of anti-prohibitionists in the city. Ultimately, the question is situated in a debate over the liberal order at the turn of the twentieth century and the proper role of the church and state in the moral formation of individuals.

Between 1890 and 1914, the Dominion, provincial, and local organizations of the Woman's Christian Temperance Union led Canada's first campaigns for anti-smoking laws. These campaigns succeeded in passing several provincial and one federal age restriction laws, yet they were considered a defeat by most WCTU supporters. The campaigns were particularly unsuccessful in Quebec. In the 1890s, when the targets of WCTU legislative efforts were provincial governments, Quebec was one of only two provinces (the other was Manitoba) which did not legislate age restrictions for smokers. In 1914 the Quebec WCTU was the only provincial union to pull out of the Dominion WCTU tobacco prohibition campaign. Support for these Dominion and provincial anti-smoking campaigns was particularly weak in Montreal. Despite these failures, the Montreal WCTU anti-smoking campaigns provide insights into at least three kinds of questions that elucidate the dynamics of what historian Ian McKay has called the 'liberal order' of governance in Canada.[2]

First, it is a useful case study of women's public activities and the difficulties which faced women who sought to influence formal politics before enfranchisement. Indeed, if, like Mary P. Ryan, we consider formal political representation in the nineteenth century a ritual of increasingly class-inclusive male power, then the WCTU was challenging fundamental assumptions underlying that ritual of male power at the heart of late-nineteenth-century liberal governance.[3] Discursively, WCTU members fastened their public campaigns to the private sphere, taking on the role of mothers concerned about what doctors considered to be the degenerative effect of smoking on boys. More concretely, social gospel-inspired churches provided women an important platform for personally participating in the public sphere.[4] Secondly, the weakness of the Montreal WCTU's legislative anti-smoking campaigns serves to highlight some of the more controversial aspects of the social gospel before the First World War. The WCTU's anti-smoking position originated in a particularly gendered vision of social gospel Protestantism concerned about national racial degeneration.[5]

Because of the WCTU's proposed infringement on individual rights – in the case of age restrictions the rights of parents and, in the case of prohibition, of smokers and commerce – its call for the state to play a role in the moral formation of individuals was far more controversial than suggested by much of Canadian social gospel historiography.[6] In Montreal, a minority of people thought the state should play this role.[7] While some historians have asserted that French Canadian opposition was the root of the failure of the anti-smoking movement, few have sought out the reasons French Canadians were antagonistic to this WCTU cause.[8] French Canadians opposed cigarette prohibition because of their Roman Catholicism, and the French language provided an insurmountable obstacle for the WCTU. Still, in Montreal, the weakness of the anti-smoking movement was the result of more than just the opposition of French Canadians. In particular, Protestant denominations that were less influenced by the social gospel also opposed prohibition measures.

Beyond this Quebec specificity, a third reason the WCTU's campaigns to restrict tobacco consumption failed is found in the dominant cultural meaning of smoking and its relationship to the liberal order. During the years immediately before the First World War, according to dominant norms, smoking was an everyday ritual of the liberal order.[9] Like no other ritual of consumption, smoking, if done 'properly,' reflected and served to legitimize beliefs about inclusion, exclusion, and hierarchy on the basis of gender, class, and race that were at the core of nineteenth-century liberalism.[10] The process of the legitimation of these values occurred in legislatures as well as on a day-to-day level. The tension between liberal preoccupations with self-possession and rationality, on the one hand, and smoking's addictive nature, on the other, made smoking a particularly useful and tenacious ritual of liberal values. The threat of addiction, of which there was an awareness in the nineteenth century, made smoking a surmountable, but not insignificant, risk, and thus a particularly meaningful display of rationality, self-control, and proper liberal masculinity.[11] The WCTU, in their opposition to smoking, was not opposing the liberal order. Rather, these women were opposing the notion that smoking was a ritual of the liberal order. In sum, by looking at the WCTU and its opponents, this essay explores the unique and contradictory liberal alliance between cultural groups in Montreal and the extent to which the liberal order shifted because of collectivist demands for a new relationship between the liberal individual (man) and the state.

Opposing Tobacco

The WCTU's concern over smoking was part of a larger concern over national physical and mental degeneration.[12] For example, smoking was seen as endangering the nation's military ability by hindering the physical development of boys. The WCTU's 'Catéchisme de Tempérance' cited a German law which forbade the sale of tobacco to minors (under sixteen years old) because smoking stunted growth and the development of German youth into strong soldiers.[13] In the House of Commons, Robert Holmes quoted a British parliamentarian who alleged that the defeat of the Spanish in the Spanish-American War and the French in the Franco-Prussian War 'was easily traceable to the habit of cigarette smoking.'[14] Another MP quoted an American doctor who claimed that three times as many recruits to the army during the Spanish-American War were rejected because they lacked 'the vitality necessary to make a good soldier' than in the Civil War, with the cause apparently being the cigarette.[15]

Another WCTU pamphlet, 'Testimony concerning the "Cigarette,"' argued that smoking put the country's businesses at a disadvantage. It cited American businessmen who would not hire employees who smoked cigarettes and Montreal MLA Michael Hutchinson, who observed, 'The boy who smokes Cigarettes [sic] is handicapped when seeking a situation. He must take second place every time; and rightly so.'[16] Thus, the nation's business would also be condemned to second place in a competitive market. Liberal ideals of self-control were front and centre in the mind of Montreal MP Robert Bickerdike when he noted that 'we are all agreed that the boy who is addicted to the cigarette habit cannot succeed in this country.'[17]

According to the WCTU, smoking also contributed to the moral degeneration of the race and nation. Smoking played a part in the construction of male delinquency, as the WCTU claimed that smoking led to boys stealing tobacco or stealing money to buy tobacco. The Reverend Elson I. Rexford of the High School of Montreal wrote that any group that worked 'to discourage the use of tobacco by our boys is entitled to receive the active support of all who are interested in the development of good Canadian Citizenship.'[18] Occasionally this was expressed in terms of race. The Montreal *Witness*, for example, editorialized, 'How infinitely more should the country sacrifice a luxury which is degenerating our race!'[19]

While the language of the WCTU and its supporters was often secular in invoking medical authorities, medical advances did not explain the timing of these anti-smoking campaigns. Rather, it was the rise of the social gospel, and its urge to create Heaven on Earth, that propelled the WCTU to organize and oppose smoking.[20] Indeed, in terms of the total Protestant population in Montreal, a disproportionate portion of the WCTU's membership came from the Presbyterian, Methodist, and smaller social gospel-influenced churches. One of the few existing Montreal WCTU membership lists broke down the 1888 membership by church: Presbyterians made up 44.8 per cent; Methodists, 24.9 per cent; Congregationalists, 9.6 per cent; and Baptists, 4.3 per cent. Anglicans, less influenced by the social gospel, made up 12.7 per cent of the membership. In comparison, the 1891 Census enumerated Montreal's Protestant population at 45 per cent Anglican, 34 per cent Presbyterian, 15.6 per cent Methodist, 3.5 per cent Baptist, and 2 per cent Congregationalist.[21]

The WCTU's criticisms of smoking were part of a female strand of the social gospel belief that stressed the role of women in reforming and protecting Canadian society. A key element of this reform agenda was altering male pastimes.[22] Indeed, WCTU literature frequently went beyond questions of children smoking to call for a reform of activities seen as masculine. In its 'Catéchisme de Tempérance,' written to be read in schools and homes, the Montreal WCTU asserted that smoking was a waste of money and that it was especially harmful to the poor as it took bread off their tables. The pamphlet maintained that smoking led men to drink and to enter vice-filled areas.[23] At the turn of the century, the WCTU also successfully campaigned against men smoking on tramways as unfair male control of space. In response, 45,000 francophone and anglophone men of all classes came together and petitioned the municipality to allow smoking.[24] Men did not respond well to women's attack on smoking. The Quebec WCTU's narcotics division superintendent remembered that, in her first three years in the position, she had learned 'to walk softly, act thoughtfully ... [and be] "wise as serpents and harmless as doves," if any real good is to be accomplished.'[25] Furthermore, she reported to her Dominion counterpart that many members 'hesitate in coming out openly on this question for fear of annoying some one [sic].'[26]

To reform men morally and protect the future of the nation would mean beginning by focusing on preventing boys from smoking. Doctors provided important support for WCTU beliefs about the dangers of boys smoking. Medical men were unanimous in their belief that smoking was perilous until boys reached maturity, at which point moderate smoking, a performance of self-control, was considered benign.[27] The WCTU claimed that it was their duty as mothers to protect boys from tobacco. Yet even WCTU members seemed to be failing in this quest to prevent boys participating in what was dominantly understood as a rite of passage to manhood.[28] Their frustration is summed up in WCTU activist Annie L. Jack's poem 'A Lesson Learned':

My boy learned to smoke,
Who taught him the filthy act?
And who will own at the judgement day
In the teaching they took a part;
I tried to keep him pure

And clean as boy should be,
But in the world he fell so low
And nothing can comfort me.

Is that the babe I've kissed?
O vile polluted breath,
And tainted blood with the poison weed,
That leads to a slow, sure death.
My bonnie, sweet-mouthed boy,
Tobacco stained to-day,
We need more strength in this hour of need.[29]

The WCTU promoted the use of the state to compensate for this fail-ure on the part of parents. This use of the state differentiated believers in the social gospel from the evangelical Protestantism and revival-ism that had developed in North America since the 1830s. Christians who adhered to early evangelical Protestantism saw the relationship between God and the individual as supreme.[30] In order for individuals to stop smoking, they had only to ask Christ for help and they would lose their desire to smoke.[31] The extent to which Christian denomina-tions supported WCTU anti-smoking motions varied according to how far these motions went in limiting individual freedoms. In the hope of saving the nation, social gospel-influenced denominations were not only willing to limit the right of parents to govern their children, they were also willing to prohibit the sale of cigarettes to adults.

The Methodist Church was the denomination most willing to take up the entire WCTU anti-smoking agenda. Not only did their Sunday Schools encouraged their pupils to take the 'Triple Pledge' against smok-ing, drinking, and swearing, their churches held an annual 'Cigarette Sunday.' This event was held across Canada, with special lessons on the evils of smoking delivered to children. In 1892 the Montreal Method-ist Conference was the first citywide church to pass an anti-smoking motion.[32] The Methodists would continue to champion WCTU anti-smoking motions when these proposals moved from age restrictions on smoking to the prohibition of the cigarette. The Presbyterians showed similar support. The Montreal *Presbyterian Recorder* published anti-tobacco articles that coincided with the Quebec WCTU's first tobacco age restriction campaigns and the church officially opposed smoking in 1908.[33] In 1912 a Presbyterian and a Methodist minister accompanied the WCTU delegation that met Prime Minister Robert Borden, calling for the prohibition of the cigarette.[34]

While these sources betray an elite bias, WCTU supporters could also be found among the working class. They expressed disapproval in the 'fire and brimstone' language historians have found to be typical of turn-of-the-century working-class revivalist groups like the Salvation Army.[35] T.C. Vickers, a worker with the CPR in Montreal, wrote Prime Minister Wilfrid Laurier in 1907, disappointed that Laurier had not introduced tobacco prohibition legislation. Vickers invoked the God-given collective right to fresh air. '[You] cannot walk the streets to Breathe the Beautiful *fresh aire* [sic] that a Loving God has made for us,' he complained. 'But some Dirty Smoker thinks he has a Perfect right to Polute [sic] it.' Vickers encouraged Laurier to convert, 'to come over on the Clean side.' For Vickers, it was not a matter of Laurier or his own opinion on tobacco, but the Lord's, and this, he told Laurier, was written in the Book of Revelation, chapter IX, verses 17 to 19:[36]

> And thus I saw the horses in the vision, and them that sat on them, having breastplates of fire, and of jacinth, and brimstone: and the heads of the horses were as the heads of lions; and out of their mouths issued fire and smoke and brimstone.
>
> By these three was the third part of men killed, by the fire, and by the smoke, and by the brimstone, which issued out of their mouths.
>
> For their power is in their mouth, and in their tails: for their tails were like unto serpents, and had heads, with them they do hurt.

Opponents of smoking were linked by a shared commitment to the social gospel. This worked in their favour in places where social gospel denominations made up a large percentage of the population. Indeed, in 1894, the Dominion WCTU reported that in Quebec the Eastern Township Unions, where social gospel Protestants were more numerous, were taking the lead in the province's anti-tobacco campaign.[37] Montreal, however, was not fertile soil for the WCTU. In 1891 denominations heavily influenced by the social gospel made up only 13.1 per cent of the population and this number was declining as the percentage of Roman Catholics rose.[38]

Opposing Prohibition

In Montreal, important newspapers opposed regulating the age of smokers, arguing that it was a case of the state usurping the rights of parents. The Montreal *Gazette*, for example, argued that the state could not fulfil these responsibilities: 'The chances are that the bill will not catch the boy. Attempts to substitute the statute book for the parental rod have not hitherto been terribly successful.'[39] Later it described banning children from theatres, invoking curfew laws, and anti-cigarette laws as 'an attempt to do by statute what can only be effectively done by home influence, by a father's or a mother's precept and advice.'[40] *Le Canada*, the Montreal Liberal Party daily, editorialized in 1907 that 'we must leave to parental authority, exercised directly or delegated to the professors and school masters, the responsibility of taking measures to eradicate a vice which does not interest society but the individual.'[41] *La Patrie* invoked the parents' rights over their children: 'Les gens ont le droit d'être libres en cette matière et pour la répression chez les enfants, c'est aux parents qu'il appartient de l'exercer.'[42]

The dominant Christian churches in the city were also reticent about the state being used to police individual morality. On the surface, the Anglican Church, the largest Protestant denomination in Montreal (10.8 per cent of population in 1891), and the Roman Catholic Church, the largest religious group in the city (73.2 per cent of the population in 1891), held similar positions on tobacco. The Anglicans gave limited support to the WCTU campaign against boys smoking, but opposed prohibition.[43] In 1899, when a motion opposing children smoking went to the floor of the Montreal Anglican Archdiocese sessional meeting, there was great controversy. Dr D.L. Davidson,[44] an Anglican with a Methodist background, declared that 'no man had a right to foul God's fresh pure air with tobacco smoke'[45] before making the following motion: 'That this Synod deplores the rapid extension and abuse of tobacco and cigarette smoking amongst all classes of the community and in particular amongst the Clergy of the Church, and amongst the young; and should express the hope that all members of the Church, Clerical, and Lay, may, by example and precept, do what they can to restrain the growing evil.'[46] Perhaps purposefully, the resolution avoided any suggestion that the state take on the role of a parent. Some openly mused about the influence of the social gospel within the Anglican Church. Dean Johnston of Montreal, for example, recounted that when he came to Canada in 1859, out of seventy clergymen in the synod, only twelve did not smoke. The same, he said, was true in 1899, yet there seemed to be 'a remarkable setting-in' against smoking and even more so against intemperance. There was a growing 'recognition on the part of the clergy that an indulgence in smoking and drinking was detrimental to the progress of Christian work.'[47] In contrast to the followers of denominations heavily influenced by the social gospel, many Anglicans would not support the prohibition of any tobacco product. Layman Mr A.G.B. Chilton maintained that smoking only fouled 'God's Fresh pure air' inasmuch as onions did. Furthermore, the Reverend Clayton, a clergyman from Bolton, did not believe that 'the person who occasionally indulged in a glass of wine or a quiet smoke was cursed by the d—l and was on the road to h—l. He strongly discountenanced the abuse of liquor or tobacco but did not believe that either were harmful if indulged in moderation.'[48] J.I. Cooper, historian of the Anglican Church in the Diocese of Montreal, has examined the diocese's attitudes to prohibition, finding that 'officially, Anglicanism did not go beyond enjoining moderation and insisting on individual responsibility.'[49]

Roman Catholics occasionally spoke out against children smoking, putting it in terms of racial degeneration. In 1887, for example, *Le Monde Illustré* gave a prize for the best essay on the 'influence pernicieuse du tabac sur l'avenir des races.' Among the judges of the eighteen entries were Abbé Marcoux, the vice-rector of Laval University, and writer Raphaël Bellemare.[50] In 1892 the archbishop of Quebec, Cardinal Elzéar-Alexandre Taschereau, supported the Quebec WCTU's call for a ban on children smoking. Many other prominent Roman Catholics added their voices to the age restriction campaign. Conservative Premier L.-O. Taillon quoted from a journal of hygiene during debate over an 1893 bill to limit smoking by boys, noting that tobacco was harmful to all and thus especially to boys. Later, the future Liberal premier F.-G. Marchand supported prohibiting children from buying cigarettes, saying that 'cigarette smoking led to the degeneration of the race.'[51]

Adult smoking, however, was never defined as a vice. In Montreal, for example, while the Roman Catholic Church was concerned about morality and especially children becoming 'le réceptacle de tous les vices,' lists of vices in the Diocese of Montreal's official declarations included blasphemy, debauchery, going to cabarets, and drunkenness – with no mention of smoking.[52] Strikingly, Roman Catholic priests and temperance organizations in Montreal confined themselves to concerns over alcohol abuse and occasionally gambling, but never smoking.[53] From 1905 to 1910, the most powerful temperance movement in Montreal, la Ligue antialcoolique, never expanded its interests to tobacco, and even its position on alcohol was for moderation not prohibition. What is more, while campaigning for the 'suppression' of alcohol, the Ligue sought to limit liquor licences, not call for prohibition.[54] The Montreal Irish Roman Catholic newspaper, the *True Witness and Catholic Chronicle*, also supported a position of moderation rather than prohibition and the editor of the *Journal de Françoise* called on the Fédération Nationale Saint-Jean-Baptiste to support age limit legislation but oppose prohibition of the cigarette. As with alcohol, it was only the abuse of tobacco that was a sin and, as such, tobacco consumption fell within a conception of liberty to consume all things that God put on the Earth.[55] Several Roman Catholic leaders opposed prohibition of alcohol on these grounds. In 1898 Canon P.-J. Saucier from Rimouski, for example, opposed prohibition because 'une loi de prohibition serait un attentat à la liberté naturelle puisqu'elle interdirait l'usage licite, en soi, d'un bien que Dieu a créé.'[56] In 1925 two French Canadian doctors echoed Saucier's argument in an article on the possible health hazards of tobacco, saying that man had the 'liberté dans l'usage des biens créés pour l'homme! L'usage très modéré du tabac est à peu près indifférent.'[57]

While both Anglicans and Roman Catholics opposed prohibition as an incursion on their rights, they arrived at this position along different paths. For many Anglicans, whether the question was prohibition of alcohol or tobacco or the excesses of capitalism, individual rights stood as a bulwark against 'Romish' despotism. In the late nineteenth century, Anglican individualists came into conflict with social gospellers who sought to improve the collective moral environment. And, while there were several social gospel advocates within the Montreal Anglican Church, proponents of individual responsibility and rights remained in control.[58]

In contrast to the Anglican position, the Roman Catholic use of individual rights to oppose the prohibition of tobacco was part of the Catholic response to what it saw as increasing materialism. The opinions of La Patrie editor J.-I Tarte illustrate this position. Tarte, a non-smoking Montreal MP, a leader of the Dominion Alliance for the Suppression of Alcohol and devout Roman Catholic, contended that because moderate smoking and drinking were not health problems, prohibition was inappropriate. Furthermore, he contended, 'prohibition has not been very popular with us in Quebec ... [not] because we drink more than the people of other provinces, but because we believe in freedom.'[59] Tarte's position as a leader of a temperance movement at the same time as he opposed prohibition may seem contradictory. In fact, it made sense within late-nineteenth-century Roman Catholic doctrine on the relationship between the church, the state, and the moral formation of the individual. The Roman Catholic Church opposed state interference in the moral formation of individuals. In the second half of the nineteenth century, as a challenge to increasingly popular secular and materialist views of the relationship between humanity and the world, Pope Leo XIII released a series of encyclicals to reassert God and the church's role in these relations. Historians Jean Hamelin and Nicole Gagnon have shown that the pope appropriated the language of the French Revolution, speaking broadly in terms of rights and liberties as well as the equality of individuals before God. This equality before God never implied social or material equality between individuals. Rather, freedom was the capacity to do right. Clerical authority was essential to this notion of liberty because it was the clergy that *taught* the individual how to make decisions.[60] At the centre of the Roman Catholic position was the belief that, through prohibition, the state was denying the church its role in building morally strong, self-governing individuals who would be able to enter a world where the state would not be the individual's only moral guide. *La Patrie*, for example, argued that to restrict personal freedoms was acceptable only in the worst scenarios, and the abuse neither of alcohol nor of tobacco was in this category of problems. What was worse, prohibition would deprive the individual of 'les fruits qu'assurerait une réforme inspirée par la modération et susceptible de rallier mieux l'appui de toute les bonnes volontés.'[61]

The fact that the Anglican and Roman Catholic churches – the two largest churches in Montreal – did not view tobacco as a danger meant that the WCTU's first task was to raise awareness. Here, Montreal's particular linguistic duality worked against the organization. Indeed, while the WCTU did have a small French division, I have found only one WCTU anti-smoking pamphlet in French, and most of their proselytizing was done in English. Much more pervasive were francophone newspaper editorials, such as those quoted above, which opposed both age restrictions on smokers as well as prohibition. Educational programs had to be a priority for WCTU members as well. J. MacL. Metcalfe, the Quebec narcotics superintendent, reported in 1894 that after sending a letter to WCTU members with the opinions of nine 'leading physicians and scientists as to the evil effects resulting from the use of tobacco,' she had many replies that they had never given the subject much thought.[62] Again, in 1895, she complained that it was still difficult to find workers because the department was 'anything but a popular one,' with some active WCTU members opposing its work and members remaining silent. Until at least 1899, the Montreal Central Union never had a narcotic superintendent and this may have contributed to the Quebec WCTU's inability to muster support for a cigarette prohibition petition in 1902.[63] The executive of the Montreal WCTU worried that '[numerous] cities in Ontario have obtained more signatures than the whole of Quebec.'[64]

Despite not having a narcotics superintendent, the Montreal WCTU sponsored educational events opposing tobacco. By 1896, the WCTU's educational campaign in Montreal included anti-smoking lectures by physicians and WCTU members and the distribution of anti-smoking literature.[65] Over the next eighteen years, the various Montreal WCTU locals in conjunction with local Methodist churches set up Anti-Cigarette and Anti-Tobacco Leagues organized primarily for boys. Among the earliest was the Westmount Anti-Cigarette Club which by 1897 had forty members, about twelve of whom attended the club's bimonthly meetings.[66] By 1905, there were three more Anti-Cigarette Leagues in Montreal, one with the Western Union, and two large leagues numbering 350 members established by the Fairmount Union. The latter organized picnics and winter socials 'to hold the boys together and ... [to give] new zeal' as well as get the interest of their parents.[67] Children who took 'The Pledge' against smoking and joined the League had their pictures published as part of the Montreal *Standard's* Anti-Cigarette Campaign.[68]

Legislative Campaigns

The Quebec WCTU's campaign to use the state to stop smoking began in 1892, and between 1893 and 1895 they had four bills presented to the Quebec legislature. Each of the bills would have made it illegal for children under fifteen to smoke '[in] any public street, road highway, or building' under the penalty of a $2-fine. Moreover, no adult could sell tobacco to anyone under eighteen without a written request from a parent or guardian.[69] These bills were part of a broader movement. In 1890 New Brunswick became the first Canadian province to set an age of majority for smokers.[70] A year later, British Columbia passed a law prohibiting minors from buying or being given tobacco, and in the spring of 1892 both Nova Scotia and Ontario followed.[71]

The Quebec WCTU would never have the legislative success of its sister associations across Canada. Still, the provincial campaigns demonstrated numerous ways women influenced the male public sphere. Indeed, in preparing the campaign in Quebec, WCTU president Mary Sanderson corresponded with the Quebec and Montreal presbyteries, the Protestant Ministerial and Methodist Ministerial Associations of Montreal, the Royal Templars and Good Templars, and each MLA asking for their support.[72] Narcotics Superintendent J. MacL. Metcalfe wrote WCTU county presidents across Quebec, urging them to lobby their MLAs, and each MLA was sent a pamphlet that detailed the harmful effects of tobacco.[73] The bill made it through the Legislative Assembly but died on the order paper in the Legislative Council.[74] Further efforts to legislate age restrictions failed to pass through the Legislative Assembly, convincing the Quebec WCTU of the futility of securing such legislation in the province.[75] It petitioned twice more after the turn of the century, but by 1907 it was opposing all attempts by the Dominion WCTU to move the fight back to the provincial level.[76]

While the WCTU faced legislative failures in provinces like Quebec and Manitoba, elsewhere it succeeded in passing age restriction laws. Yet in these provinces the laws were ineffective and tougher measures were deemed necessary. MPs from Ontario and Nova Scotia, for example, claimed that anti-smoking laws in their provinces were dead letters.[77] Deciding that age restriction legislation had proven 'worthless,' in 1899 the Dominion WCTU turned its attention to obtaining federal legislation that prohibited the manufacture, importation, and sale of cigarettes to all Canadians, a restriction of trade that fell under federal jurisdiction.[78] For the good of the country, it was argued, adult men would have to give up cigarettes. The Montreal *Witness* compared the prohibition of cigarettes to the banning of margarine. Margarine was banned 'for the sake of commerce' even though, as a cheap butter substitute, it would have nourished the 'poor man.'[79] M.K. Richardson called on MPs to cast aside 'that bugbear of interference with personal liberty.' Was self-sacrifice not, he asked, the most admired quality of the individual?[80]

In addition to pushing for prohibition rather than age restrictions, the federal campaign differed from provincial campaigns by focusing on prohibition of the cigarette rather than all tobacco products. The problem with singling out the cigarette in the 1890s was that few people smoked them. By the turn of the century, however, there was statistical evidence that cigarette smoking was on the rise. The WCTU, for example, quoted excise statistics showing a boom in cigarette sales from 76,000,000 in 1898 to 134,000,000 in 1902.[81] Cigarettes, the WCTU argued, were more dangerous than other tobaccos because the tobacco in cigarettes was milder than that used in cigars and smoked in pipes. The cigarette, the Dominion WCTU executive wrote to the *Witness*, 'whets without satisfying the appetite' and is therefore more addictive. As well, the letter continued, cigarette smoke was more likely to be inhaled, with its poisonous nicotine drawn 'into the infinitely delicate lung tissues.'[82] The focus on the cigarette had a strategic advantage. Supporters of the WCTU claimed that the prohibition motion was harmless to adult men since they would most certainly smoke other forms of tobacco. Reminding the House that there were other forms of tobacco that an individual could smoke, W.S. Maclaren noted, 'If gentlemen cannot forego the pleasure of smoking cigarettes for the purpose of helping the boys of this country, I am mistaken in the calibre of the men who occupy seats in this House.'[83]

When the cigarette prohibition petition came before the House in April 1903, WCTU representatives were in the gallery to watch over the MPs.[84] Despite their lobbying, the WCTU was still an outsider to this political process, with none of its members in Parliament and no suffrage rights for women. This gender inequality was pointed out by Mortimer Davis, the president of the American Tobacco Company of Canada, which at the time was the country's largest cigarette manufacturer. Davis wrote the minister of fisheries reminding him of his long support for the Liberal Party and of the large number of male voters who would be upset if cigarettes were outlawed. According to Davis, 36,000 merchants and wholesalers opposed the bill, and their tobacco shops were a 'rendez-vous, really, for store-keeper's customers, to hang around the store and discuss politics, etc., with their friends.'[85]

During debates on smoking over the next five years, anti-prohibitionists in Parliament argued that prohibition was a female invasion of the male sphere of politics, an affront to individual (male) liberty, and a vicious attack on male leisure activities. Some members attacked the bills as being evidence of women interfering in affairs that they did not understand. E.B. Osler, a Toronto MP, rebuffed 'my lady friends who are so interested in this matter' by stating that 'there is more evil wrought among the youth of this country, by bad cooking than by the use of tobacco.' Instead of lobbying, women should start teaching cooking courses to girls. Prime Minister Laurier, in a more diplomatic tone, echoed Osler by suggesting that the women of the WCTU would be better off educating, thus not questioning male freedoms, than pushing for prohibition legislation.[86]

Between 1903 and 1908, the WCTU succeeded in guiding four cigarette prohibition resolutions into Parliament, yet, with the exception of one, all died 'procedural deaths.'[87] The watershed moment for the WCTU and its supporters came in 1908 when the Laurier government derailed the cigarette prohibition movement. After another bill was introduced calling for the prohibition of the importation, sale, and manufacture of cigarettes, on 16 March 1908 A.H. Clarke of South Essex, part of Ontario's tobacco belt, turned the tables on the WCTU and proposed an amendment to the bill.[88] Instead of cigarette prohibition, Clarke called for changes in the Criminal Code to stop minors from smoking all types of tobacco.[89] With the support of Laurier and other ministers, the bill, which restricted anyone under the age of sixteen from buying tobacco or smoking in public, passed with a vote of 61 to 51.[90]

Taken at face value, the law seems like a victory for the WCTU. Yet this assessment must be questioned since some of the strongest supporters of cigarette prohibition, Robert Bickerdike, for example, voted against the bill.[91] What is more, we should remember that the WCTU itself had abandoned their campaigns for age restrictions because they had found these to be hollow victories. Put in the context of the Montreal (and not coincidentally Canadian) liberal order, the law was a symbolic entry of the state into a domain previous considered the sole 'jurisdiction' of parents. This was an acceptable compromise since there was some support, as I have shown, among Roman Catholics and Anglicans. It was certainly more acceptable than prohibition as it did not put the smoker's rights into question, and more importantly, it did not extinguish the right of the free exchange of commodities. The 1908 compromise demonstrated the hierarchy of rights, commercial over total parental freedom, within the Canadian liberal order.

That the victory of collective social reform over individual rights was symbolic rather than real became clear with the enforcement of this law. Though WCTU's supporters voted against the bill, the WCTU gave the new measures a period of grace to see if it would be enforced more effectively than the provincial acts of the 1890s. While the WCTU were still active in anti-smoking educational campaigns and continued to call for prohibition of the cigarette, the act gave them a new focus: agitating for enforcement of the age restriction law. Three of their significant activities were giving copies of the law to tobacco dealers, making sure they understood the law's provisions, and lobbying the police for its enforcement.[92]

In Montreal, 'the Act to Restrain the Use of Tobacco by the Young' was sporadically enforced. In the first year there was only one conviction. The following year, there were 133 convictions. But in 1911 convictions dropped to four.[93] If a child was caught with cigarettes, the offender was brought before a judge of the Recorder's Court or, after

1912, a judge of the newly created Juvenile Court. The culprit was usually reprimanded and a promise extracted not to smoke anymore. The
judge then pushed the accused to reveal the origin of the cigarettes. If
the source was divulged, the judge looked for another witness to cor-
roborate the evidence. Only after having corroboration would the judge
proceed with a prosecution of the dealer.[94] By February 1912, it was not
clear if officers were actually enforcing the law. Alderman Drummond
had to go as far as to ask council if there was a law to restrain children
from buying cigarettes in Montreal. The question wove its way though
several levels of city officials and had to go to the chief lawyer of the
city, who affirmed that indeed there was a law and all that was necessary for its enforcement were orders to enforce it from the chief of
police.[95] In 1912 convictions rose to twenty-five and in 1913 dropped to
twenty-two. In 1914, after the Juvenile Court hired two special officers,
the count rose dramatically to eighty-two.

The difficulties of convicting tobacconists pushed the police to use
entrapment to gather evidence.[96] Yet the consequences of entrapment
could be far from the intentions of those looking for better enforcement
of the law. Tobacconist James Stephen sold cigarettes to an eleven-year-
old boy only to be promptly charged with selling tobacco to a minor
by a special officer. Realizing that the boy and the police officer were
making the rounds of all local tobacconists, Stephen called his cousin,
also a tobacconist, alerting him to the coming visitors. When the boy
attempted to buy cigarettes at the cousin's tobacco store, he 'was subject to a hearty thrashing' before the officer could intervene.[97]

By 1914, perhaps with hopes of finding a more sympathetic ear with
the Conservative Party in power, the Dominion WCTU again prepared
for a campaign to prohibit the cigarette. During preparations, the Quebec WCTU fell out of line with the Dominion cigarette prohibition
efforts. President Mary Sanderson asserted that anti-smoking legislation 'had been, in her opinion, practically useless' and the provincial
narcotics superintendent argued that the tobacco prohibition campaign had received so many 'turn downs' from the government that it
would be better to spend their time, energy, and money on educational
campaigns.[98] The Quebec pullout was symptomatic of the reticence of
Quebeckers to using the state to intrude on individual rights. Sharon
Anne Cook, in her study of the Ontario WCTU during the same period,
argues that the WCTU was divided between supporters of progressive
evangelism – most obvious in the federal and provincial hierarchies
of the WCTU, which subscribed to social gospel beliefs of collective

cleansing of society – and the more traditional evangelicalism of local unions, which saw 'salvation as being personal and experiential, rather than societal.'[99] One of the dividing lines between the two positions was an interest in using the state in projects of moral regulation. In the case of the Quebec WCTU cigarette prohibition campaign, the dividing line is also apparent, with the only difference being that the provincial hierarchy took the traditional position, a position that was more easily reconciled with liberal notions of freedom of the individual.

The Dominion WCTU's cigarette prohibition campaign continued, in spite of the Quebec union's absence. But, instead of letting the question go to a vote, the Conservative government diverted the issue to a House of Commons Commission on the Cigarette that was to look into amending the 1908 age restrictions or to suggest other ways the 'Evils Arising from the Use of Cigarettes' could be prevented. The commission heard testimony from Montreal, Toronto, and Ottawa 'experts' on boys smoking. Yet no WCTU members were considered experts. Instead, officials linked to juvenile courts and reformatories as well as insane asylums gave testimony, six out of ten of them from Montreal. These reformers were interested in making tobacco age restrictions more effective rather than invoking prohibition. The commission submitted two reports without making any recommendations for change, claiming that it had heard much theory but little empirical data.[100] In June 1914 the parliamentary session ended and the committee took leave and never resumed its work, concerns over tobacco eclipsed by the First World War.

The social gospel and the WCTU were not successful in their efforts to label smoking a 'vice' on the national front. After lengthy legislative and educational campaigns, the WCTU could not convince Parliament that the cigarette was so dangerous to the country that it would have to be prohibited. The age restriction law they succeeded in passing was not enforced and would be forgotten until the 1980s.[101] Part of the WCTU's failure to pass stronger legislation may have been due to the fact that they had no members in Parliament. Indeed, with the support of social gospel-influenced churches, they had not only pushed their cause into the male public sphere of formal politics, they had also attacked an almost exclusively male habit, and in Parliament MPs expressed nothing short of anger towards these women. In the end, the Montreal and Quebec WCTU was worn down by this legislative fight to stop smoking, preferring to retreat to education campaigns and Bible studies.

There were, however, other significant obstacles to the WCTU's collective social reform in Montreal. The dominance of Christian denominations that were less influenced by the social gospel as well as the fact that most of WCTU activism was done in English made the movement weak. The Anglican Church, for the most part, did not see tobacco as a vice and, regardless, was not won over to the collectivist spirit that defined the social gospel. For them, the individual was still paramount in deciding one's own moral future. The Roman Catholic Church, on the other hand, came to a similar position regarding the individual, but from a radically different theological direction. As part of a response to growing materialism and secularism, the church reasserted itself in the everyday lives of Roman Catholics by appropriating a language of individualism that did not imply equality of individuals on Earth, but equality before God. The moral will of the individual was to be formed through church instruction, and freedom was the individual's right to make morally sound decisions. To impose cigarette prohibition was to deny the individual's right to make a moral decision as well as to limit the church's role in Quebec society. The combination of the demographic weakness in Montreal of the most important promoters of the WCTU, their unilingual nature, and the rejection, to a great extent, by the Roman Catholic and Anglican churches of state involvement in moral training of individuals meant that dominant notions about smoking being a sign of respectable and mature masculinity were less challenged by the WCTU in Quebec and Montreal than elsewhere in Canada. What is more, the Montreal WCTU anti-smoking campaigns provide insights into the alliances, compromises, and hierarchies of rights within the Canadian liberal order.

NOTES

1 I would like to thank Brian Young, Suzanne Morton, Chris Koenig-Woodyard, Steve High, Nicole Neatby, and the anonymous reviewers of the *Journal of the Canadian Historical Association* for their insightful criticisms. I am also grateful to the Fonds pour la Formation de Chercheurs et l'Aide à la Recherche (FCAR) for partially funding this research.

2 Ian McKay, 'The Liberal Order Framework: A Prospectus for a Reconnaissance of Canadian History,' *Canadian Historical Review*, 81, 4 (2000): 617–45.

3 Mary Ryan, 'Gender and Public Access: Women's Politics in Nineteenth-

Century America,' in Craig Calhoun, ed., *Habermas and the Public Sphere* (Cambridge, Mass.: MIT Press 1990), 259–88.

4 On this theme, see, for example, Ruth Compton Brouwer, *New Women for God: Canadian Presbyterian Women and India Missions, 1876–1914* (Toronto: University of Toronto Press 1990).

5 Richard Allen, *The Social Passion: Religion and Social Reform in Canada, 1914–28* (Toronto: University of Toronto Press 1971), especially chapter 1.

6 See ibid. as well as Neil Semple, *The Lord's Dominion: The History of Canadian Methodism* (Montreal and Kingston: McGill-Queen's University Press 1996); and Sharon Cook, *'Through Sunshine and Shadow': The Woman's Christian Temperance Union, Evangelicalism, and Reform in Ontario* (Montreal and Kingston: McGill-Queen's University Press 1995).

7 Fernande Roy outlines the debates around liberalism in Quebec in her *Progrès, Harmonie, Liberté: Le libéralisme des milieux d'affaires francophones de Montréal au tournant du siècle* (Montreal: Boréal 1988). Since Roy's book, others have stayed within the parameters she sets out. See Yvan Lamonde, *Louis-Antoine Dessaulles, 1818–1895: un seigneur libéral et anticlérical* (Saint-Laurent, Que.: Fides 1994); and Yvan Lamonde, ed., *Combats Libéraux au XXᵉ Siècle* (Montreal: Fides 1995).

8 Ruth Dupré, *'To Smoke or Not to Smoke: That was the Question': The Fight over the Prohibition of Cigarettes at the Turn of the Century* (Montreal: Cahier de recherche, École des Hautes Études Commerciales 1997).

9 See my 'Manly Smokes: Tobacco Consumption and the Construction of Identities in Industrial Montreal, 1888–1914,' PhD thesis, McGill University 2001. For other 'everyday rituals of political order,' see John Kasson, *Rudeness and Civility: Manners in Nineteenth-Century Urban America* (New York: Hill and Wang 1990); Keith Walden, *Becoming Modern in Toronto: The Industrial Exhibition and the Shaping of a Late Victorian Culture* (Toronto: University of Toronto Press 1997); Mary P. Ryan, *Civic Wars: Democracy and Public Life in the American City during the Nineteenth Century* (Berkeley: University of California Press 1997); David Scobey, 'Anatomy of the Promenade: The Politics of Bourgeois Sociability in Nineteenth-Century New York,' *Social History*, 49 (May 1992): 203–27.

10 My comparison of these consuming rituals is drawn from Cheryl Krasnick Warsh, ed., *Drink in Canada: Historical Essays* (Montreal and Kingston: McGill-Queen's University Press 1993); Wolfgang Schivelbusch, *Tastes of Paradise: A Social History of Spices, Stimulants, and Intoxicants* (New York: Vintage Books 1992); and Jordan Goodman, Paul E. Lovejoy, and Andrew Sherratt, eds., *Consuming Habits: Drugs in History and Anthropology* (New York: Routledge 1995).

11 Rudy, 'Manly Smokes.'

12 Matthew Hilton has made this argument for Britain. See *Smoking in British Popular Culture* (Manchester, U.K.: Manchester University Press 2000), 162–75.

13 Société chrétienne de tempérance des dames de la province de Québec (WCTU), 'Catéchisme de tempérance à l'usage des familles et des écoles de la province de Québec,' reproduced in the Canadian Institute for Historical Microreproductions (CIHM) collection, fiche 26045, 13–14.

14 House of Commons *Debates*, 1 April 1903, 827.

15 Ibid., 23 March 1904, 338.

16 'Testimony concerning the "Cigarette,"' CIHM collection, fiche 73873, 11.

17 House of Commons *Debates*, 1 April 1903, 820–1.

18 WCTU, 'Catéchisme de Tempérance,' 4 and 16.

19 Montreal *Witness*, 28 March 1903, 4.

20 In the nineteenth century, the most significant medical discovery related to tobacco was the isolation of nicotine as a poisonous element in 1828. The link between the cigarette and lung cancer was established in 1950. See the essays in Stephen Lock et al., *Ashes to Ashes: The History of Smoking and Health* (Amsterdam: Rodopi 1998). A parallel to social gospel interest in the consequences of smoking can be found in the rise of eugenics among social gospellers. See Angus McLaren, *Our Own Master Race: Eugenics in Canada, 1885–1945* (Toronto: McClelland and Stewart 1990).

21 Montreal WCTU, *Annual Report*, 1888, 19. Canada, *Census*, 1891, 204, 312–13.

22 Cook, 'Through Sunshine and Shadow,' 6, 75–133.

23 WCTU, 'Catéchisme de tempérance,' 13.

24 Rudy, 'Manly Smokes,' 67–72.

25 J. MacL. Metcalfe, 'Report of the Department of Narcotics,' Quebec WCTU, *12th Annual Report*, 1895, 65.

26 Sara Rowell Wright, 'Report of Department of Narcotics: Quebec,' *8th Report of the Dominion WCTU* (1895), 87.

27 R.B. Walker, 'Medical Aspects of Tobacco Smoking and the Anti-Tobacco Movement in Britain in the Nineteenth Century,' *Medical History*, 24 (1980): 391–402. For Montreal examples and loss of self-control as addiction, see Rudy, 'Manly Smokes,' 35–8.

28 Cook, 'Through Sunshine and Shadow,' 84.

29 Annie L. Jack, 'A Lesson Learned,' Quebec WCTU, *8th Annual Report*, 1891, 39.

30 Semple, *The Lord's Dominion*, 138.

31 H.T. Crossley, *Practical Talks on Important Themes* (Montreal: William Briggs

1895), 194–200. For more on Crossley, see Semple, *The Lord's Dominion,* 219–20.

32 *Sunday School Banner,* March 1904, iii. *Minutes of the Proceedings of the Fifth Session of the Montreal Annual Conference of the Methodist Church* (Montreal: William Briggs 1892), United Church Collection, Archives nationale du Québec (ANQ-M), 84.

33 'Dr. Richardson on Tobacco,' *Presbyterian Recorder,* December 1892, 330; 'Digest of Minutes,' Thirty-Fourth Session of the Synod of Montreal and Ottawa, p. 23, 11–0–001–03–06–001B–01, ANQ-M.

34 'To Prohibit Cigarettes,' Montreal *Weekly Witness,* 20 February 1912, 3.

35 Lynne Marks, *Revivals and Roller Rinks: Religion, Leisure, and Identity in Late-Nineteenth-Century Small-Town Ontario* (Toronto: University of Toronto Press 1996), 157.

36 T.C. Vickers to Wilfrid Laurier, 6 March 1907, Laurier Papers, Library and Archives Canada (LAC), MG 26, G, vol. 453, microfilm reel C-845, 121093–7.

37 *7th Annual Report of the Dominion WCTU* (1894), 76, MU 8398.3, Archives of Ontario (AO).

38 Canada, *Census,* 1891, 1901, 1911.

39 Montreal *Gazette,* 20 February 1893, 4.

40 'Children and Theatres,' Montreal *Gazette,* 3 April 1903, 4.

41 'The Cigarette,' translated in the *Canadian Cigar and Tobacco Journal (CCTJ),* May 1907, 17, from *Le Canada,* 12 March 1907.

42 'Contre les cigarettes,' *La Patrie,* 4 December 1907, 4.

43 Canada, *Census,* 1891, 312–13.

44 J.I. Cooper, *The Blessed Communion: The Origins and History of the Diocese of Montreal, 1760–1960* (Montreal: Archives' Committee of the Diocese of Montreal 1960), 118–19.

45 Montreal *Star,* 18 January 1899, 7.

46 *40th Annual Session of the Synod of the Diocese of Montreal,* 17 January 1899, 34–5.

47 Montreal *Star,* 18 January 1899, 7.

48 Ibid. For another affirmation in a more popular source that smoking was not considered a sin, see, 'Etiquette,' Montreal *Family Herald and Weekly Star,* 5 February 1895, 6.

49 Cooper, *The Blessed Communion,* 125.

50 X.Y.Z., 'L'Influence Pernicieuse du Tabac,' *Le Monde Illustré,* 31 December 1887, 275; *Le Monde Illustré,* 21 January 1888, 293.

51 Montreal *Gazette,* 21 November 1895, 1.

52 See *Les Mandements: Lettres Pastorales, circulaires et autres Documents publiés*

dans le Diocèse de Montreal (Montreal: Arbour et Laperle) from 1890 to 1914. For examples of lists of 'Vices,' see *Tome 11*, 'Lettre Pastorale de Nos Seigneurs les archevêques et évêques des Provinces ecclésiastiques de Québec, de Montréal et Ottawa: Dangers des Mauvaises Compagnies,' 662, Les Archives de l'Archevêché de Montréal.

53 See numerous letters in the dossier 'Campagnes de Tempérance par les évêques de Montréal: Correspondance Générale, 1882–1906.' For other Catholic temperance organizations in Montreal, see the 'Nouveau Manuel de la Ligue du Coeur de Jesus,' in the dossier on the 'Ligue du Sacre-Coeur (fédération des), 1905–1924,' and 'Société de Tempérance de l'église St. Pierre,' in the dossier entitled 'Société de Tempérance et de charité établies dans le diocèse de Montréal.' These dossiers are at the Archives de l'Archevêché de Montréal.

54 Jean Hamelin and Nicole Gagnon, *Histoire du catholicisme québécois: Le XXe siècle, tome 1, 1898–1940* (Montreal: Boréal Express 1984), 175–230.

55 'Our Ottawa Letter,' *True Witness and Catholic Chronicle*, 11 April 1903, 4; Françoise (Robertine Barry), 'Sauvons l'Enfance,' *Le Journal de Françoise*, 18 January 1908, 310; Hamelin and Gagnon, *Histoire du catholicisme québécois*, 19.

56 Hamelin and Gagnon, *Histoire du catholicisme québécois*, 198.

57 Pierre Fontanel, 'Pour et contre le tabac,' *L'École sociale populaire*, 133–4 (1925): 23.

58 For a recounting of the two positions by a Montreal church leader, see Herbert Symonds, *A Memoir* (Montreal: Renouf Publishing 1921).

59 Elva Desmarchais to Archbishop Paul Bruchési, 15 March 1907, WCTU Dossier, Les Archives de l'Archevêché de Montréal; 'Joseph-Isreal Tarte,' *Dictionary of Canadian Biography*, 13, 1013–20; 'Lois Prohibitives,' *La Patrie*, 18 October, 4; House of Commons *Debates*, 1 April 1903, 842.

60 Hamelin and Gagnon, *Histoire du catholicisme québécois*, 18–19.

61 'Lois Prohibitives,' *La Patrie*, 18 October 1907, 4.

62 J. MacL. Metcalfe, 'Report of the Superintendent of Narcotics,' Quebec WCTU, *11th Annual Report*, 1894, 79–80.

63 Montreal WCTU, *Annual Reports*, 1884–99, Rare Book Room, McGill University.

64 'Executive,' 1 December 1902, Montreal WCTU Minute Book, 1902–6, AO 5 MU 8414.6.

65 Quebec WCTU, *13th Annual Report*, 1896, 65.

66 Quebec WCTU, *15th Annual Report*, 1897, 75.

67 Quebec WCTU, *22nd Annual Report*, 1904–5, 78–9; Quebec WCTU, *24th Annual Report*, 1906–7, 66.

68 'The Standard's Anti-Cigarette Campaign,' Montreal *Standard*, 30 March 1907, 6.

69 Montreal *Gazette*, 20 February 1893, 3.

70 'A Bill Intituled [sic] an Act to Prohibit the Sale of Cigarettes to Minors,' *Journals of the House of Assembly of New Brunswick*, 1 April 1890, 60.

71 'An Act to Prohibit the Sale or Gift of Tobacco to Minors in Certain Cases,' *Journals of the Legislative Assembly of the Province of British Columbia*, 20 April 1891; 'Minor's Protection Act,' *Journals of the House of Assembly of Nova Scotia*, 25 March 1892; 'An Act respecting the Use of Tobacco by Minors,' *Journals of the House of Assembly of Ontario*, 29 February 1892, 47. Similar proposals were considered in at least eight American state legislatures; see Cassandra Tate, 'The American Anti-Cigarette Movement: 1880–1930,' PhD thesis, University of Washington 1995, 133.

72 J. MacL. Metcalfe, 'Report of the Superintendent of Narcotics,' Quebec WCTU, *10th Annual Report*, 1892–3, 65.

73 Her letters to county presidents of the WCTU produced limited effect. Out of eighty letters, she received only thirteen replies, with six of these writing that they were too busy with other WCTU business. Ibid.

74 Montreal *Witness*, 27 February 1893, 6; Montreal *Gazette*, 27 February 1893, 4.

75 *Journeaux de l'Assemblée Législative de la Province de Québec*: for the second attempt, see 10, 16, and 21 November 1893; for the third attempt, see 27 and 29 November 1894; and for the final bill, see 8 and 20 November 1895. Also, Montreal *Gazette*, 21 November 1895, 1; Quebec WCTU, *14th Annual Report*, 1897, 54.

76 Anti-smoking lobbying on the provincial level in Quebec was limited to two petitions: the first, sent on 28 February 1902, called for the prohibition of tobacco sales to anyone under eighteen and was submitted by 'Mary E. Sanderson and others'; and a similar petition was sent on 12 May 1905 by the Quebec WCTU. For the Quebec WCTU's opposition to moving the cigarette prohibition campaign to the provincial level, see their *24th Annual Report*, 1907, 12–13.

77 House of Commons *Debates*, 1 April 1903, 830.

78 Cover letter to pamphlet 'Testimony concerning the "Cigarette,"' Annie O. Rutherford, Annie M. Bascom, and Jennie Waters to MPs, 25 April 1903.

79 Montreal *Witness*, 28 March 1903, 4.

80 House of Commons *Debates*, 23 March 1904, 344.

81 WCTU, 'Testimony concerning the "Cigarette,"' back cover. For a discussion of the rise of cigarette smoking and the changing meaning of the cigarette, see Rudy, 'Manly Smokes.'

82 'The Cigarette Evil,' Montreal *Witness*, 26 March 1903, 12.

83 House of Commons *Debates*, 23 March 1904, 339–40. Others continued on the theme of only outlawing cigarettes, not all tobacco products. See *Debates*, 1 April 1903, 830–1, and 16 March 1908, 5103.

84 'Anti-Cigarette Motion Adopted,' Montreal *Gazette*, 2 April 1903, 7.
85 M.B. Davis to R. Préfontaine, Laurier Papers, LAC MG 25, G, vol. 272, microfilm reel C-802, 75090–1. The letter is undated but its positioning in the Laurier Papers suggests it was written in 1903. For more on Davis and the American Tobacco Company of Canada, see Rudy, 'Manly Smokes.'
86 House of Commons *Debates*, 23 March 1904, 354, 363.
87 This legislative path is summed up in House of Commons *Debates*, 16 March 1908, 508891.
88 On the Ontario tobacco belt, see Lyal Tait, *Tobacco in Canada* (Canada: T.H. Best 1967), 5972.
89 House of Commons *Debates*, 16 March 1908, 5123.
90 'Anti-Cigarette Bill,' Montreal *Star*, 16 July 1908, 4; House of Commons *Debates*, 16 March 1908, 51334.
91 See vote division, House of Commons *Debates*, 16 March 1908, 5134.
92 Daisy Cross, 'Anti-Narcotics,' Quebec WCTU, *26th Annual Report*, 1908–9, 64; Sophia Black, 'Anti-Narcotics,' Quebec WCTU, *27th Annual Report*, 1909–10, 63.
93 Recorder's Court *Reports*, 1909–11, Archives de la Ville de Montréal (AVM).
94 'Minutes,' House of Commons Commission on the Cigarette, 23.
95 *Minutes*, City Council, Montreal, 26 February 1912, 51; *Procès verbal*, Bureau des Commissaires, AVM, 23 March 1912, 19.
96 At the House of Commons Commission, F.X. Choquet denied using entrapment, only to be contradicted by Owen Dawson. See 'Minutes,' 23 and 45.
97 *CCTJ*, November 1913, 37.
98 Florence E. Woodley, 'Quebec Will Not Be Found Wanting,' *Canadian White Ribbon Bulletin*, April 1914, 59.
99 Cook, *'Through Sunshine and Shadow,'* 13.
100 'Minutes,' House of Commons Commission on the Cigarette, 2 and 6.
101 Robert Cunningham, *Smoke and Mirrors: The Canadian Tobacco War* (Ottawa: International Development Research Centre 1996), 35.

3 From Flapper to Sophisticate: Canadian Women University Students as Smokers, 1920–60[1]

SHARON ANNE COOK

The young woman in Image 1 who graces the advertisement for Matinée Extra Mild and Matinée Slims Cigarettes in 1987 could very easily have been a university undergraduate. Holding her long, shiny hair back with a fashionable sweat band, with her sweatshirt slung carelessly around her shoulders and her no-nonsense shirt and shorts, sweat socks, and sneakers, the young woman rides a high-end bicycle through the greenery on a glorious day. For the era, she cuts an apt image of the undergraduate woman: as serious about her fitness as she is about her education. Both the 'extra mild' and extra-long cigarettes, 'slims,' had found a market among young women concerned with their health but also intent on weight control and the performative possibilities of smoking.

By 1987, the steeply climbing rate of women's smoking in Canada was beginning to decline from the absolute apex in 1974 when almost 40 per cent had taken up the habit.[2] Although smoking by undergraduate women has continued to decline since then, cigarette use remains the number one preventable cause of disease and death in Canada, with the number of yearly mortalities somewhere around 45,000 each year.[3] Almost a quarter of young women aged twenty to twenty-four continued to smoke in 2006,[4] and this group remains the most resistant of any to smoking-cessation programs.[5] A new book considers the close interplay of obesity – or the fear of being overweight – and smoking, particularly for young women. It shows that one-third of all deaths from all causes are directly linked to smoking and obesity.[6]

What attracts young women to smoking? Is it rooted in rebelliousness, a response to advertising,[7] a desire to remain thin?[8] Or is it most accurately understood as a minor addiction, like social drinking[9]? Is

1. *Chatelaine*, November 1987, inside back cover (245). Author's collection.

it simply one of many acts bringing pleasure to the user, sanctioned in our modern society with many other similar products – soft drugs, sweets, dancing?[10]

In all likelihood, all of these factors influence some young people to begin smoking. And yet the history of smoking makes it abundantly clear that rates are directly related to many societal factors, that the act is influenced by event, legislation, and societal norms. Smoking can be reduced with strong government and educational initiatives. When taxes have been increased, rates have declined; with the publicizing of health threats, like cancer, rates have also eventually dropped.

Popular knowledge of why women in particular are drawn to smoking remains sketchy. One factor that is under-examined in the scanty literature on causation, and that is explored here, concerns the visual performance made possible through the act of smoking, a set of visual cues taught to young people through popular culture and carrying with them clear utility for the young woman aiming to construct a powerful visual identity. Most of these attractions are either ignored or uncontested in the anti-smoking literature directed to these same young women, limiting the authority of formal education in disrupting this life-threatening habit which, for many, soon emerges as an addiction. Two segments of the Canadian female population continue to smoke more heavily than most other Canadians: working-class girls and young women in higher education. This essay addresses the history of smoking among young women in higher education.

How and when did Canadian middle-class women engaged in post-secondary education first adopt smoking as a common pastime? What purposes has smoking served for the undergraduate woman in the twentieth century? On the other hand, what factors discouraged smoking before 1960? How did women learn the rituals associated with smoking? This essay will argue that, while smoking was slow at first to catch on with respectable young women, the decision to smoke supported a variety of modernist notions relating to visual identities. Young women's social capital became deeply invested in their bodily qualities in this period, including their ability to command and maintain attention through dramatic gestures associated with smoking. Smoking – or simply manipulating the cigarette or other smoking paraphernalia, such as decorative lighters – offered women the means to make, and possibly remake, a visually based identity to suit the era and circumstance. The many powerful and enduring disincentives that operated until the 1940s were swept away in the patriotic iconography of the Second World War, ushering in an era in which smoking became almost the norm.

This essay investigates the process by which smoking moved for the respectable middle-class Canadian woman from a potentially exciting act indulged in by a minority during the interwar period to one which seemed more normalized, especially for this privileged group of young women, by the 1940s. It remained so until at least the late 1980s, and even to the present day for many. Through a close reading of both textual and visual evidence, the smorgasbord of visual identities on offer to young women through popular culture will be sampled. To understand what meaning young women attached to these identity choices, products in the form of student photograph albums, undergraduates' yearbooks, and other 'candid' and posed photographic evidence from undergraduate culture will also be investigated.

As a framework for analysing both the messages offered to the undergraduate woman smoker and the meanings she made of those messages, the essay begins with a short discussion of methodological implications in using visual records for academic research. It draws on several semiotic techniques such as denotative and connotative meanings in images, and applies these to a variety of visual documents, including visual prescriptive documents such as advertisements and youth-produced and organized visual records such as yearbook and scrapbook photographs. It tracks undergraduate women's smoking between 1920 and 1960 on two Canadian university campuses, Queen's University in Kingston, Ontario, and the University of Manitoba in Winnipeg, Manitoba, and explores the process of value change as regards smoking in two distinct periods: the interwar years, the presumed first era of large-scale public smoking by women; and the Second World War and post-war era, from about 1940 to 1960. In each case, samples of the prescriptive code constructed by advertisers are presented and compared with photographic evidence produced by undergraduate smokers themselves, both 'staged' and 'candid.' Smoking as part of a liberated lifestyle of 'flaming youth' during the 1920s and 1930s was an insufficient motivation to convince many Canadian women undergraduates to smoke. Rather, it was not until the Second World War, when the range of visual identities had been extended and normalized, when many more middle-class women were engaged in paid labour, and when smoking came to be closely associated with many screen and media icons and consequently with identity performance, that smoking became normative for the still-respectable undergraduate Canadian woman. By the 1950s, smoking had become a common prop for the serious young woman. The essay concludes with a consideration of the many factors that draw women into the company of smokers in our own age, and suggests that a more socially utilitarian view must be adopted in designing any effective smoking-cessation program for young women of this group.

Smoking among Canadian Women as Depicted in the Historiography

Despite the assertion in both academic and popular literature that smoking first became common among women in the 1920s, an era of multiple and overlapping liberations – social, political, economic – in fact, the first period when large numbers of young Canadian women smoked in public was during the Second World War and its immediate aftermath. Statistics were first collected on the numbers of women smokers from the mid-1960s, so numbers for the interwar period are necessarily impressionistic and reliant on international comparisons. Yet, notwithstanding the lack of statistics for women smokers before 1935 in the United States, contemporaries asserted that the quadrupling of cigarette sales there between 1918 and 1928 was due in part to the advent of the woman smoker. One estimate puts the percentage of women smokers at 5 per cent in 1923 and 12 per cent in 1929.[11] Another source claims that 18 per cent of American women were smoking by 1935 and 36 per cent by 1944.[12] In the first survey of women smokers in Montreal, in 1947, almost half of the women who responded declared themselves to be smokers.[13] A private survey conducted by the Canadian Daily Newspaper Association in 1956 indicated that about 68 per cent of francophone women in Montreal and 28 per cent of anglophones admitted to smoking,[14] showing the ethnic and regional influences on smoking patterns. By the time official statistics for Canadian smokers were available in 1965, about 39 per cent of women smoked.[15] In none of these estimates is there a distinction by class, education, or profession. Clearly, however, until the mid-1970s, the rates of women's smoking climbed for all sectors of the female smoking public. Thus, we can safely conclude that the majority of women remained non-smokers between 1919 and 1939, with numbers rising during and after the Second World War and reaching an apex sometime in the 1970s with the Virginia Slims' population of smokers.

However, the fact that respectable Canadian women largely

eschewed smoking in the 1920s does not mean that women were blind to the many ways by which smoking allowed young women of this transitional period to imagine new expressive techniques that would mark them as modern and sophisticated, rather than backward-looking and repressed. Such was the case as well with young university men, of course, for whom smoking had long been a symbol of sophistication and maturity.[16] Joan Jacobs Brumberg has argued that, in the United States, smoking was common among college women in this period, supporting the new 'flexible personal image'[17] of the era. In Canada, Cynthia Comacchio has documented the range of destabilizing forces during the 1920s that caused many authorities to be anxious about the 'problem of modern youth,' with their presumed rejection of their parents' generational authority.[18] But Canadian historians generally agree that these anxieties exaggerated 'flaming youths" level of rebellion,[19] certainly among women. As with many other social changes, the promise encapsulated by the many rebellious acts of the era, including smoking, long outpaced the doing of them.

The literature relating to smoking until very recently has been preoccupied with the long-standing battle between governments and corporate tobacco giants in which the tobacco interests have been exposed as rapacious and unethical.[20] And such stories have been exceedingly well told: Richard Kruger's *Ashes to Ashes* won a Pulitzer Prize.[21] This study does not dispute that aggressive marketing campaigns by tobacco manufacturers have helped to convince men, women, and children to try smoking. Indeed, anyone familiar with the literature documenting the actions of tobacco manufacturers since the late nineteenth century could not reasonably conclude otherwise. However, unlike many academic works in this area, this study argues that women were willing accomplices in normalizing smoking. Women took an active role in shaping smoking's meanings, thus contributing to the smoking woman's identity. This was not a passive process whereby women were victimized, nor is it for women smokers today. Interest in the social history of smoking is much more recent.

A small international literature in social history has appeared over the past decade which includes women but which is by no means exclusively concerned with women's decisions to smoke or their representation.[22] Of particular importance, Matthew Hilton has produced an impressive cultural history of smoking in Britain, although concentrating on the male smoker. Many of his insights about the significance of visual and artefactual culture have enriched this study of women's smoking.[23] Cassandra Tate has shown how the anti-cigarette movement in the United States took on 'Big Tobacco' between 1890 and 1930 and lost. Allan Brandt's masterful *The Cigarette Century* is the latest addition to tobacco scholarship.[24] Acknowledging that smoking does support social exchange and adolescent identity formation, his analysis also positions women as mainly acted-upon, not as actors, in the performance of smoking.

Jarrett Rudy explores changing public views of tobacco consumption by women and men in Montreal between the late nineteenth and mid-twentieth centuries. Rudy's main argument is that smoking served to promote liberal ideals related to gender, class, and racial norms. These changing ideological frameworks, which stressed views of personal rights, supplanted earlier moral explanations.[25] The foremost source on the 'Canadian Tobacco War' is Rob Cunningham's study, *Smoke and Mirrors*.[26]

The literature focusing on women and smoking is even more select. Women have been explored as opponents of smoking through temperance leadership,[27] as advertising copy in the post-war consumer society,[28] and as consumers from the 1920s when increased access to motor cars and unchaperoned dance halls, as well as the advantages of the franchise, less constraining dress, and higher rates of paid employment for women, all encouraged smoking.[29] The consensus is that Canadian women of all classes took up smoking during the 1920s in a much relaxed and even enabling environment characterized by many other modernist attitudes and behaviours.[30]

Decoding Visual Evidence

Smoking has visual power, imbuing visual records with particular importance for research purposes. Nevertheless, a debate exists as to whether the effective use of visual records for academic investigation requires specific skills of 'visual literacy.' Paul Messaris argues that 'what distinguishes images (including motion pictures) from language and from other modes of communication is the fact that images reproduce many of the informational cues that people make use of in their perception of physical and social reality.'[31] Thus, we possess visual intelligence innately. Similarly, Ronald Barthes holds that the photograph is 'a message without a code.'[32] Nevertheless, the constructed nature of the visual record, together with its essential ability to either reinforce or break with unmediated 'visual orders,' suggests that attending to certain semiotic functions can facilitate productive analysis of the visual record. With this in mind, Janne Seppanen sets out the concept of 'denotation' (the visual record's obvious meaning), which is to be distinguished from 'connotation' (its 'surplus' meanings) and 'myth' (in which the 'historical' becomes 'natural').[33] One way in which the mythic meaning of the visual record can be made to appear as a natural representation of a phenomenon, rather than as one that has been carefully and consciously constructed, is by drawing out the photograph's metaphoric content. As in spoken language, metaphors elide two images, a primary one, usually the subject, and a secondary, culturally significant image which is broadly recognized. Metaphoric strategies invite the observer (or the listener, in spoken language) to apply some features of the culturally significant image to a visual record's subject, thereby creating a 'parallel implication complex,' as Charles Forceville puts it, where either or both the primary and secondary image are strengthened by the power of the association.[34] We might take one example of a powerful metaphor created in cigarette advertising, the so-called 'Marlboro Man,' where a culturally powerful and recognizable image of masculinity was carefully constructed by associating a handsome, healthy, virile western American cowboy with cigarette smoking, and smoking in a particular way. In this case, the metaphor came to be so recognizable that it assumed mythic proportions, thereby strengthening both images – that of a male smoking in this fashion, and that of the iconic Marlboro man himself: the cowboy, his hat, his stance, his cigarette 'hold.' This example reminds us, too, that powerful metaphors and myths are bound by time and place: when the actor who served as the visual image for the Marlboro Man died of lung cancer, the ad was retired, disrupting what had been a powerful and prosperous association.

Visual records come in a variety of forms, some more easily manipulated than others. This study makes use of carefully constructed visual texts, such as advertisements, and those visual records that appear to be 'candids' or largely unmediated in source or construction, such as one finds in a student-produced photograph album. It aims to 'read' both of these visual documents for purposes of the research questions set out earlier. However, it must be acknowledged at the outset that visual documents can rarely ever be considered 'unstaged.' In many instances, the greater the photographer's skill in structuring the subject, the more the product looks to be a 'candid' shot. Even in instances where photographs are genuinely extemporaneous, a selection must have been made among other like photographs of which this one was chosen. As well, the photographs have been mounted in a particular pattern, 'framed' or coupled in a particular spatial relationship with others, which influences the meanings to be made. Finally, exclusions as well as inclusions produce their own narratives and narrative shifts with a sufficient number of examples.

Smoking's Attractions for the Undergraduate Woman

Smoking's eventual popularity suggests that young women were attracted to it for a number of reasons, then as now. Moreover, as movies, billboards, periodical advertisements, and much else refined the image of the woman smoker, and as modernism chose visual markers such as changing fashion and cigarette smoking, the range of identifiable 'smoking types' broadened, thereby inviting the consumer to find at least one with which to identify. Especially beguilling for the young woman who was actively 'finding herself' was the fact that she need not choose only a single identity; with smoking, she was free to 'test drive' one or more by adopting the characteristic gestures associated with one type of public female smoker: perhaps a reflective (smoking) intellectual by day, she could experiment with the visual orders associated with the (smoking) 'vamp' for evening events or the friendly and pretty (smoking) 'girl next door,' or even take on the image of the (smoking) 'sophisticate.' All of these identity models were developed in visual detail and through repetition in the popular media, and all were within reach of the young, middle-class woman. For this period, when women lacked role models on whom to pattern their developing modern identities, the woman smoker as represented in popular culture taught the young woman how to explore new visual identities while remaining fairly respectable.

The process of visual identity-formation was closely associated with social values born in the interwar period. Brumberg argues that cultural prescriptions for young women in these years were moving from the 'good works' of the nineteenth century to the 'good looks' of the twentieth.[35] The hallmark of this 'first modern generation'[36] was an emphasis on visual bodily features, including unpocked, clear skin, shiny hair, and, most important of all, a slender profile. Smoking allowed women to control the image they projected in a number of ways: weight was thought to be more easily controlled through this form of appetite suppression; the act of lighting up and holding the cigarette aloft allowed public attention to be drawn to the carefully made-up face and manicured hands, with the exhaled smoke softening the facial contour; in the crowded and noisy public arena of the classroom or workplace, attention could be captured through wordless performance, telegraphing as well sexual allure or worldly sophistication without the need to 'find the right words.' A woman moving into the public sphere, as all university co-eds were required to do to some degree, needed to develop strategies by which she could announce her presence, capturing a place for herself and focusing attention on her physical form before uttering a syllable. As will be shown, careful attention to the details of smoking through popular cultural representations allowed respectable women to learn how to do just this.

Beyond the act of smoking itself, a woman could construct her visual identity through a vast range of smoking accessories for her appearance and home. In his study of the nineteenth-century British male smoker's 'paraphernalia of smoking consumption,' Matthew Hilton argues that the amassing of the pipes, pipe holders, storage jars, tobacco pouches, smoking armchairs, slippers, jackets, hats, and much else might seem irrational in expressing a smoker's identity, and yet, as a group, these objects constructed a 'distinctive picture of the smoker as different from everybody else.'[37] And so it was for the woman smoker. More serious than a debutante, but more stylish than her blue-stocking or temperance-oriented grandmother, the Canadian undergraduate found herself in a privileged and yet unfamiliar role within the academy. Her generation of collegians, like the English tobacco aficionado, was aiming to cut a 'distinctive picture.'

Decorative cigarette cases could set off a particular costume, and cigarette holders in fine materials like wood and ivory, or cheaply produced to match the colour and texture of an outfit, not only completed the 'look' but also extended the length of the cigarette, protecting the fingers from unsightly nicotine stains. These holders were often kept in perfumed delicate boxes.[38] Perfumed and tinted cigarette ends were produced to match a woman's lipstick or her nail enamel. Decorative cigarette containers were manufactured for the coffee table, and cigarette dishes to match fine tea sets were available. Monogrammed cigarettes were reportedly given as favours to guests, according to newspapers of the day.[39] One could buy specialized lines of clothing for smoking, including light-weight smoking tunics which mimicked mens' smoking jackets. Thus, products ranged from modest to expensive to support the woman smoker in accessorizing her dorm room or apartment.

A third attraction of smoking for women was the social facilitation it offered. Unlike the cigars or pipes favoured by men who engaged in a languorous process of stuffing the tobacco, lighting, and drawing the smoke through in an extended performance, cigarettes had the advantage of being small enough to be carried in the smart new hand-bags and to be consumed as a break between classes. Sharing a cigarette and coffee with friends created a social exchange which was inexpensive, much more socially acceptable than drinking alcohol and as short-term as one chose. Cheap, mass-produced cigarettes were available from the 1880s as a result of James Bonsack's cigarette-rolling machine.[40] The refinement of the self-striking match in the late nineteenth century meant that lighting the cigarette was a fairly reliable act too. Henceforth, the lit cigarette could act as a prop to aid discussion but not damage clothing.

Factors Discouraging Smoking

Smoking had the potential of both danger and exciting liberation. The forces holding women back from smoking included the traditional temperance message which, while on the wane, could still muster enough social sanctions to make public smoking by women an act that few would hazard. As well, smoking's long-standing negative associations with the demimonde of the theatre, petty crime, and noisy intellectuals, and the remaining positive associations of women with social purity, maternal feminism, and the Victorian doctrine of the 'angel in the house,' meant that, despite inducements to smoke, most respectable women resisted. At the same time, advertising campaigns promoting women's smoking were in their infancy and had yet to find the convincing formula that would develop by the 1940s.

By the Second World War, large numbers of middle-class women were in the workforce along with their working-class sisters, creating ideal conditions for smoking to facilitate the same type of social bonding behaviour that men had experienced in combat; popular culture had also embraced women's smoking with vigour, making a wide variety of images of the woman smoker a normalized part of the visual map. Not surprisingly, then, this was the era when many Canadian female undergraduates took up smoking, continuing in the long tradition of the female intellectual as rebel smoker through to the 1980s.

Selling Cigarettes to the Canadian Undergraduate in the Interwar Years

The conventional view, both popular and academic, is that the 1920s saw public smoking by young women become both popular and accepted as a general expression of the liberating norms of such forces as post-war urbanization, waged labour for the middle- as well as the working-class woman, secularism, the franchise, and the quiet death of maternal feminism which undid Victorian notions of respectability, particularly as they applied to women. Young women were expected to act differently from their mothers' generation, and did so to a degree, taught the new code by such prescriptive images as tobacco advertising. But the idea that social norms changed with this first decade is incorrect. The evidence suggests that pre-war standards of feminine respectability remained intact for much of the inter-war period.

Consider Image 2, a United Cigar Stores advertisement in the inaugural issue of the new Canadian women's magazine, *Chatelaine*, in 1928. The ad tries to convince young women that the respectable girl could not only safely smoke outside her home but also shop for her tobacco supplies while maintaining decorum. This advertisement is noteworthy on several levels. First, the denotated messages are unusually full. The visual arrangement shows two young and attractive women in their stylish coats, pumps, and cloche hats framing the equally young and handsome male merchant. While the women seem delighted with their purchases, the young man appears as a passive agent, staring with parted lips as he watches one woman hold her packet of cigarettes aloft. Immediately before the women are the stock-in-trade of the United Cigar Stores: box after box of ornately decorated cigar boxes which beckon to the middle-class (and middle-aged) male clientele. Within such an alien masculine space, women would justifiably feel some anxiety about their place. To answer their reasonable fear that they might feel uncomfortable, the ad devotes considerable copy to address 'Ladies' and their worries directly. Smoking at home is one thing, but buying tobacco products in public spaces puts the young middle-class woman at the mercy of a working-class male clerk who could easily insult her, intentionally or not. The ad confronts this anxiety and the young women smoker's obvious vulnerability through a carefully phrased statement. The potential woman customer is assured that her shopping experience will be pleasurable, rather than an affront to her respectability, that the clerk will act appropriately by taking sufficient notice of her so that she will not feel rebuffed, that he will provide superior products (since her novice status as a smoker might make her an easy mark to being sold inferior goods), and that he will mask the products by wrapping them neatly.

2. *Chatelaine*, March 1928, 69.

Thus, rather than the denotated message telegraphing happiness and security, the image recognizes instead the many social barriers for the young, respectable, female smoker. Included in these dangers was the implication that the smoking woman was overtly sexual, an exceedingly dangerous suggestion for any woman, particularly one who was already on a modernist track through claiming post-secondary education. The implication of sexuality is countered both by the visual arrangement and by the text. Interestingly, the advertisement underscores its naturalized depiction (and its connotative meaning) by presenting the women smokers through a photographic image rather than through line drawings, the more common device for the period. At the same time, the young woman in search of an updated visual identity would find in these two customers the visual cues of friendly confidence, the smart, stylish woman as consumer.

In fact, despite the implication to the contrary, advertisers in this period operated in a hostile climate. These young women and their anxious parents would have encountered the long-standing message in educational textbooks of tobacco's dangers for young people, both physical and moral.[41] Textbooks typically grounded discussions of smoking as physiologically dangerous to all parts of the body – the human skeleton, muscular and digestive and circulatory and respiratory systems, and sensory patterns.[42] More troubling yet, the reader was told, was both the alcohol and tobacco user's 'powerlessness to improve the character' since 'it is a habit which *grows*; and constant indulgence renders the person powerless to resist the desire.'[43] In popular literature as well, the dangers for women were argued to be far greater than for men. With her essential reproductive role, the woman smoker was accused of placing not only her body but also her morals in peril. Readers of Mac Levy's popular 1916 book, *Tobacco Habit Easily Conquered*, learned that smoking 'devitalizes and debilitates even the sturdiest and healthiest of women. It retards the normal functioning of the delicate organs. It has a harmful effect upon offspring before and after birth. It is even a potential cause of sterility itself.'[44] Consistent with this view, John Harvey Kellogg's *Tobaccoism or How Tobacco Kills* argued that tobacco 'destroys the sex glands and hinders reproduction' in men, women, and animals, the latter shown in clinical studies.[45] The 'family press' such as *Maclean's* magazine, also put the case that women were particularly at risk from smoking. Thus, any campaign to convince the educated young woman to smoke somehow had to contend with the weight of educational and popular literature, of which this is but a small sample, which stated outright that smoking was dangerous for young women and that it should be avoided.[46]

Even with clear social change, behavioural norms actually changed much more slowly, especially as regards liminal activities like public drinking and smoking for the respectable woman. Furthermore, what might have been acceptable in large Canadian cities took much longer to be accepted in small-town and rural Canada. In her recent collection of autobiographical stories, *The View from Castle Rock*, Alice Munro describes her own youth during the 1930s. Her grandmother, she notes, 'did not approve of women smoking or of anybody drinking' and in this she was in accord with her small-town neighbours. Her grandmother had a dear friend who broke these rules consistently and flagrantly, however, smoking, drinking, wearing slacks and sunglasses, and playing bridge (rather than euchre). Munro grants that, while the smoking friend 'was not an unusual woman of her time,' she was 'an unusual woman in that town.'

Searching for the Canadian Woman Undergraduate of the 1920s: Charlotte Scott Black

The 1920s represents a period characterized by dissonance between the promise offered by advertisers and the reality of the social danger presented by smoking. The result was that few Canadian undergraduates chose to smoke publicly. Instructive in this regard is the case of Charlotte Scott Black.

Raised in Winnipeg, Manitoba, Black graduated with a bachelor of science in home economics degree from the Manitoba Agricultural College at the University of Manitoba in May 1925. (In this, Charlotte was something of a pioneer. Established in 1906, the Agricultural College had been transformed into the Faculty of Agriculture in 1924, with responsibility for the new degree program in home economics.[47]) One of the convocation gifts received by Charlotte was a scrapbook, sent to her by her Auntie Maude from Los Angeles. Redolent with pride in this treasured niece, the card carries the hope that this 'little gift' will do its part in helping Charlotte to transport 'memories of [her] college life into the larger and fuller life' she was about to enter.[48]

The scrapbook became the frame for a wide variety of documents and memorabilia for this exciting milestone in Charlotte's life: postcards, letters, invitations, notations of social outings and receptions, and many photographs dating from the graduation itself, as well as events over her undergraduate years. From her carefully planned scrapbook, we learn that, in honour of their graduation, Charlotte and her classmates were invited to a reception at Government House, hosted by Lieutenant Governor and Lady Aikins, to dinners hosted by the Manitoba Agricultural College faculty and the dean of science, and to a luncheon at the lavish Fort Garry Hotel hosted by the University of Manitoba Alumni Association, among other events.

There can be little doubt that Charlotte Black and her classmates occupied a position of some status in this agricultural society. Women entered university in Manitoba in increasing numbers after the First World War, but by the 1950s they still occupied only one-quarter of the undergraduate places at the University of Manitoba.[49] This placed Charlotte in a select group.[50] Further, as a student in the 'science' program, Charlotte and her classmates had a higher status than prospective teachers of home economics, who spent only one year on campus. There is some evidence that Charlotte, or 'Blackie' to her friends, was quite aware of her social entitlement individually as well. Included in the scrapbook, for example, is an invitation to a banquet in June 1924 at the Fort Garry Hotel. The sponsor was her father's fraternal lodge, the 'Order of the Royal Purple Supreme Lodge.' Charlotte notes that she 'attended with Daddy because Mother was ill. The most awful banquet ever experienced. Danced with such things as gas-meter-men after dinner – a scorching night,' she sniffed.

Raised in comfortable middle-class homes, feted by the university and their families, and armed with a relatively rare university degree, we might assume that Charlotte Black and her friends might have adopted a common marker of modernity and feminine authority, cigarette smoking. The many photographs kept by Charlotte Black to memorialize the best of her undergraduate experience suggest otherwise, however. Leaving aside the obviously posed pictures of the happy graduands, the 'candid' photographs show a tight group of eleven young women at work and play, but with no evidence at all of smokers in the group. At leisure in a lounge, taking tea 'in Isobel's room,' lounging on the building's steps after their last lecture, shopping as a foursome, camping with the same eleven classmates, or enjoying a bonfire meal with men friends too, hiking, studying, strolling – they perch, sit with feet drawn up, hang companionably on each other, laugh helplessly at their own antics, but never, ever smoke. Some of the men sport pipes, but none of the women even play-act at smoking. It is entirely absent from this female visual space.

The denotated meanings of these photographs are clear through repeated patterns and spatial locations: university life is comfortably coeducational, for the young, and within a select number of private and public spaces. Appropriate leisured activities include studying, amiable conversations with tea, camping, or elegant dinners, always in groups of varying sizes, but apparently never with faculty members, of whom there were only two women in arts and, at times, one in home economics in this era in any case.[51] Charlotte's socializing appears to have been done almost exclusively with her peers. The connotative meanings are limited, but suggestive: the undergraduates tended not to 'date' one partner but rather socialized in groups; female graduates dressed in a virginal white 'uniform'; both leisured and academic activities remained closely tied to the natural environment of the western prairies rather than to a built landscape; and the code of respectability for the university-educated middle-class woman seemingly offered little opportunity for personal expression. In the photographs selected by Charlotte Black for her scrapbook, one young undergraduate looks very much like the next: short hair swept off the face, mid-calf skirts, shapeless tops and coats, a profusion of hats for any social event.

No one could reasonably argue that, because Charlotte Black's personal scrapbook contains no references to women smoking, no women did so. (It should be noted as well that a thorough investigation of yearbooks for a number of Canadian universities during the 1920s and 1930s turned up not a single photograph of a woman smoker, though, given the era and the fact that yearbooks were an official record, this is hardly surprising.) In fact, there is considerable evidence that undergraduate women were smoking in this period. The diary of Yvonne Blue, a freshman at the University of Chicago in 1927, suggests that sorority sisters often smoked together. Yvonne became a member of the Acoth Club and reported that the members 'talked of nothing but boys, smoked incessantly, and scattered "O my Gods!" quite liberally through their conversation.' In response, Yvonne also took to smoking, cut her hair in a severe bob, and dressed exclusively in black.[52] Oral testimony from Saskatchewan undergraduates indicates that many smokers indulged on the sly, smoking while hanging out of windows to mask the smoke, or finding secure areas on campus out of the public gaze.[53] Phyllis Lee Peterson, a student at McGill in the 1920s, remembers her 'rush down to Murray's for five or six cups of coffee on an original ten cent investment because women are not allowed to smoke at McGill and the management of Murray's is more understanding.'[54]

We can only guess at Charlotte's own opinions about the smoking woman, or her intentions as she set about creating her keepsake document. Furthermore, we cannot know if one of Charlotte's friends might have smoked, but not for the camera or not in this crowd. Evidence of female undergraduates' vocational intentions in the 1920s at Queen's University shows that the majority sought positions in teaching, one of the few professions open to women in this era for which a university degree would be advantageous.[55] It is possible that the spotless visual record kept by Charlotte and her friends was motivated in part by their vague intentions to one day teach, and therefore to be 'moral exemplars' for children.[56]

The textual record of this era suggests that smoking by university women commanded a great deal of attention and generated anxiety in the general population. Hollywood films like the 1920s *Confessions of a Co-ed: A Flaming Diary of Flaming College Youth* played in theatres across the Canadian west, and doubtless would have added to public anxiety.[57] Both the secondary and primary literature of the period leaves the impression that smoking was rampant among university women as an expression of their rejection of the conventional behaviour expected of mothers or young wives. Edward Bernays sent out the following press release to the American college market, for example: 'Seven out of every 10 coeds at Northwestern Like to Smoke. Those figures were computed on the basis of a petition signed by the women students living in houses on the women's quadrangle. The petition, in protest against the established ban on smoking, asked for the right to vote.'[58] Undoubtedly, some university-educated women did smoke in this era, but the visual and textual sources examined here suggest that smoking in public might have been less typical than we have come to believe, calling into question the amount of smoking generally.

Convincing the Undergraduate Woman to Smoke: Popular Media, 1940–60

By the Second World War, Canadians were exposed to many more images of women as smokers in a variety of types: glamorous, demure, serious, playful, sexy, and sophisticated. This is not to say, however, that public smoking by women was accepted in all social quarters; in many places, including, as described by Donald F. Davis and Barbara Lorenzkowski, buses and trams, public smoking remained a male activity. For many, the woman smoker still summoned a constellation of unseemly and dangerous connotations, as in this letter to the editor of the *Ottawa Morning Citizen:* 'smoking, drinking, wearing slacks and shorts (the latter so brief) a loose kind of conversation, yes and all this ... on street-cars.'[59] In fact, Nancy Kiefer and Ruth Roach Pierson argue that, in comparison to earlier periods, the liberated status of the female undergraduate eroded somewhat during the war years.[60]

Nevertheless, smoking by women was much more in evidence both in public and in popular culture. These commonplace acts and representations provided real-life examples of visual identities based on 'looks' that were within reach for the discerning woman consumer. The means invoked to 'sell' this message to women by the 1940s had also become more refined. Cigarette advertising of the 1920s often represented the woman smoker as a very young woman primarily in search of 'pleasure.' By the 1940s, the image was more often of an older woman who sought pleasure and sexuality, to be sure, but also represented such qualities as mature accomplishment and prosperity with her glamour.

In the array of images on billboards, in magazines, in films, and elsewhere, the consumer could easily find models to emulate showing the smoker as a woman of personal authority and sophistication, as in the 1942 'still' of Bette Davis reproduced here (see Image 3). At the same time, Davis telegraphed sexuality and slender beauty. If Bette Davis were thought to be too forward, the undergraduate could turn instead to Judith Garden (Image 4), a society florist. Conveying the many rules of smart smoking, Garden demonstrates the appropriate stance for a woman smoker: bent arm, cigarette in 'flag' position, about mid-neck. Just as Bette Davis had taught that a lady should never light her own cigarette if possible, Judith Garden's lesson was that cigarettes belonged naturally with other sophisticated skills of the prosperous middle class, like flower arranging. Reminiscent of many advertisements of the age in which society hostesses were presented as models of (smoking) sophistication,[61] Garden also offered readers of the *Ladies' Home Journal*, one of only two Canadian women's magazines of the era, the testimonial that she 'tried and compared many brands – and I learned that cool, mild Camels are the cigarette for me!' 'It's experience and taste that counts,' whether in flowers or cigarettes, she advises. These denotative lessons would elicit interest in many young undergraduate women, with media personalities like Judith Garden displaying recognizable skills in professional and personal life. All the while, Garden is glamorous and sexy. As powerful a message would have been the connotative ones:

3. Bette Davis still, in a scene from *Now, Voyager*, 1942.

LADIES' HOME JOURNAL

FAMOUS FLOWER-STYLIST

Florist with a Flair **Judith Garden** AGREES:

"Whether you're arranging flowers or choosing a cigarette . . . EXPERIENCE IS THE BEST TEACHER!"

"I tried and compared many brands —and I learned that cool, mild Camels are the cigarette for me!"

Simple French marigolds with a handful of green leaves take on a sophisticated air when they're arranged with the touch of experience!

● Into a brilliant ballroom ablaze with fabulous flowers walks a brisk, little brunette. She stoops to tilt a creamy petal; adjusts a straying leaf; nods with satisfaction. Miss Judith Garden has just set the stage for a dazzling social debut! Later . . . in her Manhattan shop (at left) . . . she designs a tiny masterpiece from a handful of rosy-red fruit, a few blossoms in a 10-cent-store container. "It isn't the cost of the blooms," says the talented Miss Garden. "It's experience and taste that counts."

More people smoke Camels than ever before!

R. J. Reynolds Tobacco Company, Winston-Salem, N.C.

MOST people, like Judith Garden, know that experience is the best teacher. That's why millions of smokers who tried and compared different brands of cigarettes say, "Camels are the choice of experience with me!" Let your own "T-Zone"—T for Taste and T for Throat—tell you about Camels. Let your taste tell you about Camel's marvelous flavor. Let your throat discover that wonderful Camel mildness and coolness. See how your own experience tells you why more people are smoking Camels than ever before!

According to a Nationwide survey:

MORE DOCTORS SMOKE CAMELS THAN ANY OTHER CIGARETTE

When 113,597 doctors were asked by three independent research organizations to name the cigarette they smoked, more doctors named Camel than any other brand.

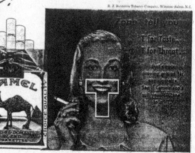

4. *Ladies' Home Journal*, November 1948, n.p.

sophistication, power, beauty, and professional status for women were aligned with smoking. Both the denotative and connotative messages would have been important to the undergraduate hoping to make her way in the professions as well as in society, at least until marriage. To buttress the smoking advertisements, the mythic status of Bette Davis and Judith Garden are also brought to bear on the message.

Metaphoric devices are especially obvious in the Judith Garden full-page advertisement: Ms Garden is posed in the centre of the collage, holding her cigarette reflectively while she contemplates the beauty of her craft. The central textual message invites the observer to construct a 'parallel implication complex' between Judith Garden and 'you,' the real subject of this advertisement and actually pictured (as Everywoman) in the lower left corner. Garden functions as the culturally relevant and recognizable reference point, but most of the text is addressed explicitly to the subject, 'you': 'Let your own "T-Zone" – T for Taste and T for Throat – tell you about Camels. Let your taste tell you about Camel's marvelous flavor. Let your throat discover that wonderful Camel mildness and coolness. See how your own experience tells you why more people are smoking Camels than ever before!' The cut-out subject box with Everywoman's image rephrases the same message as a didactic lesson:

Let your "T-Zone" tell you
T for Taste ...
T for Throat ....
that's your proving ground for any cigarette.
See if *Camels* don't
suit *your* "T-Zone"
To a "T."

In case the observer somehow misses the catechism-like lesson in which the cultural authority Judith Garden teaches the young woman why and how to smoke, the advertisement ends by invoking the eminence of medical doctors: 'According to a nationwide survey: more doctors smoke Camels than any other cigarette.' Long gone are the days when a working-class clerk will figure in a message intended for the young middle-class woman.

If the undergraduate were to leaf through the other Canadian women's magazine of the era, *Chatelaine*, in the same month as the advertising feature on Judith Garden in the *Ladies' Home Journal*, she would have found a tasteful line-drawing of a begloved and modestly hatted woman with eyes demurely downcast, but holding her cigarette in precisely the same stance as the previous two examples. Advertisements stressing the sophistication of smokers appeared in most women's and family magazines in this period. American tobacco manufacturer Philip Morris regularly ran advertisements for their Virginia Oval cigarettes, again with line-drawing images of refined women in modest hats. Some of these harkened back to Wedgewood graphics, making the connection between the refinement of smoking and expensive dishware. The distinguished magazine *Saturday Night* regularly ran advertisements for up-market Pall Mall, where well-dressed and older women were shown taking tea in elegant hotels while they smoked.[62] The alignment of 'fine mature woman–fine cigarette' was thereby underlined.

Despite the continued representation of the woman smoker in line-drawings, however, the increasingly common portrayal was photographic, where the realistic setting and other figures would lend credence to mature, middle-class women imagining themselves as part of modern society. In Image 5 the Canadian Pacific Railway profiled its Princess Lounge in the elegant Royal York Hotel in Toronto, connected to Union Station. By 1954, the women shown here are hatless but dressed in a variety of stylish yet sexy gowns. All of the women are older and suitably escorted by at least one male for each female grouping. Several of the patrons sip a drink and smoke in the prescribed way, repeatedly demonstrated, of crooked arm holding the cigarette aloft. The elegance of the furniture, the recessed ceiling, the flower arrangements, the liveried waiter, the pleasant social gathering all connote the smoker as sophisticated and sociable, characteristics that the undergraduate could well imagine for herself.

Thus, the marketing strategies of the war and post-war eras contrast in a number of ways with approaches taken during the interwar period. First, rather than presenting the woman smoker as a young and often edgy character, marketing campaigns of the 1940s to 1960s profiled women smokers as older, elegant, prosperous, and professional in bearing. Smokers are often developed as full personalities, with achievements and opinions of their own. Part of the explanation for this strategy might be the larger group of media icons who were known smokers, and who were happy to receive this free advertising for their own purposes; partly, too, this is likely a result of weakened criticism of the middle-class woman smoker, allowing positive and personalized qualities to be drawn out in media profiles. Certainly, the effect was to further normal-

5. Archives of Ontario, Canadian Pacific Railway Company, Princess Lounge
in the Royal York Hotel, C 310–1–0–36, 1954.

ize and naturalize this most historical event, presenting young women
with possibilities of visual identities which they could try on, much
like an outfit. It seems clear that the campaign to associate smoking by
both men and women with such qualities as maturity, professionalism,
sophistication, and especially social cohesion resulted in increased rates
of smoking for all sectors of society. Having visually demonstrated a
variety of achievable identities for otherwise talented and respectable
young women (and men) of the middle class, all of which were closely
associated with smoking, we can anticipate that many followed that
advice. The statistics for smoking rates confirm this trend.

Canadian Women Undergraduate Smokers Present Themselves, 1940–60

Textual and photographic evidence as well as oral testimony from the period between 1940 and 1960 indicates that both male and female smoking rates climbed steeply in this period. In addition to the earlier defined reasons for doing so was the apparent blessing of university authorities. Traditional academic strictures against women smoking at campus events became so eroded that authorities not only tolerated young women smoking but memorialized this in staged scenes.

In an earlier period, after the First World War, former servicemen returning to Canadian campuses brought with them a culture that prominently featured smoking as a male-bonding activity. Indeed, a major student strike in 1928 occurred at Queen's when university authorities attempted to reduce wartime leisure activities such as drinking and smoking on campus.[63] Following the Second World War, this landscape changed significantly. University authorities, changing their views dramatically, were now keen to demonstrate the university's modern face. Images of the female smoker were thought to be an important way to accomplish this aim. Further, this period predated the American Surgeon General's Report (in 1964) where the link was definitively made between smoking and cancer. Hence, smoking seemed to most to be a harmless and inexpensive way to spend time with others; it also appeared nationalistic, since Canada had developed into one of the major producers of tobacco. Among other inducements for the young undergraduate to take up smoking, the visual record produced by undergraduates themselves shows the presumably harmless fun of social smoking, recommending it to many.

Two photograph albums from Queen's University in Kingston, Ontario, both from the 1940s, offer evidence of just this. Despite historian Frederick Gibson's assertion that, in its early days, Queen's had a reputation for being a poor-man's institution, by the 1930s it was drawing from a solid middle-class base for its student body, with women students' families showing higher class status than men's.[64] As with the Charlotte Black scrapbook, the candid photograph allows us to peek into the world of undergraduate life for a given place and time. The camera's owner chooses what to memorialize, but the person being photographed also has agency in deciding if she will allow herself to be immortalized in this way, how she will pose herself, and what props she will choose to share the frame. Both albums contain photographs

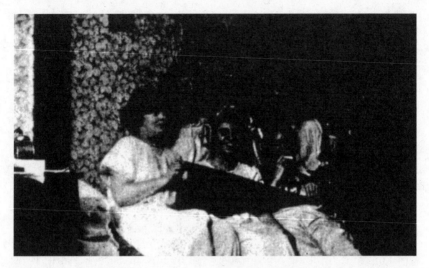

6. Queen's University Archives, Diana Wheeler Scrapbook, 1940–1, n.p.

along with other artefacts of university life: invitations to events, dance cards from formal proms, and so on. However, unlike the 1920s album from Winnipeg, cigarettes are photographed in these albums from the 1940s, and almost always playfully. It would seem that the edge had been taken off the act of women's smoking through class entitlement and repeated viewings in the media and on campus.

In Image 6, a group of young Queen's University dorm-mates from 1940–1 pile onto a bed, hair in 'rag rollers' and nightgowns donned.[65] One of the women 'smokes' a cigarette, which appears suspiciously oversize, as if it too were constructed from one of the rag rollers. Real or not, however, it is included in the photograph as a marker of innocent good times, relaxation, and, especially, social conviviality. The photograph has been mounted on heavy paper with the intention (or perhaps the act) of using it as a postcard: 'R.R.I. – 117 East Ave, Brantford.' Whether or not it was used in this way, the photograph's intended use as a public document advertises the owner's pride in the image, its public acceptability, and its denotated and connotated meanings.

In Image 7, a photograph from a second Queen's album shows two young women relaxing in a park or in some other public space. Despite the lack of captions, we can see that both are attractive, though modestly clothed for outdoor cool weather. One reads, the other holds a new puppy, and both casually smoke. Interestingly, the stance adopted

7. Queen's University Archives, Brookings Collection, Kathleen Mary Giller Album, 1940s.

8 & 9. University of Manitoba Archives, PC 80: 443:10, 4 December 1950.

210'-1

REGISTRAR'S OFFICE

DO NOT REMOVE

2368

PLEASE RETURN TO THE REGISTRAR.

From **THE REGISTRAR**
The University of Manitoba
WINNIPEG - MANITOBA

One of the reception rooms in the
University Residence, December 4, 1950.

by the young women does not mimic the screen idols with the 'flag' display of crooked arm, cigarette at mid-neck level. In both cases, the cigarette is held away from the body in one hand, with the alternate hand holding another object. The cigarette is such a normalized part of the woman's appearance that here it has lost its central framing power. The cigarette is merely one of several objects of interest in both photographs. Apparently the rules of how to smoke smartly have been loosened since the war, allowing for a broader range of expressive poses for women.

A similar message of sophisticated sociability appears in a publicity photograph for the new reception room at the University of Manitoba Residence in December 1950 (see Image 8). The Registrar's Office had arranged for a variety of posed photographs to be used to promote the university's new facility. In this image, however, the photographer chose to have one couple, on the extreme left, staged as smokers. The woman evinces the typical 'flag' posture with her partner offering a light. The controlled respectability of the event is underlined by the placement of the furniture and by the students arranged in strict pairs. Although smoking had become increasingly common by this date, the back of this photograph (Image 9) reminds us that the decision to pose a woman undergraduate smoking in 1950 in one of Canada's conservative urban centres would be noticed, and unfavourably by some. It bears the Registrar's Office stamp and this note: 'Important – do not reprint without removing cigaretts [sic] from figure second from left – parents' earnest desire.' But, even if parents did not want to admit that their university-attending daughters were smoking comfortably at the University of Manitoba, it was not the only institution to 'set up' the undergraduate smoker as an indication of modern appeal.

A similar staged photograph, this one ordered by the Queen's University administration (see Image 10), purports to show the range of student life during the 1950s at that university. The photograph collage provides pride of place in the middle to a photogenic couple at some university event, possibly a football game. In only one of the photos included in this set is anyone clearly smoking, and that is the beautiful, well-dressed woman with her hair tied smartly in a scarf and a double strand of pearls at her neck. She clings winsomely to her escort, while lifting her cigarette in the prescribed stance. As a general collage, we do not know how this set of photographs was actually utilized by the authorities at Queen's; what we do know, however, is that, by this time, smoking by women was not just tolerated, it was celebrated as nor-

10. Queen's University Archives, V28, Box 35, 'Student Life Folder,' n.d. but likely 1950s.

mal glamorous behaviour typically engaged in by the undergraduate woman.

Beyond the official photographs, how did student yearbook editors understand the role of smoking in student life? As demonstrated in the Princess Lounge depicted in Image 5, smoking had become associated with dating, allowing a woman to develop new uses for the attention-focusing cigarette. The potential for serious young women to show off their hands to good effect or contrive to gently frame the face in soften-ing smoke, or, like Bette Davis, encourage a male companion to gal-lantly light her cigarette, telegraphed important social messages – often saturated with sexual content – without her needing to say a word. The same conclusion must be drawn with more formal events associated with student clubs, such as sororities. The University of Manitoba Year-book for 1953 offered space to every fraternity and sorority on campus. Image 11 shows one of these, Pi Beta Phi, with its Open House recep-tion, and the sorority executive committee. This photograph is interest-ing both in itself and for its placement on the page with other artefacts of the sorority. The denotated meaning of the images is similar: smiling young women clad in sweater sets, curled hair, and strings of pearls grace both photographs. However, the connotation of the upper pho-tograph includes new features to explain the young woman casually smoking in the centre of the image. The upper image shows a social occasion, calling for crowds of young men and women as well as older members of the community, refreshments, and evident conviviality. When do fine young women smoke in the 1950s? At social engage-ments, formal or not, and particularly where they control the agenda, as here shown. And the social engagements can be very formal, as in Image 12, where two couples, with the women dressed in tulle and lace, enjoy each other's company, a refreshing drink – and a cigarette. In this collage, from the Queen's University Yearbook of 1957, the central female subject is centrally placed as she holds liquor glass and cigarette in one hand, a feat of both dexterity and modernism.

But for changing clothing and hairstyles, these undergraduates of the 1950s would not look out of place on today's university campus-es; in about three decades, the respectable young woman had utterly changed the notions of acceptable behaviour around the act of smok-ing. Where it had been unseemly in the 1920s, it was now smart. And there it remained until the turn of the twenty-first century.

The battle to discourage smoking among young women, especially those still in secondary school and in university undergraduate pro-

PI BETA PHI OPEN HOUSE

Founded April 28, 1867, at Monmouth College.
Monmouth, Illinois.

MANITOBA ALPHA CHAPTER
Installed, 1929.

PI BETA PHI

Executive:

Front Row— RUTH THORVALDSON, ANN MASTERMAN,
JANE EMERY. *Second Row—* SHELAGH SWAIN, NANCY
FISHER, JOYCE ROBERTSON.

ACTIVES

LYNNE ANDERSON, CLAIRE ANDERSON, JANETTE
AVERY, HELEN BRIGDEN, SALLY DANGERFIELD,
JOAN DARBEY, JANE EMERY, NANCY FISHER,
HELEN GRABOWSKI, JOAN KELLY, PATRICIA
MALAHER, ANNE MASTERMAN, MARILYN MAY,
MILDRED MCDONALD, BETTY MUIR, ANNIE LOU
ORMISTON, DIANE ORRIS, BULA PATERSON,
JOYCE ROBERTSON, GERDA SCHELL, WENDY
SMITH, EVELYN SUTER, SHELAGH SWAINE,
ELEANOR SWAIL, RUTH THORVALDSON, JOANNE
WINTEMUTE.

PLEDGES

MARION BARTLETT, RAYMA COOPER, LORNA
CRAIG, DOREEN DICKSON, RHODA FAIRFIELD,
AVRIL LAURIE, GERALDINE TOD, KATHERINE
WOOD.

11. University of Manitoba Archives, Brown and Gold Yearbook, 1953, 266.

12. Queen's University Archives, 1957 Yearbook, n.p.

grams, continues, with more public interest than at any earlier period. The current popular wisdom about rates of smoking is self-congratulatory and misleading. We are told that the most recent results from the Canadian Tobacco Use Monitoring Survey pegs the smoking rate of teenage girls (aged fifteen to nineteen) at 14 per cent, down from 18 per cent in 2003–6.[66] But, as usual, we want to know only the good news; the statistics for women aged twenty to twenty-four, undergraduate women, is much higher at 24 per cent, and the rate of pre-teen smoking continues to grow. There is now clear evidence that smokers beginning before the age of fifteen have double the risk of premature death.[67] Considering the web of historical reasons why women began smoking in the first place, including the possibilities offered of visual performance and the centrality of body image in this process, should encourage us to problematize the causal reasons for smoking. Even more important, recognizing smoking's utility to young women as well as its danger will permit us to address the attraction of smoking in a more nuanced and effective manner, putting an end to this health scourge.

NOTES

1 An earlier version of this essay was presented at the International Standing Conference for the History of Education in Hamburg Germany in July 2007. I am grateful for the many perceptive comments and suggestions received in that forum.

2 Health Canada, *Canadian Tobacco Use Monitoring Survey, 1999–2001*, 'Tracking Key Indicators,' 5.

3 See, for example, Advisory Committee on Population Health Working Group on Tobacco Control, *The National Strategy: Moving Forward – The 2001 Federal Provincial Territorial Progress Report on Tobacco Control* (Ottawa: Queen's Printer 2001), 10–11.

4 In 2006, 24 per cent of women in this age group was estimated to smoke, while 27 per cent of both males and females smoked. This figure was an increase over 2005 smoking rates. At the same time, about 19 per cent of Canadians over the age of fifteen smoked. Health Canada, Tobacco Control Programme, Supplementary Tables, *CTUMS Annual Report*, 2006, http://www.hc-sc.gc.ca/ahc-asc/branch-dirgen/hecs-dgsesc/tcp-plct/index-eng.php (accessed 17 July 2007).

5 See, for example, Health Canada, *Mixed Messages: Smoking Interventions in the Prenatal and Postpartum Periods* (Ottawa: Minister of Supply and Serv-

ices Canada 1995); Health Canada, *Tobacco Resource Material for Prenatal and Post Partum Providers: A Selected Inventory* (Ottawa: Minister of Supply and Services Canada 1995); Health Canada, *Francophone Women's Tobacco Use in Canada* (Ottawa: Minister of Supply and Services Canada 1996); Health Canada, *Women and Tobacco: A Framework for Action* (Ottawa: Minister of Supply and Services 1995); and Health Canada, *Smoking and Pregnancy: A Woman's Dilemma* (Ottawa: Minister of Supply and Services 1995).

6 Hans Krueger et al., *The Health Impact of Smoking and Obesity and What To Do about It* (Toronto: University of Toronto Press 2007), 7.

7 Kirk Makin, 'Top Court Upholds Tobacco Advertising Laws: Anti-Smoking Lobbyists Claim Ruling Opens Doors for a Full Ad Ban,' *Globe and Mail*, 29 June 2007.

8 Rob Cunningham, *Smoke & Mirrors: The Canadian Tobacco War* (Ottawa: IDRC 1996), 175.

9 See, for example, Andrew Bridges, 'Addictions: Booze and Butts: Anti-Smoking Drug May Also Curb Drinking, New Research Shows,' *Globe and Mail*, 11 July 2007, L4.

10 John C. Burnham, *Bad Habits* (New York and London: New York University Press 1993), esp. chapter 4.

11 Cassandra Tate, *Cigarette Wars: The Triumph of 'The Little White Slaver'* (Oxford: Oxford University Press 1999), 93–4.

12 Cheryl Krasnick Warsh, 'Smoke and Mirrors: Gender Representation in North American Tobacco and Alcohol Advertisements before 1950,' *Histoire sociale/Social History*, 31, no. 62 (1998): 199; Bobbie Jacobson, *Beating the Ladykillers: Women and Smoking* (London: Pluto Press 1986), 43. About 40 per cent of British women were smokers by 1950.

13 Jarrett Rudy, *The Freedom to Smoke: Tobacco Consumption and Identity* (Montreal and Kingston: McGill-Queen's University Press 2005), 148.

14 Ibid., 168.

15 Statistics Canada and Health and Welfare Canada, 'Directions: The Directional Paper of the National Strategy to Reduce Tobacco Use' (Ottawa, 1993), 10.

16 Keith Walden documents that young male freshman who dared to smoke in the presence of upper classmen were punished by hazing. Keith Walden, 'Hazes, Hustles, Scraps and Stunts,' in Paul Axelrod and John G. Reid, eds., *Youth, University and Canadian Society: Essays in the Social History of Higher Education* (Montreal and Kingston: McGill-Queen's University Press 1989), 94–121.

17 Joan Jacobs Brumberg, *The Body Project: An Intimate History of American Girls* (New York: Vintage Books 1997), 105.

18 Cynthia Comacchio, *The Dominion of Youth: Adolescence and the Making of Modern Canada, 1920 to 1950* (Waterloo, Ont.: Wilfrid Laurier University Press 2006), 11–13.

19 See, for example, James M. Pitsula, 'Student Life at the Regina Campus in the 1920s,' in Axelrod and Reid, eds., *Youth, University and Canadian Society*, 122–39.

20 Howard Cox, 'Growth and Ownership in the International Tobacco Industry: BAT 1902–27,' *Business History*, 31, no. 11 (1989): 44–67; Cunningham, *Smoke & Mirrors*; Richard Kruger, *Ashes to Ashes: America's Hundred-Year Cigarette War, the Public Health, and the Unabashed Triumph of Philip Morris* (New York: Alfred A. Knopf 1996); Robert H. Miles, *Coffin Nails and Corporate Strategies* (Englewood Cliffs, N.J.: Prentice Hall 1982); Larry C. White, *Merchants of Death: The American Tobacco Industry* (New York: William Morrow, Beech Tree Books 1988).

21 Kruger, *Ashes to Ashes*.

22 See, for example, Iain Gately, *La Diva Nicotina: The Story of How Tobacco Seduced the World* (London: Simon and Schuster 2001); Jason Hughes, *Learning to Smoke: Tobacco Use in the West* (Chicago and London: University of Chicago Press 2003); Robert H. Miles, *Coffin Nails and Corporate Strategies* (Englewood Cliffs, N.J.: Prentice Hall 1982); Kerry Segrave, *Women and Smoking in America, 1880–1950* (Jefferson, N.C., and London: McFarland and Company 2005); Penny Tinkler, 'Refinement and Respectable Consumption: The Acceptable Face of Women's Smoking in Britain, 1918–1970,' *Gender & History*, 15, no. 2 (2003): 342–60; Cheryl Krasnick Warsh, 'Smoke and Mirrors: Gender Representation in North American Tobacco and Alcohol Advertisements before 1950,' *Histoire sociale / Social History*, 31, no. 62 (1998): 183–222; Larry C. White, *Merchants of Death: The American Tobacco Industry* (New York: William Morrow, Beech Tree Books 1988).

23 Matthew Hilton, *Smoking in British Popular Culture, 1800–2000: Perfect Pleasures* (Manchester, U.K.: Manchester University Press 2000); Rudy, *The Freedom to Smoke*; and Tate, *Cigarette Wars*.

24 Allan M. Brandt, *The Cigarette Century: The Rise, Fall, and Deadly Persistence of the Product That Defined America* (New York: Basic Books 2007).

25 Rudy, *The Freedom to Smoke*.

26 Cunningham, *Smoke & Mirrors*.

27 See, for example, Sharon Anne Cook, 'Evangelical Moral Reform: Women and the War against Tobacco, 1874–1900,' in Marguerite Van Die, ed., *Religion and Public Life: Historical and Comparative Themes* (Toronto: University of Toronto Press 2001), 177–95; Sharon Anne Cook, 'Educating for Temperance: The Woman's Christian Temperance Union and Ontario Children,

1880–1916,' *Historical Studies in Education/Revue d'histoire de l'éducation*, 5, no. 2 (1993): 251–77.

28 See especially Warsh, 'Smoke and Mirrors,' 183–222. Also useful is Gately, *La Diva Nicotina*.

29 See, for example, Hughes, *Learning to Smoke*; Segrave, *Women and Smoking in America*; Tinkler, 'Refinement and Respectable Consumption; and Penny Tinkler, *Smoke Signals: Women, Smoking and Visual Culture* (Oxford and New York: Berg 2006).

30 Cunningham, *Smoke & Mirrors*; Hilton, *Smoking in British Popular Culture*; Veronica Strong-Boag, *The New Day Recalled: Lives of Girls and Women in English Canada, 1919–1939* (Toronto: Copp Clark Pitman 1988), 342–60.

31 Paul Messaris, *Visual 'Literacy': Image, Mind and Reality* (Oxford: Westview Press 1994), 165.

32 Ronald Barthes, *The Photographic Message. In Image, Music Text – Essays Selected and Translated by Stephen Heath* (London: Fontana 1987), 15–31.

33 Janne Seppanen, *The Power of the Gaze: An Introduction to Visual Literacy* (New York: Peter Lang), 122–7.

34 See Charles Forceville, 'Pictorial Metaphor in Advertisements,' *Metaphor and Symbolic Activity*, 9, no. 1 (1999): 1–29, cited in Seppanen, *The Power of the Gaze*, 123–6.

35 Brumberg, *The Body Project*, xx.

36 Comacchio, *The Dominion of Youth*, 8.

37 Hilton, *Smoking in British Popular Culture*, 35.

38 Segrave, *Women and Smoking in America*, 58.

39 Ibid., 60.

40 Tate, *Cigarette Wars*, 15–16.

41 See also Sharon Anne Cook, 'From "Evil Influence" to Social Facilitator: Representations of Youth Smoking, Drinking and Citizenship in English-Language Canadian Health Textbooks, 1890–1960,' *Journal of Curriculum Studies*, 40, no. 6 (2008): 1–32.

42 See, for example, the authorized textbook for Ontario from 1893: William Nattress, M.D., *Public School Physiology and Temperance, Authorized by the Education Department, Ontario* (Toronto: William Briggs 1893).

43 Benjamin Ward Richardson, *The Temperance Lesson Book: A Series of Short Lessons on Alcohol and Its Action on the Body: Designed for Reading in Schools and Families* (New York: National Temperance Society and Publication House 1883), 100. See also G.E. Henderson and Chas. G. Fraser, *Physiology and Hygiene Notes* (Toronto: Educational Publishing Company 1897). Emphasis in the original.

44 Mac Levy, *Tobacco Habit Easily Conquered* (New York: Albro Society 1916), 98.

45 John Harvey Kellogg, *Tobaccoism or How Tobacco Kills* (Battle Creek, Mich.: Modern Medicine Publishing Company 1922), 104.

46 See also Sharon Anne Cook, '"Liberation Sticks" or "Coffin Nails"? Representations of the Working Woman and Cigarette Smoking in Canada, 1919–1939,' *Canadian Bulletin of Medical History*, 24, no. 2 (2007): 367–401.

47 Mary Kinnear, *In Subordination: Professional Women, 1870–1970* (Montreal and Kingston: McGill-Queen's University Press 1995), 31.

48 University of Manitoba Archives and Special Collections (hereafter UMA), Mss SC 89, Notecard, Auntie Maude to Charlotte, Charlotte Scott Black, 'My Graduation Journal' (scrapbook), May 1925.

49 The percentage of women undergraduates in Ontario universities was far higher, however. In 1929, for example, 36.4 per cent of the undergraduate population was female at the University of Western Ontario. Alyson E. King, 'The Experience of Women Students at Four Universities, 1895–1930,' in Sharon Anne Cook, Lorna R. McLean, and Kate O'Rourke, eds., *'Framing Our Past': Canadian Women's History in the Twentieth Century* (Montreal and Kingston: McGill-Queen's University Press 2001), 163. By 1931, more than half of the undergraduates at Victoria College were women. Jean O'Grady, 'Margaret Addison: Dean of Residence and Dean of Women at Victoria University, 1903–1931,' in Cook, McLean, and O'Rourke, eds. *'Framing Our Past,'* 167. For Queen's University, Nicole Neatby notes that in, 1919–20, 16.3 per cent of undergraduates were women, while by 1929–30 the percentage of female undergraduates had risen to 23.5 per cent. However, for Canada as a whole, in 1920, only 1 per cent of Canadian women between ages twenty and twenty-four attended university. Nicole Neatby, 'Preparing for the Working World: Women at Queen's during the 1920s,' in Ruby Heap and Alison Prentice, eds., *Gender and Education in Ontario* (Toronto: Canadian Scholars Press 1991), 333–4, 335.

50 Mary Kinnear, *A Female Economy: Women's Work in a Prairie Province, 1870–1970* (Montreal and Kingston: McGill-Queen's University Press 1998), 59–60.

51 Kinnear, *In Subordination*, 33 and table 7, 176. See also Margaret Gillett, 'Carrie Derick (1862–1941) and the Chair of Botany at McGill,' in Marianne Goszronyi Ainley, ed., *Despite the Odds: Essays on Canadian Women and Science* (Montreal: Vehicle Press 1990), 74–87.

52 Brumberg, *The Body Project*, 106.

53 Pitsula, 'Student Life at the Regina Campus,' 135.

54 Margaret Gillett, *We Walked Very Warily: A History of Women at McGill* (Montreal: Eden Press Women's Publications 1981), 264.

55 Neatby, 'Preparing for the Working World,' 342–4.

56 Alison Prentice, 'Three Women in Physics,' in Elizabeth Smyth et al., eds., *Challenging Professions: Historical and Contemporary Perspectives on Women's Professional Work* (Toronto: University of Toronto Press 1999), 119–40.
57 Pitsula, 'Student Life at the Regina Campus,' 134.
58 Edward Bernays, quoted in Warsh, 'Smoke and Mirrors,' 198.
59 *Ottawa Morning Citizen*, 12 August 1944. Quoted in Donald F. Davis and Barbara Lorenzkowski, 'A Platform for Gender Tensions: Women Working and Riding on Canadian Urban Transit in the 1940s,' in Mona Gleason and Adele Perry, eds., *Rethinking Canada: The Promise of Women's History* (Oxford: Oxford University Press 2006), 229.
60 Nancy Kiefer and Ruth Roach Pierson, 'The War Effort and Women Students at the University of Toronto, 1939–45,' in Axelrod and Reid, eds., *Youth, University and Canadian Society*, 161–83.
61 See, for example, similar images in the American press discussed by Warsh in 'Smoke and Mirrors,' 195.
62 See, for example, *Saturday Night*, 14 August 1920, 13, where the images are in the Art Deco.
63 Frederick W. Gibson, *'To Serve and Yet be Free': Queen's University, 1917–1961* (Montreal and Kingston: McGill-Queen's University Press 1983), 68, 75.
64 Neatby, 'Preparing for the Working World,' 336.
65 In ibid., her article analysing undergraduates' lives at Queen's University in the 1920s, Nicole Neatby deplores the scanty historiography of the 1920s female undergraduate experience. However, women's undergraduate lives during the Second World War and into the 1950s have been even less tracked.
66 Siri Agrell, 'Girls Get the Message,' *Globe and Mail*, 10 July 2007, L1–2.
67 Krueger et al., *The Health Impact of Smoking and Obesity*, 15.

4 'Their Medley of Tongues and Eternal Jangle': Liquor Control and Ethnicity in Ontario, 1927–44

DAN MALLECK

In 1939 John W. MacKenzie, the superintendent of Bankfield Consolidated Mines in Geraldton, in northwestern Ontario, wrote to Edmond Odette, chief commissioner of the Liquor Control Board of Ontario (LCBO), asking him to permit beer sales in a new veterans' club in the northern boom town. This establishment would provide returned soldiers with 'a club of our own ... where they could assemble and partake in peace of such amenities of life as the club could offer[,] [which] would be much preferable to forcing these men to frequent the beer halls, for in new mining towns like Geraldton the clientele of the tap rooms includes many races and nationalities who have no interests in common with the return[ed] soldier ... such premises, with their medley of tongues, the general atmosphere and eternal jangle, are not places where our returned men should be driven for their recreation and association.'

MacKenzie's letter drew upon a number of common discourses, which he may have believed would appeal to the LCBO administration. He asserted that white, native- born Canadians naturally wanted and deserved a place of refined sanctuary, far from the troubling polyglot cacophony of the current drinking space, which was nothing more than a chaotic 'beer hall.' While he may not have known that the Liquor Control Act (1927) had specific provisions for licensing such places, he presented the proposed club as something intended for the noble soldiers who fought for King and Country. Considering much of what has been written about the relationship between native Canadians and the ethnic newcomers, one might expect the clear ethnocentric and elitist bias in this letter to have resonated positively with the board's central administration.[1] But it did not. The LCBO did not grant a licence to create a new club that would be dedicated to returned – white – soldiers. They would have to mingle with the masses.

The LCBO's rejection of MacKenzie's request would seem contrary to much of the history of ethnocentricism in Canada, but it was consistent with the board's primary mandate: preserving social order. Formed when the province ended Prohibition in 1927, the LCBO managed all sales of liquor in the province, through state-run stores, as well as overseeing the operations of private breweries, wineries, and distilleries. In 1934 its purview was expanded to include licensing of establishments for the sale of beer and wine for public consumption. The board's mission was to ensure social order by controlling access to and consumption of alcoholic beverages in Ontario, granting 'Beer Authorities' or 'Beer and Wine Authorities' to establishments it deemed acceptable.[2] To license another drinking place in Geraldton, regardless of the perceived needs of the white Canadian veterans, would create more opportunities for consuming alcohol. It would violate the idea of control ensconced in the board's very name. Besides, the board knew that white soldiers were no less troublesome than the multicultural masses MacKenzie described. The ethnocentric argument fell on deaf ears because ethnicity was not a prime category of restriction for the liquor-control authorities in Ontario.

Arguing that ethnicity was not an issue in 1930s Canada may appear to contradict much of the literature on ethnic relations in Canada. In the early part of the twentieth century, concerns about the direction in which the nation was heading, combined with growing labour militancy and (perceived) imported European radicalism, Bolshevism, anarchism, and fascism, brought discussions about ethnic out-groups, and new, potentially dangerous foreigners, to a fever pitch.[3] Studies of nation-building efforts, of white Anglo-Celtic Canadians' reaction to increasingly diverse immigration, and, more recently, of the immigrant experience and the history of ethnic communities have opened a broad understanding of the multi-ethnic character of Canadian history.[4] Donald Avery has noted that concern over white immigrants from eastern and southern European countries was assuaged with the knowledge that 'time and Anglo-Canadian institutions … would ultimately erase these differences and facilitate the absorption of all-white immigrants into the Anglo-Canadian community.'[5] Nevertheless, many agencies attempted to speed along the processes. Most studies that include a consideration of immigrants' encounters with agencies working towards assimilation have looked at ethnic groups as immigrant groups, that is, in their relationship with government immigration officials and social reformers, such as 'Home Mission' societies of evangelical churches and groups like the Woman's Christian Temperance Union.[6] But once arrived, and established within the country, the individual of different ethnic background interacted with a variety of hegemonic institutions designed to construct or preserve some 'imagined' sense of Canadianness, or at least Britishness.[7] How, then, did discourses of ethnicity and nationalism function within other hegemonic bureaucracies?

Established to reconstruct the drinking culture of Ontario along lines of moderation and order, the LCBO was one of these hegemonic agencies. The Liquor Control Act was drafted to control and shape the drinking cultures within a framework defined by white, middle-class, Anglo-Saxon, and Christian values. Its creation was part of an international shift towards introducing 'disinterested management' in the distribution of liquor. Typified by the 'Gothenburg System,' which was pioneered in the last part of the nineteenth century in Scandinavia, disinterested management sought to curb excessive drinking by eliminating the profit incentive from liquor sales. It could take several forms; while in Scandinavia it manifested itself in tight government control over all aspects of liquor sales, in Britain, during and after the First World War, it manifested itself in government oversight of liquor sales, but an oversight that remained part of market capitalism.[8] Disinterested management was considered the best alternative to the excesses of the pre-Prohibition saloon and of the illegal drinking spaces that emerged during Prohibition. It required a structured bureaucracy to oversee its operations. For this reason, Max Weber's notion of bureaucratization, which characterizes the 'ideal-typical' bureaucracy as one that is able to entirely remove subjectivity from the enforcement process, is a useful model for analysing the actions of the LCBO. Merging the ideas of disinterested management and bureaucratization with the Foucaultian language of 'governmentality,' we can view the LCBO as attempting to function as an ideal-typical bureaucracy that, by encouraging disinterested management and moderation, sought to (re)construct common ideas of proper and improper consumption of alcohol, thereby creating new 'truths' about the relationship of the individual and the alcoholic beverage. In effect, it was constructing a new drinker, and one who adhered to the values of responsible citizenship. This 'citizen-drinker' understood the importance of moderation, disassociated him or herself from the moral hazards of the pre-Prohibition saloon culture, and, to paraphrase

Robert Campbell, sat down and drank his (or her) beer but did nothing more.[9]

This essay, based upon an examination of cases in six Ontario communities, explores the intersection of government bureaucracy and ethnicity in the work of the Liquor Control Board of Ontario.[10] It argues that, while native-born Canadians' ideas of ethnic outsiders adhered to a classic ethnocentric discourse, the LCBO administration was motivated by a vision of social order that prevailed despite this discourse. Instead of discriminating based upon ethnic origins, the LCBO permitted ethnic groups to have beer drinking in their clubs and hotels as long as they adhered to its ideas of social order. Its vision was to encourage an ideal of moderation that would ensure social order but also to permit activities that, while not necessarily consistent with its ethnocentric view of proper behaviour, were not going to undermine social order. So, although the LCBO administration was attentive to ethnic difference, ethnicity itself was not a major category of exclusion, nor did ethnic difference immediately indicate lack of control in non-native Canadians, or superior drinking habits in those who claimed nativist privilege. When the Second World War began, and concerns arose over the loyalty of several ethnic communities in Ontario, the board's central value of social order ensured that increased surveillance of such individuals and groups was consistent with the public interest. But, again, as a bureaucracy focused upon managing a specific type of behaviour and social space, the LCBO limited its own work to ensuring social order. While it was aware of the need for surveillance over potential 'enemy aliens,' it left wartime security to other agencies.

Perceiving the Ethnic Other

Ethnicity and ethnic tension was not absent from the views and activities of the LCBO. In the vast correspondence it generated and collected, between inspectors and the central administration, politicians and administrators, or the general public and board administrators, an ethnocentric discourse is clear. When a hotel proprietor applied for a license to serve beer, inspectors usually visited the premises and evaluated the proprietor's viability to enforce the rules. Often the ethnicity of the proprietor would be mentioned. When Inspector Pitt, the board's most senior inspector, evaluated the proprietor of the King George Hotel in Crystal Beach, he noted that 'this man ... may be all right but I am a little suspicious of these foreigners especially in a place like Crystal Beach.'[11] On inspecting the Queen's Hotel in Port Colborne, Pitt found it to be used essentially as a boarding house for 'forty-five boarders, understood to be all foreigners, though that is not mentioned as anything against them.'[12] In evaluating the application of a Chinese man named King Lee, Essex County Inspector Reaume noted that the man was a naturalized Canadian and 'I honestly think that Lee is an honest Chinese and that the hotel would be properly conducted.'[13] Inspector Skuce noted that the proprietors of the Algoma Hotel in Jellicoe, in the Thunder Bay District, 'are Finnish peoples but very willing to co-operate in anything I ask them to do.'[14] In this district, many of the new immigrants were men working in the resource industry who were generally associated with boisterous activities (Finns were considered to be especially troublesome[15]). Skuce knew ethnic outsiders to be potentially rowdy, but he also recognized the malleability of the Algoma Hotel's proprietors. Although ethnic background was worth noting, inspectors often mentioned a proprietor's ethnicity as a way of illustrating that this person, ethnic origins notwithstanding, was a solid citizen who could be trusted with running a hotel. All of the hotels noted above received their licences.[16]

The board may not have made it a practice to discriminate based upon ethnicity, but, in many complaints that it received, nativism and ethnic difference often appeared to motivate or underpin the arguments justifying exclusion. For example, if a non-ethnic club was denied a licence to sell beer, but a local ethnic club received the privilege, native-born people might express indignation based on the idea that native Canadians deserved special treatment. MacKenzie's letter in Geraldton is an indication of this argument. Likewise, the predominantly (white) working-class Talbot Club of Windsor had a barrister write to the board arguing that his clients 'certainly are entitled to [a licence] just as much as any organization of Germans, Polish or Italians or any other nation who have already received authorities.'[17] The local member of the provincial legislature agreed, arguing that the members of this club 'are all native-born Essex county residents ... and if they do not get their license renewed it will have very serious political consequences.'[18] Proprietors of hotels used ethnicity as a point of complaint, too. One Niagara-on-the-Lake proprietor who had an application delayed noted, 'If I was an Italian or Polack I perhaps would be granted a license,'[19] while a St Catharines proprietor complained that 'there has been granted authorities to Jews, Armenians, French and Italians some who cannot speak English.'[20] The proprietor of the French Canadian Club of Windsor was less inflammatory when he argued that 'the French Canadian's [sic] of Windsor should be granted the same privileges of dispensing beer and wine in their clubs as Alien born who operate clubs in Windsor.'[21] The Windsor national Veteran's Social Club was more diplomatic but displayed similar prejudice when it observed that, since a number of Authorities had been granted to 'our foreign friends,' it seemed only reasonable that a group of men 'who went forth to fight for the democracy which we should enjoy' should receive a similar privilege.[22] They did not.

Native Canadians' concerns were rooted in a sense of nativist privilege, which was offended by the official sanction implied by a club's licence to sell beer. It is useful to consider the terminology employed by the board. The official name for the liquor licence was an 'Authority,' which meant that, given the 'Authority' to sell, the proprietor became a de facto agent of the LCBO and was expected to adhere to the parameters governing liquor sales in the province. So, when native-born applicants saw immigrants receive such a privilege, they began to question why outsiders might be permitted this type of state-sanctioned role but native Canadians were denied it. Yet the board was concerned about orderliness and respectable behaviour, not about ethnocentric privilege. Inspector Hanrahan of Essex County was confronted by one of the members of the Talbot Club about the fact that, while a local German club had received an Authority, the Talbot Club's Authority would not be renewed. Hanrahan simply replied that 'if all clubs were run like the German club I wouldn't have any trouble.'[23] Clearly, the behaviour of the proprietors and the patrons, not their ethnicity, was crucial to this inspector. Indeed, when an applicant complained to Deputy Commissioner Arnold Smith, the second-in-command at the board, that 'I feel that a Jew or a Greek can get more consideration than I can,' Smith replied sharply that 'this Board is not in any way interested in a man's nationality and do not grant authorities because of a man's religion or nationality nor do we on the other hand hold that against him.'[24]

Club Culture

One of the main sites for ethnic drinking was the ethnic social club, like the German club that Inspector Hanrahan held up as a model of propriety. From its inception, the Liquor Control Act carved out a special place for 'clubs ... incorporated or organized and operated in accordance with the regulations [and not] a club which is operated for pecuniary gain.'[25] It made special provision for 'any of the established war veterans' organizations in Canada which the Board may recognize' and 'any of the established labour organizations.'[26] It is likely that the writers of this law envisioned the civilized consumption of the occasional beer between reading the newspaper and perhaps talking politics in the mythical but rare social clubs of the English gentry, transplanted to Canada and downgraded somewhat to include the rough classes. Indeed, one of the board's unwritten guidelines for clubs was that it (usually) would not permit women to drink in the establishment (a rule that was not entrenched in the legislation, nor was it written in the Board's *Digest of Rules and Regulations*).

Yet the ideal of a gentleman's club was rarely achieved. Indeed, during Prohibition a 'club' was a euphemism for an illegal drinking space.[27] The board had considerable frustration in investigating applications for club licences, because the applicants and conditions were so varied and deviated so significantly from the ideal. Applications came from groups of workingmen like those at the Canadian Pacific Railway, whose employers frowned upon them drinking in public. They also came from a club at a race track, which could quickly transmogrify into a raucous beer hall; a club formed by a group of men who just wanted to hang out together; men's club such as the posh St Catharines Club and the Niagara Driving and Riding Club; and, of course, a number of clubs identified by ethnic origin, such as the Windsor and District Hungarian Society, the Italian Canadian Society of Thorold, and the Italian Society of Fort William. In Waterloo County, there were only three ethnic clubs that applied for licences to serve beer, and all three drew their membership from the heavily Austro-German population.

Club licences, irrespective of the ethnicity of members, were prime candidates for abuses. They were much less expensive than those of the main place where people could drink, the hotel beverage room. Whereas a hotel proprietor paid from $100 to $300 per year (the fee increased during the 1930s), a club licence was $100.[28] Moreover, hotels had to pay monthly gallonage fees, while the clubs did not. According to the LCBO, a true club had to have a constitution and a list of paid-up members and have been incorporated for at least a year. For these groups, the club beer licence was seen as a sort of courtesy, so that members could have a drink while relaxing or socializing in between carrying out other club activities. Such activities could be anything from club meetings to tennis or curling tournaments (depending upon the type of club). But between the sport or service club and gentleman's club was a wide swath of clubs whose main purpose was to provide a social space for the use of members. These organizations were often the target of complaints. Many clubs that were licensed were accused by neighbours and licence inspectors of simply being drinking establishments, run for pecuniary gain, and many of these complaints were legitimate. An inspection of the Edgewater Club in Windsor revealed that the application was 'another instance of taking advantage of the letter of the law without regard to its spirit' and that the club was being operated 'only from the motive of selling beer.'[29] The Talbot Club of Windsor sold one thousand associate memberships at twenty-five cents a piece as a 'screen for general admission of the public.'[30]

Ethnic Clubs

Concern over the veracity of a club was equally cast upon clubs whose members had distinct, self-identified ethnic origins. In 1939 the LCBO had an inspector from a different region investigate, surreptitiously, the activities of all clubs in Windsor, and he reported that the Italo-Canadian Political Club conducted activities that were more typical of those of a bad hotel beverage room: 'Women having to be helped from the Club to the Taxi Cabs on Account of being intoxicated, Neighbors being awakened out of their sleep on account of the Noise, One Man who has 2 Motherless children and not a Member was allowed to get intoxicated and the two Children would go to the Club and call their Father at the door, who would be shoved out to the children in this condition.'[31]

Windsor hotelier W.D. Roach wrote the board in 1935 complaining that the competition from the local German club, the Ostschawben Alliance of America and Canada, was severely damaging his business. 'It is nothing more nor less than a saloon,' he argued.[32] The board had its own suspicions and warned the club's management that it had to make sure it was selling to bona fide members of the club, or their guests, 'in accordance with the general usage of clubs.'[33] The inspector, counting the number of kegs of beer that the club went through in a month, did the math and knew that it was highly unlikely that 'any club that sold 58 halves in one month ... could not have been restricted to selling to members only.' But, when warned about the inspector's suspicions, the proprietor replied that 'German people are heavy beer drinkers.'[34]

As this example suggests, ethnicity did present a category of evaluation and explanation, but not necessarily one of exclusion. The only facet of the Liquor Control Act that indicates ethnic bias was the provision that only native or naturalized Canadians could receive an Authority. The remainder of the act was sufficiently vague than many kinds of behaviour that seemed normal to some groups, like the supposedly heavy drinking of German immigrants, could be deemed problematic by the board. Consequently, the board's inspectors, who (outside Toronto) were the official eyes and ears of the board in the community, were expected daily (and nightly) to make judgment calls on the specific contexts of a supposed transgression.[35] In an early examination of the Ostschwaben Alliance, Inspector Hanrahan noted that 'it is typical of [Germans] ... to keep within their group for the enjoyment of their social life' and that if there was a hotel where 'persons of their race could gather there would no longer be need of giving an authority to their people.'[36] Similarly, Inspector Ratz of Waterloo County justified the Austrian need for a beer licence by saying, 'I can readily appreciate how they feel as regard having beer in their club, to the Austrian German, beer is as essential for everyday living, as milk is to the Canadian, and since they live in a strange country, speaking a dialect distinctly different than most Germans they feel themselves out of place in a public beverage room.'[37] Here the issue was creating a space for ethnic minorities, but, even within this homogeneous ethnic environment, specific norms of the new country had to be observed.

The dynamics of control and permissiveness may be illustrated with the example of the Austrian Club in Waterloo. When the club applied for an Authority in 1938, Inspector Ratz endorsed the application, using the language of respectability, mixed with recognition of the unique requirements of this ethnic group, as justification: 'As a group they are industrious, thrifty and law-abiding citizens, who left their homes because of the unrest in Central Europe, and the horrors of war which they endured during the Great War ... A great many of them have become Canadian Citizens and express themselves quite freely as having no particular desire to return to their native land ... they are almost as a unit in helpfulness to one another, and maintain a common fund to help the sick and needy, and in a general way avoid becoming wards of the community.'[38] The central administration was not initially convinced that granting the club an Authority was a good idea, and decided to do so only when several prominent local individuals vouched for the club's members. Yet, even then, the board placed restrictions on the membership. Women would not be allowed as members, the club had to keep its membership to under 100, and it could not have 'associate' memberships, only full ones.

It would be inaccurate to assume that such regulations were placed upon the Austrian Club by virtue of the ethnicity of the applicants. Many clubs faced similar restrictions, and it appears that the board was tightening its control over all clubs owing to the tendency for them to attempt to use the beer Authority to compete for hotel beverage-room business. For example, Ottawa's Preston Social and Athletic Club, which was playing fast and loose with the rules, faced similar restrictions in 1936.[39] Kitchener's Sachsen-Schwaben Club, which claimed a membership of Yugoslavian, Romanian, and Hungarian immigrants, had just recently seen its Authority suspended because it had been allowing the general public to attend dances and had been selling two classes of membership, one for $1.00/month and one for 50 cents/ month (with varying levels of sick benefits).[40] The suspension lasted two weeks.[41] These sorts of violations made the board much more hesitant to grant any club Authorities. By 1937, when the Austrian Club made its application, the board had reduced to a trickle the number of new Authorities it was granting to hotels or clubs, explaining to many applicants that it had actually 'stopped' granting them. While this was not entirely the case, it was cutting back drastically, save for exceptional circumstances. It had determined that there were sufficient Authorities to satisfy the needs of the people in most of the communities in the province, and tended to be reluctant to grant more. Few clubs had received Authorities after the initial flurry of applications in 1934–5. The stipulations the LCBO set for the Austrian Club, then, are best viewed as an attempt to limit significantly any increase in the opportunities to drink in Waterloo.

Within six months, the Austrian Club was lobbying heavily to permit women to join their husbands in the club space.[42] The club executive, through their lawyer, argued that they had conducted their organization respectfully and demonstrated their ability to stay within the law, and that relaxing the strict regulations was not unreasonable. The crux of their argument illustrated the central place of clubs in the lives of this particular ethnic group: 'The premises occupied by the Club are a centre for the social activities of the members. They keep pretty well to themselves, and are all reputable citizens highly regarded in the community. There is considerable resentment on the part of the wives of the male members on account of the fact that they are not permitted to join their husbands in their social activities at the Club and the Club members themselves cannot see where any harm would result from enlarging its membership along the lines asked for.'[43] The Board remained adamant that this not happen, notwithstanding letters from the mayor of Waterloo.[44]

To the supporters of the Austrian Club, the club's request did not seem out of line with what other clubs were receiving in the area. It was asking that it receive the same sorts of privileges as the Sachsen-Schwaben Club, the other major Germanic ethnic club in the region. One writer argued that the Sachsen-Schwaben's members were both male and female who had equal access to the same beverage room, although this was not accurate. As noted earlier, the Sachsen-Schwaben club had experienced problems that made it a poor point of comparison for the Austrian Club. A better comparison was made by Inspector Berges, who replaced Ratz in 1939. He noted that the Concordia Club, a German club but one patronized mostly by younger, Canadian-born members, had been permitted to have dances and to sign in guests on Fridays and Saturdays. He observed that, in contrast, the Austrian Club's members were middle-aged and had wanted to have fewer heterosocial activities. This comparison, which provided an example of an orderly way of integrating men and women into club activities, appealed to the board's need to ensure social order. After reviewing the specifics of the club's modified request, the board altered the parameters of the Authority to permit dances twice a month and a specified list of occasional heterosocial activities.[45] Whether the club continued to observe these restrictions is impossible to determine, since a year later it and all other German clubs in the region were forced to close because of wartime concern about the associations of German and Italian people.[46]

As the Austrian Club's experience illustrates, while permitting a place for ethnic groups, the board did not necessarily permit a continuation of Old World drinking behaviour. What appears to have been seen as a natural community space for the ethnic group was usually restricted to men-only by the board. Thus, when the local inspector kept finding that the Hungarian Self-Culture Society of Welland was serving women, and had women on its membership rolls, the board rescinded its Authority.[47] Similarly, the proprietor of a club of Windsor Hungarians, the Independent Mutual Benefit Society, had been 'under the impression that [women] have the same rights to enjoy the privilege of having beer as the men members.'[48] Inspector Reaume entered the Ostschwaben Alliance one night to find 'the place filled [with] ... approximately, 40 women and about 100 men ... singing German songs ... to music from a five piece string orchestra accompanied by a piano.'[49]

Inspector Pitt was horrified in 1935 to find 'men and women drinking with babes in arms not over three or four months old' in the beverage room of the Polish Army Veteran's Association in Windsor.[50] In each case, the clubs faced censure or even suspension of its Authority. What is notable here is that repeatedly the ethnic clubs, which seemed to function as social centres, were being shaped along the lines of the norms of the host country, in which this sort of communal beer-hall formation was anathema.

Just as the board investigated ethnic clubs on their merits as clubs rather than as ethnic out-groups, so too these clubs were not necessarily representative of their ethnic community. Expecting the behaviour of one small group to represent the values of the entire community is problematic. Several times the board had to deal with controversy within an ethnic community, or across communities of immigrants. So it would be inappropriate to assume that the drinking cultures revealed in the investigations of ethnic clubs indicated a homogeneity of behaviour for individual ethnic groups. In a number of cases, complaints came from other members from the same ethnic community.

Complainants were concerned at the effect certain activities would have on the morality of their children, and the peace of their neighbourhoods. The pastor of the Hungarian Evangelical Lutheran Church in Windsor wrote to the board in 1935 stating that the club licence for which the Windsor and District Hungarian Society had applied should not be granted. His argument was that, in the depths of the Great Depression, the morale of unemployed Hungarians was already very low and 'they should not be exposed to more temptations than they already have.' He concluded by noting that he was anxious to 'protect the good name of the Hungarian people.'[51] A group of Hungarian ministers also protested the activities of the (Hungarian) Independent Mutual Benefit Society in Windsor, noting that 'the liquor traffic has become a menace to the youth of the community ... much good will be derived from such a revoking as it will protect the morals of our youth.'[52] That these requests came from religious leadership is notable. Was the club replacing the church as the social centre? Or was this an instance of the religious values of the host country being adopted by another great hegemonic institution, the church?

Likely the former; proximity of a licensed club could create considerable tension. The pastor of the Ukrainian Catholic Church, which was located next door to the Border Cities Polish Canadian Club in Windsor, argued that whenever an event such as a parish supper took place at the church, 'there was always an intercourse between the church and the club ... in other words, persons not members of the club were being sold beer in the club room.'[53] The Ukrainian Labor Temple was across the street from the Roumanian [sic] Beneficial and Cultural Society of Ontario in Windsor. The temple's secretary argued to the board that such proximity could 'cause us and the public patronizing our hall many difficulties, quarrels and possibly fatal accidents.'[54] A similar protest was lodged in Fort William, where the Finnish Pentecostal Church, which was across the street from an Italian branch of the Canadian Legion, stated that 'you can help us and the Church in this by not granting them a license.'[55] In all cases, the complainants expressed their concern that drinking was anathema to good behaviour, irrespective of the place of drinking in the home culture's social system.

For the LCBO, ethnicity as a category of exclusion was subsumed by a universal notion of respectability. Ethnic clubs that could impress the board's inspector and receive positive character references had a better chance of receiving an Authority than others. I have already noted the language of respectability that Ratz used to endorse the application of the Austrian Club. True, the language was patronizing, but it also employed concepts that were central to the board's mandate of social order. Members of the club were respectable people in the community, and the reference to their unwillingness to become wards of the community spoke to an ethic of independence: all good, 'British' values. In Windsor in 1934, inspectors Hanrahan and Pitt recommended that all Polish Authorities in Windsor not be renewed but that the Polish War Veterans Association receive one instead. This group, they noted, 'was a very worthy organization, doing charitable work ... and that the others do not have the backing of the Polish people.'[56] Hanrahan further noted that the Polish People's Home Association consisted of 'a very good class of people' who were 'lending their efforts to moral and educational uplift.'[57]

The discourse of respectability and social order was pervasive. While the inspectors were not the only ones who used it when endorsing an establishment's application, their assessments held more weight than those coming from citizens with a vested interest in the case. When the Hungarian Self-Culture Society of Welland lost its Authority in 1937, Barrister R. Boak Burns wrote to the LCBO asking that it be restored. He observed that the Hungarian community in that city 'are without a doubt, the best of the non Anglo-Saxon groups' and appealed for a degree of leniency: 'The majority of the members are of the labouring or heavy manual class, and there are few especially of the older members, that are completely educated in our way, and a large majority although naturalized, have very little knowledge of the English language ... [their] idea of a club and the use they make of it were certainly different form such as our own.'[58] His request, and those of other members of the community, did not sway the board, although, given that Welland had just experienced several years of labour tension that were attributed to immigrant radicalism, there may have been more to this refusal than the records suggest.[59] Similarly, a Fort William alderman characterized the Italian Society of that city as 'composed of the outstanding Italian residents of Fort William and its efforts have been ever since it was formed, to instruct the Italians who come to this City in British institutions and in what is required of British subjects and I think I am safe in saying, has met with fair success along these lines. It has carried on extensive relief and educational work in the foreign section of the city and it has taken part in supporting all municipal works and schemes of this city.'[60] Such upstanding people, who were attempting to improve the lot of their ethnic group, deserved to be supported in their efforts. Unfortunately for this club, the board did not agree, and the Italian Society did not receive a beer Authority. It would have to continue its sober activities, soberly.

Radicalism and the Fear of Disorder

Ethnic clubs and associations might have been easily connected to noble respectability, but in the political atmosphere of the 1930s ethnic identity could also imply social disorder. The growth of industrial cities and the expansion of the resource-extraction industries in Canada during the first quarter of the twentieth century had created a need for immigrant labour that resulted in the sort of multicultural communities MacKenzie railed against in his letter from Geraldton.[61] Many of these immigrants were seen as the cause of much of the labour unrest that these booming areas faced. The economic uncertainty of 1930s created and exacerbated tensions, which were fuelled as well by growing fears of anarchists, communists, and, as the decade ended, Nazis and fascists. Each of these groups was considered to have subversive elements rooted in the ethnic subcultures that the Canadian government had encouraged to immigrate in the years following the Great War. While the United States embarked on immigration restriction, for much of the 1920s the Canadian government encouraged immigration, notably for workers in resource extraction (such as in northwestern Ontario) and industry. Many of those workers ended up in factories in growing industrial cities like Windsor and Toronto.

There were two key ways that radical politics among ethnic groups entered into the LCBO's records. First, some ethnic groups were considered key to keeping radicalism at bay by representing the values of the dominant culture, as indicated in some of the letters mentioned earlier. These groups needed to be favoured and their activities encouraged and even nurtured. Second, other groups were considered to be at the centre of radical non-conformist activities. In both instances, the concern over radicalism often came from letters from the general public. The LCBO, for its part, reacted to evidence of radicalism with cautious vigilance. By the beginning of the Second World War, it was part of a larger surveillance machine intent on keeping the country safe from the ethnic enemies. However, while using its mechanisms for surveillance activities, the board did not turn its Authority-granting power into a tool of national security.

The connection between ethnicity and radicalism was familiar to the LCBO throughout the 1930s. The board's role was to protect the social order through enforcing proper drinking behaviour, and therefore it did not tie the receipt of an Authority to potential subversive activities, be it to prevent them or to stop them. In 1935, when the board decided against granting an Authority to the Hungarian Self Culture Society in Welland, a member of the society's executive wrote to the board claiming that 'this society had been largely responsible for checking the further advancement of radicalism in this city.' He argued that a comfortable and enjoyable club house with a beer Authority would permit the members to continue to carry on such good work.[62] The argument fell on deaf ears. Similarly, a barrister supporting the application of an Italian working men's club called the Port Colborne Social Club argued that failure to grant an Authority could in fact create radicalism. The board had made specific note of the inadequate club rooms, and the barrister felt this was troubling: 'They cannot understand why this should be a bar to securing a license ... It gives them the idea that the securing of a license appears to be a rich man's privilege, and the only reason that they cannot get a license is because they are labouring men. This is the sort of thing which produced communism and discontent among such people and I respectfully submit that everything in reason should be done to counteract the fermenting of such discontent.'[63] Again, the petition was unsuccessful. The LCBO did not seem to consider this sort of argument to be a valid reason for contradicting its own parameters for club Authorities. It had established a norm, and intended to preserve it.

Such arguments, that a beer Authority would act as some sort of prophylaxis against radicalism, were rare. Prior to the Second World War, intimations of the threat of radicalism usually came from people who opposed the granting of a licence to a club. Essex County, and especially Windsor, saw most of this sort of argument, and the proximity to Detroit might have been part of the reason.[64] For example, a 1938 petition to the commissioner from three pastors of a local Hungarian Church cited complaints from 'law-abiding citizens relative to anti-government agitation of communistic tendencies' taking place at the Hungarian Independent Mutual Benefit Society.[65] Following up on a complaint by a local Ukrainian Church, inspectors Hanrahan and Pitt reviewed the Border Cities Polish Canadian Club's activities, noting that 'paid agitators are brought from Detroit to address club gatherings and their utterances are of the Red and Communistic type, down with church, government etc.'[66]

The nature of complaints from the general public against ethnic clubs demonstrates how deeply imbedded in the national psyche were concerns over radicalism. While complaints (many signed anonymously) against non-ethnic clubs or hotels often included sensationalized accounts of lewd behaviour, heavy drinking, lascivious entertainment, and other forms of immorality, those against ethnic clubs frequently charged them with political radicalism and non-religiosity. For example, the Border Cities Polish Canadian Club was the target of a letter ostensibly (but not likely) from 'ladies of Catholic Church' that claimed the club 'have plenty cominnist [sic] in there' and was also non-religious: 'When you past [sic] there [sic] hall they laugh and say look crazy church people go to church.'[67] A few years later, another series of letters about the same club was sent to the board. It is likely that these letters were from a local bootlegger who was upset with competition. They accused the club of harbouring 'Commints' and 'they don't believe in church or priest.'[68] What is notable about these letters, regardless of their veracity, is the idea that the correspondent would assume the board would react severely against radicals only if they were anti-religious. Interestingly, Inspector Reaume seemed to concur with this dubious source, reporting that 'over sixty per cent of their members are "Reds."'[69] Yet, while the inspectors found such 'communistic' tendencies worth noting, they did not, apparently, view them as reasons for refusing any club a licence.

When the Second World War began in 1939, however, the importance of ethnocentric observations changed. Now, Germans, Austrians, and Italians (as well as other 'Germanic' groups) could be labelled enemy aliens, and the LCBO's activities turned to surveillance measures more integrated with those of other security branches of the provincial and federal governments. According to the *Globe and Mail,* the government crackdown on ethnic clubs began in Waterloo County.[70] As soon as the war began, the city councils passed a motion urging the Germanic clubs to close. Soon afterwards, the Concordia Club and the Sachsen-Schwaben Club, both of which had German, Yugoslavian, Hungarian, or other eastern European members, ceased operations. The Austrian Canadian Club, which had repeatedly emphasized its allegiance to Canada in representations to the LCBO, was closed by May 1940.[71] After the government made the decision to intern Italians in June 1940, the board withdrew the licences of four Italian clubs, effectively shutting them down.[72] When the Border Cities Italian Club sought to reopen in 1942, Inspector Reaume noted that 'this community would not stand for re-opening of an Italian club during this war,' a sentiment that may indicate concern over the club but that also may have been rooted in the fear that granting an Authority would cause disorder and problems in the community, especially given that such clubs were the targets of militant anti-Axis violence during the war.[73]

The board's response to the concerns over radicalism was patriotic but not, apparently, excessive. Throughout the province, practically every German and Italian club and hotel proprietor was subject to a background check with the Royal Canadian Mounted Police (RCMP). Rarely did these background checks turn up suspicious activity, but every time the RCMP officer replying to the LCBO's information request would note that a report turning up no evidence of subversive activity 'should ... not be taken as an assurance of the loyalty of the individual in question.'[74] The reactions to these background checks demonstrate a good deal about the board's position on a person's past. When investigating the proprietor of the Roma Hotel, which was renamed the Welland Hotel upon the outbreak of hostilities, Deputy Chief Commissioner Smith noted that the proprietor, a Mr M, had a bad reputation, likely because he had once shot and killed his wife. But Smith observed that the board was not interested in 'what occurred in a man's past, and would not consider cancelling the Authority for the reasons given.' Instead, 'the only reason we would wish to withdraw an Authority or License issued by this Board, would be if a man were anti-British in his leanings.'[75] Given that the board took note of but did not react to concerns over radicalism in the pre-war period, this statement suggests that, once the war broke out, the LCBO's interest in the morality of the nation shifted into an interest in its security.

Yet such concerns were not always followed with action. There were a number of instances where security concerns became a central issue to the LCBO during the war, but, rather than cancel Authorities, the board simply passed on the information. Along with the RCMP, the LCBO conferred with the Ontario Provincial Police (OPP), and in June 1940 one of its inspectors argued strongly against the granting of any licences to 'enemy aliens,' noting that one part of Windsor, where the 'Polish Falcons' had hoped to establish a club, 'is a hotbed of aliens and in my estimation should be the last place ... to issue a permit.' He took a consciously law-and-order perspective, maintaining that 'it would be in the best interests from the standpoint of law enforcement to refuse permits to organizations other than those comprised of British and Canadian subjects.'[76] The Falcons did not receive a permit. More perplexing for the board were establishments that already had licences. The OPP and RCMP were clear in their interests, noting that the Windsor and District Hungarian Society should have its licence withdrawn, 'thereby eliminating another nest for prospective fifth columnists.'[77] It was, according to the anonymous report, a centre of Nazi sympathy. The Order of the Sons of Italy in Windsor, meanwhile, as with many other Italian establishments, was considered to be housing a school where the children of Italian immigrants were taught 'the tenets and principles of Fascism.'[78] The board did not cancel that club's Authority initially, but eventually, as noted above, it rescinded four Italian clubs' Authorities in Windsor after the RCMP reported its concerns.

Conclusion

As long as ethnic groups were seen to adhere to the LCBO's vision of social order, their activities were deemed legitimate and generally accepted. The ideal ethnic club was one in which drinking was not a main goal, so groups whose members' activities centred around drinking would receive much more scrutiny than those who were doing other things, like offering mutual support in economically troubled times.

The board saw a liquor Authority as a privilege that should be granted to the deserving few. It went to tremendous lengths to ensure that the establishments that received an Authority were properly laid out to meet the demands of its regulations. It often refused new Authorities based upon the calculation that enough Authorities existed in an area to meet the needs of that area. It spent a great deal of administrative time paring away inappropriate establishments before the end of the 1930s. So, by the start of the war, it had managed to establish a fairly consistent group of authorized establishments that adhered to its expected physical and geographical expectations. It could be the case that, rather than grant new Authorities to new establishments and proceed with the effort of ensuring their conformity to the board's rules, the LCBO decided to maintain the establishments it had and ensure that they were run properly.

When the Second World War created an entirely new connection between ethnic outsiders and social disorder, the LCBO modified its perspective accordingly, but, in a style characteristic of bureaucratic sobriety, did not overreact. For the most part, it left the administration of national-security issues to other agencies. It consulted them when necessary, and respected their authority, but did not simply cut off any suspect establishment. When a new hotel proprietor with an Italian or German last name applied for a beer Authority, the board did not simply reject the application. It wrote to the RCMP to inquire if the applicant had any record of subversive activities. If the record was clean, the board would continue with its regular vetting processes.

This division of administration duties is a fundamental aspect of bureaucratization, where expertise is compartmentalized for the sake of efficiency. For one and a half decades, the LCBO had exercised its role in controlling access to liquor. It had created an increasingly dispassionate bureaucracy based much more on quantifiable data than subjective interpretation of actions. For example, its inspectors' reports changed over the decade between 1934 to 1944 from a single sheet, with half a page of information the inspector had to fill in (such as number of rooms, location of toilets, and so on) and the remainder left blank for comments, to a four-page document that required each inspector to record standardized information but provided no space for additional remarks. Such administrative standardization was characteristic of the LCBO's approach to subversive activities. In spite of offering the assurance that, of course, it would not license a subversive organization, the board seemed more interested in fitting into the broader bureaucracy than expanding its role. It would let other policing groups determine if a proprietor were a danger to society. In the face of ethnic difference, therefore, the LCBO sought to use the tools it had for the purpose it saw as its initial driving mandate: to create or instil social order by encouraging proper behaviour among all residents of the province, irrespective of ethnic background.

NOTES

1 The term 'ethnic' is problematic. I am using it loosely to define non-native-born members of society. They may have been new immigrants, or second- or third-generation ones. The issue is who was defining them. For the most part, this study looks at self-definition, for example, people who congregated in ethnic social clubs, but it also includes notions of ethnic 'otherness' that are held by individuals who consider themselves 'legitimate' citizens.

2 The law did not specify which types of establishments would receive beer Authorities to sell beer and wine to the general public, but, after the 1934 act came into force, the board announced that only 'Standard Hotels,' which was a specific designation relating to the hotel's size and the types of amenities it offered, would receive the Authority to sell beer and wine to the public; restaurants were excluded. The act also permitted clubs, steamships, and train cars to be licensed.

3 Donald Avery, *'Dangerous Foreigners': European Immigrant Workers and Labour Radicalism in Canada, 1896–1932* (Toronto: McClelland and Stewart 1979); Donald Avery, *Reluctant Host: Canada's Response to Immigrant Workers, 1896–1994* (Toronto: McClelland and Stewart 1995); Kay Anderson, *Vancouver's Chinatown* (Montreal and Kingston: McGill-Queen's University Press 1995); Franca Iacovetta, Paula Draper, and Robert Ventresca, *A Nation of Immigrants: Women, Workers, and Communities in Canadian History, 1840s–1960s* (Toronto: University of Toronto Press 1998).

4 For example, Dirk Hoerder, *Creating Societies: Immigrant Lives in Canada* (Montreal and Kingston: McGill-Queen's University Press 1999); Vadim Kukushkin, *From Peasants to Labourers: Ukrainian and Belarusan Immigration from the Russian Empire to Canada* (Montreal and Kingston: McGill-Queen's University Press 2007); Carmela Patrias, *Patriots and Proletarians: The Politicization of Hungarian Immigrants in Canada, 1923–1939* (Montreal and Kingston: McGill-Queen's University Press 1994).

5 Avery, *Reluctant Hosts*, 10.

6 Sharon Ann Cook, *Through Sunshine and Shadow: The Woman's Christian Temperance Union, Evangelicalism, and Reform in Ontario, 1874–1939* (Montreal and Kingston: McGill-Queen's University Press 1995); Mariana Valverde, *The Age of Light, Soap and Water: Moral Reform in English Canada 1885–1925* (Toronto: McClelland and Stewart 1991); Barbara Roberts, '"A Work of Empire": Canadian Reformers and British Female Immigration,' in Linda Kealey, ed., *A Not Unreasonable Claim: Women and Reform in Canada, 1880s–1920s* (Toronto: Women's Press 1979).

7 Fundamental to this idea of imagined nationhood, of course, is Benedict Anderson's *Imagined Communities: Reflections on the Origin and Spread of Nationalism*, rev. ed. (London: Verso 1983). On 'normalization,' I draw upon the work of Philip Corrigan, notably, Corrigan and Derek Sayer, *The Great Arch: English State Formation as Cultural Revolution* (London: Blackwell 1985), and also Corrigan's 'Viewpoint: Power/Difference: Some Elementary Forms of a Post-"Sociological" Modernity. Further Remarks on Moral Regulation Celebrating the End of *the* "Stratification Paradigm," *the* "Logic" of "Society" and All That,' *Sociological Review*, 39 (May 1991): 309–34. For an interesting take on another government policy that might appear mundane but functioned as a hegemonic institution, see Sean Purdy, 'Building Homes, Building Citizens: Housing Reform and Nation Formation in Canada, 1900–20,' *Canadian Historical Review*, 79 (September 1998): 492–523.

8 David Gutzke, 'Gothenburg Schemes/Disinterested Management,' in Jack S. Blocker, Jr, David M. Fahey, and Ian R. Tyrrell, eds., *Alcohol and Temperance in Modern History: An International Encyclopedia* (Santa Barbara, Calif.: ABC-Clio 2003), 274–5; David Gutzke, *Pubs and Progressives: Reinventing the Public House in England 1896–1960* (Dekalb: Northern Illinois University Press 2005).

9 Mariana Valverde examines the notion of citizenship and liquor control in her 'meta–analysis' of liquor-control history in North America. See Valverde, 'The Liquor of Government and the Government of Liquor,' chapter 6 of *Diseases of the Will: Alcohol and the Dilemmas of Freedom* (Cambridge: Cambridge University Press 1998).

10 The Niagara region (Lincoln and Welland counties), Essex County, Waterloo County, the cities of Toronto and Ottawa, and the Thunder Bay district, which included the two small cities of Port Arthur and Fort William and a number of towns, many of which were booming from increased resource extraction or mining efforts throughout the area, such as Geraldton.

11 Inspector's report, 20 June 1931. Archives of Ontario, LCBO fonds (hereafter AO/LCBO), RG 38–1–0–1496. The LCBO records for public beer

consumption consist of two main collections: the Standard Hotel files, each of which is identified by a unique file number in the Record Group (RG) 36–1; and the Establishment Files, each of which does not have a unique number and is therefore identified by the name of the hotel around 1944. So some hotels that changed name during the period under examination may have a different file name than the hotel identified in the body of this essay.

12 Dingman to Raymond, Spencer, Law, and Burr, 30 May 1929, AO/LCBO, RG 36–8 (Ritz Hotel, Port Colborne).

13 Reaume to Smith, 14 August 1937, AO/LCBO, RG 36–8 (Imperial Hotel, Windsor).

14 Authority Holder Conduct Report (AHCR), 25 February 1936, AO/LCBO, RG 36–1–0–1131.

15 Ian Radforth, 'Finnish Radicalism and Labour Activism in the Northern Ontario Woods,' in Iacovetta, Draper, and Ventresca, eds., *A Nation of Immigrants*, 293–315.

16 To clarify: prior to 1934, the board evaluated hotels to ensure that they fit the description of a 'Standard Hotel,' one of the few places that were allowed to have 'Light Beer Licenses.' So, while the two hotels mentioned as examined by Pitt did receive the board's endorsement, they did not receive the Authority to sell strong beer. No one received such permission until 1934.

17 A.F. Gignac to Edmund G. Odette, 8 December 1934, AO/LCBO, RG 36–1–0–166.

18 J.H. Clark to Odette, 11 December 1934, AO/LCBO, RG 36–1–0–1661.

19 'M.H.' to LCBO, 17 August 1934, AO/LCBO, RG 36–1–0–617.

20 Stevens to Odette, 5 April 1935, AO/LCBO, RG–36–1–0–604.

21 Raoul Renaud to 'Sinclair' [sic] Gordon (n.d.; rec'd 25 July 1940), AO/LCBO, RG 36–8 (French Canadian Club of Windsor file).

22 William Bethell to Odette, 17 July 1935, AO/LCBO, RG 36–1–0–1665.

23 Affadavit of Milton E. Peck, 11 December 1934, AO/LCBO, RG 36–0–1–1661.

24 Smith to McMullin, 18 November 1935, AO/LCBO, RG 36–0–1–1118.

25 *Consolidated Statues of Ontario*, c. 294, Liquor Control Act, s. 75(1).

26 Ibid.

27 See Nancy M. Forestell, 'Bachelors, Boarding-Houses and Blind Pigs: Gender Construction in a Multi-Ethnic Mining Camp,' in Iacovetta, Draper, and Ventresca, eds., *A Nation of Immigrants*, esp. 264–66.

28 See, for example, Reaume to Smith, 29 December 1939, AO/LCBO, RG 36–1–0–278.

29 Inspector's Report, n.d. (last quarter of 1934), AO/LCBO, RG 36–1–0–1648.

30 Inspector's Report, n.d. (c. autumn 1934), AO/LCBO, RG 36–1–0–1661.

31 M. Watson to Smith, 1 August 1939, AO/LCBO, RG 36–8 (Italo-Canadian Political Club, Windsor).

32 W.D. Roach to Smith, 3 August 1935, AO/LCBO, RG 36–1–0–1653.

33 Mair to Reaume, 27 November 1936, AO/LCBO, RG 36–1–0–1653.

34 Authority Holder's Conduct Report, 18 January 1938, AO/LCBO, RG 36–1–0–1653.

35 In Toronto the board's central administrators might visit establishments in question, whereas this rarely happened outside the provincial capital.

36 Hanrahan to Smith, 3 September 1935, AO/LCBO, RG 36–1–0–1653.

37 Ratz to Smith, 11 February 1938, AO/LCBO, RG 36–8 (Austrian Club, Waterloo).

38 Ibid.

39 Smith and Dawson (of club) to Smith, 15 September 1936, AO/LCBO, RG 36–8 (Preston Athletic and Social Club, Ottawa).

40 Ratz to Smith, 31 May 1937, AO/LCBO, RG 36–8 (Sachsen–Schwaben Club, Kitchener).

41 Authority Holder's Conduct Report, 28 November 1937, AO/LCBO, RG 36–8 (Sachsen–Schwaben Club, Kitchener).

42 Authority Holder's Conduct Report, 4 October 1938, AO/LCBO, RG 36–8 (Austrian Club, Kitchener).

43 A.W. Boos to Smith, 14 December 1938, AO/LCBO, RG 36–8 (Austrian Club, Kitchener).

44 McKernzie to J.A. Smith, 20 June 1939, AO/LCBO, RG 36–8 (Austrian Club, Kitchener). This letter from the mayor to Hydro Commissioner Smith was forwarded to the LCBO on 20 July 1939.

45 Smith to Austrian-Canadian Club, 2 August 1939, AO/LCBO, RG 36–8 (Austrian Club, Kitchener).

46 Berges to Smith, 27 May 1940, AO/LCBO, RG 36–8 (Austrian Club, Kitchener).

47 See various records in AO/LCBO, RG 36–1–0–1537.

48 Reaume to Smith, 4 December 1937, AO/LCBO, RG 36–1–0–1652.

49 Reaume to Smith, 7 March 1938, AO/LCBO, RG 36–1–0–1653.

50 John Pitt to Mair, 23 November 1935, AO/LCBO, RG 36–8 (Polish War Veteran's Association, Windsor).

51 J.L.E. dePapp to Mair, June 1935, AO/LCBO, RG 36–8 (Windsor and District Hungarian Society, Windsor).

52 Petition to Edmond [sic] G. Odette, 24 March 1938, AO/LCBO, RG 36–1–0–1652.

53 Hanrahan to Smith, 5 November 1934, AO/LCBO, RG 36–8 (Border Cities Polish Canadian Club, Windsor).

54 Emanuel Michailuk to LCBO, c. 4 September 1934, AO/LCBO, RG–36–1–0–1657.

55 Finnish Pentecostal Church to LCBO, 29 January 1939, AO/LCBO, RG–36–1–0–1145.

56 Unsigned note, October 1934, AO/LCBO, RG 36–8 (Polish War Veteran's Association, Windsor).

57 Hanrahan to Smith, 19 November 1934, AO/LCBO, RG 36–8 (Polish People's Home Association, Windsor).

58 R. Boak Burns to LCBO, 20 April 1937, AO/LCBO, RG 36–1–0–1537.

59 See Carmela Patrias, 'Relief Strike: Immigrant Workers and the Great Depression in Crowland, Ontario,' in Iacovetta, Draper, and Ventresca, eds., *A Nation of Immigrants*, 322–58.

60 Frank Cherry to Smith, 26 May 1937, AO/LCBO, RG 36–1–0–1115.

61 Avery, *Dangerous Foreigners*; Avery, *Reluctant Host*; Hoerder, *Creating Societies*; Kukushkin, *From Peasants to Labourer*; Patrias, *Patriots and Proletarians*; Forestell, 'Bachelors, Boarding-Houses and Blind Pigs'; Barbara Roberts, *Whence They Came: Deportation from Canada 1900–1935* (Toronto: University of Toronto Press 1988).

62 H.S.C.S. to Smith, 23 April 1937, AO/LCBO, RG 36 –1–0–1537.

63 Robert Forsyth to commissioner, 21 January 1935, AO/LCBO, RG 36–1–0–1534.

64 Avery notes that there were many concerns over the cross-border activities of radicals during the Depression.

65 Petition to Edmond [sic] G. Odette, 24 March 1938, AO/LCBO, RG 36–1–0–1652.

66 Report, Pitt and Hanrahan to LCBO, n.d. (1935), AO/LCBO, RG 36–8 (Border Cities Polish Canadian Club files).

67 Anonymous to LCBO, n.d. (1935), AO/LCBO, RG 36–8 (Border Cities Polish Canadian Club).

68 'Catholic Women Society' to LCBO, 21 September 1938, AO/LCBO, RG 36–8 (Border Cities Polish Canadian Club).

69 Reaume to Smith, 22 March 1937, AO/LCBO, RG 36–8 (Border Cities Polish Canadian Club files).

70 'Nazi Roundup Said Started at Kitchener,' *Globe and Mail*, 4 September 1939, AO/LCBO, RG 36–8 (Concordia Club file).

71 Berges to Smith, 27 May 1940, AO/LCBO, RG 36–8 (Austrian-Canadian Club, Waterloo).

72 On internees, see Franca Iacovetta, Roberto Perin, and Angelo Principe,

eds., *Enemies Within: Italian and Other Internees in Canada and Abroad* (Toronto: University of Toronto Press 2000). Also, V.A.M. Kemp, superintendent, commanding 'O' Division, RCMP, to Smith, 28 June 1940, AO/LCBO, RG 36–8 (Italian War Veteran's Association, Windsor); Gordon to Smith, 18 June 1940, AO/LCBO, RG 36–8 (Border Cities Italian Club, Windsor).

73 Reaume to Elmhurst, 23 June 1942, AO/LCBO, RG 36–8 (Border Cities Italian Club, Windsor).

74 This was a standardized form letter. See, for example, V.A.M. Kemp, superintendent, commanding 'O' Division, RCMP, to Smith, 26 June 1940, AO/LCBO, RG 36–8 (Drake Public House, Windsor).

75 Smith to officer commanding, RCMP, 20 June 1940, AO/LCBO, RG 36–8 (Niagara Hotel files).

76 Phil Walter, district inspector, to F.E. Elliott, LCA Investigation Branch, 6 June 1940, AO/LCBO RG, 36–1–0–1655.

77 Copy of report from OPP (by anonymous OPP investigator), 5 November 1940, AO/LCBO, RG 36–8 (Windsor and District Hungarian Society).

78 James Clark to Odette, 22 July 1938, AO/LCBO, RG 36–8 (Order of the Sons of Italy, Windsor).

5 Becoming a 'Hype': Drug Laws, Subculture Formation, and Resistance in Canada, 1945–61[1]

CATHERINE CARSTAIRS

In the early 1920s, the Canadian government passed extremely harsh drug laws, including six-month minimum sentences for possession. Over the next twenty years, opiate and cocaine use slowly declined. But in the late 1940s and 1950s a new community of users emerged in the larger urban centres. These young users were primarily working class or poor and often came from troubled family backgrounds. For them, heroin use was a way of establishing a sense of identity and community. Heroin's status as a banned substance with a frightening reputation ensured that consuming it was also an act of defiance and resistance. These young heroin users, or 'hypes,' used drugs for pleasure, but also because the harsh laws ensured that drug use provided a concrete way to resist the rules and perceived conformity of post-war society. In short, they initiated the process of using drugs as a symbolic act of resistance, carving out a cultural style that would be imitated by middle-class marijuana users in the 1960s.

Most young heroin users in Canada in the late 1940s and 1950s were working class or had grown up in poverty. Many had spent time in juvenile institutions or foster homes and some had experienced violence and abuse within their homes. Their world was a very different one from the prosperous middle-class life that was portrayed in television and magazines, and reflected the extent to which poverty and marginalization continued to affect many Canadians, even in the relatively prosperous post-war world.[2] For these marginalized young people, heroin use was a way of satisfying longings and cravings and establishing a sense of identity and community, much like any other consumer commodity. However, its illegal status and frightening reputation ensured that heroin consumption was also a significant act of defiance against the law and community norms. The expression of resistance through drug consumption was not entirely new to the 1950s (one can also see it in a more limited way in the drug subcultures of the 1920s), but the perceived conformity of the 1950s, the strict drug laws, and harsh enforcement made drug use a symbolically significant act.

Given the backgrounds of most young drug users, it would be easy to describe heroin use as an escape, but the reality was far more complicated than this. Drug users deliberately chose to violate the strong social dictates and laws against drug use and decided to use their bodies to obtain what pleasure they could. However, consuming heroin was not just about pleasure: it was about identity and community. Heroin users defined themselves transgressively through their consumption of an illegal substance. Their word for themselves, 'hypes,' stemmed from an instrument of consumption, the hypodermic needle they used to administer drugs. Heroin use allowed young people to identify as street-wise criminals: knowledgeable, tough, and fearless. It put them in the ranks of the most experienced group of offenders in Canada's criminal justice system. And it gave them access to a community of other users, who shared a love of drugs, a refusal to live by society's rules, and a great deal of companionship and support both in and out of jail. In other words, consuming heroin provided the means to create a deliberately rebellious identity.

A growing number of American historians have argued that the characterization of the 1950s as conservative and the 1960s as radical misrepresents the continuities in the post-war years. The civil rights movement, the feminist movement, and the sexual revolution all had important roots in the 1950s and earlier. And, some historians have added, our image of the 1960s as radical ignores the fact that relatively few people, even relatively few young people, were part of the New Left or the counterculture, and neglects the growing conservative movement.[3] In Canada, though, historians have emphasized the differences between the 1950s and 1960s. Doug Owram asserts that the most striking thing about the youth culture of the 1960s was how rapidly it emerged from the conservative teenage culture of the 1950s, while Myrna Kotash celebrates the period from 1964 and 1970 as a magical time of possibility and revolt.[4] And yet, if we look at rising rates of juvenile delinquency and teen pregnancy in the 1950s and early 1960s, or if we examine the growing peace movement and the ongoing student commitment to Christian social reform, it is possible to see many continuities between the 1950s and 1960s.[5] Moreover, in Canada as in the

United States, most young people did not participate in radical political movements or the counterculture. It is undeniable that drug use
exploded in the late 1960s, and that many more young people were
smoking marijuana and using heroin and speed than ever before, and
yet, here too, there is a history. The heroin users of the 1950s, much like
the Beats, were important initiators of a new cultural style.[6]

This essay relies heavily, but not exclusively, on two sets of case files.
The John Howard Society of Vancouver (JHS), a prison-reform organization that worked extensively with drug users, generated the first set
of case files, which details drug users' interactions with social workers. The second set of files was created by the federal government's
Division of Narcotic Control, which kept comprehensive files on every
person it identified to be a drug user across the country. The files contain detailed police reports of every arrest for a narcotic offence, court
transcripts, full criminal records, mug shots, and parole information.
Altogether, 556 cases were examined and coded. Additionally, I examined the bureaucratic records of the Division of Narcotic Control, media
accounts of drug use, and studies by social workers and psychiatrists.
The documents in the case files, with the rare exception of a few letters
by users themselves, were all produced by regulatory agents such as
social workers, police officers, or bureaucrats in the Division of Narcotic Control. This can be frustrating, since only rarely do direct quotes
from drug users appear, and even these are likely to have been incor-
rectly remembered. Even so, case records are a rich source for uncover-
ing individual experience. They provide a useful way to examine the
relationships between drug users and regulatory agents. Lives are lived
and identities are constructed in relation to others, and case files provide a very dramatic representation of that fact.

Drug Users: Beyond Social Pathology and Rituals of Resistance

In the late 1940s and 1950s, the academic view of drug users was that
they were 'inadequate personalities' who threatened society through
their criminal activities.[7] While this view persists in some corners today,
research on drug users has become far more diversified and complex.
In arguing that drug use was a limited form of cultural resistance in
the late 1940s and 1950s, this essay draws on several different theoretical traditions. The first is the work that emerged out of Birmingham
School of Cultural Studies on subcultures. Influenced by the Marxists
Raymond Williams and Antonio Gramsci, scholars such as Dick Heb-

dige, Paul Willis, and Stuart Hall saw resistance in the multitude of subcultures that sprang up in post-war Britain, including punks, teddy boys, and mods.[8] Rightly criticized for paying insufficient attention to race and gender and for exaggerating the possibilities of resistance, the Birmingham School nonetheless drew attention to the possibility of creating a dissenting politics in the cultural sphere. A second influence was that of the historian E.P. Thompson, who strongly emphasized the agency of marginalized peoples.[9] Thompson and the Birmingham School both enlarged ideas of what it means to engage in political activity and grounded their discussions of culture on a firm understanding of history, economics, and class.

A third influence comes from American drug ethnographers such as Harold Finestone, Alan Sutter, Edward Preble, and Dan Casey, who painted pictures of dynamic heroin users creating identities as 'righteous dope fiends' getting 'kicks' and 'taking care of business' in an alternative economy of their own creation.[10] While these ethnographers overstated their case and downplayed the very real problems faced by drug users, they nonetheless refuted the stereotype of the withdrawn, psychologically dysfunctional addict, and showed that heroin use, and a heroin-using identity, could be regarded as a creative response to inequality in American society. A more recent and considerably more nuanced example of this tradition is Philippe Bourgois's book *In Search of Respect: Selling Crack in El Barrio*, a study of crack users and sellers in East Harlem. Bourgois combines a structural perspective with the insights of cultural-production theory. His book discusses the misery and violence of life in the inner city but firmly places the blame for these problems on social and racial inequality. Bourgois also pays careful attention to oppositional cultural formation in the inner city. He regards culture as a site of resistance and self-esteem, without ignoring the self-destructiveness and familial suffering caused by drug use.[11]

Although inspired by ideas about 'history from the bottom up,' this essay is also strongly influenced by the work of Michel Foucault, whose multifarious view of power has cast a dim light on any simplistic notions of agency. Drug users' sense of themselves was influenced by social workers, police officers, the media, medical and psychiatric discourses, and other drug users. All consumption, even the consumption of banned substances, never takes place outside of power, outside of governance.[12] However, this governance is never complete. There are always forms of resistance, even though resistance generates its own governing mechanisms. The consumption of heroin in post-war society, although it had its own governing rituals, marked a refusal by young heroin users to live their lives according to the norms espoused by the media, government, police, and social workers. Perhaps a more sophisticated vocabulary is needed to describe their cultural dissent, one that better encompasses the reality of their restricted opportunities, personal pain, and the many sources of power (capitalism, the media, social workers, police, other drug users, parents, prison workers) that operated on their lives. However, in lieu of a better word, this essay will continue to use the term resistance to describe their decision to take a banned substance and to join the ranks of a clearly demarcated oppositional group.

The Canadian Heroin-Use Scene, 1945–61

Heroin users in Canada from 1945 to 1961 were a very small and homogeneous group compared to drug users in the United States or to Canadian drug users today. It is impossible to know precisely how many users there were in Canada but estimates by the police and by the Division of Narcotic Control indicate that there were probably fewer that 4,000 steady heroin users across the country. (This compares to estimates of 75,000 to 125,000 injection-drug users in Canada today.[13]) Most lived in either Vancouver or Toronto. In these years, more than one-half of all narcotic convictions took place in Vancouver, and another one-fourth took place in Toronto.[14] There were some users who had been using before the war and were considerably older. But the majority of users were part of a new generation of drug users that first began to emerge late in the war. Although these users were similar to the older generation in that they were primarily working class, there were several important differences. First of all, far more of these users were female. In 1946, 21 per cent of people convicted of a narcotic offence were female; by 1961, 37 per cent of people convicted were women. Secondly, they were predominantly white, although there were small numbers of aboriginal, African Canadian, and Asian Canadian users. Chinese users, who had previously accounted for the largest number of convictions, had all but disappeared by the post-war period – the result of the prohibition of new immigrants in 1923, deportations under the Opium and Narcotic Drug Act, and the aging of the population. The very small number of non-white users meant that there was no separate community for users who were racial minorities. Racial minorities intermarried with white drug users and spent their time on the street in the company of white users. This differed significantly from the United States, where heroin users were often drawn from members of ethnic and racial minority groups. Thirdly, illegal drug use meant heroin use. Opium use largely disappeared after 1948, replaced by a regular supply of heroin. Morphine was used occasionally, but primarily by the limited number of people who obtained prescriptions from doctors. Marijuana use was uncommon.[15] Finally, the heroin on the market was extremely weak and expensive, and few users were able to acquire substantial habits.

Drug use in post-war Canada was an extremely risky activity. Because of the tight control over narcotic prescriptions and the vigilant policing of the illicit market, it was almost impossible to be a drug user in the late 1940s and 1950s and not come to the attention of narcotic authorities. Surveillance over drug users was more carefully and successfully maintained than ever before or ever since. Penalties for possession were harsher than they are today. Minimum sentences for possession were six months, and sentences of two years were not unusual for repeat offenders. Steady users often spent more time in jail than outside it. On the street, regular users spent much of their time avoiding and occasionally clashing with and fighting the police.

Owing to the small size of the drug-using community and the strict enforcement, which forced them to be very secretive about drug use and sales, drug users tended to associate primarily with other users. In Toronto and Vancouver there were a few bars and cafés where heroin users hung out and learned who was selling and where. They bought drugs from other users, shared rooms, and made deals. Their friendships and romantic relationships were with other users. The close-knit nature of the Vancouver drug-use community becomes clear when one sees the remarkable number of drug users who had family members who were also users. Richard D.'s mother and father had both been drug users.[16] One young woman who spent her childhood in foster homes lived with her father for the first time when she was fifteen to sixteen years old. Her father had been a drug user for many years, and she claimed that she supported her father's habit by prostitution. Her mother was also a drug user and was incarcerated in the Prison for Women in Kingston, Ontario.[17] Far more frequently, siblings used. The Brewster family consisted of four boys, at least three of whom were drug users. Two of the brothers married women who were also users, meaning that the John Howard Society, as well as other social agencies, had a long history of involvement with this family.[18] Drug users usually married or lived in common-law relationships with other users.

The users began young, although they were older than many drug users today. A study of 400 consecutively convicted drug users at Oakalla Prison Farm in Burnaby, British Columbia (where many drug users served their time), concluded that 46 per cent began using before they were twenty years old, and another 32 per cent began between the ages of twenty and twenty-four.[19] Women often began even younger than men did. The files from the John Howard Society, most of which date from the post-war period, show that the average age for women to start using was nineteen, while for men it was twenty-two. Compared to today, it took time for people to come into contact with the very small community of users and it took even longer to be trusted enough to be able to buy drugs oneself.

Most drug users came from economically disadvantaged backgrounds. A study of drug users at Oakalla Prison Farm in the mid-1950s found that only one-third of drug users grew up in homes that were economically comfortable (which, according to designers of the study, indicated that these homes had 'sufficient income and accumulated savings'). Almost one-fourth lived in homes that needed welfare assistance at least some of the time.[20] A study of consecutively convicted users at Oakalla Prison Farm showed that 56 per cent of addicts who were raised in Vancouver grew up in 'the deteriorated section' of Vancouver's East End. In several cases, workers at the JHS noted that clients had been malnourished as children.[21] This was not surprising, since many of the post-war users were born in the late 1920s and 1930s and had spent their childhood during the Great Depression.

The difficulties of poverty often created other familial problems.[22] Only 42 per cent of drug users at Oakalla said that they had a 'satisfactory home life.' Only 40 per cent had both parents alive and in their home to the end of their school years.[23] Over 30 per cent reported that their father's outstanding characteristic was 'overly aggressive, quarrelsome, irritable,' while another 10 per cent complained that their father's outstanding characteristic was 'alcoholic.'[24] The case-file records show that some users had extraordinarily troubled lives. Sharon M., for example, was adopted when she was ten months old, lived with the family until she was nine, and was then placed with the Convent of the Good Shepherd until she was twelve. She kept running away from the convent and back to her foster home. She was then placed in the Girls' Industrial School, where she set a school record by running away sixty-eight times. She was released from the Industrial School just after her sixteenth birthday. She started using drugs when she was twelve years old.[25] Sharon's confrontational attitude towards authority and her rebellious attitude made using drugs appealing to her, and allowed other users to trust her at a very young age.

Cameron G. told penitentiary officials that his parents separated when he was seven years old. His father was said to be a steady drinker and a stern disciplinarian. When his parents split up, his two brothers went to live with his father while he was sent to live with his aunt. Cameron reported that his aunt was extremely strict. He first appeared in juvenile court when he was thirteen. When he was fifteen, his grandfather became ill and his aunt could no longer care for him. The Children's Aid Society sent him to a ranch north of Edmonton. When he was sixteen, a welfare agent advised him to join the army and made arrangements for him to meet the recruiting officer (this was during the war). In less than a year he was wounded and had venereal disease. He was honourably discharged at eighteen and started using sometime thereafter.[26] Cameron's history was not unusual. Many users in the case files had parents with substance-abuse problems, usually alcohol, many had lived in foster homes, and many faced serious health problems from an early age.

Aboriginal users often faced additional hardships created by racism and the often brutal policies of assimilation pursued by the Canadian government. Like many aboriginal women of her generation, Kitty H. grew up on a reserve where drinking problems were common.[27] Her mother died in a drunken brawl when she was four to five years of age, and her grandparents took her in and raised her with their own children. Her grandmother had a serious drinking problem. Kitty had tuberculosis from ages nine to fourteen and started drinking heavily herself while she was in her early teens. According to social workers, her grandmother was a nasty drunk, and Kitty ran away from home and eventually started taking drugs. She was sent to the Girls' Industrial School, and then returned to the reserve, but said she was never accepted after her jail sentence. Kitty told her social worker that 'she takes drugs when she is depressed.'[28] Separated from her family and from her community, with a long history of loss and abuse, it was not surprising that Kitty would often be depressed.

Many users had experienced physical or emotional violence. One JHS client reported that one of his first memories was his stepfather beating him. Although he was only twenty-six at the time, he claimed that he hadn't seen his parents in eight years.[29] William W. reported that his father did time in Oakalla for assaults on both him and his brother.

Eventually, when the boys were found living in a shack 'inadequately clothed and fed,' they were committed to the Children's Aid Society.[30] Johnny R. reported that his mother and father were always arguing, that his father beat both him and his mother, and that his mother was always so emotional that he couldn't talk to her. 'Under narcotics,' he confessed, 'I don't worry about nobody screaming about anything – dad used to be always screaming.'[31] It is not surprising that young people with such difficult memories would find solace in heroin use and the community it provided.

And yet few heroin users blamed their parents for their drug use. Instead, most users reported that they started using out of inquisitiveness. Pat D. told a social worker that she started using out of curiosity, and that she understood what she was getting into since she knew many addicts.[32] When asked why they had first started using, over 90 per cent of users in a study at Oakalla Prison Farm indicated that 'curiosity and desire for a new thrill' was at least part of the reason. Eighty per cent added that it was because they had been associating with addicts.[33] Sixty-eight per cent of users in the Oakalla Prison Farm study said that they had seen someone else take a fix before they first tried heroin.[34] While heroin users such as Kitty, Cameron, and Sharon may have continued using heroin to forget their problems, it was curiosity, excitement, and the possibilities of pleasure and status that led many of them and their contemporaries into drug use in the first place.

The Pleasures of Consumption

Drug users liked the way heroin made them feel. Veronica S. reported: 'If drugs were not illegal she had no desire to give them up, she likes the life, she enjoys the feeling and the greatest pleasure to her in all her life was to be able to coast under the influence of drugs.'[35] But there were other pleasures as well. All aspects of consuming heroin involved specialized knowledge and insider status, what Sarah Thornton would call 'subcultural capital.'[36] First, heroin users needed to know whom to buy from. Most drug users bought their drugs from street peddlers rather than doctors. In Vancouver, where most users lived in residential hotel rooms, peddlers often congregated in the cafés and beer parlours that surrounded the hotels at the corner of Hastings and Columbia. In Toronto, drug peddlers were more likely to sell out of their homes and apartments and on the street, although the drug trade was centred around Jarvis and Dundas. In Vancouver, sellers generally staked out a location and sold to small numbers of users at a time, whereas in Toronto the practice of arranging 'meets' with a large number of addicts seems to have been more common. While it was no secret that drugs were bought and sold at these locations, it was impossible to make purchases without being trusted. The executive director of the John Howard Society of Ontario told a conference of people concerned about the drug problem that 'any of us sitting here could not go and buy drugs at Jarvis and Shuter tonight if we tried with a thousand dollar bill in our hand.'[37] Undercover police officers discovered the same. It was almost impossible for them to make purchases until they had established themselves as members of the drug-using community.

Heroin users also needed to know what they were buying, what price they could expect to pay, and what to do with the heroin when the purchase was made. Heroin was sold in gelatin capsules. The heroin was cut with sugar of milk and other substances, and a capsule contained between one-tenth of a grain to slightly more than full grain of heroin, although this varied.[38] Individual capsules of heroin were usually double-wrapped in the silver paper from cigarette packages and users generally carried these capsules in their mouth, so that they could swallow them in the case of being seized by police. Larger numbers of capsules were wrapped in balloons, condoms, or fingerstalls (a piece of latex shaped like a finger). These could also be carried in the mouth, or inter-vaginally, or in a few cases inter-anally. The cost also varied over time and from city to city. Most sales were made at $5 or $6 per cap.[39] Heroin users were diligent about ensuring that their capsules were appropriately wrapped in foil before placing them in their mouths and fellow users policed each other to ensure that the drugs were being carried in as safe a way as possible.

Heroin was almost always injected. A few drug users took 'skin shots,' meaning that they injected it subcutaneously. Most, however, 'mainlined,' injecting the drug right into the vein. Drug-injection equipment was described as 'an outfit,' which generally consisted of an eye-dropper, a hypodermic needle, and a spoon. The contents of a capsule were placed in a spoon and mixed with water, and then heated to help the heroin dissolve. To shoot up, the drug user tied something around his or her arm, inserted the needle into a vein, and released the contents of the eyedropper into the needle. Afterwards they rinsed the syringe with water to make sure that, if police seized it, it would not analyse positively for heroin.[40] In the United States in the 1950s, renting an 'outfit' was a common way of gaining money to buy drugs.[41] In Canada, the items in an 'outfit' were legal, and single drug users were sometimes arrested with more than one outfit. However, it was common practice for users to share outfits, probably because one outfit was easier to clean, hide, or throw away if the police broke down the door. While people occasionally received shots from others, most heroin users shot up themselves and had to be familiar with all of the stages in preparing a shot, finding an appropriate vein, and using the needle effectively. These complex rituals, which took some effort to learn, lent a prestige and status to heroin use.

It was not just specialized knowledge and pleasure that gave heroin its status. Young people with experiences of crime and institutional life looked up to older users in prison and on the street, partly because drug users had a strong sense of community and a reputation for being hardened 'cons.' Becoming a heroin user allowed young 'rounders'[42] (delinquents) to identify with a group that was regarded as the most rebellious and, in many ways, the most cohesive in Canada's prisons.[43] In 1958 Rebecca R. told a social worker that 'it is because the person wants to feel part of a group that they usually become an addict.' She said that non-addict rounders were 'half baked' rounders and that unless drugs are taken 'he or she does not feel part of the group ... and it is because they want this sense of belonging that many of them turn to the use of narcotics.' She added that 'to many it was like a game, almost like winning a war, and the war was won when they were able to score and take a fix successfully ... It was somewhat this thrill of being able to win ... that made the whole idea of using drugs attractive to young teenagers.'[44] Rebecca R. was unusual in some respects. She was Jewish and middle class, while most drug users at the time were Catholic or Protestant and working class. Also, most drug users were much more circumspect in their conversations with social workers. Yet Rebecca was not alone in her feeling that heroin use in post-war Canada could give one access to prestige and excitement within the criminal background. A matron at Oakalla Prison Farm confirmed that the young inmates were 'greatly enamoured of the exciting, glamorous life of the narcotic addict. They frequently aspire to membership in the addict group.'[45]

Drug use was usually part of a long pattern of 'deviant' behaviour, and heroin use was another step in becoming a bona fide rounder. Most users had already spent time in juvenile institutions or in prison before they started using drugs. Case files from the Narcotic Division reveal that it was unusual for someone's first conviction to be for a narcotic offence, although it was more common for women than for men, perhaps because women often started using when they were younger, and because women's primary illegal activity was prostitution, which was not always policed intensively. The Oakalla Prison Farm study indicated that only 22 per cent of male drug users and 43 per cent of female drug users had no convictions before they started drug use.[46] In Vancouver, most people who later became drug users were already hanging out on the 'corner' and had come to the attention of police and social workers as juveniles. Joe W., for example, first went to the Boys' Industrial School at eight years of age for theft, and was in Oakalla for car theft by the time he was seventeen. It is not clear when he started using, but he served his first term for possession in 1957, at twenty years of age.[47]

Troy H. was a typical example of someone who had been involved in criminal activity well before he started drug use and found drug use appealing because of its status within the criminal underworld. Troy grew up in East End Vancouver with his mother and stepfather. He joined a gang when he was a teenager, and at seventeen he told JHS workers that he was not interested in becoming an apprentice or doing manual labour. He wanted a 'big job with big money' – preferably mechanics. At eighteen he was convicted of breaking and entering. By his twenties, he was selling and using drugs. In 1955 British Columbia Penitentiary (BCP) officials described him as having a 'cocky, self-assured aggressive front with a well defined generalized hostility towards authority.' In 1956, at twenty-five years of age, he was sentenced to fifteen years for possession for the purposes of trafficking. When parole was being considered in 1963, Troy told the parole representative that he needed to pursue a 'fast dollar' because it represented 'prestige in society.' At the same time, a JHS worker reported that fellow inmates at BCP saw him 'as a big-time trafficker with utter contempt for our judicial procedure' and felt that he would have considerable difficulty staying away from the addict community because of his prestige in their eyes.[48] Drug users like Troy H., with their working-class backgrounds and poor education, had little chance of achieving respect through legal work. However, among the street gangs and rounders of Vancouver's downtown eastside, they could garner status unavailable to them through any other means.

Drug users lived their lives in a community of other drug users and urban rounders. The relative homogeneity of drug users in the 1950s fostered this sense of community. The sense of community was also to some degree created by enforcement officials, who forced users to be very cautious in their dealings with non-users and created a siege mentality among them. However, it was also created by users, who had a great deal in common, including an enjoyment of heroin, sexual and marital patterns that deviated widely from the norm, sporadic work records in low-status occupations, and shared experiences in jail and prison. When psychiatrist George Stevenson conducted a study of users at Oakalla and asked them whether they preferred the company of addicts and felt a sense of loyalty to them, those who answered in the affirmative said that 'addicts help and understand each other,' 'they are the only group I can feel natural with. I am self-conscious with square-johns,' 'we're all the same – all fighting a common cause, the police and drugs,' and 'we talk the same language. We live the same life. We are all looked down on because we are addicts.'[49] John Turvey, a user in the late 1950s and early 1960s, recalled that there was a 'lot of loyalty on the street' and 'a strong sense of ethics in the community.'[50] Drug users felt themselves to be members of a community of people who shared similar values and problems.

Outside observers also frequently commented on the feeling of community among drug users. Stevenson remarked that

in many respects the addict group has resemblances to a secret society or religious cult. There is a considerable period of pre-addiction apprenticeship, an admiration of older addicts and companionship with them. Finally there is the initiation, the actual receiving of 'working tools' (bent spoon and eye-dropper syringe) and the first injection of the addict's sacramental food – heroin. Henceforward, their preferred companions are addicts. They have their secrets – sources of supply, how to avoid the police, how to get rid of evidence if the police invade their inner sanctums. They have their secret words – a cant or argot peculiar to addicts. They help one another when in distress, they talk about little else than drugs, they combine for illegal activities, they live with addicted cult members, and marry within the cult. The addict feels that he is misunderstood and persecuted by society and has hostile feelings towards society. Moreover, he regards the average hard working citizen as a 'sucker' and likes to claim that: 'everyone has larceny in his heart,' and will commit dishonest acts if reasonably sure of not being caught.[51]

Heroin users, in other words, had access to very specific knowledge about drugs, pleasure, and crime which few other Canadians possessed. Like the 'lads' described by Birmingham School theorist Paul Willis in the 1970s, who looked down on their fellow students for their lack of knowledge about sex and life, young heroin users could feel superior to 'square johns,' who know nothing about the joys of heroin or the excitement of crime.[52]

While users also fought with each other and informed on one another, the ideology of users standing up for one another was not just a myth. Drug users were usually arrested in groups and they tried to ensure that only one person would serve time for the offence. In 1952 Norman M. was in a hotel room with a female companion when the police broke in and found two capsules. The woman announced: 'Well it's my room and my coat, everything in the room is mine, he knew nothing about it.' The police decided that they did not have enough evidence to charge Norman M., even though they knew he was an addict.[53] Users outside prison often tried to make life inside prison a little more bearable. In 1954 Robert K. dropped by the JHS with a package of phonograph records for the East Wing at Oakalla.[54] (The East Wing was where male drug users served their time.) A couple weeks later, he dropped by again and asked the JHS to inquire why the records had been taken to other wings. More commonly, drug users tried to send drugs to their friends on the inside. In 1961 Dorothy T. sent a postcard to a friend of hers at the Prison for Women in Kingston. The card read: 'Thought you would like this one. Your Friend.' Some heroin was included in the compressed cardboard of the postcard.[55]

The tight community of users could be seen in their language. Today many of the users' expressions have passed into everyday language, and even at the time many of the JHS workers, police officers, and prison officials were conversant with the argot. Common expressions included 'boosting' – shoplifting, 'bum beef' – a false legal charge, 'bulls' – the police, 'pony boys' or 'harness bulls' – Royal Canadian Mounted Police (RCMP), 'score' – to make a purchase of narcotics, and 'yenny' – a strong desire for narcotics.[56] Chief George Allain of the RCMP told a 1955 Senate committee that, if most people heard a 'pusher' and a client talking about drugs, 'he would not know they were talking about drugs, because they use some kind of code.'[57] In 1968 a former undercover policeman published an article on the argot of heroin users in Toronto. This is a little later than the time period under examination here, but the language seems to be largely the same. He found that his experimental subjects spoke at a rate of approximately forty-seven words per minute. On average, 11.7 of these words were argot, making it difficult for outsiders to understand the conversation.[58] The language played an important role in identifying users to one another and making them feel as if they were part of a community with a highly specialized knowledge.

The Realities of Consumption

The exciting life of a drug user often soured as users aged. Becoming a hype can be described as a form of resistance, but remaining a hype often led to desperation and despair. Many drug users got tired of hustling and prostitution, the revolving door in and out of jail, the struggles with the police, and the realities of withdrawal. The social-work case files are filled with people who asserted that they had a strong desire to stop using. A study of 100 consecutively convicted drug users at Oakalla found that only 25 had never quit voluntarily. Forty-three had stopped using voluntarily on three different occasions.[59] Thirty-two subjects (46 per cent) in the Oakalla Prison Farm Consecutive Conviction Study indicated that they quit because they were '"fed up" with drug addict life and wished to live a normal life,' 12 (17 per cent) quit to take up regular employment, and 11 (16 per cent) quit because of fear of the police and imprisonment.[60] Malcolm N. Brandon, head of the narcotic-addiction treatment unit in Oakalla Prison Farm, wrote that most drug users expressed a wish to abstain because they did not want to go back to jail.[61] The JHS files indicate that people's reasons for quitting were more complex and often involved personal and familial concerns. Rick H. moved to Victoria in 1961 in an attempt to stop using. In a letter to his social worker, he indicated that he needed to 'straighten myself out with both my family and my own mind.'[62] Another woman complained (perhaps for the benefit of the social worker) that 'taking drugs or alcohol doesn't really solve problems, you still have your depression left, only after taking drugs you are left with a feeling of guilt which makes your problems worse.'[63] Regardless of the reason for wanting to quit, however, it is clear that many users found heroin to be burdensome and they expressed a wish to live a different sort of life.

Drug users often had poor work histories, low levels of skill and education, weak relationships with people outside the drug-using community, and serious emotional problems. It was difficult to quit using, partly because many drug users found that drugs gave them considerable pleasure and allowed them to forget, if only for a brief time, their other problems. However, it was not love of drug use alone that made it hard to quit. Drug users who quit felt extremely isolated. The same desire to be part of a group that led many into drug use in the first place made it very difficult to leave that world. Few drug users had much contact with square johns, and they frequently told social workers that they felt uncomfortable with people who did not use. Ben Maartman, the parole officer for the Special Narcotic Addiction Project (SNAP),[64] the first parole program specifically for drug users, wrote that his favourite parolee 'was convinced that he was so different from the squarejohn world that he could never fit into it and be accepted by it. Heroin was nothing compared with this problem. The drug was merely the way out from worrying about it.'[65] Drug users continued to use because their friends used. The busy life of the drug user gave them a focus and a community. Stopping drug use was as much about leaving behind an identity and a set of friends as it was about withdrawing from drugs and their effects.

Conclusion

In the years after the Second World War, the strict laws against using drugs actually made drug use appealing to a small set of people. Using heroin allowed marginalized young people to identify with a community that had access to knowledge and pleasures that few Canadians possessed, while also giving them a certain degree of power in penal institutions and a reputation for standing up to the police. Heroin permitted them to express their disdain for authority and conformity. This was exciting for rebellious young people who often already had experiences with police and institutional life. Over the long run, however, health problems, fear of arrest, and time in prison usually took its toll. One could flaunt authority by consuming an illegal substance such as heroin, but in the end this was a limited sort of resistance. Consumption had its pleasures but it was not a step towards social justice or equality.

Nonetheless, in the 1960s consuming drugs would become an increasingly important way of expressing resistance. In the mid- to late 1960s, the number of drug users in Canada exploded. Many historians of sexuality have argued that it was the working class that pioneered changes in sexuality which would later be picked up by the middle class.[66] This seems to be true in drug history as well. The working-class heroin users of the 1950s would pave the way for the middle-class marijuana smokers of the 1960s. Like the hippies that would follow them, the hypes took a deliberate pleasure in flouting the law and conventional norms and found considerable joy in their transgressive consumption. The laws against heroin use, much like the laws against marijuana use for a later generation, actually made drug use more appealing to this small community of users, even while these same laws made the life of a heroin user much more difficult.

NOTES

1 This essay is a revised version of an article with the same title that initially appeared in *Contemporary Drug Problems*, 29 (spring 2002) (copyright Federal Legal Publications). I thank *Contemporary Drug Problems* for allowing me to rethink this material. Thanks also to Chris Dummitt, whose thoughtful review of my book, *Jailed for Possession*, in *BC* Studies, 153 (spring 2007), strengthened my analysis.
2 Joy Parr, *Domestic Goods: The Material, the Moral, and the Economic in the Postwar Years* (Toronto: University of Toronto Press 1999); Valerie Korinek, *Roughing It in the Suburbs: Reading Chatelaine Magazine in the Fifties and Sixties* (Toronto: University of Toronto Press 2000); France Iacovetta, *Such Hardworking People: Italian Immigrants in Postwar Toronto* (McGill and Kingston: McGill-Queen's University Press 1992).
3 Joanne Meyerowitz, ed., *Not June Cleaver: Women and Gender in Postwar America 1945–1960* (Philadelphia: Temple University Press 1994); M.J. Heale, 'The Sixties as History: A Review of the Political Historiography,' *Reviews in American History*, 33 (2005): 133–52; Alan Pentigy, 'Illegitimacy, Postwar Psychology, and the Reperiodization of the Sexual Revolution,' *Journal of Social History*, 38, no. 1 (2004): 63–79; Charles Payne, *I've Got the Light of Freedom: The Organizing Tradition and the Mississippi Freedom Struggle* (Berkeley: University of California Press 1995).
4 Doug Owram, *Born at the Right Time: A History of the Baby Boom Generation* (Toronto: University of Toronto Press 1996), 187; Myrna Kotash, *Long Way from Home: The Story of the Sixties Generation in Canada* (Toronto: James Lorimer 1980).
5 Catherine Gidney, *A Long Eclipse: The Liberal Protestant Establishment and the Canadian University, 1920–1970* (Montreal and Kingston: McGill-Queen's University Press 2004); Ann Petrie, *Gone to an Aunt's: Remembering Canada's Homes for Unwed Mothers* (Toronto: McClelland and Stewart 1998); Jeff Keshen, *Saints, Sinners and Soldiers: Canada's Second World War* (Vancouver: UBC Press 2004), 206.

6 W.T. Lhamon, *Deliberate Speed: The Origins of a Cultural Style in the American 1950s* (Washington: Smithsonian Institution 1990).

7 George Stevenson, the author of the pre-eminent study on drug users in Canada at this time, certainly took this point of view: 'Drug Addiction in British Columbia,' unpublished manuscript (University of British Columbia 1956). The best example from the international literature is Isodor Chein et al., *The Road to H: Narcotics, Delinquency and Social Policy* (New York: Basic Books 1964).

8 Stuart Hall, ed., *Resistance through Rituals: Youth Sub-Cultures in Post-War Britain* (London: Hutcheson in Association with the Centre for Contemporary Cultural Studies, University of Birmingham, 1976); Paul Willis, *Learning to Labor: How Working Class Kids Get Working Class Jobs* (Farborough, U.K.: Saxon House 1977); Dick Hebdige, *Subculture: The Meaning of Style* (London and New York: Routledge 1999; 1st ed. 1979). Punks, teddy bears, and mods were all the names of countercultural groups in 1950s, 1960s, and 1970s London.

9 E.P. Thompson, *The Making of the English Working Class* (New York: Pantheon Books 1963).

10 Harold Finestone, 'Cats, Kicks and Color,' *Social Problems*, 5, no. 1 (1957): 3–13; Alan Sutter, 'The World of the Righteous Dope Fiend,' *Issues in Criminology*, 2, no. 2 (1966): 177–222; and Edward Preble and John Casey, Jr, 'Taking Care of Business – The Heroin User's Life on the Street,' *International Journal of the Addictions*, 4, no. 1 (1969): 1–24.

11 Philippe Bourgois, *In Search of Respect: Selling Crack in El Barrio* (New York and Cambridge: Cambridge University Press 1995). His approach is similar to that of Robin Kelley in *Race Rebels: Culture Politics and the Black Working Class* (New York: Free Press 1994).

12 Gary Wickham, 'Governance of Consumption,' in Pekka Sulkunen et al., eds., *Constructing the New Consumer Society* (Houndmills, U.K.: Macmillan 1997), 277–92.

13 Eric Single, 'Injection Drug Users Overview, Canadian Centre on Substance Abuse,' http://www.ccsa.ca/Eng/Topics/Populations/IDU/Pages/InjectionDrugUsersOverview.asp (accessed 16 November 2010).

14 Dominion Bureau of Statistics, *Annual Report of Criminal and Other Offences* (Ottawa, 1945–61).

15 Psychiatrist George Stevenson reported that very few of the subjects he studied at Oakalla Prison Farm 'have ever seen marijuana and fewer still have used it.' Stevenson, 'Drug Addiction in British Columbia,' 128.

16 Simon Fraser University Archives (SFUA), John Howard Society Case File (hereafter JHS) no. 84. All names have been changed to protect confidentiality.

17 SFUA, JHS no. 85.
18 SFUA, JHS no. 86, JHS no. 87, JHS no. 88, JHS no. 56, JHS no. 89.
19 Stevenson, 'Addiction in British Columbia,' 133.
20 Ibid., 41.
21 SFUA, JHS no. 6 and JHS no. 7.
22 A large body of research has shown a link between socio-economic status and family violence. John Hagan and Bill McCarthy, *Mean Streets: Youth Crime and Homelessness* (Cambridge: Cambridge University Press 1997), 56–63.
23 Stevenson, 'Addiction in British Columbia,' 42.
24 Ibid., 32.
25 SFUA, JHS no. 5.
26 SFUA, JHS no. 8.
27 The community breakdown caused by residential schools, displacement from their land, and Christian evangelization is well known. See Jim Miller, *Skyscrapers Hide the Heavens: A History of Indian-White Relations in Canada* (Toronto: University of Toronto Press 1989).
28 SFUA, JHS no. 2.
29 SFUA, JHS no. 58.
30 SFUA, JHS no. 9.
31 SFUA, JHS no. 10.
32 SFUA, JHS no. 65.
33 Stevenson, 'Addiction in British Columbia,' 385.
34 Ibid., 131.
35 SFUA, JHS no. 11.
36 Sarah Thornton, *Club Cultures: Music, Media and Subcultural Capital* (Cambridge: Cambridge Polity Press 1995).
37 Proceedings of the Conference on Narcotic Addiction, Niagara Falls, Ontario, 21–24 February 1963, 42.
38 Stevenson estimated that capsules contained one-tenth of a grain. Stevenson, 'Addiction in British Columbia,' 534. RCMP annual reports indicated that caps contained between one-fourth grain and one full grain. In February 1963 R.C. Hammond, the chief of Narcotic Control, wrote that 'it is doubtful if the average heroin addict in Canada is able to obtain a dosage of 1 to 1 1/2 grains per day. In fact, we are inclined to believe it is much less than this.' 'Proceedings of the Conference on Narcotic Addiction.' A 1959–60 study of heroin capsules seized in Canada determined that 95 per cent of the 229 seizures contained 24–68 mg of heroin per capsule with a mean of 46 mg. Quoted in Royal Commission on the Non-Medical Use of Drugs, *Final Report* (Ottawa, 1973), 303. One grain is 64.8 milligrams.

See http://www.tostepharmd.net/pharm/clinical/measurement.html (accessed 17 November 2010).

39 RCMP, *Annual Report for the Year Ended March 31, 1952*; RCMP, *Annual Report for the Year Ended March 31, 1955*; RCMP, *Annual Report for the Year Ended March 31, 1957*.

40 Stevenson, 'Addiction in British Columbia,' 139–40.

41 Jeremy Larner, ed., *The Addict in the Street* (New York: Grove Press 1966).

42 According to Barron H. Lerner, 'rounders' in early-twentieth-century Seattle were people 'who made the rounds of a particular community, living in lodging houses but frequently requiring admission to hospitals or jail': *Contagion and Confinement: Controlling Tuberculosis along the Skid Road* (Baltimore, Md.: Johns Hopkins University Press 1998), 29. By the mid-twentieth century in Vancouver and Toronto, rounders were people who were involved in criminal activity.

43 Claude Brown describes a similar process in 1950s Harlem in his autobiography *Manchild in the Promised Land* (New York: Macmillan 1965).

44 SFUA, JHS no. 11.

45 Dorothy Mae Coutts, 'Social Structure of the Women's Unit at Oakalla,' MA thesis, University of British Columbia, 1961, 58. The physician at Oakalla in the 1950s, Guy Richmond, agreed that 'heroin seemed to be a status symbol.' Guy Richmond, *Prison Doctor* (Surrey: Nunaga Publishing 1975), 54.

46 Stevenson, 'Addiction in British Columbia,' 113.

47 SFUA, JHS no. 82.

48 SFUA, JHS no. 83.

49 Stevenson, 'Addiction in British Columbia,' 181.

50 John Turvey in Jo-Ann Canning-Dew, ed., *Hastings and Main: Stories from an Inner City Neighborhood* (Vancouver: New Star Books 1987), 151.

51 Stevenson, 'Addiction in British Columbia,' 158.

52 Willis, *Learning to Labor*.

53 Library and Archives Canada (LAC), RG 29, vol. 3345, file 329-M-391.

54 SFUA, JHS no. 13.

55 LAC, RG 29, vol. 3348, file 327-T-182.

56 Coutts, 'Social Structure of the Women's Unit at Oakalla,' 268.

57 *Proceedings of the Special Committee on the Traffic in Narcotic Drugs in Canada* (Ottawa, 1955), 414.

58 Lloyd G. Hanley, 'Functions of Argot among Heroin Addicts,' in W.E. Mann, *The Underside of Toronto* (Toronto: McClelland and Stewart 1970), 294–307.

59 Stevenson, 'Addiction in British Columbia,' 145.

60 Ibid.

61 British Columbia Report of Inspector of Goals, 1956–7: BB39.
62 SFUA, JHS no. 32.
63 SFUA, JHS no. 50.
64 SNAP was initiated in 1962.
65 Ben Maartman, *The Strange Thing about Miracles & Other Stories* (Errington, B.C.: Fogduckers Press 1990), 15. Maartman had previously worked at the John Howard Society.
66 This argument was first taken up by Kathy Peiss in *Cheap Amusements: Working Women and Leisure in New York City, 1880–1920* (Philadelphia: Temple University Press 1986). It was also made by George Chauncey in *Gay New York: Gender, Urban Culture, and the Making of the Gay Male World, 1890–1940* (New York: Basic Books 1994).

6 'Just Say Know': Criminalizing LSD and the Politics of Psychedelic Expertise, 1961–8[1]

ERIKA DYCK

In 1962 the Canadian public learned about the tragic consequences of taking Thalidomide while pregnant and the federal government responded after some deliberation by reclassifying the drug as a prohibited substance. During those debates, federal politicians and drug regulators also considered adding LSD to the list of prohibited substances, owing to its assumed potential for harm and abuse. Medical researchers familiar with LSD felt that the proposal to include LSD with Thalidomide was unprovoked and unwarranted. The association with Thalidomide particularly stung because published studies on LSD had shown promising results in clinical experiments in an era where thousands of drugs were being tested and marketed in North America without similar scrutiny, and now these two drugs were being singled out in an unprecedented new drug schedule. Canadian-based researchers Humphry Osmond and Abram Hoffer declared: 'It seems apt that there is now an outburst of resentment against some chemicals which can rapidly throw a man either into heaven or hell, and it appears to be as irrationally based as was the Victorian resistance to the use of anesthetics ... the less experience any person has with these drugs the more apt is he to utter profound yet meaningless statements about their so-called dangers.'[2]

These kinds of comments revealed a set of concerns that intensified over the next five years and came to characterize debates over the regulation of LSD in the 1960s. In the period between 1962 and 1966, LSD's legal status hinged on its appraisal by medical investigators, but by mid-decade damning public and police reports about the dangers associated with LSD use eroded any remaining medical authority on the subject and replaced it with the need for decisive political action. Hoffer and Osmond's assessment of first-hand, personal experience versus objective or clinical expertise became a defining feature of a debate over who claimed authority in a socio-cultural climate that embraced pharmaceuticals while abhorring narcotic abuses.

A number of contradictions emerged over the course of this intense and precedent-setting debate; some of the perspectives formed a familiar chorus, which had been heard before when considering the use of other substances that flirted with both therapeutic and recreational potential. Drugs such as opium, cocaine, and Miltown had been in this position in earlier years, and in these cases medical practitioners sometimes became entangled in an illicit drug trade as they performed roles as either gatekeepers or pushers.[3]

In the latter half of the 1960s, the medical authority over LSD wavered as politicians and parents entered discussions over the value of the drug, often from entrenched positions of opposition. As the anti-drug side gained momentum, triggered in part by the Thalidomide findings but fuelled by the growing popularity of non-medical LSD use, clinical researchers searched for ways to retain their authority over 'acid.'

By focusing on the personal papers of Canadian-based LSD researchers alongside debates in Parliament and the Senate over control of LSD, this chapter examines how various players jockeyed for control over the terms of LSD's regulation. Medical researchers with vested interests in studying LSD maintained that authority for assessing its value rested in experience with the drug, both personal and that acquired through direct-observation research. Those opposing LSD's continued use suggested that personal experience undermined one's judgment; rather, authority relied upon objectivity and, thus, distance from the drug itself. In other words, those who had direct experience with the drug could not make pronouncements about its inherent risks because they had already accepted these risks by virtue of their own consumption. This fundamental discrepancy over assigning expertise descended into a public debate over the risks involved in taking LSD; one side would later adopt the 'Just Say No' slogan to represent their intolerance towards drug use, while the other side preferred 'just say know' in an effort to promote informed consumption.

Controlling Access

In 1943 LSD (lysergic acid diethylamide), originally developed as a migraine medicine, became available for scientific research, freely and legally, from the Sandoz Pharmaceutical Company in Switzerland.[4] Thousands of clinical studies took place between 1950 and 1965, many of which involved the investigators themselves consuming the drug as part of the experimentation. One of the dominant theories regarding the clinical value of LSD relied on its capacity to provide mental-health practitioners with empathetic insights into the perceptions of their patients with schizophrenia. The drug, they believed, offered the user the opportunity to experience hallucinations, sensory distortions, paranoid delusions, and more generally an altered sense of reality. These insights became critical for biochemists who believed that further chemical investigation might help to identify the patho-physiology of schizophrenia. Others felt that an LSD experience should form part of the prerequisite training for mental-health workers, including psychiatrists, psychologists, social workers, and psychiatric nurses. In short, some optimistic clinical researchers hoped that LSD might cultivate clinical compassion for institutionalized people who had customarily been misunderstood in part because of their altered sense of reality.[5]

LSD also fit within the paradigmatic shift that was taking place in mid-century psychiatry that embraced pharmaco-therapies as a means of 'curing' and managing illness.[6] Hundreds of new drugs flooded the marketplace in the 1950s and, within that mix, LSD appeared unspectacular. In terms of its therapeutic applications, researchers tested its benefits for a wide range of ailments, from homosexuality to depression, and from compulsive disorders to addictions. It gained clinical ground throughout North America and parts of Europe for its use in treating alcoholics, who were given a massive dose which often produced a spiritual and/or intensely self-reflexive reaction that sometimes led to sustained periods of sobriety. The experience itself became the therapeutic modality, which distinguished LSD from contemporary medications that more often operated on the physiological level. By contrast, advocates of psychedelic interventions concentrated on the clinically monitored psychological experience as the locus of therapy.[7]

Several researchers whose work relied on safe access to LSD supplies looked to the drug's manufacturers for guidance on assessing the risks involved with their studies. Sandoz Pharmaceuticals in Switzerland was the main manufacturer and maintained national distribution branches around the world. In Canada, the local Sandoz distributor was located in Dorval, Quebec, and remained the sole LSD distributor in the country during this period. This company worked directly with medical researchers to provide the drug to bona fide medical investigators after a careful review of the applicant's qualifications and proposed research. Initially, this process proceeded without additional government surveillance, but by 1963 the Canadian government had introduced an additional measure that required researchers to apply for access through the federal health minister. The government thus tightened its grip on LSD regulation by clamping down on the distributors and medical researchers engaged in studying the drug.

The personal records of psychedelic drug investigators involved in the debate reveal their attempts to work simultaneously with distributors and policy makers to design regulations based on an intimate understanding of LSD. Psychiatrist Humphry Osmond expressed his frustration trying to maintain medical authority among the medico-scientific establishment while experimenting with the drug himself and sometimes seeking collaboration with non-medical people in an effort to better understand the drug's capacities. He therefore felt that he needed drug regulations that were flexible enough to incorporate non-medical perspectives and non-therapeutic trials into the research methodology. But, while Osmond appreciated input from literary figures such as Aldous Huxley and Gerald Heard that added to his collection of LSD narratives, he was also deeply suspicious of individuals who sought to profit from the drug, whether in pharmaceutical or spiritual exploits. He likewise corresponded with people such as Timothy Leary and Allen Ginsberg, and implored them to handle the drug responsibly rather than sully the potential for serious research in exchange for selfish personal gain. Although Osmond sympathized with some of the emerging cultural critiques expressed by the younger generation during the 1960s, he remained cautious and even somewhat elitist about who should be free to experiment with LSD.

As authorities tightened controls on the drug by closely monitoring medical experiments and the legal distributor, the black market in illicit drug production and abuse expanded after 1963. A number of scholars have drawn attention to how the criminalization of drugs drives illicit drug-taking activities deeper underground. This situation has frequently caused law-enforcement agencies to adjust their policing methods and develop special drug squads and undercover investigation units to identify the illicit subterranean networks. Part of this process has also traditionally involved targeting particular neighbourhoods and/or profiling particular racial and social characteristics based on cultural assumptions about drug use. For example, another contributor to this volume, Catherine Carstairs, has shown how police forces in Vancouver relied heavily on assumptions about Chinese males and their connections to opium smoking in an effort to control the opium trade. In spite of evidence showing opium use among whites, particularly those seeking opium for medically sanctioned pain relief, the focus of police efforts reinforced a racialized view of opium consumption.[8] A similar approach functioned in the case of LSD; as the legal channels of experimentation faced external scrutiny, the illegal channels flourished and shifted political and police attention to young Canadians.[9] Another feature of clandestine drug-seeking and drug-taking activities is an increased level of risk, whether in the form of physical harm, transgressions of the law, or the concealment of health hazards associated with the need to suppress drug consumption.[10] One of the consequences of concealed drug consumption, often out of fear of criminal conviction, has resulted in the inability of the health-care system to respond appropriately to the needs of the drug user. Drug policies have then had the unintended effect of hampering medical practitioners from providing many preventative services or lower-risk interventions because of the criminal consequences of detection. Even putting aside concerns of addiction, drug policies have often placed medical practitioners in a difficult position in terms of addressing the health risks associated with drug use.

From Experimental Drug to Narcotic

The political decision to reclassify LSD as a narcotic changed the context of medical authority. In the years leading up to this decision, which was ultimately finalized in 1968, government officials first concentrated on the relationship between the manufacturer and the medical community before seeking input from the Royal College of Physicians and Surgeons about whether or not the experiments themselves carried any medicinal value. At that point, the policy debates centred around questions of utility, in terms of clinical benefits of the drug and whether that potential might outweigh broader harms to the public. Regulation and control focused on limiting the independent distribution powers of Sandoz Canada and trusting the medical profession in its capacity to determine the health benefits and risks of new drugs. In fact, government officials felt the state had an obligation to protect the medical community and help shield its authority in this arena.

Although this approach held sway when LSD emerged in the political debates in 1962 alongside Thalidomide, the next few years brought very different circumstances. In 1966, when discussions over reclassification emerged again, a black market in LSD was undeniable; figures such as Timothy Leary made public appearances urging people to 'turn on' by taking LSD; television and newspaper reports publicized information about the drug, which many authorities felt titillated audiences; and the medical community began displaying internal divisions over the therapeutic use of these psychedelic substances. The terms of regulation and control changed significantly in this altered context and required new rules of engagement.

One distinguishing feature of LSD that separated it from other recreationally used and abused substances in the 1960s, including drugs such as marijuana, amphetamines, and heroin, was the effect itself. LSD allegedly caused consumers to experience a profound psychological experience, and one that did not produce addiction according to contemporary clinical reports. Many investigators puzzled over the way to explain the experience, which many felt was indescribable; indeed, researchers looked for opportunities to collaborate with artists and writers in an effort to describe LSD's effects. Osmond, who coined the term 'psychedelic' in 1957 to define the sensation of the LSD experience, maintained that the reaction had 'mind-manifesting' qualities, while others insisted that LSD experience was primarily spiritual and still others felt that LSD affected one's deep sense of being, or ontological perspective. A 1959 report by psychologist Duncan Blewett and psychiatrist Nick Chwelos catalogued the most commonly reported reactions and recorded them in a *Handbook for the Therapeutic Use of LSD*:

1. A feeling of being at one with the Universe.
2. Experience of being able to see oneself objectively or a feeling that one has two identities.
3. Change in usual concept of self with concomitant change in perceived body.
4. Changes in perception of space and time.
5. Enhancement in the sensory fields.
6. Changes in thinking and understanding so the subject feels he develops a profound understanding in the field of philosophy or religion.
7. A wider range of emotions with rapid fluctuation.
8. Increased sensitivity to the feelings of others.
9. Psychotic changes – these include illusions, hallucinations, paranoid delusions of reference, influence, persecution and grandeur,

thought disorder, perceptual distortion, severe anxiety and others which have been described in many reports.[11]

The complicated nature of the experience encouraged clinical investigators in the 1950s to focus especially on the application of this drug to psychotherapy because of its capacity to affect thinking and feeling, but throughout this period they remained reluctant to limit its research potential, with the result that it stayed in an experimental category.[12] The experience, however, also later appealed to people outside the medical setting, which alarmed authorities and drew attention to the need to develop laws constraining its non-medical use.

Several medical investigators were intrigued by the drug's effects and developed protocols for experimentation both for self-discovery and for therapeutic potential. While some clinical researchers felt that this kind of inquiry suited the contemporary focus on pharmacology, others felt that LSD, with its hallucinogenic and 'psychedelic' properties, had no inherent medical value. Clinical attitudes towards the drug revealed deeper attitudes about the nature of drug research, but, during the first phase of the debate, members of the medical community nonetheless agreed that this issue belonged within the parameters of medicine and science.

By 1962, when the subject of reclassifying LSD first arose alongside discussions over the regulation of Thalidomide, LSD had been more or less confined to the clinical context.[13] In December of that year the Canadian federal government introduced legislation to amend the Food and Drugs Act, which would place LSD and Thalidomide on Schedule H, making it a prohibited substance. This move would ban the distribution, preparation, manufacture, preservation, packaging, labelling, storing, and testing of these drugs.[14] The second reading of the Bill (C-3) began with a lengthy report from the minister of national health and welfare, J.W. Monteith, who, after explaining the Thalidomide issue, turned his attention to LSD. He expressed the need for caution, stating that 'it would not be proper to remove a drug from medical availability except in the most extraordinary circumstances ... we would wish to have the advice of the most competent authorities.'[15] He then drew attention to the clinical optimism surrounding LSD experimentation, and suggested that perhaps the drug should remain available, under controlled circumstances, for further medical investigation. After all, he added: 'In the course of nearly 11 years, some 2,000 new drugs have passed through the screen of our new drug regulations and have been placed on the market in Canada with great benefit to Canadians.'[16] He concluded by recommending that Canada look to the Royal College of Physicians and Surgeons in Canada and to regulation practices in the United States for guidance on handling new drugs.

In the discussion that arose in the House of Commons after the minister's speech, members were unusually supportive. H.C. Harley, MP for Halton, described in detail the kinds of medical studies that currently used LSD to great benefit, then criticized the health minister for singling out LSD: 'We all read in the newspapers about people taking what are referred to as "goof balls" [barbituates] ... one of the common drugs on the market ... the minister has not suggested that we take barbiturates off the market; therefore I think we should be very careful, when we do take drugs off the market, to leave some method open by which they are still available for worth-while and experimental purposes.'[17] Guy Marcoux, MP for Quebec-Montgomery, used this discussion as an opportunity to display his ideological distaste for state control and instead emphasized the need to rely on medical authorities to make decisions regarding the safety of new drugs.[18]

David Orlikow, MP for Winnipeg North (whose wife, Val, would later be treated with LSD for post-partum depression by Montreal-based psychiatrist Ewen Cameron), weighed into the debate with a plea to identify the right kind of clinical experts: 'responsible, objective and conscientious authorities.'[19] He worried about the corrupting influence of drug companies and implored the government to help provide protection for prescribing doctors. As the discussion continued, this point received further elaboration: 'If a doctor, pharmacist or other person named in selling, dispensing or disposing of a prohibited drug, then there is power for the inspectors to move in and to take that drug but that, if it is merely a case of possession, there is no authority at the present time.'[20] Another MP, Stanley Knowles, commended the government on its decision to delay the final reading of the bill until receiving a report from the Royal College of Physicians and Surgeons. 'I recognize the fact that it is standard procedure for the government to ask parliament to give to the government the power to make regulations ... usually this is done because we know nothing of what is in the government's mind ... in this particular case, the government itself does not know what is in its mind.'[21]

The tenor of this debate in 1962–3 concentrated on how to control the distribution of a substance that might have harmful effects by working closely and cooperatively with the medical community. The case with

Thalidomide involved allegations from angry parents, and precedents set in other national jurisdictions; the need for the government to protect the public on this issue emerged clearly. But the inclusion of LSD in this bill did not immediately generate a consensus in the House of Commons. As several members recognized, LSD's potential for danger was known by the medical profession, but there was still significant optimism surrounding its potential therapeutic benefits. And, even if the drug remained available to researchers in the clinical setting for experimental purposes, the new legislation would restrict its application as a therapy. The divisions over this subject, in combination with the report from the Royal Commission of Physicians and Surgeons, resulted in an amendment to the legislation that permitted the continued clinical use of LSD.

Abram Hoffer, a psychiatrist working in Saskatoon, and one of Canada's leading researchers on LSD, complained that the proposed legislation threatened to undermine professional medical authority. In a letter to his colleague, Humphry Osmond, he spelled out his critique: 'I agree that questions of safety and toxicity should be rigorously controlled, but I believe the question of efficacy should be left entirely in the hands of the medical profession who are competent to judge whether their inpatients are improving. The new act restricts drug trials to qualified investigators, but there is no definition of who is a qualified investigator.'[22] In spite of the government's desire for input from such practitioners, some, like Hoffer, felt constrained.

The medical community defended its prerogative to determine the value of new drugs. In spite of the degree of uncertainty about LSD's effects, the majority of research articles in mainstream medical journals pointed to the clinical benefits, particularly those arising from the alcoholism trials.[23] Hans Lehmann, one of the primary advocates of chlorpromazine (an anti-psychotic medication) and one of Canada's leading psychopharmacologists, published a review of new drugs in psychiatry where he included LSD: 'This type of drug is used mainly for experimental purposes, in the study of phenomena of artificially produced mental disorders and to investigate the accompanying physiological processes. However, in certain carefully selected cases, an experienced psychiatrist also may make therapeutic use of these drugs.'[24] The absence of negative results in published medical reports and reassurances from leading psychopharmacologists in the field meant that the medical community's position seemed unified and credible.

Reports outside Canada matched these perspectives. In 1960 Sidney

Cohen, a psychiatrist at the Wadsworth Veterans Administration Hospital in Los Angeles and an adjunct professor of medicine at the University of California, Los Angeles School of Medicine, conducted a thorough investigation of the medical literature on LSD and surveyed research units in North America experimenting with the drug.[25] Through his own experiences, Cohen had grown increasingly concerned by the feeling of emptiness, loneliness, and sometimes despair reported to him by his LSD subjects after the trials. He published the results of his survey in the *Journal of Nervous and Mental Disease*. His report covered over twenty-five thousand experiences (volunteers and patients) with either mescaline or LSD. Based on the responses he received and the literature available, Cohen concluded that no published medical article or questionnaire respondent encountered harmful physical side effects from small doses of LSD. Larger doses, it seemed, produced more variable results, including intense paranoid thinking and acting out. Adverse reactions also occurred among neglected subjects, where investigators refused to interact with the subject or when the subject engaged in self-experimentation alone. Cohen's study identified the occurrence of negative reactions under certain circumstances, but overall it concluded that the drug was relatively safe.[26]

The medical consensus on LSD, prior to the Thalidomide controversy, seemed to accept its role in a variety of experimental and therapeutic contexts, leaving discretion to the medical community over its applications. Its identification as a potentially dangerous drug, alongside Thalidomide, in 1962 seemed out of step with these sentiments. Thalidomide, in comparison, was known by 1962 to cause severe birth defects and spontaneous abortions. Medical reports substantiated a more benign view of LSD and even upheld the right of the medical community to determine the risk calculus when assessing future drugs. Ultimately, the government relaxed pressure on the medical community and instead tightened the grip on the manufacturers and distributors of LSD.

Acid in the Streets

When local and national media reported on LSD, they often drew upon information supplied by medical reports. The drug was routinely introduced to the public as a new psycho-active substance with clinical potential, but by 1963 this situation had begun to change.[27] Within a year, new players began influencing the public discourse on LSD.

In particular, self-proclaimed gurus such as Timothy Leary and Allen Ginsberg made regular public appearances encouraging drug use. A black market in psychedelics developed at the same time, putting pressure on Sandoz and the medical community to identify the leak in the system. LSD, or 'acid,' as it increasingly was known, became a popular recreational drug and its growing abuse exposed a number of severe health risks that had not been encountered in the clinical environment. Newspapers and television programs frequently reported dramatic consequences associated with LSD use, including blindness, violence (including homicidal and suicidal behaviour), depression, recklessness, and even insanity. The medical community was unprepared for these kinds of reactions and struggled to maintain its authority in the face of the growing alarm of parents, police, and government officials, who collectively looked for someone to blame for introducing this drug to young Canadians.

In April 1963 the Psychology Department at Harvard University fired Timothy Leary for his 'unscientific' studies with psilocybin and LSD and for failing to fulfil his academic duties.[28] The news of Leary's dismissal spread across North America and raised concerns about the kinds of mind-experiments taking place at premier research institutions. For Leary, however, losing his position at Harvard merely catapulted him into the public spotlight where he struggled to remain for most of the rest of his life. Maintaining a vast network of friends and wives, Leary charismatically captured the spirit of the counterculture with his vocal liberalism and his insatiable appetite for cultivating inner freedom through drugs. Collaborating with many American cultural icons of the period – Allen Ginsberg, Aldous Huxley, Michael Hollingshead, Jerry Garcia, Richard Alpert (Ram Dass), Ken Kesey, Eldridge Cleaver, the Weathermen, and a host of others – Leary promoted LSD use with perhaps an unrivalled amount of cultural capital. His status as a psychologist confused some and outraged others since his convictions conveyed the appearance of professional currency. Although Leary's antics did not reach their peak until the end of the 1960s, his influence on the public discourse surrounding LSD use was profound.

Whether coincidentally or not, the same year that Leary lost his position at Harvard University, police units in Canada and the United States identified a black market in LSD.[29] Police also seized other kinds of hallucinogens, such as morning glory seeds, which caused effects that resembled those of LSD. American psychiatrists and the Food and Drug Administration found a number of hallucinogens being used

recreationally, including ololiqui and lysergic acid.[30] While the medical reports on the LSD experiments continued to stress positive results,
the emergence of a black market in hallucinogens put pressure on the
medical community, Sandoz, and the government to keep strict controls on these substances. Other hallucinogens were likely being manufactured illegally, or at least obtained illegally, but LSD had only one
legal manufacturer in Canada and therefore its use outside the clinic
raised concerns among LSD researchers.

Anticipating external scrutiny, Humphry Osmond contacted his
psychedelic colleagues and LSD's chief manufacturer and distributor,
Sandoz. Although they could not entirely rule out the possibility that
Sandoz-produced LSD was leaking into a black market from medical laboratories, Osmond felt that the medical community was not to
blame.[31] Albert Hofmann of Sandoz agreed with Osmond. His labs
had determined that approximately fifty other psychologically active
substances closely resembled LSD, and he suspected that many of
these other substances circulated in the black market, being pedalled
as acid.[32] It was quite possible that a black market in hallucinogens
existed and that in this context 'LSD' or 'acid' had become a generic
label describing psycho-active substances that caused hallucinations.
Osmond implored his medical colleagues, and psychedelic researchers
in particular, to cooperate with the legal authorities in order to avoid
fuelling the misconception that medical lysergic acid was circulating in
a subterranean drug economy.

Naturally, the government first looked to Sandoz and psychedelic
researchers to provide an explanation for the non-medical access to
LSD. Although Sandoz was under strict legal orders to distribute LSD
only to qualified, licensed medical practitioners for clinical purposes,
other manufacturers had tried to gain a share of the clinical market.
Al Hubbard, an investigator working at Hollywood Hospital in New
Westminster, British Columbia, admitted that he had actively sought
alternative supplies.[33] He leaned on his fellow investigators throughout
North America to share their stores, but he also identified rival companies that were attempting to create their own versions of LSD. In 1959 he
had found a biochemist who agreed to make LSD for him. He wrote to
Hoffer, his colleague in Saskatoon, stating, 'He [the unnamed biochem-
ist], of course, did secure some from Sandos [sic], and then worked out
a system for making it. He is not like the Los Angeles group, however,
and is not in it for the money, but does supply it to competent right
motivated researchers who cannot get it from Sandos.'[34] He later found

another such source in Seattle, and then another in England, both of which sold LSD (unlike Sandoz, which made it available to researchers for free, so long as researchers met all of the licensing and registration requirements).[35]

Not all of Sandoz's competitors generated a stable product. Hoffer wrote to Hubbard in 1958, stating : 'I have just discovered a new source of LSD and it is Lights Organic Chemicals, Poyle Trading Estate, Colenbrook, Buchs, England. The price is about 35 cents per ampoule.'[36] But, after comparing this new product with a Sandoz sample, Hoffer found the new version inferior. With concern over liability, Hubbard agreed to return the supplies, telling Hoffer that 'if there is any doubt about it at all we have too much at stake to risk tampering with it.'[37] The proliferation of competitors raised suspicions about the quality and quantities of LSD available to researchers, not to mention the question of access to the drug for non-medical investigations and the legal nature of these distribution networks.

The growing availability of LSD, ostensibly for medical purposes, gave governments good reason to worry about its capacity to maintain legal control over its distribution. Hubbard, who did not himself have medical qualifications, confided to Hoffer that he had actually obtained LSD from several other different suppliers over the years, including biochemists at the University of British Columbia and the Delta Chemical Company in New York, and he knew of several others who made their own LSD or mescaline though he remained wary of some of these sources, which he felt provided inferior products. Hubbard also admitted that he had passed on supplies to a number of others, including 'various students' at the University of British Columbia and the General Hospital in Vancouver.[38]

Sandoz soon grew concerned that it was being blamed for contributing to the proliferation of lysergic acid and other hallucinogens. In 1962, in an effort to cooperate with authorities, Sandoz, after responding to a request from the Canadian government, temporarily withdrew LSD from the market to prove that its supplies were not the only ones in circulation.[39] Four years later, the American branches followed this move, claiming that the unforeseen development of a black market in LSD in combination with unanticipated negative physiological effects had encouraged the company to abandon this line of research altogether.[40]

The issue intensified and demanded legal attention when the American government identified more users, and as it traced traffickers into Canada. In 1965 two Canadians were indicted for smuggling LSD into the United States in sugar cubes. A federal investigation revealed that 'its manufacture is apparently not difficult ... because the formula is known and the chemicals are available.'[41] According to instructions later published in *The Anarchist's Cookbook*, acid could be made at home after obtaining morning glory seeds or baby Hawaiian wood rose seeds.[42] Given the accessibility of these instructions and the apparent ease of concoction, homemade versions of acid became available, with an alarming capacity to evade detection.

Osmond was deeply concerned about the status of LSD, and he used his personal connections with psychedelic experts, and his qualifications as an internationally renowned researcher, to implore policy makers to find a reasonable way to control this substance. He deplored the growth of an underground market in LSD and felt that such a development would prove lethal for the continued, legal use of the drug. In part, he blamed Timothy Leary's approach to popularizing psychedelics. Writing to Hofmann in 1966, Osmond complained that he felt that Leary was attempting to create some kind of community tied together culturally by its use of LSD. 'The problem [for Leary] which seemed most tricky was getting sufficient supplies of lsd 25 and you [Albert Hofmann] were of the opinion then that smuggling or an underworld connection was likely, or possibly a leak from a supplier. This has never satisfied me ... because it would be a weakness in the maguis supply line that could be damaging, even fatal.'[43] He continued by stressing that he had been 'extremely careful not to acquire illegal lsd 25.'[44]

Osmond felt that clinical researchers would bear the brunt of blame in this situation if medical authorities did not stand up to Leary and support the legal restrictions on LSD use. After spending an evening with Leary, Osmond wrote to Hofmann and expressed his frustration with Leary's cavalier attitude:

His [Leary's] viewpoint was much against us medical men and he made his case well and clearly ... what he is saying is that he aims at producing a situation where it is *moral* among young (under 25) people to take lsd25 etc, in defiance of their elders and immoral not to do so ... I do not find the authorities' actions appealing and I doubt whether they have really grasped the nature of the problem. If a guerilla war of this kind might develop I would do all I can to prevent so destructive an intergenerational conflict ... However, you and I are in a rather unusual position because, in a way we are responsible for the fact that the fight developed, our legitimate and well intentioned efforts produced Timothy's crusade and hence the vigorous response to it.[45]

Osmond was not alone in this battle, but the growing availability of the drug, in combination with an explosion of publicity about the non-medical use and abuse of LSD, made it difficult for him and his fellow psychedelic investigators to maintain credibility. While he blamed Leary for recklessly promoting the recreational use of psychedelics, he also sympathized with the desire to experiment with LSD, especially for people seeking an experience that could be both humbling and insightful. In an effort to try to understand the perspectives of the young, illegal users, Osmond met with a self-identified drug dealer. The young chemistry student, as it turned out, claimed to have made twenty or thirty different hallucinogens, including LSD. He told Osmond that he wanted to promote psychedelic use 'to change society for the better and to save mankind from the danger of the bomb and from the dangers of a mechanistic and inhuman conformism.'[46] He did not seek remuneration for the distribution of his drugs, and believed that the authorities would not be able to penetrate effectively their underground circulation. Osmond assessed the drug dealer as 'an ethical man who wishes to better society by molding it to his particular notions.'[47] Although Osmond confronted the young man with the inherent immorality of his actions, he sympathized with his philosophical and political objectives.

Believing that psychedelics had some potential for stimulating political action, Osmond nonetheless remained uncomfortable with the notion of illegal and unregulated use. His own political views and his open attitude towards radicalism led him to sympathize with some of the recreational drug users' aims. 'The huge power of these substances,' he claimed, 'in a semi-political movement would arise from the commonality of the experience which they can impart – the sense of sharing similar worlds and goals and of being part of a larger whole in a way in which no amount of meetings can do.'[48] He agreed, in part, with the drug dealer's position that, since the government could not control these substances, they should concentrate on their production to ensure that only good drugs were available and that profit-seekers did not control the trade with inferior products. The meeting, although instructive, left Osmond deeply concerned about the likelihood of designing an effective strategy for controlling the distribution of LSD and minimizing the risks associated with its recreational use.

Osmond forwarded his own recommendations for regulating LSD

to the chief of psychopharmacology at the American National Institute of Health, Jonathan Cole. After acknowledging that psychologically active substances circulated in the black market, he recommended that the Food and Drug Administration employ psychedelic experts to test the alleged LSD supplies. He felt strongly that the widespread suspicion that LSD proliferated in these underground channels had led to a lack of scientific research on the topic, when in fact policy makers required such studies in order to propose suitable legislation. To that end, he recommended obtaining samples from the black market to test in three independent labs. His main concerns stemmed from his fear that the chemistry students and illicit drug dealers were gaining the upper hand on the experts in terms of the kinds of substances in circulation. He concluded his letter, pleading this point: 'The gifted amateurs have been moving ahead at a rather alarming rate. It is not, from all reports, that the substances seem to be particularly harmful, they don't seem to be any worse than LSD; but to me the really serious thing is that if we fall technically far behind the amateurs, they will take absolutely no notice of us for we shall have lost any expertness in their eyes.'[49]

He also appealed to Senator Robert Kennedy, whom he viewed as a progressive, young American leader. In his letter, written in May 1966, Osmond carefully distinguished the importance of continuing clinical psychedelic research from the pressing need to curb the dangers associated with the unregulated production and distribution of psychedelic-like substances. He urged Kennedy to consider the essential contributions of medical experts in determining the most sustainable resolution to the drug panic. In the case of LSD, Osmond explained, the real medical experts were practitioners with personal experiences; those without these critical insights seemed more susceptible to the public's alarmist views.[50] The crux of the problem, according to Osmond, concerned the proliferation of allegedly hallucinogenic substances in the black market. Legislative measures targeting LSD, therefore, missed the central issue and unnecessarily constrained legitimate research.[51]

By the mid 1960s, Osmond felt that legislators had developed their own mechanisms for producing risk assessments, and that they were about to make a decision on this issue without sufficient input from the medical community, particularly those clinical researchers who had real experiences with LSD. The problem, he contended, was not that medical experimenters freely distributed psychedelics, but rather that

growing pressure on researchers curtailed legitimate studies and incapacitated professionals from analysing the real dangers of black-mar-
ket substances. The inadequate findings indicated that neither medical
authorities nor consumers really had any way of determining what
combination of substances constituted an illicit dose of acid.

LSD and the Counterculture

By the spring of 1966, LSD had acquired a reputation for infecting
young minds with anti-authority attitudes and for causing physiological damage to users. At that time, the drug remained legal throughout North America if taken under the direction of medical authorities,
but its status quickly changed as regulators questioned the integrity of
psychedelic investigators and as those investigators grew suspicious
about the intentions of their colleagues.[52] Popular publications concerning LSD abuse proliferated, while medical authorities who strongly believed in the healing properties of psychedelics searched for
allies and looked to distance themselves from others who, they felt,
were behaving irresponsibly. Timothy Leary resurfaced in the public
at this time, tarnished (or validated) by his multiple arrests for marijuana possession, and, for some, assumed a martyr position as an LSD
apostle, poised to shepherd a new generation towards inner freedom
through psychedelics. Leary had long since abandoned the discipline
of psychology after being fired from his post at Harvard University
and now sought media attention as a cultural icon and a psychedelic
guru.

The number of news reports on LSD in the *New York Times* jumped
from five in 1965 to over five hundred in 1966. There was a comparatively lower rate of increase in the *Globe and Mail*, but its editors altered
the tone of the articles on LSD dramatically.[53] The content of articles in
the Canadian press as a whole shifted from the earlier focus on LSD in
medical research to a growing sense of alarm over recreational LSD use
and its health risks. The stories about LSD moved to the front pages
and opened with striking headlines presenting the frightening consequences of abusing this drug. Purported evidence of its dangers included descriptions of subjects who experienced extended psychotic states
or committed murder and suicide or engaged in various sorts of risky
behaviour, including promiscuous sexual activities, vandalism, theft,
and experimentation with harder drugs, such as heroin and cocaine.
Reports also indicated that LSD use led to political dissent and inhibit-

ed interest in economics, politics, and the law.[54] The sensational reports about LSD reinforced the idea that it was responsible for a whole range of activities that threatened social order. These kinds of headlines eroded the image of medical and political control over LSD consumption and instead highlighted the chaotic consequences of a non-compliant generation of drug abusers. The increased publicity and news of health risks forced policy makers to open a new discussion about the regulation of new drugs.

In the spring of 1966, another debate over the control of LSD was held in Parliament. Member of Parliament Frank Howard initiated the discussion and requested a statement from the government on how it planned to address the issue: 'What steps are being taken to detect the possession of this drug [LSD], to prevent its further dissemination and to prevent trafficking in it?'[55] A few days later, Allan MacEachen, minister of national health and welfare, presented his statement, in which he explained that the drug continued to be available on an investigational basis:

> In 1963 the sale and distribution of this drug was prohibited except for the small quantities provided by the manufacturer of the drug to institutions approved by the minister for clinical investigations and research ... there is only one manufacturer of this drug in Canada, and there has been no suggestion that any of the supplies of this drug which have appeared in the illicit underworld market are connected in any way with this company. It appears that LSD is being smuggled into Canada for illegal sale. In prohibiting the sale of the drug except under the conditions I have mentioned, there was not at that time any thought that the drug would lend itself to illicit trafficking. Developments, however, in recent months have unfortunately shown a growing interest in the drug by persons not under medical care. The hallucinogenic effects of this drug have received wide publicity, giving the impression that such effects are intensely pleasurable and not in any way harmful to the individual. This is not so ...
>
> The RCMP, who are concerned with this problem, are doing their best to eliminate illicit supplies and we have under consideration, in consultation with that force, special measures which will permit more effective control of LSD than is possible under existing legislation.[56]

MacEachen's statement summarized the situation concerning LSD, including its growing recreational appeal and the identification of an illicit trade, but he avoided blaming either Sandoz or the medical community by suggesting that LSD had been brought into Canada by illegal means. He left the impression that the problem could be controlled through legislative measures that isolated the production and dissemination of the drug. His analysis suggested a profound misreading of the situation.

Nonetheless, MacEachen's assurances worked to placate the growing alarm, at least in the House of Commons, for the time being. One member commended MacEachen for his management of the problem, and added: 'The RCMP are endeavouring to prohibit the smuggling of LSD into Canada, and I think the control of its production under one manufacturer does give complete control through all legal channels.'[57] But, as others pointed out, the legal manufacture and distribution of the drug was not the most pressing concern: 'The real danger of this drug lies not in the control of its lawful manufacture and importation but the ease with which it can be made by amateurs and made available to younger people for the production of kicks. It is ignorance of this kind in younger people that produces the actual danger.'[58] Combating this rather elusive threat, MP William Dean Howe recommended a coordinated public-education campaign as the most effective strategy for minimizing harms caused by the non-medical consumption of LSD. At this point in the debate, legislators continued to shield the medical community and frequently referred to the benefits of clinical investigations with LSD, but separated its legal use from its illegal use in terms of consumers, producers, and associated health risks.

Meanwhile, publicity about LSD intensified. Policy makers regularly referred to the media's influence as a significant factor in the escalation of interest in LSD. One MP complained that the Canadian government was slow to realize the 'immense amount of power it has distributed to the producers [of the CBC] to shape Canadian public opinion.' He went on to show how this power had been used to provide an unbalanced account of the LSD issue in a one-hour documentary aired in English and French, 'which did nothing to solve the problem created by this drug in Canada. In fact, it probably aggravated the situation.'[59] Members debated the merits of the television programs on LSD and worried that even ones that exposed the dangers of taking the drug titillated viewers.

Others found direct media evidence that encouraged drug use: 'It [*The Sheaf*, the University of Saskatchewan student newspaper] advertises a series of long playing records by Dr. Timothy Leary who has been something of a high priest to the cult built round the use of LSD.'[60]

Later in the same speech, MP Howard Johnston drew attention to a *Globe and Mail* article discussing the appearance of Allen Ginsberg on a CBC program: 'The headline says, "Ginsberg Asks LSD For All." The individual mentioned has come to Canada and has been given a tremendous amount of free publicity. I suspect he was even paid for his services to CBC.'[61] A few months later, opposition leader John Diefenbaker raised a similar point: 'My question has to do with a program on CTV called "W5" which has to do with marijuana and LSD and could not but have the effect of encouraging experimentation by young men and women across Canada.'[62] The increasing publicity, and especially that which did not explicitly condemn the use of the drug, alarmed policy makers and gave rise to the need for tighter regulations.

By the spring of 1967, the non-medical use of LSD in Canada reached alarming proportions, and news of personal tragedies associated with its use prompted policy makers to change its legal status. Diefenbaker spelled out his recommendation to reclassify LSD as a prohibited substance and place it under the Narcotic Control Act. The proposal, introduced as Bill S-60, was considered by a cabinet committee, while the solicitor general worked with the RCMP to apprehend individuals who appeared on television and admitted to having tried LSD.[63]

At this point, the Senate joined the discussions and considered the implications of sending young Canadians to jail if LSD was reclassified as a narcotic. Some senators felt that people who took LSD were likely 'sick' and therefore required medical help, not criminal sentences; others believed that it was 'a crime to send a person that young to jail unless the person [was] a bona fide criminal.' The terms 'sick' and 'criminal' were not defined.[64] One senator maintained that 'he has sons and daughters of his own and he regards this as such a terrible thing that he may send the accused to the penitentiary.'[65] This statement provoked further discussion as senators considered the consequences of sending university students to jail, and perhaps their own children. After some deliberation, the senators agreed that the regulation should be amended to include options for medical and psychiatric treatment instead of jail time, thus reinforcing the middle-class character of the problem.

Particularly troubling to the senators was the 'sensational and ghoulish character' of certain CBC television broadcasts and magazines.[66] Outlets such as CBC, CTV, *Life Magazine*, and the University of Toronto, which hosted a psychedelic festival in 1967, outraged many senators, who felt that such publicity confused young Canadians and encouraged them to try LSD: 'It has become fashionable in the press and on television to glamorize the life of an LSD addict as one of leisure and as the ideal life to follow.'[67] For these reasons, the penalties for use, they felt, should not be severe because the youth consumers were likely naive: 'There are tens of thousands of these young people using this drug who really are doing so with innocent intentions.'[68] Others did not share the need to protect the youth: 'These beatniks in the Yorkville area ... have this haunted, goofy look. They seem almost to be depraved, and one thing they have in common: to look at them you cannot tell who is a man and who is a woman.'[69] The lively Senate debate focused primarily on the need to alter the public discourse on LSD by clamping down on irresponsible journalists. The participants displayed some sympathy for the young, naive users, but none for a medical community that had failed to forecast these problems. The debate in the House of Commons echoed these themes, blaming the media and searching for a legislative solution that minimized the dangers to young Canadians, with limited regard for the continuation of medical research with LSD.

During the second reading of Bill S-60, senators agreed that they had consulted sufficient medical and legal information to reach a consensus. There was agreement among the experts that the dangers of the drug outweighed its benefits and that 'stricter controls to this dangerous, indeed ghastly, drug' would help to curb the risks to the public.[70] Based on these external reports, the senators stressed that 'practically without exception the drug is declared to be dangerous and, in fact, a terrible menace, especially in the case of young people seeking thrills.'[71]

As this bill went through another round of revisions in the spring of 1967, Senator Hartland de M. Molson, from the Molson Brewing family, weighed into the discussions. At that time he was the chairman of the Standing Committee on Banking and Commerce and he introduced a further set of restrictions surrounding the potential for trafficking. In his statement to his fellow senators, he suggested that 'in addition to the evils of trafficking in these substances and the damage of using them, there was another feature which in the course of amending this bill it would be wise to incorporate, namely that of dealing with the matter of promotion of the use of or trafficking in these drugs.'[72] The senator with the closest ties to the alcohol and brewing industry squarely targeted the issue of distribution and promotion of any substance that might fall into this category of restricted substances.

In 1968 Bill S-60 was passed, but, rather than placing LSD under the

Narcotic Control Act, which would essentially criminalize all users of the drug, it consigned LSD to a special category of the Food and Drugs Act, alongside a list of restricted substances, including N-diethyltryp-tamine (DET), N-Dimethyltryptamine (DMT), and methyl-deimeth-oxyamphetamine (STP, MDMA).[73] The move effectively restricted the use of LSD by putting it in a category with other psychotropic sub-stances that fell into the grey area between potentially therapeutic and potentially recreational. The decision was in keeping with international trends, which stressed the need to establish much stricter controls on the regulation of these psych-active substances.

The medical community had failed to reach a consensus on the thera-peutic benefits of LSD and advocates of psychedelic research blamed journalists for irresponsible reporting and further chastised the gov-ernment for responding to the media rather than listening to psych-edelic experts. In the parliamentary debates over the legal status of the drug that occurred in 1966 and again in 1967–8, reactions often centred around the publicity, without paying sufficient attention to the actual medical literature, in spite of claims to the contrary. Several psychedelic investigators abandoned their LSD studies during this period, citing negative publicity as a major reason for that decision. Indirectly, they felt, the sensational media coverage caused friction with colleagues who increasingly believed that psychedelic research was unscientific; it made obtaining grants more difficult; and volunteer subjects had almost invariably heard about the drug and signed up for trials seeking a euphoric experience.[74] Although the published, peer-reviewed medi-cal literature on LSD at the end of the 1960s supported the need for continued investigations, in light of the publicity and cultural reaction, even dedicated psychedelic researchers could not sustain their cred-ibility. Some, like Osmond, believed that eventually the moral furore would dissipate and LSD could become the subject of medico-scientific inquiry again.[75]

Conclusion

For over forty years the legal status of LSD remained firm, but medical researchers in 2007 began revisiting the relationship between scientific expertise, based on medical evidence, and drug regulations. A group of scientists in the United Kingdom published in *The Lancet*, a lead-ing international scientific journal, the results of an investigation into the use of evidence for informing drug policies. Focusing particularly on the assessment of harm that informs the drug-classification system, they concluded that 'the current classification system has evolved in an unsystematic way from somewhat arbitrary foundations with seemingly little scientific basis.'[76] By defining harm as a composite of factors including intoxication, damage to family and social life, and costs to society in terms of health care, social care, and policing, the group of over seventy experts who contributed to the study agreed that alcohol and tobacco are much more harmful than drugs currently ranked in categories that carry more extreme legal penalties for their use.[77] Their study revealed a considerable degree of consensus among medical and scientific researchers concerning the social harms of these drugs. Surmising that the lobbying efforts of the tobacco and alcohol industries undoubtedly played a role in the drafting and passage of the Misuse of Drugs Act in Britain, the authors contended that the absence of medical scientists in policy discussions has led to a framework of penal regulation that is no longer based on scientific evidence.

The regulation of drug use, they maintain, is rather arbitrary and lacks a scientific foundation; this situation is especially true for psychedelic drugs. Drugs such as LSD and Ecstasy (MDMA), according to these investigations, have been placed in the highest risk categories without sufficient evidence to indicate that they cause sufficient harm to necessitate such a ranking. Conversely, alcohol and tobacco remain in lower harm categories while this scientifically evaluated harm study ranked them much higher, fifth and ninth respectively.[78] These findings illustrate the enduring disjuncture between political and scientific pronouncements of risk.

LSD has reappeared in medical investigations since 2005, but questions abound as to whether the drug can be controlled and by whom. During the 1960s, the growth of a black market in psychedelics in combination with a degree of cultural liberalism towards drug use stymied policy makers, police, and clinicians in their capacity as authorities charged with controlling drug abuse. Since then, a concerted public-education campaign and an American-originated 'war on drugs' has provided North Americans, especially young men and women, with a clear message about the dangers of abusing drugs. The 'Just Say No' campaign, which developed in the 1980s, grew out of the legacy of political decisions made in the 1960s and 1970s, which increasingly focused the decisions around matters of public policy rather than on medical input or scientific studies of health risks. And, as the 2007 *Lancet* study indicates, commercial interests have significantly crept into the equation, justifying the continued legal status of substances such as alcohol and tobacco.

In the 1960s Humphry Osmond recommended a pragmatic approach to decisions about drug regulation, one that relied on political, cultural, *and* medical knowledge; in his mind, by *knowing* the risks and benefits of drugs, politicians, doctors, and users could fashion the best way of ensuring control and compliance. Today, physicians who are familiar with the kinds of illicit drugs available are better equipped to address the health complications of users. With another batch of psychedelic investigations on the horizon, it is worth reviewing the story of LSD in the 1960s for a better understanding of the challenges to authorities that such drugs represent.

NOTES

1 I am grateful to Ed Montigny and my fellow contributors who provided valuable feedback on this chapter and to Patrick Farrell for his research assistance.
2 Saskatchewan Archives Board (hereafter SAB), A207, box 37, 233-A, 'LSD' report from Hoffer and Osmond, c. 1962, 1–2.
3 Examples of literature examining these other cases include: Carolyn Jean Acker, *Creating the American Junkie: Addiction Research in the Classic Era of Narcotic Control* (Baltimore, Md.: Johns Hopkins University Press 2002); Joseph Spillane, *Cocaine: From Medical Marvel to Modern Menace in the United States, 1884–1920* (Baltimore, Md.: Johns Hopkins University Press 2000); Andrea Tone, *The Age of Anxiety: A History of America's Turbulent Affair with Tranquilizers* (New York: Basic Books 2009); David Herzberg, *Happy Pills in America: From Miltown to Prozac* (Baltimore, Md.: Johns Hopkins University Press 2009); Catherine Carstairs, *Jailed for Possession: Illegal Drug Use, Regulation, and Power in Canada, 1920–1961* (Toronto: University of Toronto Press 2006); and Stephen Snelders, Charles Kaplan, and Toine Peters, 'On Cannabis, Chloral Hydrate, and Career Cycles of Psychotropic Drugs in Medicine,' *Bulletin of the History of Medicine*, 80, no. 1 (2006): 95–114.
4 See Albert Hofmann, 'Discovery of D-Lysergic Acid Deithylamide LSD,' *Sandoz Excerpta*, 12, no. 1 (1955): 1.
5 See Erika Dyck, *Psychedelic Psychiatry: LSD from Clinic to Campus* (Baltimore, Md.: Johns Hopkins University Press 2008), chapter 2.
6 See, for example: David Healy, *The Creation of Psychopharmacology* (Cambridge, Mass.: Harvard University Press 2002); David Healy, *Mania: A*

Short History of Bipolar Disorder (Baltimore: Johns Hopkins University Press 2008); David Herzberg, *Happy Pills in America* (Baltimore: Johns Hopkins University 2009); Edward Shorter, *A History of Psychiatry: From the Era of the Asylum to the Age of Prozac* (New York: John Wiley 1997); and Tone, *The Age of Anxiety*.

7 Erika Dyck, '"Hitting Highs at Rock Bottom": LSD Treatment for Alcoholism, 1950–1970,' *Social History of Medicine*, 19, no. 2 (2006): 313–29.

8 Carstairs, *Jailed for Possession*, 92–114.

9 Marcel Martel, '"They Smell Bad, Have Diseases, and Are Lazy": RCMP Officers Reporting on Hippies in the Late Sixties,' *Canadian Historical Review*, 90 no. 2 (2009): 215–46.

10 See ibid. and Caroline Jean Acker, 'Portrait of an Addicted Family: Dynamics of Opiate Addiction in the Early Twentieth Century,' in Sarah Tracy and Caroline Jean Acker, eds., *Altering American Consciousness: The History of Alcohol and Drug Use in the United States, 1800–2000* (Amherst: University of Massachusetts Press 2004), 165–81.

11 University of Regina Archives, 88–29, Duncan Blewett Papers, Writings of Duncan Blewett, 'Interim Report on the Therapeutic Use of LSD' (1958), 4–5. The same list is in the Handbook included in chapter 2 of this work, entitled 'Nature of the Drug Reaction.'

12 A later article described (though I am sure there are many such descriptions) a number of recreational LSD 'trips.' See L.S. Drey, 'Psychedelic Experiences I Have Known,' *Canadian Dimension*, 8, no. 6 (1972): 14–19.

13 Of course, this is difficult to substantiate, but newspaper reports do not seem to show concern – in fact, they remain relatively positive about the drug.

14 *Statutes of Canada*, 1962–3, vol. 1, 119.

15 House of Commons *Debates*, vol. 1 (1962), 977 (J.W. Monteith).

16 Ibid., 978.

17 Ibid., 980 (H.C. Harley).

18 Ibid., 981 (Guy Marcoux).

19 Ibid., 1524 (David Orlikow).

20 Ibid., 1551 (Gordon Aiken).

21 Ibid., 1567 (Stanley Knowles).

22 SAB, A207, XVIII, 12a, Hoffer to Osmond, July 1962.

23 For example, see J.R. Ball and Jean J. Armstrong, 'The Use of LSD 25 (D-Lysergic Acid Diethylamide) in the Treatment of the Sexual Perversions,' *Canadian Journal of Psychiatry*, 6, no. 4 (1961): 231–5; S.E. Jensen and Ronald Ramsay, 'Treatment of Chronic Alcoholism with Lysergic Acid Diethylamide,' *Canadian Journal of Psychiatry*, 8, no. 3 (1963): 182–8; T.F.

Ward, 'A Psychiatric Panorama: Review Article,' *Canadian Medical Association Journal*, 86 (1962): 23–9.

24 H.E. Lehmann, 'New Drugs in Psychiatric Therapy,' *Canadian Medical Association Journal*, 85 (1961): 1148.

25 Steven Novak, 'LSD before Leary: Sidney Cohen's Critique of 1950s Psychedelic Research,' *Isis*, 88, no. 1 (1997): 88.

26 Sidney Cohen, 'Lysergic Acid Diethylamide: Side Effects and Complications,' *Journal of Nervous and Mental Disease*, 130 (1960): 30–40.

27 For example: 'Propose Use of Powerful Mind-Changing Drugs,' *Toronto Star Daily*, 28 March 1961, 28.

28 Richard Greenfield, *Timothy Leary: A Biography* (Orlando, Fla.: A James H. Silberman Book / Harcourt 2006), 194–6.

29 'Small Black Market Reported in LSD,' *News Call Bulletin—San Francisco*, 4 January 1963.

30 'Potency of Morning Glory Seeds Probed,' *Globe and Mail*, 12 July 1963, 3.

31 SAB, A207, XVIII, 22.b, Osmond to 'Al,' 25 April 1966.

32 Osmond recounts this discussion later in a letter warning the National Institute of Health about these conditions. SAB, A207, XVIII. 26.b, Osmond to Dr Jonathan Cole, chief, Psychopharmacology Service Centre, National Institute of Health, 9 February 1967.

33 SAB, S-A 207, III, 109, A. Hoffer to A. Hubbard, 8 June 1956.

34 SAB, S-A 207, III, 109, A. Hubbard to A. Hoffer, 17 February 1959.

35 It is unclear whether either, both, or neither of these sources had any direct relationship with Sandoz. Hoffer tested the products in his lab and found both to be sound, but he could not determine whether or not they were the same quality as the Sandoz-produced LSD. See SAB, S-A 207, III, 109, A. Hoffer to A. Hubbard, 16 December 1958.

36 SAB, S-A 207, III, 109, A. Hoffer to A. Hubbard, 27 June 1958.

37 SAB, S-A 207, III, 109, A. Hubbard to A. Hoffer, 20 May 1959.

38 SAB, S-A 207, III, 109, A. Hubbard to A. Hoffer, 17 September 1959.

39 'Drug Used in Mental Ills Is Withdrawn in Canada,' *Globe and Mail*, 21 October 1962, 30.

40 'Sole U.S. Distributor Surrenders Its Right to Handle Drug LSD,' *Globe and Mail*, 14 April 1966, 1.

41 'U.S. Jury Indicts 2 as Smugglers of Mind Drug,' *New York Times*, 15 October 1965, 47.

42 William Powell, *The Anarchist's Cookbook* (Fort Lee, N.J.: Barricade Books 1971). Although this book was not published until 1971, it seems likely that recipes for LSD were available as early as 1963. It is, of course, difficult to locate written sources to confirm this belief, but, through a combination of

newspaper reports and anonymous oral interviews, it is clear that black market, kitchen, 'bathtub,' or 'basement' LSD became available in the early part of 1963. In fine print, Powell's guidebook warned that some seeds might be coated with a substance that, when subjected to the process of turning them into LSD, made the end product poisonous.

43 SAB, A207, XVIII, 22.b, Osmond to Hofmann, 25 April 1966.

44 Ibid.

45 SAB, A207, XVIII, 22.b, Osmond to Hofmann, 25 April 1966.

46 SAB, A207, XVIII, 26.d, Osmond's report of a meeting with 'the alchemist,' 30 April 1967.

47 Ibid.

48 Ibid.

49 SAB, A207, XVIII, 26.b, Osmond to Jonathan Cole (NIH), 9 February 1967.

50 SAB, A207, XVIII, 23.b, Osmond to Robert F. Kennedy, 24 May 1966, 4.

51 Ibid. Emphasis in original.

52 In the United States, LSD's legal experimental use was confined to investigations within Veterans Administration hospitals and projects approved by the National Institute of Mental Health.

53 For example, see 'Ottawa Seeks Closer Control on LSD Sales,' *Globe and Mail*, 5 February 1966, 4; 'RCMP Start LSD Probe to Halt Illegal Trafficking,' *Globe and Mail*, 11 February 1966, 35; 'The Big Turn-on Goes to College,' *Globe and Mail*, 21 March 1966, 21; 'LSD Subject Arraigned in Murder: DA Convenes Talks in New York on Hallucinatory Drugs,' *Globe and Mail*, 15 April 1966, 16; and 'LSD Fascinating to Collegians, Alarms U.S. Parents and Police,' *Globe and Mail*, 25 April 1966, 4.

54 *Final Report of the Commission of Inquiry into the Non-Medical Use of Drugs* (Ottawa: Information Canada 1973), appendix on hallucinogens.

55 House of Commons *Debates*, 13 May 1966, 5100 (Frank Howard).

56 House of Commons *Debates*, 16 May 1966, 'Statement on Control of Drug LSD by A.J. MacEachen, Minister of National Health and Welfare,' 5156.

57 House of Commons *Debates*, 16 May 1966, 5157 (J.W. Monteith).

58 Ibid., 5157 (William Dean Howe).

59 House of Commons *Debates*, 11 July 1966, 7501–2 (Howard Johnston).

60 House of Commons *Debates*, 21 November 1966, 10157 (Howard Johnston).

61 Ibid., 10158 (Howard Johnston).

62 House of Commons *Debates*, 13 February 1967, 12945 (J.G. Diefenbaker).

63 House of Commons *Debates*, 20 March 1967, 14174 (J.G. Diefenbaker).

64 Senate *Debates*, 26 April 1967, 1846 (M. Hollett).

65 Ibid. (Malcolm Hollet).

66 Ibid., 1821 (Gunnar S. Thorvaldson).

67 Ibid., 1824 (Orville H. Phillips).
68 Senate *Debates*, 20 April, 1967, 1814 (David Walker).
69 Ibid., 1817 (David Walker).
70 Senate *Debates*, 25 April 1967, 1821 (Gunnar S. Thorvaldson).
71 Ibid. (Gunnar S. Thorvaldson).
72 Ibid., 1845 (Hartland de M. Molson).
73 *Statutes of Canada*, vols. 17–18, 1968–9, 991–5.
74 SAB, A207, III, A, box 53, Charles C. Dahlberg, Ruth Mechaneck, and Stanley Feldstien, 'LSD Research and Adverse Publicity' (1967), 2; and Robert E. Mogar, 'Research in Psychedelic Drug Therapy: A Critical Analysis,' *Research in Psychotherapy*, 3 (1968): 500.
75 SAB, A207, XVIII, 26.b, Osmond to Abram Hoffer, 6 March 1967.
76 David Nutt et al., 'Development of a Rational Scale to Assess the Harm of Drugs of Potential Misuse,' *The Lancet*, 369 (2007): 1047–3, 1047.
77 Ibid., 1048.
78 Ibid., 1050. The list of substances, in sequential order of assessed risk, is: heroin, cocaine, barbiturates, street methadone, alcohol, ketamine, benzodiazapines, amphetamine, tobacco, buprenorphine, cannabis, solvents, 4-MTA, LSD, methylphenidate, anabolic steroids, GHB, Ecstasy, akyl nitrates, and khat.

7 Setting Boundaries: LSD Use and Glue Sniffing in Ontario in the 1960s[1]

MARCEL MARTEL

When thinking of the 1960s, terms such as counterculture and marijuana go hand in hand. Although marijuana captured public attention and scientists debated its health risks, many individuals, and in particular youth, experimented with other drugs. The head of Ontario's Alcoholism and Drug Addiction Research Foundation,[2] H. David Archibald, acknowledged the proliferation of chemical and non-chemical drugs and called this new reality 'the age of drugs.'[3]

In addition to marijuana, reports on the use of LSD (lysergic acid diethylamide) and glue sniffing triggered fear among social actors who dealt with young people. Both these latter substances crossed the boundaries of legitimate use because users were not supervised by the medical establishment, in the case of LSD, or the substance was used for a purpose other than the one for which it was conceived, as in the case of commercial airplane glue. The list of social actors who intervened in the debate was impressive because it included parents, municipal politicians, media, boards of education, industry representatives, and scientists.The public debates over LSD use and glue sniffing raised the question of who had the authority to intervene and define what constituted legitimate and illegitimate use of LSD and glue. On this last point, and despite their differences in terms of financial and human resources, ability to influence and shape the views of others, and ideology, all these social actors were convinced that they had the right to intervene and that consequently their interventions were legitimate. Believing that their social and political responsibilities conferred upon them a certain authority, they called for government interventions such as a ban on the sale of airplane glue to minors and jail terms for LSD users. In pursuing these campaigns, they tried to shape public perception on the issues and influence the views of other social actors, in particular state officials.

In addition to the issue of defining what constitutes legitimate and illegitimate drug use, this essay revisits the theory of 'moral panic' and explores how it applies to the response of society and in particular certain state organizations to this issue in the 1960s. The conclusion set out here is that the theory of moral panic does not adequately explain how the Ontario government handled LSD use and glue sniffing. Although different social actors tried to shape the understanding that the Ontario government had of these practices, they had unequal means and access to the government. In the case of both LSD and glue sniffing, the Ontario government came under pressure but, in each case, was swayed less by those stirring up moral panic than by its own experts at the Addiction Research Foundation of Ontario, who believed that education and health-oriented solutions rather than repression were the best course of action.

Brief Overview of Moral Panic Theory

Since the publication of Stanley Cohen's *Folk Devils and Moral Panics: The Creation of the Mods and Rockers* in 1972, the theory of moral panic has been employed in the field of drug studies. It offers a useful analytical tool in understanding why drugs used for recreational purposes trigger strong opposition in society, why media coverage insists on the negative aspects of drug use, and why the outcome in terms of public policies (i.e., repression) is predictable, at least in most Western countries.

Although the 1960s offer plenty of evidence of crises over values and social order, an episode of moral panic did not occur each time there were fears concerning new social practices or behaviours. This raises the question of selectivity and why certain issues fail to capture public attention. Possible answers are found by focusing on the abilities of social agents to sustain their agenda over a long period of time, broaden their support, or mobilize quickly and effectively.

Kenneth Thompson provides an interesting working definition of episodes of moral panics. These episodes of panic are called moral because they relate to social issues and how a society defines its values, practices, and order. As stated by Thompson, such episodes generate a specific type of discussion and argument because they trigger 'strong feelings of righteousness.'[4] Inspired by Cohen's book, Thompson identifies the different steps that characterize an episode of moral panic.

The first step or stage of an episode of moral panic is when there is 'something or someone ... defined as a threat to values or interests.' The something refers to a social practice such as drug use for non-medical purposes, alcohol, prostitution, and so on, and the someone to a specific group targeted because their members used drugs, drank alcohol, or had sex. The social practice or the group in question is perceived, constructed, and depicted as a threat by certain social actors who are highly sensitive to these issues and are compelled to intervene because they feel that values that they cherish and champion are threatened. Such social actors are referred to as moral entrepreneurs or 'moral crusaders, who attempt to rouse public opinion through the media and by leading social movements and organizations to bring pressure on the authorities to exercise social control and moral regulation.'[5]

In the process, fear is generated as the issue attracts attention in the public domain. At the same time, the social actors responsible for triggering the panic express hostility towards the social practice or group that is being targeted. In many instances, this hostility is translated into the depiction of a social and moral threat. Although, in many cases, the social practice or group targeted involves or consists of only a few people, the social actors depict this practice or group in exaggerated terms since they have the potential of becoming mainstream, creating havoc, and challenging and ultimately changing social values. In other words, there is a disconnect between the facts and what is said and printed about the targeted social practice and/or group.

The second stage is when the threat constructed by social actors who are disturbed by what they see, hear, or read is 'depicted in an easily recognizable form by the media.' Often the media disseminate social anxieties that are disproportionate to the actual threat. Since the threat is now in the public domain, there is, according to Thompson, 'a rapid build-up of public concern.'[6]

The public concern, or third stage of the process, generates other societal reactions. Among them, there is an expectation on the part of many that those who are in a position of authority, locally, regionally, or nationally, will respond to the threat being manufactured.

The last stage of an episode of moral panic relates to the results, but here scholars disagree. For Thomson, the panic either 'recedes or results in social changes.'[7] For Erich Goode and Nachman Gen-Yehuda, the status quo is reinforced, especially if the episode of moral panic involves drug use.[8] In such a case, repressive public policies are implemented. For instance, in Canada the federal government has adopted repressive drug public policies since the beginning of the twentieth century when it legislated for the first time on the recreational use of opium. Another scholar, Kenneth J. Meier, insists that these type of public policies, which are very popular among moral entrepreneurs, are actually inefficient since they fail to change the targeted behaviour.[9]

In the case under study here, public discussions of LSD use and glue sniffing for recreational purposes offer many interesting parallels with the theory of moral panic. Furthermore, discussions of these social practices in Ontario in the 1960s brought together the media, the public, social agents such as parents, state entities such as school boards and municipal councils, and government authorities. However, the outcome in terms of public policies was not necessarily repression.

'We Will Hear a Lot More about This Drug and Its Illicit Uses in the Future': Constructing LSD as a Serious Social Threat

In his presentation as part of an educational course for coroners in May 1966, Dr Beatty Cotnam, from the Ontario Ministry of the Attorney General, stated that LSD was 'the *most dangerous* of all the under-the-counter drugs available today.' Using American data, Cotnam depicted the drug's effects in worrisome terms. 'LSD produces bizarre-psychic effects with extreme and distorted sensations of color, taste, sight and sound to the point where there is a complete breakaway from reality while still conscious.' Indeed, LSD's effects were so powerful that 'a few pounds of it dropped in the water supply of a major city would be sufficient to disorient millions of people for hours or days.' Why would some people try this 'terrible' drug without proper medical supervision, Cotnam asked? In offering his answer, he could not conceal his strong views on the subject: 'This is part of a sickness in our society today. Many people are taking all sorts of substances … to escape from reality and seek new adventures in the unknown.' Although the drug was popular in the United Stated but not in Canada, Cotnam warned everyone that they should not take comfort in this fact. On the contrary, he argued that 'we will hear a lot more about this drug and its illicit uses in the future!'[10]

At the time, Sandoz Pharmaceuticals in Switzerland had the rights to distribute LSD to laboratories and research centres in Canada. In his presentation, Cotnam reassured his audience by stating that none of the company's products ended up on the black market.[11] However, like many other companies in Western societies, Sandoz was nervous because the United Nations Economic and Social Council, which monitored drug production, strongly encouraged countries to limit LSD to research and medical purposes.[12] This could only mean state interference and regulation of an economic sector dominated by the private sector. For the industry, calls by social agents for an LSD ban meant a direct attack on an economic activity – the manufacturing of chemical drugs – that should remain free of state control.

In his conclusion, Cotnam predicted that more and more stories would be published about LSD and indeed Ontarians did hear more about this drug. In 1966 there was a story in *Chatelaine* magazine about how LSD helped a woman alcoholic stop drinking.[13] But it was a conference on drugs held in Toronto that generated the most responses as well as concerns since LSD was no longer being used exclusively for scientific research; instead, it was increasingly being used for pleasure, or in the quest for personal or religious meaning, by a particular group, mostly young, middle-class individuals.

Called Perception '67, the conference was organized by the University College Literary and Athletic Society at the University of Toronto. It offered its participants various activities such as a performance by the New York rock group *The Fugs* at Convocation Hall, an exhibit by Toronto artist Michael Hayden called *Mind Excursion* that simulated a drug experience, and panels featuring American beat poet Allen Ginsberg and Dr Humphry Osmond, a scientist known for his work on LSD.[14]

In the days leading up to the conference, the fact that Dr Timothy Leary was listed as one of the panellists cast a shadow over the event, with municipal politicians, Toronto newspapers, and university administrators expressing their displeasure over the presence of what they labelled an undesirable guest speaker. In an editorial entitled 'No Welcome Mat for Leary,' the *Toronto Star* made a clear demarcation between legitimate and illegitimate use of LSD. The drug had a purpose: to be used in the treatment 'of some forms of mental disease.' Its use for personal pleasure was unacceptable. If Leary came to Toronto and encouraged many impressionable youth to try LSD, there was, according to the *Star*, 'the possibility of real harm, and even tragedy.' Because of that, the *Star* felt that forbidding Leary from addressing the crowd was a legitimate restriction.[15] Fears about Leary lessened after officials from the federal Department of Immigration announced that the American counterculture icon could not attend the event. Leary was barred from entering the country because of his drug conviction.[16]

Despite this controversy, Perception '67 received favourable reviews, particularly from Robert Fulford, a *Toronto Star* columnist, and Barbara Frum, a *Chatelaine* reporter.[17] Speakers tried to reassure participants about the effects of LSD use. Some argued that it enhanced creativity and others encouraged participants to put pressure on politicians to amend the drug legislation, especially as it applied to marijuana. As for Leary, he was supposed to address the participants in a pre-recorded speech but the tape did not arrive on time, prompting the festival organizers to point an accusatory finger at Customs officers for interfering with the activities of Perception '67. Instead, his 'high deputy,' as the *Toronto Star* called Richard Alpert, addressed the participants.[18]

Almost a month after the conference, Perception '67 was back in the public domain after a deadly incident that played on the fears surrounding LSD use. In 1967 newspapers published front-page stories about the death of a twenty-year-old music student, John Stern, on 18 March. The *Toronto Daily Star* reported the story under the headline 'Viaduct Death Fall Ends "Trip" on LSD for Music Student.'[19] According to this newspaper, Stern was a 'depressed' student who plunged from the Bloor Viaduct after taking LSD. For its part, the *Toronto Telegram* clearly laid the blame on the drug: '"LSD disciples helped to kill my son" [said] father.' The victim's father was categorical when asked about the cause: his son took LSD and his drug experiment led him to commit suicide by jumping off the Bloor Viaduct. Furthermore, the father blamed the disciples of LSD and 'every publication that in any way glorifies this drug as a magic gift that can broaden and enlighten anyone.' The *Telegram* reminded its readers that the deceased attended Perception '67 and one of the speakers, Dr Alpert, encouraged individuals to take LSD. The newspaper even contacted Alpert and asked him if he felt responsible for the tragic event. In response, Alpert declined to accept any responsibility for the tragedy, stating that 'it's extremely difficult to pin such a death exclusively to LSD.' He added that 'his group never at any time urges people to take LSD.' The boy's father insisted that his son's death should awaken politicians and compel them to ban LSD except for medical use.[20]

The father's call for government action received support from the *Toronto Telegram*. In his column, Frank Tumpane wrote that the time had come for the federal government to act and keep LSD out 'of the hands of the immature and the irresponsible charlatans who urge them to use it.'[21] Police were quick to point out that they were unable to stop youth from using LSD since the federal government had classified the drug as a prohibited substance. This meant that LSD could be used for scientific research but there were no penalties for its possession, unlike marijuana, cocaine, and other drugs classified under the Food and Drugs Act and the Narcotic Control Act. For police, the solution was the classification of LSD as a narcotic.[22]

Buried in the *Toronto Telegram*'s story was a reference to another suicide that was attributed to LSD. The suicide of Henry Borycki on 3 January did not receive the same media coverage as that accorded John Stern's death, which raised the issue of various social actors' selective use of information when fanning the flames of moral panic. Why did Stern receive so much media and public attention? Did Stern's father play a pivotal role by being so outspoken, as opposed to the silence of Borycki's parents? (As mentioned by the *Globe and Mail*, Stern's father was the president of a business-consultancy firm.) At the coroner's inquiry into Borycki's death in February, it was revealed that the case was reopened because of allegations that the death resulted from LSD use. Those who testified at the inquiry revealed that Borycki had a history of depression but he was also known as a LSD user in Yorkville. However, Dr Fred Jaffe, the pathologist who performed the autopsy, found no traces of the drug in the body of the deceased. Although he indicated that it was impossible to find the drug in question because most users took only a small quantity, he ruled out the possibility that LSD played a role in this tragic death.[23]

In reaction to John Stern's death in March 1967, a reader wrote to the *Toronto Telegram* denouncing the media treatment of the incident. He pointed out that many other deaths due to drugs such as alcohol or to car accidents occurred on a regular basis but did not receive the same kind of extensive coverage.[24] An underground newspaper, *The Satyrday*, reported that Stern was seen often in Yorkville and was a regular user of LSD. 'He was known by many as "Stern the Burn," a reference to his connection with the dopy business in Yorkville.' These elements of the story were ignored by mainstream newspapers, as noted by Stuart Henderson in his analysis of Yorkville in the 1960s.[25] At the coroner's inquest into Stern's death, some witnesses testified that the victim consumed LSD. As in the case of Borycki, tests to detect LSD in the deceased were negative. For his part, pathologist Raymond Cromarty indicated that 'LSD is used in such small quantities that it would be very difficult to detect' and did not rule out that a car struck the young man. Despite these reports, the jury blamed LSD in Stern's death and recommended the creation of educational programs about the dangers of this drug for young people. Certainly, expert witnesses influenced the recommendation about educational programs since they warned that any attempt to make LSD an illegal substance would be counter-productive. Such legislative action would only make the substance more attractive to young people.[26]

In the months following Stern's tragic death, LSD stories did not disappear from the media. On the contrary, they resurfaced from time to time, often to highlight the dangers of the drug's use. For instance, at a two-day conference on children's learning problems in January 1968, Dr J.S. Prichard, a neurologist at the Hospital for Sick Children, used the opportunity to warn youth that they should not take LSD, 'not even ... one dose,' because it 'breaks in chromosomes' and causes 'severe mental illnesses.'[27] On 13 August 1968 the *Globe and Mail* published the conclusion of a coroner's jury which, after hearing testimonies from drug experts and a drug user, concluded that the death of a young man that occurred on one of the Toronto Islands was due to LSD use; he had climbed a 'guardrail on an observation pier at Central Island and jumped. His body was recovered a short time later in 15 feet of ... water.'[28] A couple of months later, the *Toronto Telegram* published a short story about a young man accused of armed robbery at a department store in Sudbury. He claimed that he was under the influence of LSD when he committed the alleged crime. For those who associated drug use and crime, the story substantiated their concern.[29]

In the case of the Toronto Islands death, as in the earlier ones, parents, police, scientists, and media highlighted the dangers of using LSD without any medical supervision. Since the death of the young man was equated with non-medical use, these social agents felt that they ought to intervene. In the case of parents, they knew what was best for their kids, and LSD was certainly not a good substance to be taken. In the view of police officers entrusted with maintaining public order, LSD use for recreational purposes resulted in disorder and danger. As for scientists, they seemed divided on the issue. Although some were cautious in not linking LSD experiences to death, others argued in favour of restricting its use to capable and knowledgeable scientific experts. And for a media eager to report on any aspect of the new social practice of LSD use for recreational purposes, the death of the young Torontonian provided an opportunity to voice the concerns and fears expressed by various social agents. Since LSD use had made another noteworthy entry into the public domain and the event in question had involved, once again, a tragic death, the debate caught the attention of provincial politicians.

There were few debates in the Ontario Legislative Assembly in these years about drug use for recreational purposes, but the one that followed John Stern's death demonstrated the influence of the media. Politicians felt that they had to make their opinions known to the public, in particular to social agents who contributed to the awareness of the dangers of LSD. By doing so, they demonstrated to their constituencies that they cared about drug issues and recognized the government's responsibility to act.

Provincial politicians debated the issue in March 1967 following news reports about Stern's death. They were quick to condemn LSD users and proponents, and pleaded for action. Although some MPPs used this death as a pretext to condemn all drug use for non-medical purposes, most who took part in the debate focused on LSD. The debate offered no reassuring words for those who were not familiar with the issue, since MPPs insisted on the awful dangers this chemical entailed for its users.[30]

The Ontario government had limited ability to regulate LSD use. It could choose to make possession of LSD a criminal offence, as the provincial governments in British Columbia and Alberta had done in 1967.[31] However, the Criminal Code resides in federal not provincial jurisdiction. Furthermore, many experts expressed the view that prohibition was not the proper way to handle the concerns and fears expressed by parents and other social agents about LSD use. For instance, Morton Shulman, chief coroner for Metropolitan Toronto in 1967, rejected a ban.[32] Moreover, the Ontario government relied on the advice of the Alcoholism and Drug Addiction Research Foundation, which viewed drug use as a health issue.

In 1949 the Ontario government had established the Alcoholism Research Foundation (ARF), which became well known for its research on alcohol and rehabilitation programs. In 1961 the government included other drugs as part of the ARF's mandate and changed its name to the Alcoholism and Drug Addiction Research Foundation.[33] Renamed again in 1967 as the Addiction Research Foundation (ARF), the organization disseminated its research findings widely and, in its earlier incarnation as the Alcoholism Research Foundation, had created educational programs in 1953 aimed at youth and parents which were used by several school boards in Ontario and other provinces. Above all, the ARF believed that science had the ability to offer an unbiased understanding of issues such as why people used drugs for recreational purposes, how to prevent the development of dependence on drugs, and how to help those suffering from such an addiction. In other words, it believed that the scientific approach offered the best understanding of such a complex issue as drug use for medical or non-medical purposes alike, since some individuals could develop a dependence or abuse drugs prescribed by the medical community. The ARF felt that its findings were objective, a view shared by many other scientific organizations similar to the ARF at the time.[34]

In a report written in either 1967 or 1968, the chief coroner of Ontario stated that 250 deaths attributed to drug use and 137 deaths due to alcohol intoxication had been investigated in Ontario. Among these 387 cases, 'only a small number of deaths' – he did not specify how many – were related to LSD or glue.[35] Clearly, as the ARF realized, there was much uncertainty in these figures. Invited to intervene on the LSD issue, the ARF encouraged the government to avoid any hasty decision because so much was still unknown – such as how many people were using LSD; how many had a bad experience resulting from LSD use; if a LSD experience necessarily led to a bad experience; or if regular LSD use led to dependence or, even worse, experimentation with other drugs and sometimes with more addictive drugs. Unless research on LSD use was allowed, it would not be possible to give advice to the government on a proper course of action. Consequently, public-policy choices such as a ban, repression, and jail terms were inadequate. At the time, alcohol and drug education was a minor element in the school curriculum. According to the ARF, spending more time on drug education was the most promising prevention strategy.

The government was not oblivious to the moral panic sweeping across society, but, in the very act of turning to the ARF for advice, it demonstrated that experts, not the voices of alarmism, would be most influential in determining policy. In any event, as Erika Dyck explains in her essay in this volume, the federal government settled the LSD issue by amending the Food and Drugs Act in 1969 so that possessing LSD and trafficking in it were now criminal offences. Yet the victory of those campaigning against LSD was not unqualified. Under the 1969 amendment, the penalty for possession of LSD was a fine of up to $1,000 or six months in jail or both;[36] however, the penalty was not as severe as it was for marijuana and other narcotics. In other words, the moral panic had succeeded, but only partially.

Handling Glue Sniffing: Rejection of Repressive Policies

In 1966 and 1967 another drug captured the attention of many people.

Although there were few media reports, the media construction of children and adolescents sniffing glue centred on the dangers and risks associated with the practice. In May 1966 the *Globe and Mail* and the *Toronto Star* stated that there were 400 children in the east end of Toronto who sniffed glue. The following May, the *Star* reported the death of Norman Michael Cook, a fourteen-year-old boy, who died of asphyxiation because of a plastic bag around his head. His father found two airplane glue tubes next to his dead son. According to the newspaper, this was the first death attributed to glue sniffing in Toronto. At the coroner's inquiry, a witness stated that numerous youth – no exact figure was given – sniffed glue at Parkdale Public School, the school attended by Norman Cook, and that Friday night was known as 'glue sniffing night.' The jury recommended that possession and inhalation of toxic solvents become an offence and that airplane glue be kept behind the counter in retail stores. In October 1967 an expert from the Clarke Institute of Psychiatry stated that glue sniffing was more dangerous than marijuana. A month later, a Toronto Board of Education trustee argued that the police could not stop youth from sniffing glue.[37]

These stories fuelled fears about the dangerous effects of glue sniffing and prompted concerned parents and individuals to press the Toronto School Board to take action. Since the board did not have the constitutional authority to ban or restrict the sale of airplane glue, parents and other individuals and groups focused their attention on the Ontario government, expecting that politicians at Queen's Park would implement the solutions they proposed. Social organizations such as the Toronto Kiwanis Club, inspired by the example of similar groups in the United States, argued for a ban on the sale of 'the ingredient in glue that causes the harm.'[38]

Under pressure from residents, the City of Toronto asked the provincial government to do something to stop glue sniffing. Since children and adolescents could easily obtain the substance from stores, the time had come to ban or restrict the sale of glue, given that shopowners were apparently unwilling to take it upon themselves to limit the sale of glue to adults only.

In November 1967 William R. Callow of the city's Legal Department wrote to Attorney General Arthur Wishart suggesting that, if the province was not planning to do anything 'to prohibit the sale of glue to anyone under the age of 18 years in an effort to prevent the practice of glue sniffing by young people,' it should give the municipal government the power to act in this area. In his response, the attorney general informed the city that the government had excluded the option of a ban.[39] According to the minister, a ban was pointless since other substances could be used instead of glue, thereby undermining the attempt to discourage adolescents from glue sniffing.[40]

With the attorney general unwilling to give the City of Toronto the power to regulate glue sniffing, municipal politicians approved a motion on 31 January 1968 encouraging the federal government to amend the Criminal Code in order to ban the sale of glue to individuals under the age of eighteen. In order to broaden support for its action, the city sent its motion to the Canadian Federation of Mayors and Municipalities, the Association of Ontario Mayors and Reeves, and the Ontario Municipal Association. The City of Toronto also pursued the issue further by suggesting that a letter from the parent or guardian of a child or an adolescent should be required for buying glue.[41]

Representations by parents, clubs, and the City of Toronto did not fall on deaf ears when they reached the premier's desk. Premier John Robarts was concerned about the glue-sniffing issue, especially after receiving a letter from the Toronto Kiwanis Club. In a letter to Attorney General Wishart, he asked for suggestions on how to 'combat this very distressing situation.'[42] The attorney general's office, for its part, believed that the government had limited options on the issue of model-airplane glue. First, the federal government was better equipped to handle the matter because glue sniffing, while being a local phenomenon, required a national solution, concerning as it did every citizen and possibly affecting every Canadian youngster. Moreover, if model-airplane glue were banned, individuals might use other substances that would have the same effects.[43]

The Ministry of Health reached similar conclusions. In a letter to the attorney general, Health Minister Matthew Dymond rejected a ban since children and adolescents could turn to other substances such as gasoline. Another possibility, adding an irritant to glue, had the potential of creating serious problems for those who did not misuse glue since 'many people make their living from skills and crafts where the use of glue is absolutely essential.' Consequently, 'why should they suffer because of a few "kooky kids"?' the minister asked.[44]

The Ministry of Health relied on the expertise of the ARF, which encouraged the minister and the government to be cautious. Banning the sale of glue or imposing jail terms on a child or an adolescent for glue sniffing were regarded as unwise and ill-conceived. The ARF used its influence to undermine the positions put forward by the City of

Toronto and later by the Board of Education by claiming that there was no hard evidence demonstrating a significant increase in glue sniffing. In fact, it argued the opposite. N. Rae Speirs, a teacher-training consultant at the ARF and former director of physical and health education for the Toronto Board of Education, wrote a report which constituted a careful deconstruction of the glue-sniffing fear. He argued that it was very difficult to come up with an assessment of how many individuals sniffed glue. 'It makes good newspaper copy, but the actual number of people affected is not known,' he said. Since newspapers were quick to create the impression that there was a new trend among school-children, Speirs pointed out that the three cases reported in a Toronto school were in fact 'three separate reports on one boy.' Furthermore, the number of those who practised glue sniffing was miniscule in comparison with those who used alcohol or other drugs. Speirs wrote that there were 'approximately 100,000 alcoholics, an estimated 10,000 to 20,000 persons who [were] addicted to prescription drugs and somewhat more than 1,000 narcotic addicts.'[45]

What about the health effects of glue sniffing on its users? Here, too, Speirs was cautious in his analysis. The long-term effects were still unknown because of the novelty of the practice. Yet Speirs listed various possible effects, including 'withdrawal into fantasy' and 'aggressive behavior' that could lead 'to bizarre conduct.' For those who were sniffing glue, was there a danger of becoming dependent? Once again, Speirs cautiously reminded people that there was no clear consensus. Although there were some dangers, the idea that glue sniffing led to the use of other drugs was excluded. 'Whenever a new case of glue sniffing is reported to his case workers, the child is already well-known to them as a multi-problem individual.' Nevertheless, in his conclusion, Speirs encouraged the provincial government to take action without highlighting specific options.[46]

One of the solutions under consideration by the ARF was adding an irritant to glue. However, the industry did not favour this solution because it would increase manufacturing costs, and, furthermore, no one knew what concentration of irritant should be added. Still, the ARF encouraged companies, notably LePage, to pursue research on adding an irritant to glue in order 'to either close the door completely [to it] or at least narrow the potential approach.'[47] On the whole, the industry became an ally of the ARF on the issue. Glue manufacturers were not thrilled by the possibility of state interference. A ban constituted a major economic danger that could jeopardize this industrial sector. Other forms of regulation were judged inappropriate and constituted an unjustified case of state interference. For the private sector, the sale of glue should remain free of state interference. Though it was not enthusiastic about the idea of adding an irritant to glue, it thought that the ARF's emphasis on education and treatment constituted a better solution.

In March 1968 the ARF informed the government that it would carry out a study on glue sniffers during the summer. In addition, it again disputed the account that many young people were sniffing glue. Its own assessment, based on meetings with individuals who were involved with adolescents in Toronto, demonstrated that the number of young people involved in glue sniffing was declining.[48] Since glue sniffing was an indication of a larger problem on the part of those who engaged in the practice, health solutions were required, such as treating those who had the habit. The ARF rejected a ban, pointing out that it would not solve the problem since children and adolescents could resort to other substances. As it did during the LSD scare, the Ontario organization advocated educational programs. The ARF believed that, by increasing the time spent on drug education in class, young people would become aware of the dangers of licit and illicit drugs. However, educational programs should not have an alarmist tone. For instance, in the case of glue sniffing, teachers should merely point out in a matter-of-fact way the harm that sniffing solvent could do to humans.[49]

In his replies to those who wrote to him on the subject, Premier Robarts repeated the arguments of the ARF and the attorney general's office.[50] These arguments were already familiar to the Toronto City Council because it had received the Speirs assessment in January 1967.[51] Robarts and Wishart reminded municipal politicians that the province did not have the constitutional power to amend the Criminal Code and wondered what would be achieved by banning airplane glue if it did. Such a solution meant that many would be punished for something done by a few kids. According to the attorney general: 'In prohibiting the sale of this substance to persons under the age of 18 years, we are, in fact, preventing all of our young people from purchasing the substance for model building which in itself is one of the greatest recreational activities which youngsters have in a creative field. It might be unfortunate to put obstacles in the way of the legitimate use of this product particularly at a time when we are trying to keep youngsters in fields of constructive endeavour.'[52]

Unable to change the views of the provincial government, the City of Toronto modified its strategy. In November 1968, along with the

Municipality of Metropolitan Toronto, the city encouraged the Toronto School Board to put in place an educational program that would emphasize the dangers of glue sniffing.[53] Yet, if the attorney general's office thought that the issue would quietly die, it misjudged or misread the situation. Over the ensuing months, calls for a ban continued.

In March 1968 the Toronto Board of Education again wrote to the attorney general asking for action on the part of the province on this issue.[54] Since the federal Liberal government had no intention of addressing the problem of glue sniffing, the board believed that it had to put pressure on the provincial Conservative government. It sent two letters and made a phone call requesting a meeting with the attorney general, which he finally agreed to in June.[55]

The Board of Education submitted its brief in June 1968. Although educating youth about the dangers of glue sniffing was a responsibility of the board, the authors of the brief argued that government action was needed. In order to persuade the government to intervene, the board maintained, without giving any specific data, that there was 'increasing [glue-sniffing] use in the Metropolitan Toronto area' and elsewhere in Ontario. It provided a list of dangerous health effects on children and adolescents that included 'loss of co-ordination, difficulty in speech, double vision, and buzzing in the ears' and also 'temporary damage to kidney, liver, and blood.' It reiterated its request for a ban on the sale of glue to children and adolescents. Anticipating the argument that it could not be done, the brief cited the case of Houston, Texas, and its 1967 by-law that banned the sale, 'giving or delivery of glue and cements containing any of 12 solvents to persons under 21 years of age.' In its conclusion, the brief stressed that this issue had to be tackled since 'sniffing airplane glue is just a first step with a maladjusted child heading towards more sophisticated drugs and the subsequent suicides, jails, etc.'[56]

Attached to the board's brief were the assessment prepared by Speirs that had guided the ARF in its advice to the minister of health, the March letter sent by the attorney general, and copies of the legislation passed by the Alberta and British Columbia legislatures banning possession of drugs, including LSD and marijuana. Although the Speirs report undermined many of the arguments put forward by the Board of Education about a glue-sniffing epidemic, the board likely included it since it contained an appeal for action on the part of the Ontario government.

The attorney general's continued silence bothered the Toronto Board of Education, which sent a new letter in July asking for an official reaction to its brief. 'Exactly four weeks ago our representative submitted a brief to you urging you to consider the immediate implementation of provincial legislation to control the sale and/or use of glues containing toluene or other toxic components to minors ... May we please hear from you in this regard?'[57] Given the directive to ignore any call for action on this issue, the attorney general informed the board that its brief was under study.[58]

In addition to the Toronto Board of Education, organizations such as the Ontario Provincial Council of the Catholic Women's League of Canada, municipalities such as Timmins and Ottawa-Carleton, and the Ontario School Trustees' Council wrote to the attorney general on the issue, urging the provincial government to take action. For their parts, two mothers met with the attorney general on 30 May 1968 and asked him to prevent kids from sniffing glue.[59]

Yet, despite letters and briefs, the attorney general's position did not change. The Ontario government would not ban the sale of glue. With regard to the ARF, its solutions revolved around studies on glue sniffers in order to ascertain the possible physical and mental damages that the practice involved, as well as the educational programs and treatment that might be most effective in combating the problem.[60]

Conclusion

The debates on LSD use and glue sniffing provided several social agents with the opportunity to be heard and to shape the debate and its outcome. They did it because they believed that they had the authority to do so and because, in their estimation, they could draw the line between legitimate and illegitimate drug use. However, they were not successful in forcing the provincial government to adopt a course of action that reflected their interests and views.

Parents intervened in the debate because their parenthood gave them authority over what was good and bad for their children. In the cases of LSD use and glue sniffing, they judged that these social practices were illegitimate unless, as in the case of LSD, the drug was taken under medical supervision. Why was LSD use so upsetting for some parents? For them, it caused the deaths of young people. For instance, the father of a young Toronto man who killed himself, supposedly under the influence of LSD, asked who in his right mind would let people take a substance that caused death?

The way newspapers reported LSD use and glue sniffing helped set the boundaries of what constituted legitimate and illegitimate uses of these substances and highlighted the dangers and risks. In the case of LSD, it was illegitimate and dangerous unless taken under medical supervision. Glue was legitimate if used in the construction of airplane and car models. Any other use was illegitimate since it constituted a danger to its users.

The Toronto Board of Education felt empowered by the glue-sniffing issue. It was convinced that it had the right to intervene since it had the responsibility to inform students of the dangers of glue sniffing. Furthermore, schoolyards were not playgrounds for glue sniffers. The board lobbied the provincial government to support its view that the use of glue for purposes other than what its producers intended was illegitimate.

Toronto municipal politicians joined the movement as well, motivated by the fact that they had the responsibility to provide a safe environment for their residents. Since retailers were reluctant to ensure better control of the sale of glue to children and adolescents, municipal politicians did not hesitate to ask for the power to ban the sale of glue to minors within their territory unless the provincial government implemented a province-wide ban or restriction. However, the Ontario government refused to do so.

Industry felt compelled to intervene since its economic survival was at stake. With regard to LSD use and glue sniffing, industry rejected any form of state control. The illegitimate use of its products had two possible outcomes, one being more lethal than the other. The worst-case scenario was a direct threat to the very existence of the companies involved in the manufacture of LSD or glue; the least damaging scenario was government control and regulations that interfered with industry's activity, such as determining how much it could produce and sell. Industry lost the battle over LSD when the Canadian government and the international community outlawed the drug, in 1968 and in 1971 respectively. It was more fortunate in the case of glue.

With regard to both LSD and glue sniffing, a variety of social actors brought pressure to bear on Ontario government officials. Yet these actors had unequal access to government authorities because of varying financial and human resources, ability to sustain a campaign of persuasion, and ideology. Government authorities mediated the assorted interests involved by taking into consideration the views expressed by these social actors, the nature of the federal system, and also expert advice such as that provided by the ARF. Some of these interests, notably the ARF, were definitely more influential than others. The Ontario organization stressed the fact that LSD and glue should not be singled out because they had received extensive media coverage. Alcohol and prescription drugs, among other substances, were just as dangerous, but they were easily available and not labelled dangerous. Despite the dangers that these drugs represented, they seldom received much attention from individuals, interest groups, and the media. The ARF's role was to encourage politicians to exclude repressive public policies. Education and treatment were better solutions and the Ontario government should implement them.

Owing to the nature of the Canadian state, it was the federal government that had the power to make the possession of LSD a criminal offence. Although some social agents put pressure on both the provincial and federal governments, any government action was welcome if it meant making LSD use a criminal offence, as the governments of British Columbia and Alberta had done. According to moral-panic theory, the outcome was predictable: LSD had to become an illegal substance by being included on the list of prohibited substances used for recreational purposes, alongside other drugs such as marijuana and cocaine. However, when the federal government intervened on the LSD issue, it chose to put the substance in a different category. And so, while the LSD episode of moral panic resulted in the drug being made a prohibited substance, it did not reinforce the status quo since the penalties for LSD use were not as severe as in the case of marijuana. In fact, the course of action chosen by the federal government gave ammunition to those who asked for change in the status of marijuana. If it was possible to do it for LSD, why should the federal government not do the same for marijuana?

In the case of glue sniffing, the episode of moral panic did not lead to repressive measures in Ontario. Although newspaper reports depicted the practice as dangerous and very risky, the lobbying of parents, the City of Toronto, and the Toronto School Board was not persuasive enough. Since there was no international control system to regulate the production of glue, the international community did not influence how national and/or provincial states dealt with glue sniffing. The glue-sniffing case demonstrates some of the limits of the moral-panic theory and forces us to pay attention to the influence and power that bureaucrats have in shaping public-policy choices.

NOTES

1 I would like to thank Jamie Trepanier who acted as a research assistant on this project.

2 As explained below, the organization's name changed over time – first the Alcoholism Research Foundation (ARF, 1949), then the Alcoholism and Drug Addiction Research Foundation (ADARF, 1961), and finally the Addiction Research Foundation (ARF, 1967). Given that the name changed from ADARF to ARF in the time period under consideration, I refer to the 'ARF' throughout this chapter for simplicity.

3 Centre for Addiction and Mental Health Archives (CAMH), Addiction Research Foundation (ARF) Collection, Box 64–09, file: Foundation-Federal Government Relations, H. David Archibald, 'Approach of the Addiction Research Foundation of Ontario to the Problem of Drug Dependence and Abuse.' Formed in 1998, CAMH is an umbrella organization embracing the Alcoholism and Drug Addiction Research Foundation, the Clarke Institute of Psychiatry, the Queen Street Mental Health Clinic, and the Donwood Institute.

4 Kenneth Thompson, *Moral Panics* (London: Routledge 1998), 8.

5 Ibid., 12–13. Thomson was inspired by Howard Becker's book *Outsiders* (New York: Free Press 1963), 147–8.

6 Thompson, *Moral Panics*, 8.

7 Ibid.

8 Erich Goode and Nachman Ben-Yehuda, *Moral Panics: The Social Construction of Deviance* (Oxford: Blackwell 1994), 229.

9 Kenneth J. Meier, *The Politics of Sin: Drugs, Alcohol, and Public Policy* (Armonk, N.Y.: M.E. Sharpe 1994).

10 Library and Archives Canada (LAC), R-923, vol. 12, file 12–5, Dr H.B. Cotnam, supervising coroner, Continuing Education Course for Coroners, 6 May 1966. In his subsequent lectures, Cotnam was not very vocal on the LSD issue.

11 Ibid.

12 LAC, RG 25, vol. 10488, file 45–9–1–1, part 2.2, resolution adopted by the United Nations Economic and Social Council, 16 May 1967; LAC, RG 25, vol. 10487, file 45.9.1, part 1, resolution adopted by the United Nations Economic and Social Council, Plenary Meeting, 23 May 1968.

13 Andrea Dickson, 'How LSD Ended My Alcoholism,' *Chatelaine*, 39, no. 1 (1966).

14 *Toronto Star*, 10 February 1967, 24; 13 February 1967, 1.

15 *Toronto Star*, 6 February 1967, 6.

16 *Toronto Star*, 9 February 1967, 35.

17 Robert Fulford, 'I Went through the Mind Excursion ... and Liked It,' *Toronto Star*, 11 February 1967, 1; Barbara Frum, 'How to Take a Trip the LSD Way,' *Chatelaine*, 40, no. 6 (1967).

18 *Toronto Star*, 11 February 1967, 26; 13 February 1967, 4.

19 *Toronto Daily Star*, 20 March 1967, 1.

20 *Toronto Telegram*, 20 March 1967, 1–2.

21 *Toronto Telegram*, 21 March 1967, 33.

22 *Globe and Mail*, 21 March 1967, 4.

23 *Toronto Telegram*, 20 March 1967, 2; *Globe and Mail*, 8 February 1967, 1.

24 'Improper Use,' letter to the editor, *Toronto Telegram*, 23 March 1967, 6.

25 *Satyrday*, second issue, 1967, quoted in Stuart Henderson, *Making the Scene: Yorkville and Hip Toronto in the 1960s* (Toronto: University of Toronto Press 2011), 301–2.

26 *Globe and Mail*, 12 April 1967, 5; 29 April 1967, 2; 13 May 1967, 1; *Toronto Daily Star*, 12 May 1967, 1.

27 *Globe and Mail*, 29 January 1968, 13.

28 *Globe and Mail*, 13 August 1968, 1.

29 Sheila Gormely, 'LSD Trip Used as Defence in Armed Robbery Case,' *Toronto Telegram*, 18 October 1968, 1–2.

30 See Marcel Martel, *Not This Time: Canadians, Public Policy, and the Marijuana Issue, 1965–1975* (Toronto: University of Toronto Press 2006).

31 Archives of Ontario (AO), RG 4–2, file 366.3, Legislative Assembly of Alberta, c. 63, An Act to amend the Public Health Act, April 1967; Legislative Assembly of British Columbia, c. 37, An Act respecting Proscribed Substances, March 1967; Documents attached to the Brief to Arthur A. Wishart, attorney general for the province of Ontario from the Board of Education for the City of Toronto, June 1968.

32 'LSD Prohibition Would Do Harm,' *Vancouver Sun*, 12 April 1967, 15.

33 AO, RG 3–26, box 123, file: Alcoholism and Drug Addiction Health, April 1963–December 1965, H. David Archibald, executive director, ARF, to D. Richmond, Prime Minister's Office, 26 November 1964.

34 See Bruce L.R. Smith, *The Advisers: Scientists in the Policy Process* (Washington, D.C.: Brookings Institution 1992).

35 AO, RG 4–2, file 445.3, Dr H.B. Cotnam, supervising coroner, province of Ontario, 'The Drug Scene or Syndrome Marijuana.' Although there was no date on the document, Cotnam likely made his statement in either 1967 or 1968.

36 *Toronto Daily Star*, 21 August 1969, 1; 22 August 1969, 1. On the issue of

LSD use in Canada, see the excellent book by Erika Dyck, *Psychedelic Psychiatry: LSD from Clinic to Campus* (Baltimore, Md.: Johns Hopkins University Press 2008).

37 *Toronto Daily Star*, 18 May 1966, 1; 26 May 1967, 1; 27 May 1967, 1; 7 November 1967, 1; *Globe and Mail*, 18 May 1966, 1; 27 June 1967, 5; 17 October 1967, 5.

38 AO, RG 4–2, file 366.3, A. Gordon Burns, president, and H.S. Dunham, MD, chairman, Boys' and Girls' Work Committee, Kiwanis Club of Toronto, to Premier John P. Robarts, 6 December 1967.

39 AO, RG 4–2, file 366.3, William R. Callow, city solicitor, Legal Department, Toronto, to Attorney General Arthur Wishart, 14 November 1967; Wishart to Callow, 23 November 1967.

40 AO, RG 4–2, file 366.3, Wishart to Gaston Demers, MPP, Nickle Belt, 21 November 1967.

41 AO, RG 10 1–1, box 34, file 34.24, C.E. Norris, city clerk, City of Toronto, to Wishart, 1 February 1968; AO, RG 4–2, file 366.3, William R. Callow, city solicitor, City of Toronto, to Wishart, 2 February 1968.

42 AO, RG 3–26, box 125, file: Alcohol and Drug Addiction, December 1967–January 1969, Memorandum from Robarts to Wishart, 12 December 1967.

43 AO, RG 3–26, box 125, file: Alcohol and Drug Addiction, December 1967–January 1969, Memorandum from Wishart to Robarts, 20 December 1967.

44 AO, RG 4–2, file 366.3, Health Minister Matthew Dymond to Wishart, 28 December 1967.

45 AO, RG 4–2, file 366.3, report on glue sniffing by N.R. Speirs, teacher-training consultant, ARF, June 1968.

46 Ibid.

47 AO, RG 4–2, file 366.3, H. David Archibald, executive director of ARF, to J. Keith Russell, Lepage's Ltd, Toronto, 29 March 1968; CAMH, box 59–16, file: Foundation Response to Rapid Growth in Drug Use, Archibald to Health Minister Matthew Dymond, 25 November 1968.

48 AO, RG 42, file 366.3, handwritten notes, 1 March 1968, Department of the Attorney General; AO, RG 3–26, Wishart to Robarts, memorandum on glue sniffing, 5 March 1968; AO, RG 3–26, vol. 125, file: Alcohol and Drug Addiction, December 1967–January 1969, H. David Archibald, executive director, ARF, to W.C. Bowman, director of public prosecutions, 1 March 1968.

49 AO, RG 3–26, vol. 125, file: Alcohol and Drug Addiction, December 1967–January 1969, Wishart to Robarts, memorandum on glue sniffing, 5 March 1968; AO, RG 10–1, box 39, file 34–24, H. David Archibald to W.C. Bowman, director of public prosecutions, 1 March 1968; 'Glue Sniffing in Metropolitan Toronto,' statement by ARF, 8 January 1968.

50 AO, RG 4–2, file 366.3, Robarts to A. Gordon Burns, president, Kiwanis Club of Toronto, 8 January 1968.

51 Speirs submitted his report to the Committee on Housing, Fire and Legislation of the City of Toronto: City Council Minutes, Toronto, 1968, vol. 1, June 1968–June 1969, Appendix A, Housing, Fire and Legislation, report no. 1.

52 AO, RG 4–2, file 366.3, Wishart to C. Edgar Norris, city clerk, Department of the City Clerk, 12 February 1968.

53 AO, RG 4–2, file 366.3, George M. Foster, metropolitan clerk, Municipality of Metropolitan Toronto, to Wishart, December 1968; City Council, 12 March 1969; City Council Minutes, Toronto, 1969, vol. 1.

54 AO, RG 4–2, file 366.3, Graham Gore, director of education, to Wishart, 19 March 1968.

55 AO, RG 4–2, file 366.3, Ying L. K. Hope, chairman, Board of Education, Toronto, to Wishart, 10 May 1968; Hope to Wishart, 24 May 1968; phone call by Hope to Wishart's office, 30 May 1968.

56 AO, RG 4–2, file 366.3, brief to Wishart from the Board of Education, June 1968; Hope, Board of Education, to Wishart, 4 June 1968.

57 AO, RG 4–2, file 366.3, Hope to Wishart, 2 July 1968.

58 AO, RG 4–2, file 366.3, Wishart to Hope, 9 July 1968.

59 AO, RG 4–2, file 366.3, Mrs J.J. Matthews, resolutions convener, Ontario Provincial Council, Catholic Women's League of Canada, Ontario Provincial Council, to Wishart, 6 April 1968; Wishart to G.B. Chevrette, deputy clerk, Office of the Clerk Administrator, Town of Timmins, 17 September 1968; Regional Municipality of Ottawa-Carleton to Wishart, 12 November 1968; CAMH, box 59–16, file: Foundation Response to Rapid Growth in Drug Use, H. David Archibald, ARF, to Heath Minister Dymond, 25 November 1968; *Globe and Mail*, 30 May 1968, 5.

60 AO, RG 10–6, box 170, file 1722, H. David Archibald, ARF, to K.C. Charron, deputy minister of health, 10 February 1969.

8 From Beverage to Drug: Alcohol and Other Drugs in 1960s and 1970s Canada

GREG MARQUIS

In 1967 noted American addiction expert David J. Pittman, in 'The Rush to Combine,' criticized the trend towards merging research on and treatment of alcohol and illicit drugs.[1] The development that helped to trigger Pittman's article was the renaming of one of North America's most influential addiction research organizations, Ontario's Alcoholism and Drug Addiction Research Foundation (ADARF), as the Addiction Research Foundation (ARF).[2] Originally set up to research and assist with the treatment of alcoholism, in 1961 the Alcoholism Research Foundation had been given an additional mandate, to work on drug addiction. The gist of Pittman's critique was that alcohol addiction was sufficiently important and unique to merit its own conceptual and professional domain. More specifically, he questioned the alleged similarity of the pharmacological effects of many illegal drugs (such as stimulants) and alcohol (a depressant) and of the personalities of drug and alcohol abusers. From the standpoint of psychology, the 'rush to combine' was particularly problematic. Furthermore, there was, in 1967, little empirical evidence to support unifying research and treatment of these problems.[3]

In 1968 the changes at the ARF, whose roots extended back to the late 1940s, were defended in print by Robert E. Popham, Jan de Lint, and Wolfgang Schmidt. The ARF, as its earlier name implied, had been involved with drug issues in terms of research and clinical services for several years. Up to the early 1960s, there was little Canadian research on narcotic drug use, and even less on non-criminal addicts.[4] In 1963 the foundation opened a new narcotic addiction outpatient unit in Toronto and by the mid-1960s it was concerned with wider drug abuse problems, including amphetamines and barbiturates.[5] In 1968 Popham and colleagues accepted many of the 'dissimilarities' pointed out by Pittman, but argued that both alcohol and drug addiction, traditionally moral and legal issues, needed to become 'treatment problems.' Furthermore, 'mixed addiction' often was encountered in treatment populations and a 'total health' approach was likely the most successful route to rehabilitation.[6] The 1966 ADARF *Annual Report* had previewed another justification for the changes – the World Health Organization expert committee had recently reclassified alcoholism as 'drug addiction-alcohol type.'[7]

This article examines an important development in research on and treatment of alcohol problems in late-twentieth-century Canada, the 'alcohol and other drugs' movement. In terms of addiction studies, the term 'alcohol and other drugs' can have varied meanings. One has to do with multiple or poly drug use – the degree to which individuals use alcohol, barbiturates, opiates, tobacco, and other licit or illicit drugs and the resulting pharmacological interaction.[8] For purposes of this study, alcohol and other drugs, or AOD, refers to the movement starting in the late 1960s that promoted the concept that ethanol alcohol was a harmful drug from the point of view of public health. The article first examines the construction of research and treatment in the period prior to 1970 when the emphasis was on the individual alcoholic. Next it discusses the emergence, in the late 1960s and early 1970s, of the illicit drug issue, which produced arguments for both criminalization and decriminalization. The final topic is the genesis and impact of the alcohol and other drugs approach up to the early 1980s.[9] The basic argument is that alcohol as a socially harmful drug, much like the earlier definition of alcoholism as a disease of the few, did not exist as a social problem until defined as such by experts and lobby groups. It was a message that politicians accepted only half-heartedly.[10]

The 'Non-Drug' Drug

One important strand of temperance ideology, represented by the Woman's Christian Temperance Union in the late nineteenth century, was that alcohol was a drug, even a 'racial poison.'[11] WCTU 'antinarcotics' work among children and youth targeted alcohol, opiates, and other illicit drugs and tobacco. The move from Prohibition to government sale of liquor in most of Canada in the 1920s and the United States in the 1930s, and the growing acceptance of the disease concept of alcoholism in the 1940s and 1950s, seriously undermined the authority of traditional and 'scientific' temperance. The latter, which exerted a limited impact on North America's public schools, attempted to use empirical evidence, often with a mixture of emotional scare tactics, to prove that alcohol was a narcotic or poison. In its simplest message, that abstinence was best, temperance teaching warned that even one drink was harmful to the physiology of the body.[12] With the defeat of Prohibition, and the increased popularity of cigarettes, terms such as 'drug' and addiction tended to focus on narcotics and a small, criminalized urban subculture.[13]

Although provincial governments tolerated limited temperance teachings based on abstinence in the schools in the decades prior to the 1960s, they also taxed, sold, or regulated alcohol at both the wholesale and retail levels.[14] Given the compromises of 'repeal' in the 1920s, and the lingering strength of temperance feeling, provincial liquor control commissions treated beverage alcohol up to the 1960s as a dangerous substance, but not as a 'drug.' This philosophy was best summed up in the 1955 Bracken report on liquor 'control' in Manitoba.[15] Government liquor stores and private taverns, clubs, and licensed restaurants were placed under a legal regime that stressed 'orderly' drinking. Alcoholism was blamed not on 'the bottle,' but 'the man.'[16] The alcohol industry was more than comfortable with the theory; the Association of Canadian Distillers later denied that alcohol itself was 'a health problem.'[17] The most popular and prestigious response to alcoholism, the self-help organization Alcoholics Anonymous, counselled abstinence for the minority of problematic drinkers, but did not denounce drinking or alcohol per se. The Manitoba Alcoholism Committee in the 1950s announced that it would do nothing 'to promote or prevent the sale of alcoholic beverages.'[18] In short, because of its cultural acceptability, alcohol, despite its psychoactive properties, became a 'non-drug' drug.

The cumulative effect of the alcoholism movement of the 1950s and 1960s was a medicalized approach that attributed alcohol problems not to manufacturers, distributors, or the state, but to diseased or at-risk individuals. On this issue both Alcoholics Anonymous and the alcohol beverage industry agreed. In the words of the Alcoholism Foundation of Alberta in 1955, in an age of liberalization, successful alcoholism programs required 'a non-controversial approach.'[19] In the 1950s and 1960s, the challenge for the treatment community, such as provincial alcoholism commissions, was to identify and treat larger numbers of alcoholics, most of whom, according to the new alcohol knowledge, were unaware of their sickness.[20] Although the ARF and other elements of the alcoholism sector attempted to stress the broader societal risks associated with increased consumption rates, the emphasis in prevention and treatment remained on the individual drinker. In contrast to addiction to illegal drug use, problem categories such as alcoholism or chronic drinking were less harshly moralistic and judgmental and more likely to win political support for treatment and rehabilitation.[21]

In Canada, the institutionalization of addiction research, treatment, and education is reflected in the history of the Alcoholism Research Foundation, created as an agency of the Ontario government in 1949. Initially the emphasis was to have been on treatment, and resources were dedicated to this end for more than two decades, but the foundation became a world-renown centre for research and dissemination of new ideas on alcohol and drug use. The ARF quarterly *Addictions* and its newspaper *The Journal* circulated to tens of thousands of social work, medical, and counselling professionals and para- professionals, including those in the United States. The foundation also ran an extensive treatment branch, with 6,000 patients handled in twenty-five Ontario municipalities in 1968.[22] Regional programs were designed to act as catalysts for local community groups to take over direct delivery of direct clinical services, a process that gained momentum in the 1970s. Other provinces established or modified existing alcohol and drug commissions from the 1950s to the 1970s. Quebec's version was OPTAT, Office de la Prévention et du Traitement de l'Alcoolisme et des Autres Toxicomanies.[23]

The Illicit Drug Threat Emerges

Despite demands for partial decriminalization, the issue of illegal drug use was largely in the hands of police, prosecutors, judges, and prison officials, not doctors or psychologists. Much like the United States, Canada had inherited a largely penal approach to illicit drug use and addiction. In the early twentieth century, Chinese users of opium were the main targets of drug enforcement.[24] In the decades after the Second World War, the authorities used the Narcotics Control Act to control the more visible 'skid-row' users of heroin as well as importers and dealers. The work was carried out by RCMP and local police drug squads, and the Division of Narcotic Control of the Department of National Health and Welfare maintained files on known addicts. As of 1969, the division had files on 4,060 addicts, (including 3,733 'criminal' addicts). The estimated number of addicts was low, perhaps equivalent to 1 per cent of the number of alcoholics in Canada. In 1955 a Senate committee that recommended stricter drug laws reported that marijuana use was not a problem in Canada.[25] For two decades following the war, 'drugs' were associated with 'social outcasts and visibly deviant groups' and public treatment programs were largely limited to the corrections sphere.[26]

In the late 1960s and early 1970s, illicit drug use, especially by Canadian youth, became an objective reality and the focus of a subjective moral panic. In 1969 there were only 2,000 convictions for marijuana and hashish offences. Although the numbers were relatively low and most convictions resulted in probation or fines, youthful cannabis users were displacing 'junkies' as the typical drug offender.[27] Numbers of prosecutions began to grow in the late 1960s. In 1976, 96 per cent of federal drug offence convictions, and 83 per cent of federal drug offences reported to the police in 1982, were cannabis-related.[28] The issue was politically sensitive because most marijuana users were casual and few had criminal records. Most police officials maintained a hard line on the issue and argued that marijuana was a 'gateway' substance that led to LSD, cocaine, and other 'hard' drugs and that the drug culture was linked to crime. Regional variations were noticeable; police in Quebec, for example, were less likely than those in Ontario to lay charges for possession of cannabis. Lawmakers, magistrates, the media, academics, and non-governmental organizations held varied views on the issue.[29]

The drug issue was also fuelled by concerns over youth subculture, notably the 'hippie' phenomenon, rising levels of violent and economic crime, and the rapid pace of social change. Although legal, medical, and social evidence was marshalled against and in favour of softening drug laws, the debate hinged on cultural or moral values, not science. The key issue by the early 1970s, from the point of view of police, lawmakers, educators, and parents, was the rapid proliferation of marijuana and other soft drugs. Law and order opinion was also concerned about LSD. From a public-health point of view, the use of licit drugs (barbiturates, amphetamines) for non-medical purposes, prompting fears of a chemically dependent society, was equally or more troubling than the rising popularity of cannabis.[30] Social problems generated research opportunities for addictions experts, including the small army of ARF scientists and social scientists. By the late 1960s the foundation was exploring not only the specific actions of various drugs on users, but also 'the social and psychological influences on the users.'[31]

Liberal interpretations embraced the notion of a 'generation gap' as an attempt to explain youthful rebellion that included music, clothing, sexuality, and recreational drug use. The general director of the Canadian Mental Health Association explained the 'drug scene' around 1970 in terms of the search by youth for 'harmony and acceptance' and an idealism threatened by parental materialism and 'copouts.'[32] A more likely explanation of what David Courtwright calls the 'marijuana complex' was the size of the Baby Boom generation, which in Western societies was identified, at least in the mass media, with 'expressive individualism, hedonism and sexual liberation.'[33] M.-A. Bertrand, a Quebec criminologist who was a member of the Le Dain Commission, opined that the late 1960s drug issue had been constructed as an 'artificial problem' by politicians and other interests in order to blame 'youth, not adults' for social problems.[34]

The Baby Boom clearly was an opportunity for experts and the helping professions to colonize new social problems and build networks. In the addictions field, the 'numbers game' of alcohol problems was part of the strategy for enlarging budgets, expanding research, and developing programs. The ARF demonstrated to the public and the provincial government that the rate of alcoholism in Ontario rose by 60 per cent from 1951 to 1965.[35] The drug issue presented similar opportunities for medical and social science. In order to understand youth subculture and the allegedly mushrooming illicit drug phenomenon, addiction researchers and public-health agencies began to study the hippies in their natural setting (such as Toronto's Yorkville area in 1967–8) and work with community-based clinics, counselling services, and hostels set up primarily for youth. The Canadian Medical Association called for 'street-level centres and services.' On the political side, the commitment of federal and provincial resources to youth issues such as drug counselling, 'drop-in centres,' and hostels was also a strategy for attracting the votes of tens of thousands of new-enfranchised young people.[36]

Illicit drug use in Canada for the decades prior to the 1990s peaked in the late 1970s (overall alcohol consumption levels peaked in the mid-1970s). Later research suggested that the drug panic of the late 1960s and early 1970s had been overblown. For example, in 1986, only 6 per cent of Canadians (most of them under thirty and single) reported using marijuana or hashish within the past twelve months. Studies indicated that most users of illicit drugs were casual or experimental in their habits.[37] The long-running Ontario Student Drug Use Survey suggested that alcohol was the drug of choice for those under nineteen. By the late 1970s, more Canadians were drinking and they were drinking larger quantities (11.8 litres per capita in Ontario in 1978).[38]

Drug policy, however, responded not to epidemiological studies, but public perception. In the early 1970s the federal health minister stated that marijuana had become a symbol of the 'alienation' of youth from Canadian society. Political interest in partial decriminalization stemmed from the fact that tens of thousands of young, middle-class citizens were acquiring criminal records for simple possession of 'soft' drugs.[39] The debate on the decriminalization of marijuana prompted the Trudeau government in 1969 to appoint the Le Dain Commission, a $4-million inquiry into the Non-Medical Use of Drugs (NMUD). The interim report, following current World Health Organization thinking, identified alcohol as North America's greatest 'dependence problem' and noted that tens of thousands of Canadians were jailed yearly for public drunkenness.[40] The final majority report of the commission, issued in 1973, represented a 'de-escalation' in that it recommended decriminalization of simple possession of marijuana. Responding to the issue of youth and drugs, Ottawa in 1971 set up a NMUD directorate within the Department of National Health and Welfare.[41] Initially focused on illicit drugs, the directorate funded research and pilot programs on education, awareness, prevention, and treatment. During the 1972 federal election campaign, Prime Minister Trudeau had spoken on the seriousness of alcohol problems to Canadian society. Following criticism in 1972–3 that the issue of alcohol abuse was being ignored, Health and Welfare, and provincial ministries, became more active.[42]

Redefining Drug Problems

The Le Dain Commission's *Interim Report*, which appeared in April 1970, noted that alcohol use was so integrated into Canadian society that many people did not even consider it to be a drug.[43] Judging by media coverage, political speeches, and information requests, the Canadian public was more concerned with 'youth' drugs such as marijuana and LSD. Yet, as Le Dain Commission research suggested, both licit and illicit drugs had been defined legally and culturally, not by pharmacological criteria. Amphetamines, barbiturates, tranquillizers, sleeping pills, anti-depressants, and analgesics, for example, were available over the counter or through a doctor's prescription and were widely used. Grouping these substances with alcohol, as well as cocaine, heroin, marijuana, and hallucinogens, was an attempt to draw society's attention to broader questions of 'substance abuse,' a problem whose scope supposedly was widening each year.[44] The commission defined a drug as 'any substance that by its chemical nature alters structure or function in the living organism.'[45] Montreal psychiatrist Dr J. Robertson Unwin used the term 'chemical promiscuity' to describe the increased use of licit drugs.[46] An epidemiological approach emphasized not drug or alcohol abuse by the few, but the negative public-health effects of increased societal reliance on psychoactive substances.

By the late 1960s, the ARF, in the face of this 'chemical threat,' was committed to reducing consumption of all psychoactive substances. This was also the message of the *Final Report* of the Le Dain Commission.[47] During the same period, the federal government began to examine health prevention issues surrounding tobacco, with a resulting 1971 law that regulated television, radio, and print media advertisements.[48]

Drugs, Society and Personal Choice, by Kalant and Kalant, was a classic statement of early 1970s 'non-judgmental' discourse on the pros and cons of a chemically dependent society. The book sold 30,000 copies within two years. The authors, pharmacologists associated with the ARF, were responding to the vigorous public discussion that accompanied the hearings of the Le Dain Commission. The broader view of addiction or dependence adopted a moral relativist stance, but it represented an enlargement of professional expertise over social problems. As 'realists,' the authors believed that the balance between controls and liberalization depended on cost-benefit analysis. In the introduction, ARF Executive Director David Archibald, much like a modern sex educator, explained that the book refrained from infringing on the individual's 'right and duty to make up his own mind, once he is fully informed.'[49] Kalant and Kalant, in their treatise on 'drug citizenship,' attempted to set a wider context for debate:

> The great majority recognize that most people who use alcohol do so in moderation, without any apparent ill effects from it. The majority would also recognize that some people use alcohol to excess and suffer mental and physical ill effects as a result.
>
> Most people would agree that those who drink to excess have an alcohol problem. In contrast, a great many people feel that any use of such substances as marihuana, LSD or other drugs which have not been traditional in our society, and for which there is at present no medical use, is a problem.[50]

Critics of the penal approach to dealing with illicit drugs concluded that North America had 'made peace' with alcohol through a combina-

tion of 'regulation, treatment and social toleration.'[51] The AOD movement, in contrast, attempted to convince legislators, the media, and the
public that alcohol was a serious drug problem.[52] This was a daunting
task because of: 1) the moral panic surrounding drug use best symbol-
ized in the United States by the Nixon administration's 'war on drugs';
2) cultural toleration of alcohol in an age of increasing liberalization
and relaxed public morality; 3) the ambivalent role of the state as both
guardian of public health and law and order and regulator and economic beneficiary of beverage alcohol sales.

In a number of jurisdictions, voluntary organizations and bureaucrats seized on the AOD message. In New Brunswick, where political support and public funding for treatment was lagging in the early
1970s, it proved useful in promoting the concept that alcohol was one of
the top health threats. One New Brunswick study, which attempted to
quantify alcohol's burden on society, concluded that 'the costs of dealing with the problems of alcoholism to date have been staggering, and
the programmes apparently ineffective.' In those jurisdictions where
public treatment programs were not as developed as elsewhere, the
emphasis remained on the addicted alcoholic.[53] Throughout the 1970s,
in addition to alcoholics, according to addictions experts there were
larger numbers of at-risk or problem drinkers. The ratio of problem
drinkers to alcoholics in early 1970s Ontario was estimated at 2–1. The
alcoholic was a person who had lost control; the problem drinker (5–9
per cent of the drinking population in a given year) lacked a physiological or psychological dependence on alcohol, but nonetheless drank
harmful amounts.[54] The Manitoba Alcoholism Foundation in 1974, in
a position paper on 'chemical abuse,' suggested that the province contained 16,000 'alcohol dependent' drinkers and 30,000 who consumed
hazardous amounts.[55] A former Alberta addiction program administrator warned in 1974 that one million Canadians 'problem drinkers'
directly affected ten million additional citizens, which made alcohol
abuse the nation's 'most devastating illness.'[56]

The research basis of the new approach was the 'single distribution' or consumption model of measuring alcohol problems. Prior to
late 1960s, the most common measure of the incidence of alcoholism
had been the 'Jellinek formula,' which was based on rates of cirrhosis
deaths.[57] Pioneered by French researcher S. Ledermann in the 1950s,
the distribution model considered broader epidemiological patterns
of consumption, and their health effects, rather than simply examining the limited minority of alcoholics. Researchers associated with the

ARF were among the first in North America to examine the 'distribution of consumption' among the general population of drinkers, and how changes in price or availability affected public health. De Lint and Schmidt, using actual customer purchasing information from the Liquor Control Board of Ontario, revealed that a small minority of customers were heavy drinkers but that most drinkers were light or moderate consumers.[58] Later work involved follow-up studies of several thousand patients treated in ARF Toronto clinics from 1951 until 1963. Also known as the 'Toronto' or 'Canadian' model, its key point was that an increase in per capita consumption would increase the percentage of heavy drinkers, and of alcohol problems across a wider segment of the population.[59]

The model also suggested that decreases in price and increases in availability had a direct impact on consumption and public health. This focus on alcohol consumption challenged the narrow view of classic alcoholism theory.[60] The associated policy suggestions included price or taxation increases, controls on advertising, and limits on access to alcohol, such as manipulating the hours of liquor stores and bars or raising the legal drinking age. Despite public perception to the contrary, the real price of alcohol fell during the 1960s and 1970s, making it more accessible. In the early 1970s alcohol advertisements on television were outlawed in British Columbia, Saskatchewan, and New Brunswick and debates on the subject were taking place in Manitoba and Ontario. In 1972 the ARF advocated doubling the price of fortified wine (a staple of skid row drinkers) and raising the price of spirits and beer. Various alcoholism experts denounced the claim of Canadian brewers that beer was a 'socially responsible' beverage of 'moderation' that should enjoy taxation advantages.[61]

Social scientists and other addiction researchers and treatment professionals began to have second thoughts about the wisdom of liberalization. The new restrictionist movement, which some dubbed 'neo-temperance,' was most evident in Ontario, where researchers began to call for increased controls on beverage alcohol.[62] By the early 1970s, government policy was ambivalent if not confusing. On the one hand, elements of public opinion and legal culture were supporting a liberalization of liquor sales and licensing. On the other hand, governments, advised by public-health and addictions experts, were loath to be seen as publicly encouraging increased consumption. In Ontario, public-health concerns led to the announcement, in late 1972, that the Davis government would conduct an alcohol policy review.[63] A parallel but related effort that embraced a medical model of alcohol problems was the partial decriminalization of public intoxication, with the province, the ARF, and non-governmental organizations running a system of detox centres and post-detox halfway houses (thirty by 1976).[64]

The culmination of several years of research reports, the ARF made recommendations in 1978 for 'stricter controls over the alcohol industry.'[65] The report, gathered in advance of a parliamentary debate at Queen's Park on the drinking age and related matters, attempted to explain to legislators that it was necessary to think beyond alcoholism and chronic drunkenness to the broader picture. The consumption model was its key paradigm. Not knowing that per capita alcohol consumption was about to fall, the researchers projected a 50 per cent increase by the mid-1980s, with a corresponding rise in health problems. The five main policy suggestions were a freeze on further liberalization, a health-centred pricing policy, an increase in the legal drinking age, the discouragement of 'lifestyle' liquor advertising, and a strong education and awareness effort.[66]

The brief produced a counterattack from the Brewers of Ontario, entitled 'Ontario Deserves Something Better from the Addiction Research Foundation.'[67] With millions of dollars of revenues at stake if governments tightened up alcohol distribution, industry remained vigilant and earned public goodwill through 'moderation' campaigns. In 1973 executives from the distilling giant Seagram, in correspondence with the executive assistant of Ontario's minister of consumer and commercial relations, had privately criticized the research assumptions of the ARF, singling out the work of de Lint and Schmidt as particularly misguided. Critics of neo-temperance often pointed out that in Scandinavian counties where controls were stricter, rates of clinical depression and suicide were higher than in Canada.[68]

One public-health message that the AOD movement attempted to disseminate was that alcohol was a greater threat to youth than drugs and that parents and 'over 30' Canadians, who were enjoying the mixed benefits of liberalization and falling prices, were hypocritical in their attitudes towards drugs other than alcohol and tobacco. This message was particularly visible in articles, editorials, and cartoons in the ARF's publication The Journal.[69] The foundation had youth drinking and drug surveys that dated back to 1968. Executive Director Archibald noted ironically in 1973 that Toronto parents panicked when surveys suggested that 20 per cent of high school students had used marijuana, but were relieved to hear that 80 per cent had consumed alcohol.

Throughout the decade of the 1970s, the incidence of teenage drinking as reported in these surveys increased.[70]

In the midst of media hype over drugs, the growing popularity of youth drinking often was glossed over. The chief inspector of the Nova Scotia Liquor License Board in a 1973 memo identified the lowering of the drinking age to nineteen in 1971, the opening of beverage rooms to female patrons, and a more permissive trend in 'social habits' as reasons why beverage rooms and lounges had become the '"in" place for young people to gather.'[71] Thanks to the demographic patterns, affluence, and changing cultural norms, which included mixed gender socializing, the Baby Boom generation was a 'wet' generation. Reductions in the minimum drinking age usually followed reductions in the voting age. In Manitoba, where the legal drinking age had been lowered from twenty-one to eighteen in 1970, beer was the preferred drink of young people.[72]

AOD arguments faced opposition from conservative opinion that tended to view illicit drugs such as marijuana, cocaine, and LSD as moral threats and licit drugs as acceptable risks, pharmacological or sociological evidence notwithstanding. There was also resistance from vested interests. A classic debate took place in 1972 when a beverage alcohol industry representative squared off against Wolfgang Schmidt, a social scientist associated with the ARF who subscribed to neo-temperance policies. According to M. McCormick, senior vice president of the House of Seagram, consumption itself had no role in alcohol problems: 'alcohol per se is not the cause of alcoholism.' McCormick, shielded behind the disease theory of alcoholism, rejected increased spending by industry on education and awareness and higher taxes on spirits and health warning labels on bottles. In his view, 96 per cent of drinkers were risk free, while the 3–4 per cent of drinkers who were alcoholics were immune from prevention campaigns. The increasingly liberal general public, furthermore, would resent 'moralizing' by neo-temperance advocates.[73] In a similar vein, the Brewers Association of Canada argued that drinking problems could be minimized if the public was encouraged, through taxation policies, to drink more beer as opposed to spirits and wine. Sales statistics indicated that, by the early 1970s, more than half of the alcohol (by volume) consumed in Canada was produced by the breweries. The brewers argued that per capita consumption of alcohol had peaked in the mid-1970s, that Canadians by international standards were moderate drinkers, and that more spirits and wine were being consumed.[74]

In the late 1970s, the ARF, which had dedicated six out of nine long-term objectives to alcohol-related problems, addressed the issue of the objectivity of a provincial Crown corporation in recommending social policy (in this case, policies that affected the private sector). Foundation president John Macdonald defended the foundation's policy formulation role on the basis of its legislative mandate to disseminate information on preventing alcohol and drug addiction. Unlike other provincial health foundations (cancer, mental health) concerned with primarily with treatment, the ARF was drawn into an advocacy role that appeared to go beyond the supposedly neutral approach of most provincial agencies. One of its alcohol objectives was to achieve a 'plateau' in per capita consumption (which represented a partial retreat on the late 1960s goal of discouraging consumption).[75]

In terms of limiting alcohol's harm to society, other than enforcing Criminal Code and provincial measures against driving while impaired, and maintaining controls on advertising, provincial governments did little beyond funding studies and authorizing health prevention messages.[76] By the early 1980s, for example, four provinces outlawed electronic media advertisements and three banned print-media advertisements produced within the province. The Canadian Radio-television and Telecommunications Commission banned radio and televisions ads for spirits and permitted provincial governments to regulate ads for beer and wine. In provinces such as Manitoba and Ontario, alcohol ads could be broadcast on television only late at night. The appearance of lifestyle advertising of beer in the 1970s was a source of concern among addictions experts and educators. The lower legal drinking age, and a rise in traffic fatalities, were topics of controversy throughout the 1970s, and following the initial spate of liberalization, a number of provinces (and most American states) raised the minimum age.[77] In 1977 the Addiction Foundation of Prince Edward Island, a Crown corporation, supported an abortive bid to raise the legal drinking age to nineteen. A Manitoba advisory committee, claiming that 70–80 per cent of the adult population was at risk, made a similar recommendation in 1981.[78]

The anti-impaired driving and health promotion campaigns, undertaken by the federal and provincial governments, took place against a backdrop of a new interest in individual responsibility for health and fitness, as evidenced by concerns over tobacco, lack of physical exercise, and poor diet. Health reformers were attempting to impart the message that risky lifestyles, not the level of health services, dictated the overall health of society. In 1972 ARF advertisements warned people who consumed six drinks daily that their health might be in danger and the Canadian Medical Association urged members to notify patients of the health risks associated with heavy drinking. Heavy drinking was defined as consumption of five or more drinks at a single time, with one drink equalling one bottle of beer or glass of draught, one glass of wine or wine cooler, or 1.5 ounces of spirits. Prevention messages also stressed that one alcoholic affected several other people – at home, at work, or at school.[79] Risk was no longer confined to 'becoming alcoholic'; it included cirrhosis, cancer, psychiatric disorders, and other health issues. The ARF's task force on treatment service for alcoholics estimated that 15–20 per cent of hospital beds in Ontario were occupied by patients with alcohol-related problems, at a cost of $450 million.[80] The Alcoholism Foundation of Manitoba, contributing to a provincial liquor policy review in 1980, recommended that any liberalization of regulation should be tested against public-health objectives.[81]

In the 1970s, alcoholism and drug treatment programs and professional associations, following the ARF model, began to merge. The Canadian Foundation on Alcohol and Drug Dependencies, a non-governmental organization founded in the mid-1960s, was later renamed the Canadian Addictions Foundation. In Quebec, treatment was rolled into the growing system of community health centres.[82] There were political, administrative, and budgetary reasons behind organizational and program mergers, and there was also a change in terminology to conceptualize the issue of treatment for psychoactive drugs. Experts were less comfortable with terms such as alcoholism and did not agree on either the causes or the cures of alcohol misuse. Problem definition in the 1970s increasingly spoke of 'substance abuse' and 'chemical dependency' rather than addiction.[83] At the same time, separate alcohol and drug treatment 'empires' continued to exist.[84]

In Canada, the timing and sequence of these changes was somewhat complex. In many cases provincial agencies, often assisted by federal-provincial cost-sharing programs, provided funding to community organizations and 'innovative services.' Ontario, which had been attempting a unified approach since 1961, continued to lead the way in terms of research and dissemination of new ideas on treatment and prevention. In 1974 the ARF defending unified approaches to drug abuse as less insular, less competitive, and more fiscally responsible.[85] In Nova Scotia, the provincial Drug Dependency Commission (formed in 1971) was tasked with general anti-drug education as well as providing services for the province's 18,000 alcoholics (early 1970s estimate).[86] By the early 1980s, the New Brunswick Alcoholism and Drug Dependency Commission maintained three rehabilitation centres and eight treatment centres.[87] In Manitoba in the early 1970s, up to twenty agencies dealt with alcohol and drug problems. Alberta founded an Alcohol and Drug Addiction Commission in 1970; by 1974 it had a budget of $3 million and more than 200 staff members. British Columbia's Narcotic Addiction Foundation and Alcoholism Foundation as of 1973 competed with an Addiction Foundation, dedicated to community-based approaches. The two organizations later merged.[88]

Federal initiatives, notably the hearings, research studies, and reports of the Le Dain Commission, supported broader 'health' approaches to drugs and alcohol. When the NMUD directorate had been set up by Health and Welfare Canada in the early 1970s as a reaction to the 'drug crisis,' it had been on the cutting edge of the AOD movement. The move reflected concern not with only with drugs and alcohol, but also the perceived excesses of post-industrial North American living: smoking, overeating, lack of physical exercise, and the over-prescribing of medication. Three years and three directors later, the role of the agency was described as 'murky' and its profile as low. From a constitutional point of view, there was little reason for the federal government to be involved in the public-health side of the drug issue, yet Medicare provided a handy precedent. According to the NMUD director general in 1974, the federal role in terms of the non-medical use of drugs was to 'develop knowledge' and to exercise 'influence' through research (15 per cent of the budget in 1973–4) and 'innovative services' (85 per cent of the budget).[89] In 1975, for example, the NMUD directorate announced a three-year plan to support aboriginal communities in developing community alcohol abuse prevention and treatment programs.[90]

During the 1980s, tobacco emerged as the 'star' of the AOD (now ATOD) approach. ARF studies of the subject began in the late 1970s; according to the 1978–9 *Annual Report*, smoking was a form of 'drug intake.'[91] Unlike the positioning of alcohol in the late 1960s and early 1970s, which took place in an era of rising per capita consumption, health promotion concerns regarding tobacco emerged as smoking was becoming less popular (50 per cent of the adult population in 1965, declining to 32 per cent in 1980).[92] The total consumption model developed by alcohol researchers was applied to this new public problem. The Canadian Centre on Substance Abuse was founded in 1990 to study the abuse of tobacco, alcohol, and illicit drugs. Its major prevalence study estimated that the cost of these substances to Canadian society, through lost productivity, health care costs, and criminal activity, was $18.45 billion in 1992. Together they were allegedly responsible for 20 per cent of all deaths in 1992, and 10 per cent of hospital admissions. Of the three, tobacco supposedly was the most harmful, with a societal cost of $9.5 billion, followed by $7.5 billion for alcohol and only $1.4 billion for illicit drugs.[93]

Conclusion

The decade of the 1960s ended with 'common-sense' political and public anxieties about the 'drug problem' and a more sophisticated expert debate about chemical promiscuity. The liberalization of alcohol controls in the 1960s and 1970s was not uncontested. Public health and safety, not morality, became the source of opposition. Addiction experts promoted AOD to slow down the perceived excesses of liberalization, which, compared to traditional alcoholism messages, were cast as threats to society as a whole. According to Heron, the neo-temperance researchers of the 1970s could not fully explain the consumption trends of the era, and politicians for the most part ignored their warnings.[94] Unlike the more narrowly focussed anti-impaired driving movement, AOD, at least as applied to alcohol, was unable to build a broader political coalition.[95] Alcohol, unlike narcotics or marijuana, could not be fully demonized. As it evolved, the AOD message could be interpreted in more than one way. Embraced by exponents of what later would be termed harm reduction, it supported warning labels on alcoholic beverage containers and higher prices in order to discourage consumption of licit drugs. Many of these same advocates supported medicalization of illicit drug problems and the partial decriminalization of personal marijuana use. AOD lived on in federal, provincial, and municipal anti-tobacco policies, which have included increased taxation, warning labels and public service advertisements, a minimum age for buying tobacco products, and no-smoking areas on public property and commercial premises. AOD also was useful to 'hawks' in the war on drugs, who opposed the decriminalization of soft drugs and supported penal sanctions and enforced treatment of addicts or substance abusers. Both sides of the substance abuse debate in the 1980s were manifestations of a revived politically motivated 'health moralism.'[96]

NOTES

1 David J. Pittman, 'The Rush to Combine: Sociological Dissimilarities of Alcoholism and Drug Abuse,' *British Journal of Addiction*, 62 (1976): 337–44.
2 Ron Roizen, 'Merging Alcohol and Illicit Drugs: A Brief Commentary on the Search for Symbolic Middle Ground between Licit and Illicit Psychoactive Substances' (1993), *Alcohol Sociology*, http//www.roizen.com/ron/.
3 Pittman, 'The Rush to Combine.'
4 Two exceptions were George Stevenson, 'Drug Addiction in British Columbia: A Research Survey,' unpublished manuscript (University of British Columbia 1956), and the work of the Narcotic Addiction Foundation of British Columbia.
5 ARF, *Annual Report*, 1955–60; ADARF, *Annual Report*, 1961–6. During the 1960s, the ARF became involved in the experimental maintenance of heroin addicts on methadone.
6 Robert E. Popham, Jan de Lint, and Wolfgang Schmidt, 'Some Comments on Pittman's "Rush to Combine,"' *British Journal of Addiction*, 63 (1968): 25–7.
7 ADARF, *Annual Report*, 1966, 11.
8 Multiple drug use became a concern of researchers in the late 1960s: *Cannabis: A Report of the Commission of Inquiry into the Non-Medical Use of Drugs* (Ottawa: Information Canada 1972), 15–28.
9 By the 1980s, the approach was recast as 'ATOD,' alcohol, tobacco, and other drugs. For an overview of historic patterns in defining drugs and addiction, see David Courtwright, 'Mr. ATOD's Wild Ride,' keynote address, International Conference on Drugs and Alcohol in History, London, Ontario, 14 May 2004.
10 For a sociological view of the construction of social problems, see Malcolm Spector and John I. Kituse, *Constructing Social Problems* (New York: Aldine de Gruyter 1987).
11 See the *Canadian White Ribbons Tidings*, the Canadian WCTU organ, for the 1920s.
12 Jonathan Zimmerman, *Distilling Democracy: Alcohol Education in America's Public Schools, 1880–1925* (Lawrence: University of Kansas Press 1999); Greg Marquis, 'The Canadian Temperance Movement: What Happened after Prohibition?' unpublished paper, 2000.
13 Harry Levine, 'The Disease Concept of Addiction: Changing Conceptions of Habitual Drunkenness in America,' *Journal of Studies in Alcohol*, 39, no. 1 (1977): 143–74; Courtwright, 'Mr. ATOD's Wild Ride'; William White, 'The

Lessons of Language: Historical Perspectives on the Rhetoric of Addiction,' in Sarah W. Tracy and Caroline Jean Acker, eds., *Altering American Consciousness: The History of Drug Use in the United States, 1800–2000* (Boston: University of Massachusetts Press 2004), 33–60.

14 For an overview, see Craig Heron, *Booze: A Distilled History* (Toronto: Between the Lines 2003).

15 Manitoba, *Report of the Manitoba Liquor Enquiry Commission* (Winnipeg, 1955). For British Columbia, see Robert Campbell, *Demon Rum or Easy Money: Government Control of Liquor in British Columbia from Prohibition to Privatization* (Ottawa: Carleton University Press 1991); *Sit Down and Drink Your Beer: Regulating Vancouver's Beer Parlours, 1925–1954* (Toronto: University of Toronto Press 2001); Greg Marquis, 'Civilized Drinking: Alcohol and Society in New Brunswick, 1945–1975,' *Journal of the Canadian Historical Association*, 2000, 173–205.

16 Mariana Valverde, *Diseases of the Will: Alcohol and the Dilemmas of Freedom* (Cambridge: Cambridge University Press 1998); Greg Marquis, '"A Reluctant Concession to Modernity": Alcohol and Modernization in the Maritimes, 1945–1980,' *Acadiensis*, 32, 2 (spring 2003): 31–59.

17 Archives of Ontario (AO), RG 31, Ministry of Consumer and Commercial Relations, box 29.

18 Public Archives of Manitoba (PAM), GR 1546, 5–19, Ministerial Advisory Committee, J.R. Boyce, 'A Statement of Intent: Alcohol and Drug Programs and Services in Manitoba,' December 1974.

19 PAM, GR 1648, Manitoba Liquor Enquiry Commission, file 35M, Alcoholism Foundation of Alberta, 2 June 1954.

20 Nova Scotia Archives and Records Management, RG 74, Interim Report of the Alcoholism Research Commission, typescript, January 1961, 53–5.

21 Roizen, 'Merging Alcohol and Drugs,' 4–5; Greg Marquis, 'Inventing the Alcoholic: Canadian Public Policy and the Individualization of Deviance,' unpublished paper, 2001.

22 ARF, *Annual Report*, 1955–60; ADARF, *Annual Report*, 1961–7; ARF, *Annual Report*, 1968, 11.

23 Ibid., 1975–6, 3, 33–4; 1978–9, 47. Despite this shift, more than one-third of the operating budget in 1978–9 supported treatment.

24 Reginald Smart, *Forbidden Highs: The Nature, Treatment and Prevention of Illicit Drug Abuse* (Toronto: Addiction Research Foundation 1981), 216; Carolyn Strange and Tina Loo, *Making Good: Law and Moral Regulation in Canada, 1867–1939* (Toronto: University of Toronto Press 1997); 9–91; Clayton James Mosher, *Discrimination and Denial: Systemic Racism in Ontario's Legal and Justice System* (Toronto: University of Toronto Press 1998), chapter 6.

25 ADARF, *Annual Report*, 1966, 13–14; Canada, *The Non-Medical Use of Drugs: Interim Report of the Canadian Government Commission of Inquiry* (London: Penguin Books, 1971), 211, 243–4. The Health Departments Bureau of Dangerous Drugs had files dating back to 1962 on 'thousands' of 'known and suspected' Canadians, mainly heroin addicts, who used illicit drugs. The information allegedly was gathered from the RCMP, police drug squads, treatment centres, pharmacists, physicians, and parole authorities: ARF, *The Journal*, 3 (June 1974), 2.

26 Klaus Makela et al., *Alcohol, Society and the State* (Toronto: Addiction Research Foundation 1981), 65.

27 Canada, *The Non-Medical Use of Drugs: Interim Report*, 260.

28 *The Journal*, 6 (September 1977), 3; Canadian Centre for Justice Statistics, *Canadian Crime Statistics 1988* (Ottawa: Statistics Canada 1989), 47.

29 For police attitudes, see Greg Marquis, *Policing Canada's Century: A History of the Canadian Association of Chiefs of Police* (Toronto: University of Toronto Press 1993), 267–8, 298–302, 435–46, 354, 386–7, 396–7.

30 Harold Kalant and Oriana Josseau Kalant, *Drugs, Society and Personal Choice* (Toronto: Paperjacks 1971), 1–4. Concern over abuse of licit drugs led to the formation of the Council on Drug Abuse (Canada) by pharmaceutical manufacturers, distributors, and retailers.

31 ARF, *Annual Report*, 1968, 23.

32 J.D. Griffin, 'Foreword,' in Sheila Gormely, ed., *Drugs and the Canadian Scene* (Toronto: Pagurian Press 1970), v. 'Copouts' referred to compromises, acts of hypocrisy, and general acceptance of the dehumanizing conformity of post-1945 society.

33 David Courtwright, *Forces of Habit: Drugs and the Making of the Modern World* (Cambridge, Mass.: Harvard University Press 2001), 45.

34 *The Journal*, 3 (February 1974), 2.

35 Canada, *The Non-Medical Use of Drugs: Interim Report*, 188–90; ARF, *Annual Report*, 1952–66. See also *Annual Report*, 1979–80, 1–2.

36 Gormley, *Drugs*, 176; *Halifax Chronicle Herald*, 23 January 1971. In the late 1960s and early 1970s, the ARF, for public-health purposes, also studied the consistency or purity of common 'street' drugs.

37 Marc Eliany, *Licit and Illicit Drugs in Canada* (Ottawa: Health and Welfare Canada, 1989), v.

38 Eric Single, Norman Giesbrecht, and Barry Eakins, 'The Alcohol Policy Debate in Ontario in the Post-War Era,' in Eric Single, Patricia Morgan, and Jan de Lint, *Alcohol, Society and the State 2* (Toronto: Addiction Research Foundation 1981), 129; Centre for Addiction and Mental Health, *Drug Use among Ontario Students, 1977–2003* (Toronto: CAMH, 2003).

39 In 1972 the Department of Justice urged Crown prosecutors to recommend, in narcotics cases where the charge was simple possession, absolute or conditional discharge: *The Journal*, 3 (July 1974), 2.

40 *Halifax Chronicle Herald*, 27 January 1972.

41 Gormley, *Drugs*, xv; *Final Report of the Commission of Inquiry into the Non-Medical Use of Drugs* (Ottawa: Information Canada 1973).

42 *The Journal*, 1 (September 1972), 3; *The Journal*, 2 (January 1973), 1; *The Journal*, 3 (February 1973), 5.

43 Canada, *The Non-Medical Use of Drugs: Interim Report*, 63.

44 ARF, *Annual Report*, 1969, 1970. This was the approach of the Mulroney government's National Drug Strategy, launched in 1987: Eliany, *Licit and Illicit Drugs*, i.

45 *The Journal*, 3 (November 1974), 1.

46 Ibid.

47 ARF, *Annual Report*, 1970; Canada, *Final Report of the Commission of Inquiry into the Non-Medical Use of Drugs* (Ottawa: Information Canada 1973), 19.

48 Debra Scoffield, *Public Policy and Alcohol Consumption in the Maritime Provinces* (Halifax: Atlantic Provinces Economic Council 1976), 40.

49 Kalant and Kalant, *Drugs, Society*, vi.

50 Ibid., 2. The non-coercive tone of the book echoed that of the Interim Report of the Le Dain Commission.

51 Dianna Gordon, *The Return of the Dangerous Classes: Drug Prohibition and Policy Politics* (New York: W.W. Norton 1994), 106.

52 *The Journal*, 1 (June 1972), 3; *The Journal*, 1 (July 1972), 5; David J. Pittman and William J. Staudenmeir, '20th Century Wars on Alcohol and Other Drugs in the United States,' in Peter J. Venturelli, ed., *Drug Use in America* (Boston: Bartlett and Bartlett 1994), 149–56.

53 *Halifax Chronicle Herald*, 29 April 1970; Report of the New Brunswick Study Committee on Alcoholism to the Minister of Health, April 1972; Marquis, 'Civilized Drinking.'

54 *The Journal*, 2 (August 1973), 2; ARF, *Annual Report*, 1972–3, Table V. For the American Psychiatric Association DSM-IV definition of 'substance dependence,' see James Inciardi, *The War on Drugs III* (Toronto: Allyn and Bacon 2002), 5–6.

55 PAM, GR 1546 S-19, Alcohol Foundation of Manitoba, 'A Statement of Intent: Alcohol and Drug Programs and Services in Manitoba,' December 1974.

56 *The Journal*, 3 (August 1974), 3.

57 ARF, *Annual Report*, 1972–3, Table VIII. See also R.E. Popham, *Alcohol and Alcoholism* (Toronto: University of Toronto Press 1970).

58 J. de Lint and W. Schmidt, 'The Distribution of Alcohol Consumption in

Ontario,' *Quarterly Journal of Studies on Alcohol*, 29 (1968): 968–73. In this study, sales slips indicated that 25 per cent of population purchased 40 per cent of Liquor Control Board of Ontario sales.

59 Reginald Smart and Alan C. Ogborne, *Northern Spirit: A Social History of Alcohol in Canada* (Toronto: Addiction Research Foundation 1996), 74–5, 173; ARF, *Annual Report*, 1968, 24; Kalant and Kalant, *Drugs, Society*, 101–5. See also *The Journal*, 6 (July 1977), 9. For an early example of consumption research, see J.R. Seeley, 'Death by Liver Cirrhosis and the Price of Beverage Alcohol,' *Canadian Medical Association Journal*, 83 (1960): 136–66.

60 Ron Roizen, Kaye Middleton Fillmore, and William Kerr, 'Overlooking Terris: A Speculative Reconsideration of a Curious Spot-Blindness in the History of Alcohol-Control Science,' *Contemporary Drug Problems*, 26 (winter 1999): 577–606.

61 *The Journal*, 1 (June 1972), 2; *The Journal*, 1 (July 1972), 1; *The Journal*, 2 (January 1973), 3; *The Journal*, 2 (February 1973), 5; *The Journal*, 2 (August 1973), 7.

62 David J. Pittman, 'The Neo-Temperance Movement,' in *Society, Culture and Drinking Patterns Revisited*, 775–90.

63 AO, RG 31, box 25, Statement by the Minister of Consumer and Corporate Relations, 24 November 1972; box 41, John T. Clement to Fred A. Burr, 4 September 1973; box 41, M.J. McCormick to John T. Clement, 21 February 1973; Submission to Cabinet: Legislation: Act to Amend the Liquor License Act.

64 K. Bottomley, N. Giesbrecht, P.J. Giffen, S. Lambert, and G. Oki, 'A History of Recent Changes in the Social Control of Public Inebriates, with Special Reference to Ontario and Toronto,' Addiction Research Foundation substudy, 1976, 813.

65 Single et al., 'The Alcohol Policy Debate,' 137–8. In 1978 a columnist in the ARF *Journal* criticized Quebec's decision to allow wine to be sold in corner stores. Much like classic temperance opinion, neo-temperance held that increased availability meant increased abuse. *The Journal*, 6 (April 1978), 6.

66 'A Strategy for the Prevention of Alcohol Problems: Background Information and Recommendations for the Parliamentary Debate on Control Measures,' *The Journal*, 6 (July 1978).

67 *The Journal*, 7 (April 1979), 8–12. The debate continued in *The Journal*, 7 (May 1979).

68 AO, RG 31–1, box 40, M.J. McCormick to Russell Cooper, 31 May 1973; Russell Cooper to M.J. McCormick, 29 June 1973; box 29, Y.M.W. Griffin to Russell Cooper, 22 May 1973.

69 *The Journal*, 1 (July 1972), 5. See also Kalant and Kalant, *Drugs, Society*, 4.

70 *The Journal*, 2 (September 1973), 1.

71 Nova Scotia Gaming Authority, G.W.R. Anderson to Hugh Tinkham, 30 August 1973.

72 Manitoba, Report of the Ministerial Advisory Committee on Liquor Control (Winnipeg, 1981), chapter 11, A4.

73 *The Journal*, 1 (July 1972), 7, 15. See also 2 (July 1973), 1.

74 Brewers Association of Canada, *Perspectives on Beer in Canada* (Ottawa, 1979); ARF, *Annual Report*, 1974–5, Table II. The brewers lost one battle in 1980 when the federal government budget equalized taxation on beverage alcohol by volume – long a demand of the distillers.

75 ARF, *Annual Report*, 1978–9, 1–6; 1979–80, 2–3, 7.

76 In 1981 Single wrote that the Ontario government had ignored the major recommendations of the ARF but had implemented most of the policy changes suggested by the alcohol, tourism, and hospitality industries: 'The Alcohol Policy Debate,' 148–9. One exception was the government's decision to raise the drinking age to nineteen in 1979.

77 Manitoba, *Report of the Ministerial Advisory Committee on Liquor Control* (Winnipeg, 1981), chapters IX–XI. Manitoba raised the age from eighteen to nineteen. Media controls applied only to commercials printed or broadcast within a specific province. During the period in question, North American distillers, through an industry agreement, refused to advertise on radio and television.

78 ARF, *Annual Report*, 1974–5, 3–4; *The Journal*, 6 (July 1977), 3; Report of the Ministerial Advisory Committee, 9. See also R.G. Smart, 'Changes in Alcoholic Beverage Sales after Reductions in the Legal Drinking Age,' *American Journal of Drug Abuse*, 4, no. 1 (1977): 107.

79 *The Journal*, 1 (June 1972), 8; (July 1972), 1, 5, 7, 9, 15. See also *Rapport de la commission d'enquête sur le commerce des boissons alcooliques* (Quebec, 1971), 33–8.

80 ARF, *Annual Report*, 1979–80, 5.

81 PAM, GR 1546, 5–19, Alcohol Federation of Manitoba, Submission to the Ministerial Advisory Committee on Liquor Control Matters, June 1980.

82 Heron, *Booze*, 364.

83 William White, *Slaying the Dragon: The History of Addiction Treatment and Recovery in America* (Bloomington, Ill.: Chestnut Health Systems 1998), 196–7.

84 For Manitoba in the 1970s, see PAM, GR 1546, Ministerial Advisory Committee on Liquor Control Matters, Brief 5–7, Alcoholism Foundation of Manitoba.

85 *The Journal*, 3 (August 1974), 2. ARF budgets, after years of steady growth, began to fall behind inflation in the mid-1970s.

86 *The Journal*, 2 (February 1973), 13. In 1972 the commission estimated that alcoholism affected 15 per cent of the province's population: Commission on Drug Dependency of Nova Scotia, *Annual Report*, 1972 (Halifax, 1972).

87 Alcoholism and Drug Dependency Commission of New Brunswick, Year End Report, April 1983–March 1984: 'Summary of Statistics for Rehabilitation and Outpatient Services' (Fredericton: typescript 1984).

88 *The Journal*, 2 (April 1973), 7; *The Journal*, 3 (May 1974), 4; PAM, GR 1546, 5–19, Ministerial Advisory Committee, Boyce, 'A Statement of Intent.' In the early 1970s, the Alcoholism Foundation of British Columbia estimated that the province contained 44,000 alcoholics: *A Comprehensive Plan for Alcohol Control* (Victoria: Alcoholism Foundation of British Columbia 1972).

89 *The Journal*, 3 (June 1974), 7.

90 'Native Alcohol Abuse Program – Joint Effort,' *Saskatchewan Indian*, December 1975, 13.

91 ARF, *Annual Report*, 1978–9, 10–12.

92 Elinay, ed., *Alcohol*, 14.

93 Presentation by M. Perron, chief executive officer of the Canadian Centre on Substance Abuse, to the Senate Committee on Illicit Drugs, 10 June 2002, Ottawa, http://www.cssa.ca.

94 Heron, *Booze*, 368.

95 For the importance of political alliances to successful social movements, see Anne-Marie E. Szymanski, *Pathways to Prohibition and Social Movement Outcomes: Radicals, Moderates and Social Movement Outcomes* (Durham, N.C.: Duke University Press 2003).

96 See Zimmerman, *Distilling Democracy*, Preface.

9 Considering the Revolving Door: The Inevitability of Addiction Treatment in the Criminal Justice System

DAWN MOORE

For more than half a century, the Canadian criminal justice system has been intent on 'closing the revolving door on crime by curing addiction.'[1] Underlying the long-standing practice of criminal-justice-based addiction treatment are two key assumptions: first, that drug use actually causes crime; and second, that curing drug use will also cure offenders of their criminal behaviours. As the entrenchment of addiction treatment in the justice system continues through the advent of mechanisms such as drug-treatment courts, specialized treatment prisons, and conditional sentences mandating addiction treatment, there is good reason to pause and pay careful and critical attention to these phenomena. While such treatments of therapeutic initiatives suggest that grave concerns emerge from wedding treatment and justice, it seems prudent, in the face of apparently imminent clawbacks to Canada's relatively liberalized drug policies and the rise of 'tough on crime' political sentiment, to resist the temptation to throw out both therapeutic baby and bath water. In light of the fact that such initiatives often extend much needed social services to the socially marginalized while also, in some cases, working to keep selected individuals convicted of a criminal offence out of the prison system, I present here tempered criticisms which also recognize how these initiatives work to redefine the ways in which we think about progressive drug policies.

My argument is that the treatment of drug addiction is as much (if not more) politically and culturally contingent as it is rooted in any kind of etiological truth. I craft my account first by offering a brief history of addiction treatment in the Canadian justice system that reveals the practice's political and cultural heritage. This is followed by a survey of extant literature casting doubt on the claim that addiction is inherently linked to crime. I close with a consideration of the future of Canadian drug policy, specifically questioning the potential for 'progress' in what appears to be an increasingly regressive climate.

A Brief History

Before the Second World War, addiction treatment was not a feature of criminal justice practice in Canada. While drug use was clearly linked with criminal behaviour[2] and the treatment of addiction[3] was a growing industry, treatment was not located in the justice system until the war's end. Much of what facilitated the introduction of addiction treatment into the criminal justice system was the widespread adoption of the medical model.

Enrico Ferri, a key figure in the early biological-positivist school of criminology, describes the medical model as follows: 'As medicine teaches us that to discover the remedies for a disease we must first seek and discover the causes, so criminal science in the new form which it is beginning to assume, seeks the natural causes of the phenomenon of social pathology which we call crime: it thus puts itself in the way to discover effective remedies.'[4] Through the medical model, interventions with lawbreakers evolved and criminal justice systems became increasingly interested in psychological and psychiatric assessments, pharmacotherapies, and electroshock treatments.[5] Much of this interest rested on the constitution of particular pathological identities which, once ascribed to offenders, mobilized particular kinds of interventions designed to cure the ailment thought to cause the criminality.

Although comparatively late to adopt this approach to punishment (especially when measured against their American counterparts), Canadian justice officials took up the medical model in different jurisdictions, largely as a response to the perception that prisons were increasingly harsh, brutal places lacking the very basics of human-rights protections. While there is a dearth of comprehensive chronicles of punishment in both the federal and provincial systems in Canada during this time, the extant accounts indicate that the medical model was desired and adopted in both political and administrative rhetoric.

The rise of the medical model facilitated the establishment of a disease paradigm of drugs and crime.[6] P.J. Giffen, Shirley Endicott, and Sylvia Lambert document the emergence of this particular type of thinking whereby drug use (specifically heroin use) is considered a disease that spreads in its own right and also advances the criminal behaviour that is its constant companion.[7] Emerging out of this perceived drug-crime nexus were the country's first treatment prisons and in-house treatment programs, initiating a multi-purpose vision of a penal system. Punishment could now be used to cure one individual pathology (addiction) and thus individual criminality.

In 1951 the government of Ontario opened the treatment-oriented Alex G. Brown (AGB) Memorial Clinic in the Mimico Reformatory. Originally mandated to treat alcoholics, AGB expanded in 1956 to treat drug addiction and then again in 1965 to treat paedophilia. The function and design of AGB conforms almost perfectly to the description of penal-welfarist practices set out by David Garland.[8] Garland assigns a number of axioms to the welfarist project, reflecting an initiative designed to effect social reform through the appreciation of state responsibility to care for and cure the criminal. In this project, social work and psychiatric/psychological expertise are pre-eminent.

AGB imagined the criminal addict most clearly as a welfarist penal subject.[9] In the three- to six-month treatment program, prisoners were immersed in a treatment milieu where everything they did was meant to facilitate their recovery. Then as now, the grammar of treatment was not simply about stopping an individual from using drugs but rather about a much bigger project of teaching good citizenship.[10] The starting point for this regime was the assumption that the criminal addict is sick and in need of total intervention in order to be rehabilitated. For example, in an AGB information booklet, new residents were encouraged to engage in all aspects of the treatment program (including arts and crafts and 'industrial therapy'). Full engagement meant following the strict prison schedule, meeting dress codes and codes of cleanliness, and seeking help for feeling 'uptight.' Residents were told when they might drink coffee and lie on their beds, and when they were required to watch films dealing with 'people and their feelings.'[11]

In Ontario, outside of AGB, no in-house interventions were offered to either addicts or alcoholics incarcerated in the province's jails and reformatories.[12] Probationers and parolees, at that point governed by the Ministry of the Attorney General, did receive addictions-related programming as well as other vocational and psychological interventions. These interventions, along with probation and parole supervision, were regularly provided by not-for-profit organizations like the John Howard Society or benevolent religious organizations. Self-help groups like Narcotics Anonymous (newly introduced to Canada) also offered interventions for those with addiction problems. AGB, however, remained the lone treatment institution in the province until the 1970s.

Ontario was not the only jurisdiction in the country that took the initiative to develop in-house addiction-treatment initiatives. Correctional Services Canada (CSC) opened the medium-security Matsqui prison just outside Vancouver exclusively for the treatment of addicts. The program at Matsqui was famously chastised by the Le Dain Commission for succeeding only in producing 'well educated, well adjusted dope fiends.'[13]

British Columbia had a comprehensive plan for penal reform earlier than did Ontario and was quick to create treatment initiatives aimed at drug addiction. In the early 1950s, the province established a heroin-addiction treatment wing in the Oakalla Prison Farm in Burnaby. This initiative expanded in the 1960s to a series of organized 'Narcotics Research Units' for both male and female prisoners. Treatment in these centres followed the same kind of therapeutic community-treatment modality targeting the same kind of criminal addict found at AGB.

The latter half of the century brought forth notable shifts in the ways in which addiction treatment was carried out. Following widespread public and academic critique of institutionalized psychiatric treatment,[14] the clinical model of treatment gave way to a more holistic, if still disjointed, strategy for curing people of their criminality. Such shifts in sentiments on best practices did not, however, mark the end of interest in the addict as a target of criminal justice intervention. On the contrary, interest in this character was galvanized by a tide of public and political anxiety over the rising scourge of drug use in Canadian cities. As is true for the history of drug regulation in English-speaking Canada more generally, the most active and influential jurisdictions were British Columbia and Ontario.

In Ontario, the changing political tide as well as an emerging interest in rehabilitation led to a sizeable restructuring of the penal system. In 1970 AGB was slated for closure. The facility was thought to be too small to accommodate the growing need for treatment spaces within the penal system. The Ontario Correctional Institute (OCI) opened in 1973 to replace AGB and offer the province's first psychological-assessment unit.[15] Inheriting AGB's mandate to treat alcoholics, addicts, and paedophiles, OCI was also intended to become a major research centre for correctional treatment. It modelled itself after therapeutic communities like Daytop and Synanon[16] (which had gained popularity in the

United States) and also built on the existing treatment model at AGB. This meant that, despite changing locations, the welfarist mentalities about the criminal addict endured. Group and individual therapy, art and music therapy, and vocational and educational programming were all part of the interventions initiated at OCI. In 'encounter sessions' prisoners confronted each other about their addictions and criminal behaviours and took responsibility for their actions. On the ten-year anniversary of OCI, Alf Gregerson, past assistant superintendent, reflected on the decidedly welfarist treatment philosophy popular during his time: 'My idea of treatment is to dig down until you find something good in a person, that I could not find something good in. It is true that in some persons the good you might find will provide only a pitiful small lot to build on, but such is the game we are in. Winston Churchill once said, "there is a seam of good in every man," I believe that to be true.'[17]

To a lesser extent, the Vanier Institute for Women, the only prison in the provincial system to incarcerate women exclusively, also followed OCI's treatment mandate. The prison, built adjacent to OCI and sharing staff and resources, housed the women in 'family'-grouped cottages intended to facilitate their treatment.

Therapeutic-treatment milieus developed less intentionally in other prisons in the province. The Rideau Correctional Centre near Ottawa, for example, placed a great deal of emphasis on the treatment of alcoholism and later included drug addiction. Rideau adopted a significantly different approach to treatment based on a more behaviourist school of intervention, setting the foundational ideas on which the vast majority of current interventions would be built. The program initially combined behavioural modification and electroshock therapy. By the late 1970s, psychologists at Rideau and the nearby Ottawa Carleton Detention Centre (OCDC) offered programming on 'Anger Management' and 'Lifeskills.'[18] Many of the standardized, actuarial assessment tools still in use today were first developed at Rideau.

In British Columbia, the heroin-treatment program at Oakalla continued through the 1970s, reflecting similar changes in treatment milieu as well as understandings of addiction as those found in Ontario. Facing re-emerging crises concerning the province's concentrated population of heroin users in downtown Vancouver, the government did make a fleeting attempt to mandate treatment through the 1978 Heroin Treatment Act. This act, which criminalized the state of addiction and shunted police-identified habitual users into state-run treatment facilities, was short-lived. Less than a year after it was enacted, the legislation was struck down by the courts on the grounds that forced-treatment laws were a contravention of human rights.

Despite the recession of the early 1980s and the marked cuts to social spending that accompanied it, the topography of criminal-addiction treatment changed very little through the decade. The main addiction-treatment prisons continued to operate in their respective provinces and community punishment also placed a great deal of focus on addiction treatment.

The 1990s marked a major turning point in correctional discourses and practices throughout the country. The Ontario regime underwent the most considerable changes. Beginning with a project of 'correctional renewal' in 1996, the Conservative government of Mike Harris carried out its tough-on-crime platform, favouring austerity and 'truth in sentencing.' In practice, these rhetorical changes meant the closure of a number of smaller prisons, the creation of five 'mega-jails,' cuts to institutional programming, and the virtual elimination of parole.

In order to maintain focus on treating addicts, however, the province changed the ways in which it talked about and dealt with drug users in conflict with the law. Addictions treatment came under the umbrella of 'effective and efficient corrections.' Treatment continued to be a viable and desired response to crime because certain forms of treatment could be administered in a timely fashion and were argued to be cost-effective. Specifically, the modality of cognitive behavioural therapy (CBT) and the idea of targeted interventions, initiated a decade earlier at Rideau, began to pervade the system.

Underlying these schools of thought is the assumption that criminal behaviour is reducible to a set of 'criminogenic factors' which are directly and etiologically linked to crime. The solution to the crime problem rests in addressing these factors and changing them in people. Handily, each of the criminogenic factors (anger, substance abuse, poor life skills, etc.) is explained largely by thinking errors or faulty cognitions. The thrust of CBT is to correct these thinking errors by teaching people how to think differently.[19] This pedagogy can be carried out in standardized programs delivered in a classroom setting to virtually any group of people in a short period of time (usually eight to twelve weeks). Coupled with individualized follow-up sessions, cognitive behavioural programming became a panacea for the crime problem.

It is not surprising that substance abuse is found among the criminogenic factors, nor is it unexpected that it should be the most targeted factor for intervention. Under a system that values efficiency and effectiveness over all else, substance use is the one readily measurable factor whose intuitive link to crime makes it appealing. While the measurement of anger or the quality of one's friends leads the scientifically inclined into the mire of subjective assessment, we are well equipped to chart the presence or absence of drug use (or its increase or decrease) through now simple tests such as urinalysis.[20] It is then a relatively straightforward project to prove the effectiveness of a substance-use program by simply revealing the presence or absence of a substance in a person's body.

By the end of the 1990s, CBT-based interventions were proliferating in criminal justice, and the presence of in-house substance-abuse treatment programs was apparent in the federal system as well as in most provincial systems on both the institutional level and in the community. This popularity of targeted interventions and addiction treatment therein endures to present day. The federal government's new anti-drug strategy (announced 4 October 2007) is a case in point. The budget affixed to the strategy allots just under $45 million to treatment and prevention programs, with the specification that all treatment must be seen to be effective.

In 1997 Canada's first drug-treatment court (DTC) opened. Based on their American counterparts,[21] the Canadian DTCs offer an intensive, judge-supervised treatment program for individuals facing non-violent and non-trafficking offences with a predicted custodial sentence. For the most part, DTCs cater to those with proven addictions of at least six months to either crack (cocaine), opiates, or methamphetamine. The courts vary in their goals for clients. All require stable periods free of the person's drug of choice, secure housing, and employment or education, but some courts (like Vancouver's) will allow court participants to complete the program while still using marijuana. The courts run as an amalgam of therapeutic and legal processes, with judges, lawyers, and therapists blending roles in order to guide the individual through a juridico-therapeutic process. They are located in the broader movement of therapeutic jurisprudence, an initiative that reimagines the space of the courtroom as a space of healing and relies heavily on the modality of CBT alongside traditional interventions such as Narcotics Anonymous in order to move people along their treatment paths. To date, the courts report varying degrees of success.[22]

The Culture and Politics of Addiction Treatment

The very fact that addiction treatment remains so central in the criminal justice system even as its modalities shift calls into question the etiological link between addiction and crime. After more than half a century of trying, addiction treatment is no better equipped to cure crime than it was in its prototype days at the AGB clinic. Yet, while addiction treatment's effectiveness for any population is routinely questioned, its effectiveness with regard to the criminal justice system is still stuck in the 'what works/nothing works' debates of the 1970s.

There is no good reason to dispute a connection between drug use and criminality. The fact that drug use is a crime in and of itself is sufficient to establish a link between the two. Substantiating causality in this relationship, however, is an impossible feat, a true chicken-and-egg conundrum. In isolation of all other factors (and every good social scientist knows that factors cannot be isolated), how are we to prove that an individual's addiction preceded (and thus caused) his criminal behaviour? The best scientific method we have to establish such a link would be something akin to a life-course survey in which the individual is asked a series of questions about his life including age at which he first started using psychoactive substances and age at which he first began committing crime. Doubtless there is information to be gained from such a survey but it hardly provides definitive evidence of causality. Surveys that ask people to recall their personal histories suffer from considerable validity flaws. In addition, such surveys ask people only a narrow range of questions about their lives, effectively eliminating the possibility that other events (such as a mother's illness) or systemic concerns (like poverty or racism) might have generative capacity in an individual's life. Thus, even if measures such as individual life histories may ascertain which came first, how are we to isolate drug use and criminality from a bevy of other factors that are correlated with both? That is, even if we can establish that most people start using drugs before they start committing crime (which has not been conclusively established in the literature), how can we make this link causal to the exclusion of other factors such as poverty, histories of abuse and trauma, and so on? Literature on people in conflict with the law reminds us that such experiences (both life traumas and social and economic marginalization) are common to many criminalized peoples. If this is the case, then why focus on drug use as the source of criminal behaviour to the exclusion of other factors?

This question is answered in part through the popularized literature on criminal psychology that now proliferates in criminological discourses. The new bible of criminal justice interventions, *The Psychology of Criminal Conduct (PCC)*, tells us that the focus on individual factors like addiction and not structural factors such as poverty is based on a utilitarian choice. Poverty, according to the *PCC*, is a 'static' factor in criminal behaviour, that is, something that cannot be changed and as such well beyond the ken of criminal justice intervention. Addiction, in contrast, is a 'dynamic' factor, one based so exclusively on individual causality that it is assumed to be readily altered if only correct interventions are administered. Thus, according even to the psychology literature, addiction is a logical target in attempts to alter criminal behaviour not because there is any hard evidence to link it to crime, but because it is one of the only concrete factors linked to criminal behaviour that we can actually do anything about. Of course, structuralists and post-structuralists alike are quick to remind us that poverty is no more static than addiction.[23] The problem is not that we can do nothing about poverty. Rather, pervasive discourses and ideologies steer us away from poverty towards individualized causes. This myopia dictates a system of intervention that is unable to address all but the most psychical aspects of criminality. Crime is quite literally all in your head. As such, it is the addict and only the addict who chose to use drugs (thus committing himself to a life of crime), and, it follows, this same individual need simply be taught to make different choices so as to extract himself from criminal behaviours. There is no coddling in this model of criminal justice intervention. Users in conflict with the law are not invited to explore their histories of trauma or their feelings of isolation with a therapist. Instead, they are merely taught the skills needed to help them make the right choices, in a way that is efficient, effective, and decidedly not soft on crime. Thus, without understanding the broader socio-structural context in which addiction treatment emerges and endures, we are not well equipped to understand fully just why it is that addiction treatment takes centre stage in criminal justice interventions.

When the Alex G. Brown treatment clinic opened in the 1950s, the welfare state was in its heyday. Cradle-to-grave mentalities pervaded governmental practices and the penal system was not immune. Thus, accompanying the medical model was the strong sense that the penal system had to do more than simply punish, it now had to take part in the project of making good citizens. To do this, practitioners focused on a number of initiatives designed to treat the whole person. Addiction treatment by the 1970s was a holistic enterprise that encouraged people to embrace bigger projects of citizen building by wholly revising themselves to fit into a broader, normalizing project.

Flash forward to the 1990s. The political climate was then notably different. Many claim that in this decade neo-liberalism replaced the welfare state, and, while in Canada Keynesian practices were not as ferociously attacked as in the United States and the United Kingdom, the effects of the rising popularity of neo-liberal ideas were apparent at all levels of government and certainly in the penal system. The days of coddling prisoners were over, replaced (as in Ontario) with a strong ethic of austerity and/or (as with the federal government) a commitment to 'evidence based,' efficient, and effective corrections.

These sizeable changes did not erase the addict as a target of criminal justice intervention; instead, they further entrenched that approach. By the late 1990s, virtually every prison and community corrections organization in the country offered some sort of addiction-treatment program and the DTC movement was rapidly gaining momentum. Why?

The answer belies what popular rhetoric about the 'punitive turn' in punishment suggests. Contrary to claims regarding the rise of hyper-draconian practices, the idea that correctional organizations ought to have a positive role to play in responding to crime never went away. After all, even hyper-punitive states like Texas still refer to the positive project of corrections. The simple act of warehousing lawbreakers does not appear to have a great deal of sway in popular discourses in most jurisdictions. In Canada this is certainly true, since even the most conservative jurisdictions in this country place a great deal of emphasis on the corrective capacity of the criminal justice system.

Canada's new anti-drug strategy is a good illustration. Introduced by a government whose election campaign promised a series of 'tough' reforms of the criminal justice system, the strategy highlights three areas of concentration: treatment, prevention, and enforcement.[24] While the enforcement branch promises significantly harsher penalties for trafficking, cultivation, and manufacture of illicit substances (the supply side), the demand side (individuals buying drugs for personal use) notably escapes increased criminalization. Instead, demand is targeted through youth-oriented prevention programs and population-specific treatment programs tailored to specific ethnic groups or fashioned in accordance with drug of choice. Notably, treatment is receiving three times the amount of new funding allotted to prevention and $10 million more in new funding than is marked for enforcement.

Treatment, therefore, is a formidable part of the Canadian response to drug use but one that does not follow the relentless and seemingly inevitable lineage of 'best practices.' Treatment is as much about politics as it is about making people better. The political appeal of treatment is perhaps intuitive. Crime is constituted as a perennial problem of modern societies[25] even if empirical knowledge about criminal behaviour suggests that the 'crime problem' is somewhat mythological. Sensible solutions to chronic, stylized crime problems are also perennial features of modern societies. If the narrative of crime is also the narrative of drug addiction, then it follows that addressing addiction will address crime. Also, if crime is caused by the individual problem of drug addiction, then it is not caused by broader failings of government such as weak social-safety nets or vast economic inequalities. Finally, framing the crime problem as a drug problem is politically manageable. Ultimately, we can do something about drug addiction, we can treat it, we can cure it.

But this political thesis only tells part of the story of why addiction treatment remains so central to the justice system. Drug use is not only politically useful, it is also culturally resonant. The stunning presence that illicit substances have (and have maintained) in Western culture for the past 100 years directs us to at least flag here the cultural importance of the figure of the drug user as she sits in relation to the criminal justice system.

Giffen, Endicott, and Lambert[26] tell us that much of the impetus behind the drug panics of the 1970s was born of growing public fear of the rise of 'hippie' culture. Parents and police alike feared children's and teens' attachment to so-called hippie hang-outs like Toronto's Yorkville because they assumed that the age-old fate of youth using illicit drugs (sexual ruin, moral depravity, mental illness, etc.) would befall any teenager who wandered into these morally void neighbourhoods. A deviant child is lost because of her involvement in the drug subculture, since drug use was (and still is), after all, a gateway (if not the express train) to individual demise. Most social histories of drug use remind us that the regulation of certain substances had nothing to do with their pernicious effects and everything to do with the cultural meanings affixed to them.

Much of the cultural meanings connected to both the umbrella term 'drugs' and specific substances remain stalwart. The cultural link between drugs and crime is a case in point. One need only browse the titles at a local DVD rental shop to be convinced that drug use is steadfastly linked to criminal behaviour. *Traffic, 21 Grams, Requiem for a Dream,* and TV shows like *Weeds* and *The Wire* all firmly fix the links between drug use and criminal behaviour. *Trainspotting,* now a cult-movie classic, stands as the foundation piece for these kinds of representations. The film follows the brutal lives of four heroin addicts as they careen head-on into a brick wall of human misery.

Such representations are not limited to the realm of fiction. The news media is also replete with images and messages of the scourge of drugs and crime. For example, as I write this morning, the Life Section of the *Globe and Mail* carries a feature on Vancouver's infamous downtown eastside, headlined 'There Is Love Down There.' The article marvels at how human beings are able to behave like anything other than animals when they are homeless and drug-dependent. A typical downtown eastside tale of a stabbed heroin dealer is countered with the 'surprising' account of one homeless and diseased man giving another his last cigarette.[27] This same morning, the local radio report features a 'town hall' meeting hosted by the Ottawa Police Services Board. The meeting focused on the city's response to drugs and mainly took aim (at least as the news report represented it) at Ottawa's controversial crack-pipe program. The story featured five different voice clips from residents complaining about drug dealers and users in their communities. Citizens fretted over a looming crime problem that would surely accompany this present addiction outbreak even as none related actual experiences of criminal activity. If the drug-crime nexus is a touchstone of Western culture, then of course it stands to reason that addiction treatment ought to be part of our justice system: as a logical, lasting, and effective way to eliminate the dual scourges of drugs and crime.

So, despite faulty logic and the lack of empirical evidence, drug treatment is a talisman of contemporary criminal justice. Readers familiar with addiction, having worked with addicts or been addicted themselves, may well wonder at this point why justice-based treatment is something worth worrying about. Certainly, in many instances addiction is a state that has wretched if not deadly implications. Philosophical critiques about the constitution of addiction aside,[28] there is no debate that for some people addiction begets a dismal existence worth escaping. Having worked with addicts and users for over a decade, I have no doubt about the veracity of these claims. Addictions can be awful and for many people addiction treatment is a helpful, desired, and ultimately beneficial option.

Treatment and Justice: Three Concerns

I do not want to conclude this essay with an anti-treatment polemic; instead, I want to offer three concerns that arise when wedding treatment and justice. The first concern is that, in its bid to cure crime, the justice system runs the risk of treating people who are not, in fact, drug addicts. Second, the elision of treatment and justice conflates powerful institutions, running the sizeable risk that the use of power will become oppressive. Finally, combining treatment and punishment can work to erase the punitive features of the justice system, creating the impression that treatment based in the justice system is not punishment. This is a dangerous and false assumption.

Treating Addiction That Is Not There

The criminal justice system's fixation on treating addiction creates the perfect climate in which to categorize individuals as addicts whose substance-use patterns belie the label. I argued above that the system is committed to the notion of doing positive work with people in conflict with the law, that is, the system is committed to making people better and therefore non-criminal. In order to ensure that people get better, they must first be sick. Thus, the illness or pathology of the person in conflict with the law must be 'discovered' before it can be cured. In some cases, the pathology presents itself in the form of mental illness or sexual deviance, triggering a certain set of justice-based interventions. But, in the vast majority of the cases and quite disproportionately from the rest of the population, the pathology 'discovered' in the individual is substance abuse.

While the population of individuals in conflict with the law is by no means a reflection of the overall demographic make-up of society, a comparison of addiction epidemiology within and outside the justice system helps to ground this argument. The Correctional Service of Canada (CSC) claims that approximately 80 per cent of people in its care are in need of substance-abuse programming. Yet, according to the 2004 epidemiology report of the Canadian Centre on Substance Abuse (CCSA), 3 per cent of the population indicated they had used one of heroin, hallucinogens, cocaine, crystal methamphetamine, or Ecstasy in the past year.[29] Of that 3 per cent, 36.7 per cent reported experiencing one or more 'harms' associated with that use (losing friends, health, housing or financial problems, etc.). Overall, of the population surveyed by CCSA, just under 1 per cent reported any problems at all related to their illicit-substance use. The constituency of cannabis users had even lower rates of adversity.

If the CSC claim is accurate, then the difference in problematic substance-use rates between the greater population and the population of people in conflict with the law is staggering and certainly supports the suggestion that drug use causes crime. Close examination of the means by which problematic substance use is discovered within the population of people in conflict with the law suggests, however, that these rates do not necessarily constitute an accurate reflection of the extent of addiction.

Problems related to illicit substance use are not the same as addiction. The CCSA survey, for example, lists a bevy of problems which users might link to their substance use (physical/health problems, loss of employment, etc.), but nowhere does it explicitly ask users to define themselves as addicts. This catch-all category of problematic substance use is familiar to those acquainted with the DSM IV. This authoritative source for psychiatric and psychological illnesses lists no fewer than forty substance-use-related disorders, many of which are subcategories of the broader, umbrella maladies of substance-use disorder, substance dependence, and substance abuse. Of these, only substance dependence is diagnosed through the presence of physical symptoms (in the form of withdrawal). The other pathologies listed in the DSM are all behaviourally related. Critical literature on clinical and diagnostic medicine reminds us that behavioural symptomatology is far removed from the kinds of standardized, rigorous criteria meant to be applied to medical pathology, meaning that (as is the case with many mental illnesses) the label of substance-use disorder opens itself easily to subjective application.[30]

The subjectivity of the assessment for substance-use-related disorders is even more profound when placed in the context of criminal justice systems. For the most part, medical criteria are applied loosely if at all in determining whether or not an individual in conflict with the law is in need of addiction treatment or some other sort of substance- use interventions. The diagnosis that an individual has a substance-abuse problem in need of intervention can be made simply by a judge at the time of sentencing, by a probation officer after first meeting with an individual, or even by an arresting officer. In all of these instances, a justice official without medical training is vested with the authority to prescribe a treatment program to someone in conflict with the law.

In my recent research on probationers enrolled in a government-based substance-use intervention program, several of the men I interviewed indicated that their probation officers had decided that they had substance-abuse problems simply because they admitted to recreational drug use or they had been using illicit substances around the time of the offence (either before or after). In these cases, the presence of substance use (regardless of its nature, duration, or even, in some cases, proximity to an offence) was enough to convince probation officers that substance use was indeed a causal factor in the person's criminal behaviour and one in need of intervention. Likewise, the advent of the conditional sentence in Canada[31] empowers judges to sentence offenders to treatment based on court reports and evidence presented at trial. In the same vein, the DTC movement relies on the initial assessments of arresting officers and crown attorneys to determine whether or not an arrestee has an addiction warranting intervention.

In all these instances, the diagnosis of a substance-related problem, a conclusion supposed to be reached through clinical assessment, is made by untrained justice officials working either on the basis of their own common sense or (as is the case with probation officers) on the basis of limited training and with the assistance of simplified actuarial assessments. Under this system, virtually anyone who has used a substance at any time in her life can, if read in a certain way, have her behaviour understood as problematic and linked to (or more precisely caused by) her substance use.

Amplifying the Power to Punish

The institutions of therapy and justice are both powerful institutions in their own rights. Each institution, in respect of their respective weights, also has particular checks and balances in place to make sure that those who come before it do not find themselves victims of the institution's undue exertion of power. A number of such checks are available but for my purposes I wish to focus on only two: the notion of the best interest of the client as articulated in therapeutic milieus, and the notion of due process familiar to legal proceedings. I choose these because both are meant to serve as power regulators, organizing an institution's power in such a way that it does what is right for the parties involved and not for the institution itself, and also because both are foundational principles to their respective institutions.

Social workers, psychiatrists, and psychologists providing therapeutic services are bound by their respective regulating bodies to work in the best interests of the people they serve. Obviously, this notion of best interest is an entirely subjective idea that opens itself for contestation perpetually. When therapeutically oriented actors find themselves working in and for justice-based organizations, the notion of best interest must be negotiated within the parameters set out by the justice system. Curiously, then, actions such as incarcerating someone against his will or disclosing personal information about him without his consent, actions that are read in most circles outside the justice system as decidedly *not* in a client's best interest, somehow become part of the best interest of the person who is in conflict with the law.

In DTC, for example, the authority to incarcerate is one of the therapist's tools. Thus, a person who is not showing adequate progress in her treatment regime may have her therapist recommend and/or request detention as a means of 'shaking up' the person. Rarely is a therapist's recommendation in this regard not followed.[32] Likewise, a psychologist writing a risk-assessment report on a prisoner is making the determination of just how securely this individual must be held and also, in the case of a parole report, as to whether or not the individual is deserving of freedom. Such determinations, made by the same people who are in place to offer therapeutic guidance and interventions to an individual, reinvent the therapist as both helper and punisher, a dangerous combination.[33]

On the other side of this coupling, I am certainly not the first to raise concerns about the compromise of due-process protections through the amalgamation of justice and therapeutic practices. Advocates of unadulterated courtrooms and determinate sentences alike argue that the justice system has no place in the psyches of those found to contravene the law.[34] The Criminal Code is simply a code of behaviour, not a mental state. Consequently, to allow justice to make determinative decisions about an individual or guide its dealings with a lawbreaker based on assessments of anything other than culpability calls into question the even application of the law. In Canada, laws allowing for the detention and forced treatment of addicts have been routinely struck down because they are seen to infringe unfairly on basic human rights and offend the concept of due process. At the same time, however, court and penal practices do routinely detain for the purpose of treating addicts.

The Case for Treatment over Punishment

Underlying these criticisms is the normative and even moral question about whether or not we ought to use the criminal justice system as a venue for addiction treatment. At first blush, the obvious answer is no. My argument thus far leads to the conclusion that the justice system is just that, a justice system. To deploy its authority for any other purposes, especially those crossed with the therapeutic, is to amplify coercive governing powers while veiling the punitive in the shroud of the healing. But this conclusion does not fully take account of our current political context, nor does it satisfactorily address the lived reality of many people's lives.

There are any number of truisms about the current state of drug-control policy in the global North and particularly in North America. The 'war on drugs' is a failure. Countless people use illicit substances without any problem or apparent detriment to their health or quality of life. Establishing markers of successful treatment options is hard. It is harder still to say definitively what kind of interventions actually work. Also, addiction can be awful. Addiction often accompanies other sorts of hardship including trauma histories, poverty, and illness. And, perhaps most important, despite all this, both American and Canadian governments plan to continue criminalizing drug users. In Canada, the Conservative government dashed all hope for progressive drug-law reform when it pulled marijuana decriminalization from the order table in 2007.

There are also any number of truisms that apply to the lived reality of many individuals with substance-use-dependency concerns. Housing is scarce, physical and mental illness, as well as social stigma, are common if not the norm, long waiting lists are commonplace for all manner of social services, and criminalization is likely, and for many inevitable. Social marginalization is often accompanied by profound health problems, victimization, and isolation, all of which exacerbate already dire circumstances.

Given these realities, criticisms of initiatives designed to deliver much needed social services to any marginalized person regardless of his or her addiction status must be tempered. The value of the justice system's ability to provide resources such as therapeutic support, housing, and health care is not insignificant. Accordingly, the criticisms I offer here are not intended as justifications for the revocation of therapeutically oriented justice programs. My point is not that the justice system or those who work within it are somehow malevolently intentioned in the quest to treat addiction. On the contrary, my own observations lead me to conclude quite unequivocally that those advocating therapeutic interventions are often among the most progressively and liberally minded (albeit paternalistic) of all the individuals working within the system. I am also quite confident that the motivation behind such interventions is the desire not only to protect public safety but also to ameliorate the lives of those marginalized individuals who come into conflict with the law. However, as with any melding of therapeutic and juridical powers, there are good reasons to approach addiction-treatment initiatives with caution.

The bigger worry is not whether or not these programs exist, because they do and will likely continue to do so for a goodly amount of time. The concern, rather, is that such initiatives are often mistakenly read as the antithesis of punishment, thus satisfying the need to push for progress in drug policy. Treatment and punishment are not inherently or even commonly opposed. Above I attempted to illustrate the ways in which I see treatment and punishment as intertwined in criminal justice addiction programs. It is important to recognize that the endurance and expansion of addiction treatment in the justice system does not signal a softening or a net narrowing of the justice side of drug policy. That is, offering addiction treatment as part of the justice system does not mean that the justice system is used less as a means to respond to drug use. The point may be rather obvious but it bears repeating. To use the justice system as a means of dispensing addiction treatment is to criminalize the drug involved. This criminalization is bound not to 'best practices' but rather to political and cultural influences on and understandings of the links between drugs and crime. Criminalization has certain effects that move drug policy further into the realm of justice and thus out of the realm of decriminalization and ultimately public health. The danger, then, is not that these programs exist, but that people need to be criminalized in order to gain access to them.

Again, the latest anti-drug strategy serves as an illustration of the point. The previous drug strategy was based (loosely) on the four pillars (harm reduction, treatment, prevention, and enforcement). The new strategy has lost one pillar entirely (harm reduction). Canadian drug policy has always been based on an oscillation between health- and justice-based responses. In the decade before the new strategy was introduced, marijuana was legalized for medical use and marijuana laws concerning possession came remarkably close to decriminalization. The country's first safe-injection site was opened, needle-exchange programs became commonplace in most major cities, and some jurisdictions (like Ottawa) were also offering a crack-pipe program. On a global scale, Canada was recognized as one of the leaders in progressive drug policy. On the heels of such developments (and in the wake of both House of Commons and Senate reports calling for even more progressive reforms to drug policy), the current changes to drug policy had to maintain some progressive elements. Today's iteration of the drug strategy has the effect of redefining progress as treatment (and to a lesser extent prevention) while maintaining a heavy (and larger) emphasis on enforcement and all but eliminating harm reduction.

The current emphasis on treating drug addiction through the criminal justice system has deep historical and cultural roots that are also reflected in contemporary drug policy such as the latest anti-drug strategy and expanding initiatives including the drug- treatment courts and prison-based treatment programs. The fact that these programs offer much needed social services signals their importance. At the same time, the link between drugs and crime is problematic and causality is impossible to establish. Today, as in the past, programs are closely aligned with prevailing political sensibilities, reminding us of the extent to which 'best practices' are guided by governing rationalities. In addition, treatment programs based in the justice system constitute an amplification of powers that can end up being punitive and coercive as well as ethically problematic. As such, therapeutic initiatives ought never to be read as the antithesis of punishment. They are instead complements to the practice of punishment, aligned with its corrective arm but punitive nonetheless. This does not mean that addiction programs located within the justice system lack progressive elements. They do appear, however, to have become the only progressive element of Canada's drug policy, coinciding with an apparent displacement of harm reduction and decriminalization.

Conclusion

History is our greatest teacher. The history of treating addiction in Canada reveals a politically and culturally relative tale of control measures that pay only lateral and fading attention to socio-structural concerns. In fact, the social slowly evaporates in this history, replaced by the pathological individual as the target and raison d'être of anti-drug legislation and juridical-therapeutic interventions. The positioning of the drug addict at the centre of criminality redefines and limits what can be taken as 'progressive' drug policy. As criminalization is ramped up, the hopes and aspirations of those seeking reform to drug laws are pared down since energies must be directed towards holding on to what has been achieved rather than gaining new ground.

NOTES

1 Paul Bentley, 'Canada's First Drug Treatment Court,' *Criminal Reports*, 31, no. 5 (2000): 257–74.

2 Virginia Berridge and Griffith Edwards, *Opium and the People: Opiate Use and Policy in Nineteenth and Early Twentieth Century England* (London: Free Association Books 1981); P.J. Giffen, Shirley Endicott, and Sylvia Lambert, *Panic and Indifference: The Politics of Canada's Drug Laws: A Study in the Sociology of Law* (Ottawa: Canadian Centre on Substance Abuse 1991); Wayne Morgan, *Drugs in America* (Syracuse: Syracuse University Press 1981).

3 William White, *Slaying the Dragon: The History of Addiction Treatment and Recovery in America* (Bloomington, Ill.: Chestnut Health Systems 1998).

4 Enrico Ferri, *Criminal Sociology* (New York: Agathan 1967), 18.

5 Kathy Kendall, 'Psy-ence Fiction: Governing Female Prisons through the Psychological Sciences,' in Kelly Hannah-Moffat and Margaret Shaw, eds., *An Ideal Prison? Critical Essays on Women's Imprisonment in Canada* (Halifax: Fernwood 2000), 82–93; Joe Sim, *Medical Power in Prisons: The Prison Medical Service in England, 1774–1989* (Philadelphia: Open University Press 1990).

6 Catherine Carstairs, *Jailed for Possession: Illegal Drug Use, Regulation, and Power in Canada, 1920–1961* (Toronto: University of Toronto Press 2005).

7 See Giffen, Endicott, and Lambert, *Panic and Indifference*.

8 David Garland, *The Culture of Control: Crime and Social Order in Contemporary Society* (Chicago: University of Chicago Press 2001).

9 Ibid.

10 T. Miller, *The Well Tampered Self: Citizenship, Culture and the Postmodern Subject* (Baltimore, Md.: Johns Hopkins University Press 1993).

11 Archives of Ontario, RG 20–155–0–11, Printed Materials: Rules, Regulations and Manuals, Alex G. Brown Memorial Clinical Information Booklet, n.d.

12 Maeve McMahon, *The Persistent Prison? Re-thinking Decarceration and Penal Reform* (Toronto: University of Toronto Press 1992).

13 Justice Gerald Le Dain, *Commission of Inquiry into the Non-Medical Use of Drugs* (Ottawa: Government of Canada 1972), 12.

14 Erving Goffman, *Asylums: Essays on the Second Situation of Mental Patients and Other Patients* (New York: Garden City Publishing 1961); Ken Kesey,

One Flew over the Cuckoo's Nest (New York: Viking Press 1969); Sim, *Medical Power in Prisons*.

15 While fairly innovative for its time, the assessment unit is a common feature of penal establishments in Canada. Usually a separate section of a larger prison, the assessment unit is the prisoner's first point of contact with the penal system. Typically, prisoners go through a period of assessment (anywhere from a few weeks to several months depending on sentence length) in which they are subjected to a series of actuarial assessments intended to assess their risk levels and also their programming needs.

16 These facilities, largely led by ex-addicts, often offered spiritually based treatments and commanded the total surrender of the individual to the dictates of the program. They were heavily moralistic and frequently worked on the philosophy that you had to break the individual down in order to build her/him back up again (White, *Slaying the Dragon*, 246).

17 *Correctional Update*, 12, no. 2 (May 1984).

18 Ministry of Correctional Services, *Newsletter*, 1, no. 5 (October, 1973).

19 Aaron Beck, *Cognitive Therapy and Emotional Disorders* (New York: International Universities Press 1970).

20 Of course, there are also any number of problems affixed to the use of urinalysis. See Dawn Moore and Kevin Haggerty, 'Bring It on Home: Home Drug Testing and the Relocation of the War on Drugs,' *Social and Legal Studies*, 10 (2004): 377–95.

21 Steve Belenko, *Research on Drug Courts: A Critical Review* (New York: National Centre on Addiction and Substance Abuse 1999).

22 The question of how success is established and measured plagues the courts in the same way as it plagues the penal system. See R. Martinson, 'What Works? Questions and Answers about Prison Reform,' *The Public Interest*, 35 (1974): 22–54.

23 Jonathan Simon, *Poor Discipline: Parole and the Social Control of the Underclass, 1890–1990* (Chicago: University of Chicago Press 1993); Alan Young, *Justice Defiled: Perverts, Potheads, Serial Killers and Lawyers* (Toronto: Key Porter 2003); Zygmunt Bauman, 'Social Issues of Law and Order,' *British Journal of Criminology*, 40, no. 2 (2000): 205–21.

24 Those familiar with the former drug strategy will note the remarkable absence of harm reduction in the current initiative.

25 Garland, *The Culture of Control*; Simon, *Poor Discipline*.

26 Giffen, Endicott, and Lambert, *Panic and Indifference*.

27 *Globe and Mail*, 21 April 2008.

28 M. Valverde, *Diseases of the Will: Alcohol and the Dilemmas of Freedom* (Cambridge: Cambridge University Press 1998).

29 http://www.ccsa.ca/NR/rdonlyres/6806130B-C314-4C96-95CC-075D14CD83DE/0/ccsa0040282005.pdf (accessed 6 December 2010).

30 Caroline Acker, *Creating the American Junkie: Addiction Research in the Classic Era of Narcotic Control* (Baltimore, Md.: Johns Hopkins University Press 2002); Bonnie Burstow, 'Feminist Antipsychiatry Praxis: Women and the Movement(s) – A Canadian Perspective,' in Wendy Chan, Dorothy Chunn, and Orbert Menzies, eds., *Women, Madness and the Law: A Feminist Reader* (London: Glasshouse 2005), 245–58; Ian Hacking, *The Social Construction of What?* (Cambridge, Mass.: Harvard University Press 1979; Nikolas Rose, *Inventing Our Selves: Psychology, Power and Personhood* (Cambridge: Cambridge University Press 1998).

31 Julian Roberts, 'Reducing the Use of Custody as a Sanction: A Review of Recent Strategies,' *Judicial Studies Institute Journal*, 5, no. 2 (2006): 121–34.

32 Dawn Moore, *Criminal Artefacts: Governing Drugs and Users* (Vancouver: UBC Press 2007).

33 Kelly Hannah-Moffat, *Punishment in Disguise: Penal Governance in Canadian Women's Prisons* (Toronto: University of Toronto Press 2001).

34 Bruce Arrigo, *Punishing the Mentally Ill: A Critical Analysis of Law and Psychiatry* (Albany, N.Y.: SUNY Press 2002); James Nolan, *The Therapeutic State* (New York: NYU Press 1998).

10 Biopolitics, Geopolitics, and the Regulation of Club Drugs in Canada

KYLE GRAYSON

On the morning of 16 March 2008, 14 Division of the Toronto Police Service in conjunction with the Toronto Drug Squad, Emergency Task Force, Gun and Gang Task Force, Organized Crime Enforcement, Toronto Anti-Violence Intervention Strategy Rapid Response Unit, Police Dog Services, Forensic Identification Bureau, Ontario Provincial Police Biker Enforcement Unit, Toronto Emergency Services Unit, Toronto Transit Commission's Special Constable Services, University of Toronto Police, and the Toronto Fire Services conducted a raid on the Comfort Zone club.[1] The club was located at 480 Spadina Street, close to the corner of a busy downtown intersection, and the raid was authorized in order to execute a warrant to search the premises for illegal drugs. Prompted by the January 2008 overdose death of a twenty-six-year-old man who had allegedly purchased drugs while at the Comfort Zone and who later died at a private home in a different municipality, the police action was the culmination of six weeks of intensive undercover operations. Thirty-three people were arrested on mostly minor criminal charges (predominantly simple possession). Police claimed to have seized $33,000 worth of illicit drugs (in street value) from the premises, which they described to the media as a 'drugs flea-market.'

The authorities presented the raid as a textbook example of a successful tactical counter-narcotics operation in response to a threat identified in the community. For others, Project White Rabbit (as code-named by the police) was a heavy-handed fiasco. Storming the club with guns drawn, police ordered patrons to lie face down at gun-point. Individuals were handcuffed and forced to remain lying down until ordered up for searching and identity verification. With approximately 150 people detained on the floor, reports emerged that it took as long as three hours to complete the process. Once processed and found to be clean, patrons faced the indignity of walking through the media gauntlet outside. Pictures of otherwise innocent individuals dotted the twenty-four-hour news coverage of the drug raid.

Furthermore, troubling allegations emerged that several individuals sustained injuries during the raid and that some of the patrons had pre-existing medical conditions such as respiratory difficulties which were ignored. Moreover, complaints of police brutality including multiple instances of beating and kicking restrained persons began to be publicly voiced via Internet chat rooms frequented by members of the Toronto clubbing community. Yet there was very little public outcry. The actions of police were largely defined as necessary given the environment within which the raid was conducted. Others argued that, by giving the Comfort Zone their patronage, individuals had granted licence for this type of police intrusion into their everyday lives; merely being present at the location was taken as an indication of being guilty of something.

The events of 16 March and the ways in which they have been interpreted provoke two significant questions. What socio-political conditions made the raid possible and how did it become possible for the operation to be understood as a legitimate response to drug use in a night club? Would the media, politicians, and general public have been as accommodating to the indiscriminate arrest and detention of individuals if the target had been different? For example, what if the police raided a Catholic church at gun-point during Sunday Mass, handcuffing and detaining all the parishioners because of previously alleged sexual misconduct within the building by the priest? Would the media and members of the public approve? Based on the reasoning underpinning the Comfort Zone raid, should we expect large-scale raids on Canadian brokerage houses and indiscriminate arrests within their premises when traders have allegedly engaged in insider trading? In a sense these scenarios are rhetorical. However, the fact that they seem so far-fetched while the Comfort Zone raid outlined above has been presented as prudent clearly underlines the need for a closer analysis of the concepts, discourses, and 'logics' (to use a Foucauldian term) of the regulation of club drugs in Canada.

The starting point for the analysis that will follow is that both Canadian regulations and what these regulations are said to be preventing and/or responding to are the products of processes of social construction.[2] In other words, there has never been a necessity for Canadian state and society to respond to issues of illicit-drug use, production, and distribution through a legal framework outside the ways in which these phenomena have come to be understood as a threat within key (political) discourses. This chapter analyses the processes of threat formulation and legal regulation through recent responses to 'club drugs.'[3] On the one hand, there is not much of a story to tell. Most of what have been identified as 'club drugs' within the Canadian drugs discourse were made illegal well before any reported use in Canada. These additions to the list of scheduled substances were at various junctures an aspect of bringing Canadian law in line with outstanding international treaty commitments and/or extending the schedule of prohibitive substances to cover close derivatives of drugs that were already illegal. What is far more interesting than this historical background is how ongoing representations of 'club drugs' as threats to Canadian society, and the accompanying response of the Canadian state, reflect what Michael Dillon has called the toxic combination of geopolitical and biopolitical approaches to security.[4] Thus, this chapter will focus on how biopolitical and geopolitical logics are shaping approaches to the 'club drug' phenomenon. The approach will be largely from a macro-level, with preliminary observations intended to provoke further in-depth empirical analysis of the socio-political contours of specific cases like that of the Comfort Zone raid. In other words, what is presented here is suggestive of an approach than may reveal different kinds of logics in the construction of an aspect of Canadian drug regulation writ large rather than any definitive answer to the questions raised.

It also bears noting that 'club drugs' is a term with no universally agreed-upon definition; it has constituted an ever shifting terrain of substances dependent on the specific social context and institutional sites tasked with their regulation.[5] What the analysis undertaken here will clearly demonstrate is that the list of substances designated as 'club drugs' should be considered secondary to the risks that are associated with these substances – such as sexual deviancy – and the 'geographing' of their use to specific, clearly delineated spatial entities outside the confines of proper society: the nightclub and/or rave.

What Is Biopolitics?

According to Michel Foucault, new logics regarding governance were generated with the establishment of liberal regimes beginning in the late eighteenth century.[6] These logics posed a novel question that had not yet been considered by those tasked with mastering the art of governance. That question was a simple one: For what purpose must we govern? Under the ancien régime, the answer precluded the question: the purpose of governance was to contribute to the aggrandizement of the state and the sovereign through the application of juridical power, primarily over the experience of death. In other words, the managerial class in the interests of the sovereign would harness means of coercive power and punishment in legal and extralegal forms to ensure that subjects acted in an orderly fashion – primarily conceived in terms of contributing to the maintenance of the current political order. The exercise of power under these conditions was naked, visible, brutal, and overtly cruel, a characterization made abundantly clear in Foucault's *Discipline and Punish* with its graphic account of the public execution of an alleged regicide in eighteenth-century France.[7]

But, according to Foucault, political and economic liberalism led to a significant transformation in the parameters within which the logics of government operated. Although the aggrandizement of the state never fully retreated – it in fact became a governing logic for geopolitical strategies among states – and the exercise of juridical power remained, the new emphasis on freedom and the articulation of what were to be understood as clear limits on state intervention into the domains of individual political and economic liberty meant that the game of governance had changed. No longer was the primary instrument of the art of government to be the (non)application of sovereign power over death, as put forward in juridical codes. Rather, the art of government was to establish the means by which life could be fostered, improved, and allowed to flourish.[8]

With the concurrent establishment of nascent-knowledge regimes including actuary sciences, statistics, medicine, sociology, and psychiatry, the art of government became increasingly concerned with the management of population.[9] Population was not necessarily equated with the population of a particular bounded territorial entity but rather concerned masses of individuals who could be grouped together based on specific characteristics identified by classification schemes arising from the new sciences (e.g., homosexuals, habitual criminals, the working poor).[10] The point was to manage these populations in order to maximize biopower, that is, to ensure that their everyday activities, behaviours, and lifestyles were contributing to a newly conceptualized political economy of life worthy of life.[11] And the means of promoting biopower would become what we now refer to as security apparatuses:

a grouping of heterogeneous elements deployed for the purposes of protecting the core of life worthy of life.[12]

Thus, it is over the ensuing two hundred years that we begin to see states promoting public-health schemes and public education, launching public works (particularly in the areas of sanitation and sewage), professionalizing police services and physicians, opening sanatoriums, operating asylums, and reconfiguring prisons. A task of government, one given the status of a worthy goal in and of itself, thus became to foster specific forms of living (e.g., healthy living, educated living, heterosexual living, lawful living). The boundaries of this task were to be found only through technology, knowledge, and the calculation of probability as to what interventions would generate success at a reasonable cost.[13]

It is analytically important to note how the governmental concern with biopolitics, that is, producing lives that are worthy of life, necessarily requires that populations be given the freedom to live and to transform, with the hope that transformation will lead to improved ways of living.[14] Thus, in this sense, the traditional analytic dichotomy that sets freedom in opposition to the law and/or security misrepresents the dynamic at play; freedom is achieved through the provision of a security that disallows dangerous forms of living. As Foucault reminds us, freedom is allowed to operate only so long as it does not become defined as a risk to 'species life' itself and does not jeopardize the ongoing production of effective forms of biopower. So, while the new institutional forms, types of knowledge, discursive formations, and policies that arose with the Enlightenment and liberalization were (and in many cases continue to be) seen as progressive developments, we must not lose sight of the relations of power that made these developments possible and those that allow for their continuing operation on the 'underside of the law.'[15]

It is these relations of power that constructed shifting biopolitical rationalities built upon the foundations of regimes of truth, disciplines, power-knowledge, and practices of surveillance and security. In turn, these have produced particular forms of subjectivity (both for individuals and at the level of population) that have inscribed bodies with characteristics that determine which institutions, mechanisms, processes, and types of knowledge will be applied to rationalizing people's lives. Thus, a series of routine questions arise from the entrenchment of biopolitics as a form of governmentality: Who must be free to live? Who must be monitored? Who must be controlled? Who must be corrected? Who must be punished? Who must be left to die?

What Is Geopolitics?

Traditionally, geopolitics has been defined as the ways in which political relationships are formed and shaped by economic and demographic factors linked to geography. The importance of geography is determined not just by what is contained within clearly demarcated boundaries and the spaces within them (e.g., states and their topographic features), but also by where these clearly demarcated spaces are located relative to other clearly demarcated spaces. As a regime of knowledge, geopolitics has attempted to hypothesize about how these various factors contribute to specific political outcomes in regional and global theatres. Certain spaces are seen as being of strategic importance while others are considered marginal. Some spaces are said to inherently contain threats while others present opportunities. The success of this knowledge production hinges upon the assumptions of geopolitics – particularly the geographical elements – being taken as natural factors that cannot be disputed or interpreted differently. Thus, geopolitics is often presented as a specific form of politics in which iron-clad laws (in the scientific sense) should underpin the strategies and tactics of the prudential policy maker in increasing the power of the state.

This descriptive and prescriptive vision of geopolitics occludes the significance of subjectivity to any geopolitical imagining of spaces, their characteristics, and their political significance. Gilles Deleuze and Felix Guattari have argued that the earth is always coded in terms of meanings that are subjectively constructed by the observer in order to divide different classifications of people into separate spaces.[16] Geopolitics is therefore intertwined within global and local power relations that seek to seize space, discipline space, and organize space in order to fit it within specific cultural visions and material interests.[17] Seizing, disciplining, and organizing all involve a degree of struggle, for, as Gearóid Ó Tuathail argues, 'it is ... a conflict between competing images and imaginings, a contest of power and resistance that involves not only struggles to represent the materiality of physical geographic objects and boundaries but also the equally powerful and, in a different manner, the equally material force of discursive borders between an idealized Self and a demonized Other, between "us" and "them."'[18]

Geopolitics, then, is a form of knowledge linked to wider and deeper currents of power in (global) society that seeks to put forward a particular vision of the world – one rich with culturally contingent values and understandings – as a universally valid and objectively grounded form of knowledge. In making these claims, geopolitical narratives subjectively construct relationships between people/spaces and the 'inherent' meanings that we are supposed to take from them. This move is especially significant in terms of the coding of 'safe' and 'risky' (if not 'threatening') spaces, with biopolitics often constructing the characteristics of the peoples said to inhabit them. Therefore, geopolitics at its most extreme is about the cartographic representation of good spaces and evil spaces. Of these evil spaces, distinctions are made between those that can and/or should be subject to corrective measures, and those that lie beyond the probability of any form of redemption. Most important, these 'renditions of the world can tell us as much about those who have created the maps as the subjects and objects that are conditioned by the mapping process.'[19]

Applying Biopolitical and Geopolitical Rationalities to the Regulation of Club Drugs in Canada

Focusing on the biopolitical and geopolitical dimensions of drug regulation provides important insights into the ways in which club drugs and those people said to use them have been managed in Canada. The biopolitical imperative to promote life worthy of life necessitates that some ways of living be promoted while others are managed to make them more amenable to the dominant forms of living. If forms of life cannot be made amenable, then biopolitics requires that either a form be left to die or (mirroring juridical forms of power) that it be exterminated before it proliferates and contaminates the 'species.' Thus, these biopolitical strategies are a central aspect of club-drug regulation in Canada, where the use of such drugs has been discursively represented by authorities as a lifestyle in and of itself. Moreover, a nexus of unacceptable risk to Canadian life is said to be constituted by the sexual deviancy and disease cultivated by club drugs, as though these substances have agency in and of themselves. Beyond the conceptual argument, empirically I have shown elsewhere that there is a long history of biopolitical regulation of illicit drugs in Canada beginning with the application of the rationales of the Canada First Movement and Social Gospel at the dawn of the twentieth century to combat suspected opium use.[20]

While geopolitics has traditionally been seen as primarily operating external to the territorial boundaries of the nation-state, the division, classification, and coding (often through biopolitical rationalities) of spaces and people within the state is a common occurrence. Conceptually, criminological analyses have been interested in finding the epicentres of criminal activity beginning with the rise of concentric zone theory in the 1940s (if not earlier). Practically, geopolitical strategies in Canada with respect to illicit-drug use have been in place since the very early targeting of opium dens by reformers and the regulations this gave rise to, including the prohibition on single Caucasian women living in close proximity to Vancouver's Chinatown, as uncovered by T.L. Chapman.[21] Geopolitical representations have been used by the Canadian state as a means by which to position areas inside the sovereign territory as outside this territory in terms of cultural dispositions. This outside within the inside becomes the locale within which Ó Tuathail's demonized Other threatens the integrity of an idealized Canadian Self.

With both biopolitics and geopolitics appearing to rest on slightly different forms of governmental rationality, how is that they are linked to form 'a toxic combination'? The ways in which their logics, rationalities, and preferred means of action will join together will ultimately depend on the problem to which they are purporting to respond and the context within which they are operating. However, in broad strokes, the geopolitics of Canadian drug regulation has been about containing drug activity within specific spaces, preventing its proliferation into new domains, and (if possible) aiming to regain control of these spaces by eradicating the drug activity said to be indigenous to them. Biopolitics becomes a complementary means of preventing proliferation, often in cleverly concealed forms, by using power in ways not identified with sovereign authority (e.g., the law, public health, or the police) to initiate transformation in the populations that are said to inhabit these spaces. It is only when biopolitical calculations of risk have been determined and the forms of life within these spaces have been made worthy of life either through transformation or elimination (whether direct or indirect) that there can be any thought of readmitting these spaces within Canada proper. Until that point, they are outliers, foreign and dangerous.

Having briefly sketched out a response to why these approaches are suitable to the study of illicit-drug regulation in Canada, I shall return to the first question: What do these approaches add to the study of illicit-drug regulation in Canada? Primarily, both approaches expand the scope of traditional understandings of the form and exercise of power in Canadian society to minute aspects of daily regulation of social life which we often overlook or fail to pay much attention to. In other words, they help to make strange those things with which we have become far too familiar. By revealing the ways in which power operates outside the realms of official policy making, lawmaking, and policing, biopolitical and geopolitical approaches demonstrate the diverse bodies of knowledge, institutions, logics, and means by which 'club drugs' as a classification of substances become designated as a particular type of problem in everyday life. Moreover, once problematized, these conceptual frameworks allow us to see how the precise actions undertaken rely on understandings and cultural meanings for their justification and legitimacy that are far more generalized in their application than the specific case itself. At their root, biopolitical and geopolitical analyses open the possibility of providing an account of what Canada (state and society) understands itself to be. In doing so, there is the chance to gain a deeper appreciation of all of the contingencies at play.

Club Drugs and the Contingent Construction of Threat

There are myriad ways in which illicit drugs can be constructed as a security threat that necessitates forms of regulation both legal and otherwise. Authorities and moral entrepreneurs are always able to correlate, if not directly link, dangerous medical consequences, deviant behaviours, identities, and political effects that are claimed to stem from the production, trade, and consumption of specific substances. Club drugs have been no different in this respect, being associated with a host of negative consequences from brain damage in users to the degeneration of Canadian society. But it is not just the threats said to emanate from club drugs that are important; equally significant are how biopolitical and geopolitical rationalities are central to the presentation of the threats said to be inherent within club drugs.

What is perhaps the most striking aspect of the construction of club drugs as a threat to Canadian society is the way in which the classification itself harbours an overt geographical positioning of the drugs: these are CLUB drugs, that is, drugs that are said to be primarily (if not exclusively) used within nightclubs and raves as opposed to any other spaces that one could imagine (e.g., pubs, health clubs, boardrooms, private homes). But, given that the medical evidence cannot provide scientific proof of the drugs determining the behaviour of the users, Dawn Moore and Mariana Valverde have argued that a geopolitical logic is employed by authorities to present these substances as a threat.[22] Utilizing Mikhail Bakhtin's concept of the chronotope, they contend that central to the regulation is the creation of a unit of space/

time that is said to exist prior to any attempt at regulation (e.g., the club or rave).[23] This space is then used as a container to 'unify and give an identity to otherwise heterogeneous and/or ill-defined risks, including pharmacological risks.'[24] In other words, the chronotope is a 'specific spatio-temporal logic that unifies otherwise heterogeneous substances and activities.'[25]

This is not to say that the deployment of chronotopes is accurate. With respect to 'club drugs,' Canadian authorities at the turn of the twenty-first century consistently conflated the unique spaces of rave and club in order to construct a single threat matrix that was able to draw upon the worst dangers found in both. For example, the Toronto Police conducted raids on a series of after-hours nightclubs (i.e., establishments that served alcohol beyond legal serving times) in 2000 and seized a cache of firearms. Within media reports, these spaces were described as 'rave-clubs,' allowing for gun violence to be attributed to raves at a time when the police were seeking tough regulations/by-laws on raves, including a ban on the events being held on public property.[26] These practices of conflation are reminiscent of broader geopolitical discourses during the Cold War that failed appreciate the deep differences between the Soviet Union and China for many decades.

From the geopolitical logic associated with constructing club drugs as a threat it follows that there is something about the space of the club itself and the times in which it operates that heightens the dangers of club drugs. As Moore and Valverde note, the temporal logic is fairly easy to discern: most clubs operate at night, generally a time that has traditionally been perceived as being more pregnant with risk. Rhetorically, public authorities have presented fairly dramatic descriptions of the activities going on within these spaces, from Julian Fantino's claim of kids squirming in vomit while high on Ecstasy to the RCMP's more measured though no less problematic claim that 'the main hours of a rave are conducive for stimulatory hallucinogenics such as MDMA ... and MDA.'[27] But what is less clear is what is specific to the club space itself that heightens the dangers of club drugs.[28]

The presence of youth and other marginalized segments of society (historically within the space of clubs this has been sexual and/or racial minorities), generally perceived as being more prone to various forms of risky behaviour, would be an obvious starting point.[29] However, at least with rave and clubs that play electronica (of one form or another), the perception of the media and of public authorities has been that this population is primarily white and middle class.

The norm that clubs are places that people go to abandon the usual social restrictions on the expression of personal feeling through dance, a form of activity that has become increasingly rare in a society where such things are uncommon, might be another; in other words, from a biopolitical standpoint, activities outside of pre-established norms become seen as threats in part because, by falling outside of norms, they make it increasingly difficult to discern probabilities and therefore control any potential risks that may be generated from them. To put it crudely, people going out to specific spaces in the wee hours of the morning to socialize and dance simply does not compute. Therefore, it must be a danger with potentially grave consequences.

The important point is that the geographing of clubs as a site of heightened and unacceptable risk with specific forms of drug use – note that alcohol and tobacco are not framed as club drugs – means that threats not generally thought to occur regularly within the broader contours of Canadian society (such as date rape or poly-drug use) are all seen as being endemic to the space of clubs. Thus, club space is assumed to be a container of licentious behaviour that does not occur in Canadian society more widely. Yet no reasons are ever given in policy documents and public statements for why this is the case.

In traditional geopolitical discourses, it is often the topography or geographic location of particular spaces that are said to provide specific (strategic) significance to them. Transposing these kinds of justification to the space of club, is it the design of clubs (e.g., layout) or their sensory environment (e.g., intermittent lighting and loud music) that make them encourage risky behaviour? Some insight is offered by the comments of Detective Sergeant Egidio Roseto, who was involved in the Comfort Zone raid. In an interview with the *Toronto Star*, he remarked that the interior of the club was 'an absolute jungle. It's pitch black. It's very hot. The lights are black lighting from the ceiling. It's very, very dirty.'[30] Therefore, the geopolitical positioning of a range of substances under the banner of the club, a grouping whose links are tenuous at best, creates the perception identified by Moore and Valverde that a set of risks are possible only within the club environment. These representations all contribute to a particular bandwidth of policy possibility and reveal the ways in which biopolitical and geopolitical rationalities may intersect in club-drug regulation.

The missing link may be the biopolitical classification of populations; clubs become a container for a collection of risky groups who then make the environment extraordinarily dangerous. In attempting to calculate the probabilities of risk of club (and rave) attendance, public authorities have identified and classified specific populations who inhabit these spaces. For example, in the pamphlet *Designer Drugs and Raves*, the RCMP outlines four major population classifications of individuals who attend raves and/or nightclubs:

- 'The Candy raver: a younger group [who] dress in baggy clothing, wear candy necklaces and jewellery, suck soothers, eat suckers, carry glowsticks, and wear stickers/sparkles/glitter ... They like to draw attention to themselves. Not all are drug users.'
- 'Club kids [who] wear expensive clothing, usually a lot of black or dark colours, tend hang out in gangs or groups ... [use mainly] heroin, cocaine and alcohol ... [and] attend weeknight club parties.'
- 'The Bar star who attends raves after clubs close.'
- 'The Party kid: many do use, however, they're into the scene for the music and the "vibes," not just the drugs; listen to the music outside of raves.'[31]

For anyone who has frequently attended a rave or nightclub, these categorizations make very little sense. But similar to the way in which a marketing firm might construct population profiles based on consumption patterns to target individuals with certain characteristics, or political parties create demographic classifications to target in election campaigns (e.g., 'soccer moms'), the RCMP is constructing populations which various institutions (not, to say the least, the RCMP itself) will target and place within a set of power relations in attempts to act upon their actions. These institutional attempts can range from trying to reduce the risks or harms of their supposed club-drug use to eliminating the possibility for them to use club drugs.

The construction of populations is also directly linked to the risks produced and/or engendered in groups of individuals by what is characterized as either their general behaviour or their shared vulnerabilities. In the pamphlet *Chemical Drug Trends*, the RCMP draws upon an existing biopolitical classification, gay/bisexual men, to emphasize poly-drug use within the clubbing environment (specifically circuit parties) and what it claims is a clear link to high-risk sexual activity (unprotected anal sex with partners of unknown HIV status).[32] This is a triple-move that, in its lack of differentiation, ends up constructing three populations as being of high HIV/AIDS transmission risk through the practice of unprotected anal sex: gay men, bisexual men, and poly-drug users. The possible forms of biopolitical regulation in this case are almost secondary to the representations of these populations within the mind of the general public, allowing for the extension of one type of traditionally perceived deviant behaviour onto another. Unfortunately, one gets the sense that an implicit argument is being made with respect to a population (i.e., the poly-drug user) that, it is believed, should be disallowed, with the only question being whether this should be through forceful correction or malignant neglect.

With heterosexual relations, the mode of sexual deviancy said to inhabit club space is that of chemically aided sexual assault. Yet authorities are rather vague on its prevalence, and instead deflect the standard burden of proof with the argument that it 'is a real problem, the full extent of which is difficult to measure. Many victims do not report incidents immediately, or at all, making it difficult to accurately measure this type of assault.'[33] Despite the lack of any concrete empirical evidence about the likelihood of occurrence of date rape in clubs as compared to other social spaces (both public and private), clubs are represented as the place in which a (female) person is most likely to be induced into an unwanted state of intoxication by a stranger who slips her a club drug without her consent, leading to an assault at some later time when the victim is incapacitated. Again, this would seem to be directly related to the construction of a club as a particular type of geopolitical space. As such, Moore and Valverde argue that 'certain sets of events that do not loom threateningly most of the time are regarded as probable in that particular chronotope; among them, women are thought to be at great risk of being drugged and raped even by their good friends. This logic is chronotope-specific: the use of drugs for rape purposes is never portrayed as happening in the daytime in coffee shops or in doctor's offices.'[34]

But what becomes particularly interesting is that, rather than identify and classify a population of rapists that requires specific forms of biopolitical regulation, this logic transposes these deviant characteristics onto the club drugs themselves. It does so by granting them a degree of agency that becomes a major contributor to the practice of drug-facilitated sexual assault. It is the specific drugs, not the perpetrator, that intends to incapacitate. For Moore and Valverde, this granting of agency is illustrative of an explicit dynamic at play that excludes broader and deeper examinations of how other gender power relations are located in practices of sexual assault, and of the ways in which a drug's agency is understood as a certain kind of social problem requiring certain kinds of action.[35]

Focusing on the production of populations and spaces leads to an awareness of the power relations at work in their management and regulation. Populations need not be managed through the use of force; this can also be achieved through the provision of help and advice which remains born of a desire to control risky populations with the hope of transforming them into something more safe (if considered possible). This awareness, for example, produces a very different analytic purchase on the grass-roots movements dedicated to providing harm-reduction materials and medical information to club goers about club drugs: such activities are neither devoid of power nor power neutral.[36] Rather, they represent a different type of (biopolitical) power relationship within the regulatory dynamics of club drugs.

The Synthesis of Geopolitical and Biopolitical Forms of Club Drug Regulation

Biopolitical and geopolitical rationalities have constructed a threat matrix through which the Canadian authorities can interpret the dangers said to be posed by club drugs. How, then, are these interpretations of danger put into practice? Moreover, what are the sleights of hand that become necessary to maintain the amenability of existing relations of power to these regulatory practices?

Much like other illicit drugs, club drugs have not experienced sustained medical and scientific investigation into their physiological effects and potential uses. There is some knowledge of their short-term risks but little consensus on the individual (e.g., existing medical conditions) and environmental (e.g., ambient temperature) factors that may increase or reduce the manifestation of risks in certain contexts. Research that has been undertaken has been suspect in both intent and methodology, often funded by states with strong prohibitive inclinations and conducted by scientists willing to produce the negative findings desired by major funding agencies.[37] Whereas the long-term effects of activities like smoking are widely known, with general scientific consensus about the associated harms, the long-term effects of MDMA (Ecstasy), ketamine, or GHB are largely unknown.

This point is being raised not as a call for further medical research or to identify how practices of pseudo-science have skewed Canadian practices of illicit-drug regulation. Rather, the lack of information on the longer-term medical effects is highlighted because it poses a significant challenge to the biopolitical rationalities involved in illicit-drug regulation. Primarily, without existing data or the opportunity to create a data-set by tracking the health of these users over a period of time, it becomes impossible to construct the sort of risk probabilities upon which biopolitical calculations rest. In the absence of this information, biopolitics has relied upon the moralizing aspects of the broader Canadian drugs discourse as a substitute. As Moore and Valverde report, 'information about the risks of such drugs as Ecstasy and Rohypnol is usually presented in a highly mixed format that includes scientific data presented in charts alongside moralizing melodramatic narratives.'[38] But one suspects that this hybrid will be able to sustain itself for only so long and that one may see a push in Canada to fund more research into these drugs as part of a revamped Canadian drug strategy. This does not mean that these moralizing narratives will be replaced. A greater body of evidence may be desired to demonstrate their validity as well as to establish a clearer picture of probabilities, risks, emerging populations, and threats.

As mentioned above, geopolitical rationalities have framed the club-drug issue as one that at the moment is largely confined to specific spaces but that has the potential, in the very near future, of proliferating beyond these spaces and contaminating Canadian society at large. Thus, much as Western Cold War geopolitical thought operated through an immediate grand strategy of containment, so too does Canadian geopolitical thought with respect to club-drug regulation. The *problematique* is one of how to best contain club-drug use within the space of clubs in order to prevent its spread into new locales such as university dormitories, schools, and house parties. Furthermore, mirroring concerns over marijuana production, the RCMP has suggested that the popularity of club drugs has resulted in the proliferation of drug production to the point where any suburban neighbourhood could be a manufacturing site and subject to a range of associated risks from noxious fumes to chemical fires.[39]

In the mid- to long term, the geopolitical logic put into practice is to shrink the availability of spaces that make club-drug use possible. However, in the case of the Comfort Zone, police were flustered after the raid to find out that they were actually powerless to stop the club from continuing to operate despite laying thirteen by-law charges against its management, including 'operating an entertainment establishment without a license.'[40] Two tactics have become apparent over the past two decades. The first has been to eliminate the ability to operate outright by prohibiting the creation and/or existence of the spaces themselves. However, because of the fluidity of space, as noted by

Moore and Valverde through their use of the chronotope concept, and the conflation of spaces as noted above, this is very difficult to achieve in practice. Other (economically) viable spaces deemed acceptable aspects of authorized ways of life could fall under prohibition.[41] Thus, an outright prohibition flanked by an army of exceptions has not been the preferred means of control.

The second tactic has been to make regulatory standards impossible to reach apart from those spaces whose owners/operators can afford to meet the costs involved. Some of these regulations are framed in terms of harm reduction, such as the provision of drinking water, functioning washroom facilities, air conditioning, and trained medical/security staff. Other regulations, though, are primarily structured to eliminate spaces without the need for a public display of force such as a raid or series of arrests. For example, City of Toronto regulations for the operation of raves require the presence of paid-duty police officers at a level determined by the division chief of the area in which the event is to take place – a decision that cannot be appealed by a rave promoter. This regulatory framework has proved to be an extremely effective means of discouraging promoters and owners of spaces that might house raves from organizing these events. It has been a major (though not sole) contributor to the decline of the rave in Toronto.

Thus, the synthesis that has occurred in Canada with respect to biopolitics and geopolitics in the regulation of club drugs has been in terms of providing safer venues through a series of regulations designed to reduce the harms and harmful behaviours said to inhabit these spaces.[42] But, because risks can never be eliminated, biopolitical and geopolitical rationalities continue to provide an imperative for intervention in these spaces at moments when it is thought that an opportunity exists to re-colonize them in a different form.[43] In Toronto, the growing number of residents flocking to expensive condominium developments located in the entertainment district, and the ensuing complaints about noise, drug use, and disruption, have now given authorities an additional justification for geopolitical intervention into the spaces of the club. This leads to the question of whether one will see the concentration of clubbing events in an ever diminishing number of venues within the downtown core based on a synthesis of biopolitical and geopolitical logics.[44]

Conclusions?

Given the exploratory nature of this chapter, it would be problematic to claim that any definitive conclusions have been reached. At best, I would want to claim that the argument put forward here about the centrality of biopolitical and geopolitical thought to the practices of Canadian drug regulation requires continuing investigation in the area of club drugs and beyond. Moreover, an account of how practices of resistance either contribute to or disrupt illicit-drug regulation is beyond the scope of this chapter.[45] However, I do think that one tentative finding comes out of this brief exercise. It should be kept in mind that biopolitical rationalities (i.e., the identification and classification of populations, some notion of life worthy of life, some calculation of risk, an understanding of the probabilities for conversion, and some cost-benefit analysis of potential interventions), geopolitical logics (i.e., locating epicentres of use, containing use, combating proliferation), and resulting relations of power run through any approach taken to illicit drugs, however progressive it may appear on the basis of first principles. Thus, there is an analytic imperative to go beyond the standard processes of adjudication to identify what are claimed to be good and bad approaches to illicit-drug regulation. Instead, the focus should be on showing the potential dangers inherent within any approach and determining the circumstances under which the relations of power underpinning it become oppressive.

NOTES

1 Toronto Police Service, News Release: Project White Rabbit: 14 Division, 2008.
2 Processes of social construction can range in these instances from the transformation of social mores to the creation of moral panics at the individual and collective levels.
3 These are also interchangeably referred to within the academic and policy literature as 'synthetic drugs' or 'designer drugs.' The use of the term 'club drugs' in this chapter is a move to highlight the explicit spatial understanding of where this classification of drugs is primarily consumed, an understanding that is implicit in the terms 'synthetic drugs' and 'designer drugs.'
4 Michael Dillon, 'Governing Terror: The State of Emergency of Biopolitical Emergence,' *International Political Sociology*, 1, no. 1 (2007): 9.
5 In the medical and sociological literature, the substances most subject to this classification include MDMA, GHB, ketamine, and Rohypnol. Other

substances that quite regularly have fallen under this designation include methamphetamine, cocaine, and LSD. There is also a long list of derivative substances of MDMA, labelled by the RCMP as 'drugs of deception,' which have also been referred to as club drugs, including 2-CB, MDA, MMDA, PMA, and MDE.

6 See Michel Foucault, *The History of Sexuality: An Introduction*, 3 vols., vol. 1 (New York: Random House 1990); 'The Birth of Biopolitics,' in P. Rabinow and N. Rose, eds., *The Essential Foucault: Selections from Essential Works of Foucault 1954–1984* (New York: New Press 2003), 202–7; 'Governmentality,' in ibid., 229–45; and *Society Must Be Defended: Lectures at the College de France 1975–1976*, trans. by D. Macey (New York: Picador 2003).

7 Michel Foucault, *Discipline and Punish: The Birth of the Prison*, edited by A. Sheridan (New York: Pantheon Books 1977).

8 Paul Rabinow, Paul Rose, and Nikolas Rose, 'Introduction: Foucault Today,' in Rabinow and Rose, eds., *The Essential Foucault*.

9 Dillon, 'Governing Terror' and 'Governing through Contingency: The Security of Biopolitical Governance,' *Political Geography*, 26 (2007): 41–7.

10 Michael Dillon and Luis Lobo-Guerreo, 'Biopolitics of Security in the 21st Century: An Introduction,' *Review of International Studies*, 34, no. 2 (2008): 265–92.

11 A different way of thinking about biopower is that it is the ability to foster life or to disallow life to the point of extermination. The point is to transform life (more broadly) into something that has been calculated as good.

12 Rabinow and Rose, *The Essential Foucault*, xxix.

13 Dillon and Lobo-Guerrero, 'Biopolitics of Security.'

14 Ibid.

15 Foucault, *Discipline and Punish*, 223.

16 Gilles Deleuze and Felix Guattari, *A Thousand Plateaus: Capitalism and Schizophrenia*, trans. by B. Massumi (Minneapolis: University of Minnesota Press 1987); and Ferguson Kennan, 'Unmapping and Remapping the World: Foreign Policy as Aesthetic Practice,' in M.J. Shapiro and H.R. Acker, eds., *Challenging Boundaries: Global Flows, Territorial Identities* (Minneapolis: University of Minnesota Press 1996), 165–92.

17 Gearóid Ó Tuathail, Simon Dalby, and Paul Routledge, eds., *The Geopolitics Reader* (London: Routledge 1998); and Gearóid Ó Tuathail and Simon Dalby, eds., *Critical Geopolitics* (London: Routledge 1998).

18 Gearóid Ó Tuathail, *Critical Geopolitics* (Minneapolis: University of Minnesota Press 1996), 15.

19 Kyle Grayson, *Chasing Dragons: Security, Identity, and Illicit Drugs in Canada* (Toronto: University of Toronto Press 2008), 60.

20 Ibid., 100–13.
21 T.L. Chapman, 'The Anti-Drug Crusade in Western Canada, 1885–1925,' in D. Bercuson and L.A. Knafla, eds., *Law and Society in Canada in Historical Perspective* (Calgary: University of Calgary Press 1979), 100–21.
22 Dawn Moore and Mariana Valverde, 'Maidens at Risk: "Date Rape Drugs" and the Formation of Hybrid Risk Knowledges,' *Economy and Society*, 29, no. 4 (2000): 514–31.
23 For Bakhtin, a chronotope was 'the spatially specific temporality that defines and is constituted by each major literary genre.' See Moore and Valverde, 'Maidens at Risk,' 516.
24 Ibid., 518.
25 Ibid., 517.
26 Rather than correct this mischaracterization, I maintain it throughout this paper. The purpose is to show the kinds of policies that become possible when raves and clubs are seen as the same type of venue.
27 Royal Canadian Mounted Police, *Designer Drugs and Raves*, 2nd ed. (Vancouver: Royal Canadian Mounted Police 2001), 5.
28 With virtually no empirical research on this specific point available to draw upon, my remarks can be only suggestive.
29 Tara McCall, *This is Not a Rave* (Toronto: Insomniac Press 2001); Simon Reynolds, *Generation Ecstasy: Into the World of Techno and Rave Culture* (New York: Routledge 1999); Mireille Silcott, *Rave America: New School Dancescapes* (Toronto: ECW Press 1999).
30 Tracy Huffman and Nick Pron, 'OD Death Spurred Dance Club Raid,' *Toronto Star*, 18 March 2008, http://www.thestar.com/news/gta/article/347162 (accessed 1 April 2010).
31 RCMP, *Designer Drugs*, 6.
32 RCMP Drug Awareness Service, *Chemical Drug Trends: British Columbia* (Vancouver: Royal Canadian Mounted Police 2003).
33 RCMP, *Designer Drugs*, 42.
34 Moore and Valverde, 'Maidens at Risk,' 517.
35 Ibid., 524.
36 Examples would include the Toronto Rave Information Project (TRIP) and the Calgary chapter of the American organization DanceSafe. Even RCMP materials purport to be providing information that could reduce risk, though this is primarily couched in terms of convincing people not to consume club drugs at all.
37 A series of scandals regarding the research results of a Johns Hopkins University investigation team led by Dr George Ricaurte is particularly instructive. Ricaurte had received nearly $10 million in funding from the

National Institute for Drug Awareness, an agency of the U.S. government, and all of his findings with respect to links between Ecstasy use and Parkinson's Disease were found to be unsubstantiated. See Donald G. McNeil, 'Report of Ecstasy Drug's Great Risks Is Retracted,' *New York Times*, 6 September 2003, http://www.nytimes.com/2003/09/06/health/06ECST. html?pagewanted=1 (accessed 1 April 2010).

38 See Moore and Valverde, 'Maidens at Risk,' 515. This calls into question the claims of Dillon and others that the creation of populations occurs only at the precise moment when a grouping is constituted as such in shared characteristics found through specific biopolitical calculations (based on data). Instead, it points to a transitional process whereby governing authorities must rely on previously articulated identities before transposing them into populations for the purposes of biopolitics.

39 RCMP, *Designer Drugs* and *Chemical Drug Trends*.

40 Of particular significance was that the property did not serve alcohol nor did it have a licence to serve alcohol from the Liquor Licence Board of Ontario, thereby excluding the owners from a series of costly charges. As a result, police continued to target patrons, conducting two further raids on 23 March 2008 and 6 April 2008. These raids generated far less media attention and resulted in charges being laid against four people. For more details, see the following at CityNews.ca (all accessed 12 May 2008): 'Comfort Zone Busted for the Third Time,' 6 April 2008, http://www.citynews. ca/news/news_21419.aspx; 'Police Raid Popular Afterhours Club Comfort Zone,' 16 March 2008, http://www.citynews.ca/news/news_20656.aspx; and 'Three More Arrested in Comfort Zone Raid,' 23 March 2008, http:// www.citynews.ca/news/news_20895.aspx. See also Huffman and Pron, 'OD Death.'

41 For example, events associated with Caribana and Pride would have fallen afoul of the initial rave ban in public buildings in Toronto. Then again, perhaps this was part of the point?

42 One wonders if these sleights of regulatory hand as opposed to more direct displays of force are in any part a reflection of the perception that, as a population at large, club goers and ravers are mainly white, middle-class youth?

43 For example, a Shopper's Drug Mart was the first enterprise to occupy the space that once housed the notorious nightclub Industry on King Street West in Toronto.

44 The case of New York City under the reign of Rudy Giuliani might prove instructive here. In what proved to be a highly effective way of reducing the number of nightclubs in Manhattan, venues were required to apply

for a cabaret licence (at a considerable cost) if they wished to be legally allowed to have more than three patrons dancing at one time. The by-laws were strenuously enforced and many establishments shut down, changed into restaurants/pubs/bars, or were forced to post signs reminding patrons not to dance!

45 For more detailed accounts of the practices of resistance, see Grayson, *Chasing Dragons*; Sean P. Hier, 'Raves, Risks, and the Ecstasy Panic: A Case Study in the Subversive Nature of Moral Regulation,' *Canadian Journal of Sociology*, 27, no. 1 (2002): 33–57; and Brian Wilson, 'The Canadian Rave Scene and Five Theses on Youth Resistance,' *Canadian Journal of Sociology*, 27, no. 3 (2002): 373–412.

Afterword: A Personal Reflection on the Law and Illicit-Drug Use

ALAN YOUNG

In reading the diverse set of essays that comprise *The Real Dope*, I was both delighted and dismayed. I was delighted because I believe it is important that scholars study and report upon the short history of our drug and alcohol policies so that the public can better understand the ill-advised and ill-informed nature of our domestic drug policy. I was also dismayed because, as I read each essay, I was painfully reminded of the primary reasons why my professional work in trying to reform our drug laws has largely been an exercise in futility.

For the past two decades, I have devoted most of my professional life to defending cannabis criminals and to constructing a viable legal and constitutional challenge to the authority of the state to dictate private consumption choices. Working on marijuana legalization has been like living the torment of Sisyphus. In ancient Greek mythology, Sisyphus was punished for exposing some of Zeus' lecherous secrets. He was condemned to an eternal life of endless labour by having to roll a marble boulder to the top of a hill, only to have the boulder plunge back down every time he reached the summit. Since the Le Dain Commission recommended decriminalization of marijuana use in 1972, the Canadian government has promised and proposed reform of the law on many occasions, but every time it comes close to achieving this goal, those in power let the boulder tumble down the hill and the activists and reformists are forced to start over again. The essays contained in *The Real Dope* confirmed in my mind that the reason the boulder constantly slides down the hill is because the state and its agents can easily defeat drug-law reform by alarming the public with lies, exaggerations, and false alarms.

The essays in this collection provide historical overviews which outline developments in public policy, law, and opinion in relation to diverse licit and illicit substances including tobacco (Rudy; Cook), heroin (Carstairs), alcohol (Malleck; Marquis), LSD (Dyck; Martel), and 'club' drugs (Grayson). The consistent thread connecting these pieces is the recurring need of government and other moral entrepreneurs to falsely demonize drugs in the crusade to maintain standards of sobriety. For example, we find that tobacco smoking was held to be responsible for major military defeats, since it was considered a 'luxury which is degenerating our race.'[1] All in all, it becomes readily evident from this collection that 'drug policy... responded not to epidemiological studies, but to public perception.'[2] Science became a tool of propaganda in the development of drug policy by policy makers who had no personal or professional experience with the very substances they sought to demonize. As Humphry Osmond, who coined the term 'psychedelic' to describe his research findings with LSD in the 1960s, noted: 'The less experience any person has with these drugs the more apt is he to utter profound yet meaningless statements about their so-called dangers.'[3]

One has to wonder why drug use is so rampant in North America in the face of official scare tactics and propaganda. If our society is ever going to gain some control over drug abuse, we have to understand why people choose to consume substances despite the claims of risk and danger. Sharon Anne Cook's essay looks at this question in relation to why women choose to smoke cigarettes despite warnings, and this is the type of analysis that is needed to understand the type of drug policy we must create if we truly wish to maintain low consumption rates for licit and illicit drugs. Ironically, Catherine Carstairs shows that the consumption of heroin in post-Second World War North America was partly motivated by the user's desire to construct a 'deliberately rebellious identity.' Accordingly, Carstairs concludes that 'strict laws against using drugs actually made drug use appealing to a small set of people.' If drug laws do not convince people of the evils of drug consumption, and in fact may actually make drug use more alluring, then one has to seriously question why the state continues to be engaged in a legal war on drugs. It may be that the war-like policy defies rational assessment and that its foundation lies within 'a framework defined by white, middle-class, Anglo-Saxon, and Christian values,' as Malleck shows was the foundation for liquor-control policy once the temperance crusades died down earlier in the twentieth century. However, it would be a mistake to assume that the irrationality of drug policy is predicated on an unconscious effort to instil Christian values of sobriety. These values are not uniformly shared among all Christians and it is likely that drug policy serves a more sinister official purpose. In discussing how the treatment of addiction became inextricably linked with criminal justice policies, Dawn Moore insightfully notes that, when 'crime is caused by the individual problem of drug addiction, then it is not caused by broader failings of government such as weak social-safety nets or vast economic inequalities.'

Curiously, this collection of essays does not extend to a discussion of the most commonly used illicit drug in the world – cannabis sativa. Although there are approximately 170 million cannabis users around the world,[4] in many ways the cannabis issue has become a Canadian issue. First, Canadians are the largest consumers of marijuana in the industrialized world, with only the people of Ghana, Zambia, and Papua New Guinea consuming more.[5] Second, Canada is one of only a few jurisdictions in the world that authorizes the production and consumption of marijuana for medical purposes.[6] Third, Canadians, and their elected representatives, are still engaged in the ongoing debate as to whether marijuana should be decriminalized or legalized. To extend the coverage of this collection, I wish to provide in this afterword a brief outline of the state of affairs in Canada with an illicit drug which is apparently enjoyed by millions in this country. The story has its complexities and ambiguities, but the short history of marijuana in Canadian public policy strongly confirms Marquis's point that empirical data and sound scientific analysis do not inform the drug-policy debate and that public perception and public fears (largely stirred up by state agents) have been largely responsible for the development of our incoherent drug policies.

With little fanfare, marijuana became a prohibited substance in 1923. Even though it had been used for sacramental, medicinal, and recreational purposes for 10,000 years,[7] when Parliament decided to criminalize marijuana use in 1923, few members of Parliament had even heard of this drug. In fact, in 1923, few Canadians were using it, and until the explosion of the counterculture in the 1960s, there were only a handful of recorded convictions for the use or sale of marijuana. After eighty-five years of chasing the cannabis criminal, we have seen consumption of marijuana skyrocket, with an estimated two to three million Canadians indulging in this 'vice' despite the presence of draconian criminal sanctions.[8] The only legacy left from this battle with marijuana consumers is the expenditure of billions of dollars in our pursuit of the cannabis criminal and the saddling of over 600,000 Canadians with criminal records for possession of marijuana.

The prohibition on marijuana consumption is unlike any other prohibition found in Western liberal democracies. In many, if not most, of the cases before the courts, we find law-abiding, productive citizens being transformed into criminals by police, prosecutors, and judges who might have indulged in the very same 'criminal' activity at some time in their lives. In order to justify inclusion of marijuana as a prohibited substance in the 1920s, public officials and media representatives were required to construct an outrageous 'dope fiend mythology' to frighten the masses and convince them that they should look to the government for protection. Judge Emily Murphy, the first woman judge in Canada, wrote in her book *The Black Candle* (1922) that 'persons using this narcotic ... lose all sense of moral responsibility. While in this condition they become raving maniacs and are liable to kill or indulge in any form of violence to other persons, using the most savage methods of cruelty.'[9] Similarly, the *Toronto Star* reported in 1938 that marijuana will 'send a large proportion of the Dominion's population to the insane asylum.'[10]

Although there are few people in 2008 who believe this hyperbolic drivel, there still remains a sense among Canadians that Parliament would not retain the prohibition unless marijuana use presented some significant danger. However, there simply is not any evidence of significant danger. Nevertheless, valiant efforts are still made to convince Canadians that marijuana will destroy the fabric of Canadian society. For example, in 2007 *Globe and Mail* columnist Margaret Wente made the claim that the increased potency of contemporary pot has made the substance far more dangerous than the hippie pot of the 1960s.[11] Her column is strewn with hyperbole and colourful language like 'scourge,' 'devastating,' 'haunted,' and 'destroyed.' Sadly, her provocative vocabulary is simply a rhetorical device to hide the fact that there is no pharmacological support for her assertion that increased potency increases any potential harm. In her zeal to demonize the 'new' marijuana, she has also failed to note that the testing protocols for a quantitative assessment of Tetrahydrocannabinol (THC) – the main psychoactive substance in cannabis – have dramatically changed in the past ten years such that all testing in the 1960s and 1970s grossly underestimated the potency of the hippie pot. She also fails to note that increased potency is not a problem for a substance like marijuana because marijuana does not have a documented and known lethal dose. Accordingly, increased potency cannot lead to overdose and death as with other illicit drugs.

Despite false claims by drug warriors, there is no convincing evidence that marijuana use leads to irreversible physical or psychological harm (although it must be recognized that heavy smoking of any substance will lead to pulmonary problems). There is no convincing evidence that marijuana is physically addictive or criminogenic. There is no evidence that marijuana is a gateway or stepping stone to the use of more dangerous drugs. Of course, there are some people who abuse marijuana, just as there are people who abuse the multitude of junk-food products available on the free market, but this a reflection more of the reckless nature of certain consumers than of the insidious properties of the drug. The bottom line is that we have more to fear from problem drinkers than we do from Cheech and Chong types who get high, giggle, and gyrate to rock music.

The refusal to believe that marijuana is harmful is not a pipe dream of spaced-out and aging hippies (if they still exist). Virtually every commission of inquiry in the Western world has reached this conclusion. Starting with the 1893 Indian Hemp Commission, every time a government has established a commission of inquiry to study the issue, the commission has concluded that the marijuana problem is a tempest in a teapot and that marijuana use should not be considered a criminal activity. This consensus emerged in the 1944 La Guardia Report (United States), the 1967 Presidential Commission on Law Enforcement (United States), the 1968 Report by the Advisory Committee on Drug Dependence (United Kingdom), the 1972 President's Commission on Marijuana and Drug Abuse (United States), the 1972 Inquiry into the Non-Medical Use of Drugs (the Canadian Le Dain Commission), and the 1979 Report on the Non-Medical Use of Drugs (Australia). Like déjà vu, at the beginning of the twenty-first century our government appointed a Senate and a House of Commons Committee to study the problem once again and the Senate proposed full legalization, while the House of Commons meekly endorsed decriminalization.[12]

Displaying utter contempt for democratic principle, the Canadian government (and its mentor, the U.S. government) simply shelved these reports, allowing them to collect dust while hundreds of thousands of North Americans are still being persecuted simply because they prefer to intoxicate themselves with marijuana and not just with alcohol, tobacco, or caffeine. It is a strange world indeed when one's choice of intoxicant becomes the dividing line between law-abiding and criminal activity in a world in which the consumption of intoxicating substances, for better or worse, has become an ordinary fact of life.

People begrudgingly accept some erosion of democratic principle and some curtailment of legal rights during an emergency situation or during war. So it should come as no surprise that politicians have employed the metaphor of a 'war on drugs' to justify disregarding the popular will of the people and the conclusions of informed scholars and scientists. When Richard Nixon, Ronald Reagan, and Brian Mulroney issued their declarations of the war on drugs, it was not because marijuana was truly perceived to be an enemy of the people. It was a signal that the government was willing to resort to propaganda to sustain the highly intrusive and powerful law-enforcement agencies which were set up to combat marijuana use. Without conducting any reputable scientific research, the Canadian and American governments continued to assert that marijuana consumption would lead to social harms far worse than the ten horrific biblical plagues. Drug users are blamed for every social ill and every manifestation of urban decay. Violence, indolence, ignorance, and all manner of physical and psychological injuries were – and still are – attributed to marijuana use despite the fact that many marijuana users are now highly respected leaders in the worlds of business, law, and medicine.

North America is becoming increasingly isolated in its punitive response to marijuana use. The Netherlands, Belgium, Germany, Italy, Spain, South Australia, and the Australian Capital Territory have all moved towards decriminalization in recognition that the war on marijuana consumers is both a failure and an injustice. While other Western liberal democracies have seen fit to rethink their approach to soft-drug use, North American drug policy still lingers in the afterglow of the Reagan 'just say no' approach to the issue, and, as with many other issues of public policy, Canada cannot sever the umbilical cord that connects us to American folly. When Nancy Reagan coined the expression 'just say no' in the 1980s, North America took one giant step backward in the development of a rational approach to social problems. The 'just say no' approach to drug use is as sensible and sophisticated as having psychiatrists deal with patients suffering from clinical depression by telling them to 'just cheer up.'

In my view, there are no compelling reasons to maintain our current policy of futile prohibition and legal threats. I believe there are six incontrovertible reasons why we should put the tiresome marijuana debate to rest once and for all, by truly giving Canadians the liberty to grow and use the marijuana plant for personal use, whether recreational or medical. First, it is a plant. Criminal law should be reserved for serious predatory conduct, and only in the world of science fiction can a plant become a predator. Second, since the 1894 Indian Hemp Commission, virtually every royal commission and governmental committee, internationally and in Canada, has recommended that marijuana use be decriminalized. Some have even called for outright legalization. It is an affront to democracy to spend taxpayers' money continuously on comprehensive and informed reports which are ignored for no apparent reason. Third, most of Europe and Australia have decriminalized marijuana use and there is no reason to believe that the liberalization of the law in these countries has wreaked social havoc. In fact, it is interesting to note that consumption rates in decriminalized jurisdictions are significantly lower than in the penal colonies of Canada and the United States.

Fourth, the use of marijuana poses few societal dangers. It is not a criminogenic substance. For most people, marijuana provides a form of deep relaxation and sensory enhancement and it does not have the unpredictable, disinhibiting capacity of alcohol. No one is getting mugged by Cheech and Chong, and contrary to the false alarms sounded by public officials, marijuana is not significantly responsible for vehicular carnage. A drug can possess criminogenic potential only if it is a disinihibitor like alcohol or if it has addictive potential. Addiction leads to compulsive behaviour which will often be criminal in nature. There is little evidence that marijuana is addictive even though there are many chronic users who experience psychological dependency, which is no different from the compulsive jogger who must continue the daily regimen of exercise despite failing knees.

Fifth, marijuana is relatively harmless for the user.[13] Admittedly, smoking has some pulmonary risks, but it is strange to think that the blunt instrument of criminal law should be used to induce good health. We don't throw junk-food makers and their consumer victims into jail despite the enormous burden these junkies place on the health-care system. Criminal law is not the remedy for gastrointestinal distress, nor is it a rational solution to curbing chronic bronchial inflammation. The solemnity and majesty of the criminal law is trivialized when it is used to prevent Canadians from becoming a nation of coughers and wheezers.

Of course, every month we are bombarded with a media report of some new study linking pot to hemorrhoids or some other health risk. The public must exercise care and caution in reading these studies. More often than not, the study is reporting inconclusive findings from overdosing rats and monkeys or it is a methodologically flawed exercise commissioned by agents of the state. Marijuana activists and users, like myself, are accused of disregarding mounting evidence of the ravages of marijuana, but we've heard this all before. The doom-and-gloom prognosis of cancer or immune impairment or cognitive decline has never materialized and has never been replicated in credible, human-population studies.

Marijuana has been smoked for thousands of years and surely, if it were a dangerous substance, there would be some epidemiological evidence of increased morbidity or mortality among the smoking population. This evidence simply does not exist, but the failure to prove that the evils attributed to marijuana are nothing more than speculative just compels agents of the state and their scientist-handmaidens to look harder and harder for harms that do not exist. Many research scientists should hang their heads in disgrace for allowing science to become a tool of propaganda, and it is regrettable that the media has also become a pawn in the propaganda war on drugs.

My final reason for denouncing the use of criminal law to manufacture cannabis criminals is that the majority of Canadians do not support criminalization of pot use. Since the 1970s every public-opinion poll has shown that close to 70 per cent of Canadians do not support the current law.[14] Some Canadians support decriminalization and some support legalization, while only a minority of Canadians express support for our current prohibitory policy. Democracy is an illusion when the state can maintain a criminal prohibition on an activity enjoyed by three million Canadians and tolerated by an overwhelming majority. Public policy should not be built on the foundation of a vocal minority of cranky but sober Canadians who do not want others seeking pleasure in exotic ways.

Even if marijuana use and production entailed more significant harms, this would not necessarily warrant state intrusion into our private choices. There is nothing in this world that is perfectly harmless. Even flush toilets and articles of clothing can wreak havoc. Studies show that 40,000 Americans injure themselves on their toilet seats every year and 100,000 injure themselves on their clothing annually,[15] yet no one has tried to demonize Sir Thomas Crapper or outlaw pant zippers.

Young Canadians have been paralysed by cross-checks administered in the course of hockey games. We accept and tolerate these risks because we believe there is social utility in having flush toilets, clothing, and competitive sports.

Yet when it comes to marijuana, we appear unwilling to tolerate any level of risk. When you sort through the bogus studies and the scientific jargon, you will find that all credible pharmacologists conclude that the moderate use of marijuana causes no harm and that any suspected harms will be found only among chronic, daily users. Less than 5 per cent of users are chronic, and even within this population the suspected harms are not uniformly present.[16] The magnitude of harm is so insignificant that the continuing state opposition to marijuana use clearly lies not in concern for public health and welfare but rather in the moral opposition to non-alcohol intoxication.

Most people believe that Canada has stalled on the path of law reform because it has been overwhelmed by the stench of American criminal justice policy, but I think our confusion has more to do with our moral ambivalence towards hedonism and the alteration of consciousness. North Americans like to see their vices on the silver screen and not in real life, and we like to leave consciousness-expanding experiments to great thinkers like Aldous Huxley. The ordinary person is condemned to a life of sobriety save and except for the joys and sorrows of alcohol inebriation.

We have wavered in repealing a bad law because our culture does not believe there is any social utility or value in drug experimentation and alteration of consciousness. Even though most animals seek out intoxicating substances, we still cling to the notion that non-medical drug use by our species is always a degenerate and self-indulgent waste of time. State officials continue to construct false alarms of harm and danger in order to mask their real fear that drug use may foster critical thought and alternative visions of reality. Experimentation with pot will not lead most people to a dramatic change of consciousness and character, but, as with most illicit drugs, the temporary alteration of perception may nourish the capacity for critical thinking. It is no surprise that drug experimentation in the 1960s was associated with questioning authority and Timothy Leary's mantra of 'tune in, turn on and drop out.' The criminal prohibition of marijuana is all about thought-control.

It doesn't matter if someone smokes marijuana or if someone has dedicated his/herself to a life of total abstention; everyone should

be alarmed whenever state officials weave a tapestry of lies to justify punishing people. Even if one does not believe that people should
have the right to make autonomous choices about what they do with
their minds and bodies, one should still worry about a government
that governs through moral panic rather than the rational development of public policy. No doubt there will be many Canadians who
frown upon the pursuit of intoxication, especially this form of intoxicating activity; however, I would still like to believe that Canada is a
free and democratic country, and the fact that many Canadians frown
upon rodeos or violence in hockey does not provide a justification for
banning all violent sports and forcing all Canadians to play golf. Freedom of choice is a defining feature of democratic political theory, and
this freedom should not be limited save and except for the most compelling of reasons.

In the *The Real Dope* collection, Line Beauchesne's essay engages this
very question of the proper role of criminal law in governing private
choices and placing limits on liberty. She concludes that 'opting for
legal liberalism in dealing with drugs, as in any other area of public
policy, is a necessary ideal in a democratic society.' I agree with Professor Beauchesne's assertion, but it is becoming readily apparent that
legal liberalism may be a favourite only among scholars, for among
lawmakers and judges it is treated as an empty concept. In challenging the constitutional validity of our marijuana laws, I once raised the
concept of liberalism to argue that the only proper role of criminal law
is to prevent harm to others or to society at large. I then argued that
the empirical data does not support the claim that marijuana is sufficiently harmful to society to warrant criminal sanction and that criminal law cannot be used for paternalistic reasons to protect the health of
Canadians. John Stuart Mill would have turned over in his grave upon
witnessing the dismissive and casual attitude of the Supreme Court of
Canada to the idea that legal liberalism is the foundation for all criminal prohibitions.

My argument was that the 'harm principle' is a principle of fundamental justice under section 7 of the Canadian Charter of Rights
and Freedoms and that a criminal offence must be invalidated by the
courts if it is shown that the impugned conduct does not lead to harm
to others (including societal harm). The Supreme Court rejected this
argument, and the reasons for judgment display a confused and incoherent theoretical vision of the role of criminal law in modern society.
The Supreme Court of Canada's decisions in *Caine, Clay,* and *Malmo-*

Levine[17] have received extensive academic commentary[18] and I will not spend much time dissecting either the cases or the commentary here. In a nutshell, these cases simply give Parliament carte blanche in its criminal law power with absolutely no recognition that any carte blanche grant of power will eventually come back to haunt the grantor.

In the context of obscenity and freedom of expression, the Supreme Court noted that the lawmaker is entitled to enact criminal law if there is a 'reasoned apprehension of harm.'[19] The standard is low and it is inconceivable that lawmakers could not show a reasonable apprehension of harm as the basis for enacting most criminal offences. Technically, this statement was made in the assessment of whether obscenity prohibitions were a reasonable limit on freedom of expression under section 1 of the Charter, and some review of the merits and objectives of the law will always be necessary to determine if a violation of free expression can be justified. In the marijuana cases, it was argued that this low-threshold test of a reasonable apprehension of harm should also be employed as a constitutional barometer of whether the enactment of a law is in accordance with the principles of fundamental justice.

The lower courts accepted that the 'harm principle' was a principle of fundamental justice,[20] but these courts concluded that there was sufficient harm associated with the use of marijuana to satisfy the dictates of the principle. Surprisingly, the Supreme Court of Canada did not resolve the challenge solely on the basis that there did exist reasonable evidence of harm, but took the additional step of rejecting the harm principle for not being a legal principle for which a societal consensus exists. The Court concluded that Parliament is not restricted to the enactment of criminal laws which prevent harm to others and that the goals and objectives of criminal law are multifaceted and diverse. Parliament can create criminal law for paternalistic reasons or to protect societal core values even in the absence of tangible harm to the state or citizen. In addition, Parliament need not justify its decision to criminalize on the basis of any of these diverse objectives. At their essence, these cases release the state from any meaningful obligation to justify its criminal law power.

The harm principle was rejected as a principle of fundamental justice primarily because the Court believed it has not been recognized since time immemorial as a legal principle by courts of law. Without clear judicial recognition, this fundamental political principle animating modern political life in most Western democracies was relegated to the world of academic scholarship. Surely judicial decisions are not a proxy for societal consensus and principles of fundamental justice should be animated by the entire legal topography including scholarship, government reports, and empirical studies. Political theory should have a role to play in constitutional adjudication. As George P. Fletcher has noted, 'the political theory we choose will invariably shape our answers to innumerable questions about what should be punished, when nominal violations are justified and when wrongdoing should be excused.'[21]

It is puzzling that the Supreme Court did not acknowledge the significance of J.S. Mill, Jeremy Bentham, and Cesare Beccaria in assessing whether the harm principle was fundamental. Ultimately, the political theories supporting constraints and limits on the enactment of criminal law became reflected in contemporary scholarship, law commission reports, and government reports.[22] This movement from theory to practice provides the Court with the type of evidence needed to show societal consensus. Yet the Court ignored the fact that 'apart from the libertarians and communists at the extremes, the vast majority of us are unreflective liberals. We are suspicious of common law crimes and accept at face value Mill's principle that the state should punish only to prevent harm, and we take these two positions to be an adequate theoretical foundation for our work.'[23] Without engaging the nuances of political theory, it is hard to argue against the political ascendancy of liberalism, however conceived, in the modern era.

Perhaps the judicial forum is ill-suited for the resolution of most public-policy debates, but one is left to wonder why the legislative branch of government has been so reluctant to take action. It must be recognized that there is an extensive body of literature calling for decriminalization or legalization of illicit-drug use, especially marijuana. Even hard-line conservatives have begun to jump on the decriminalization bandwagon. You can comb through the literature and you will be hard-pressed to find many commentators supporting the current prohibitory policy. In fact, reading the literature will make you wonder why the prohibitions have been maintained, since it appears that virtually everyone who takes the time to study and cut through state-sponsored propaganda ends up disheartened and disillusioned about contemporary drug policy.

Beyond my earlier assertion that North American society does not recognize the value of intoxication or mind-altering experiences, I wish to return to the point made by Dawn Moore about the politically expedient value of relying upon drug use or abuse as the explanation for societal failings. The impulse to scapegoat is strong. People crave answers in the face of terror. Scapegoating an innocent victim allows scared people to regain an illusion of control over their lives. People believe that every horror has a cause. The universe must be ordered. Nothing is random. Everything is controlled by some cosmic law of cause and effect. The ancient Greeks confronted a famine by sacrificing a scapegoat to whatever petulant god was wreaking havoc with the environment. Of course, this was practically useless but psychologically effective in allaying fear and appeasing the need to take action. Until the Reformation, communities would put rats, pigs, and cows on trial for tragic events within the community. An animal has no soul and thus is vulnerable to demonic possession, so when a real culprit could not be found, or when a plague would not subside, there was always a soulless animal to put on trial and execute. This impulse to transfer evil onto an innocent victim continued well into the nineteenth century with the law of deodand – in British law, the deodand, or the instrument of crime like a knife or gun, had to be forfeited to Her Majesty and ultimately destroyed. The taint of crime infected even an inanimate object and the object had to be destroyed to prevent the taint from spreading like a virus. In the mid-twentieth century, we witnessed the greatest spectacle of scapegoating imaginable – the Holocaust. And in the later twentieth century, the modern state singled out the drug user as a scapegoat for urban decay.

It is a wonderful historical irony that the Greek scapegoat was called a *pharmakos*. As renegade psychiatrist Thomas Szasz likes to point out, 'the root of modern terms, such as pharmacology and pharmacopoeia, is therefore not "medicine," "drug" and "poison," as most dictionaries erroneously state, but "scapegoat."'[24] Those morally debased men and women who get stoned by partaking in the current illicit pharmacopoeia are today's *pharmakos*. Our cities are in decay, crime is rampant, and teenagers are educational failures. Why? It must be because people are taking drugs. State officials need people to believe that those who are shooting junk, smoking pot, or snorting coke are destroying the fabric of society by doing so. Billions of dollars are pumped into the war on drugs on the basis that casting out the drug user will lead to a modern, urban renaissance. This type of money is not spent on low-cost housing, employment opportunities, or education. It is spent on ridding society of the people who are apparently destroying our great society. I have never doubted that the state has cleverly converted the drug user into the *pharmakos* in order to cover up its inability to combat most social ills.

Admittedly, when you move from marijuana to heroin the risks associated with use are magnified, but instead of calling in Big Brother to scapegoat the smack-user, the increased risks simply require greater prudence and responsible planning by the drug user. People will pave their own roads to heaven or hell. In a free society, the path taken in search of paradise is a personal decision. You may end up in a detour and paradise becomes hell, but that is the price we pay for freedom. Freedom does have costs and some people will cause themselves harm, but should the vast majority of drug users, who exercise responsible choice, be demonized because a small percentage of their drug-taking colleagues are irresponsible or ill-suited for illicit-drug use?

The pursuit of intoxication is not a manifestation of sickness in modern society. Historically, drugs were an integral part of all pre-industrial religious experiences. Shamans could heal by entering into trance-like states induced by plant hallucinogenics. Tribes could achieve moments of great unity and communion by collective rites of passage through intoxication. I know that people largely dismiss shamanism as superstition and thus dismiss the relevance of the drug-taking components of these ancient rituals. Nonetheless, the historical and cultural prevalence of intoxicating activities does suggest that the pursuit of intoxication is an integral component of the human condition. Perhaps it is even an instinctual drive. Dr Robert Siegel has made a compelling case that the use of drugs is a fourth drive after hunger, thirst, and sex.[25] How else can one explain rats dancing around intoxicated after eating cannabis seeds, or boars digging up and eating the hallucinogenic Iboga plant, or cattle tripping out on locoweed, or snails getting stoned on coca leaves? Every species, from the smallest to the largest, looks for intoxication by ingesting plant products. Getting stoned is not solely related to some frivolous recreational activity of the jaded, postmodern urban dweller. For many people and for many animals, from the beginning of time, getting stoned has been as important as getting sex. Sex ensures the future existence of a species and drug-taking forays into paradise help the species get through the mundane drudgery of the present.

The law cannot curb the instinctive drive to get high. In previous centuries, rulers occasionally tried to prohibit mind-altering pursuits. When the Western world was first introduced to coffee and tobacco, rulers prohibited the use of these 'vicious' substances, but the prohibitions were always short-lived and quickly forgotten. Why would we resurrect a prohibitory policy which has always failed in past centuries? As a species we've done wonderful things with science and technology, but in terms of public policy we are often just groping in the dark.

As for the future, my dismay in reading the collection of essays contained in this book arose from my fear that reading about the historical evolution of our drug policy will not serve to protect us from repeating the folly of the past. However, with marijuana, there still remains some hope for progressive change. The state-sponsored image of deviancy cannot be dispelled solely by reliance upon empirical data and scientific analysis, since most people do not have the time, or the interest, to decipher the jargon of pharmacologists or psychologists. Most of us rely upon the sound-bite construction of deviancy uttered by politicians who usually have hidden agendas and an unthinking reverence for waging war as the metaphoric solution for all social problems. The state's construction of the deviant can be dispelled only when the hundreds of thousands of aging lawyers, doctors, corporate executives, and religious leaders acknowledge that they can and do enjoy illicit drugs without necessarily becoming the state stereotype of the dishevelled and degenerate drug abuser. When the late Pierre Berton boldly acknowledged his love of the cannabis plant and demonstrated his joint-rolling prowess on television with Rick Mercer, this single act of courage had greater potential to dismantle the war on drugs than the collective hubris of thousands of youthful activists taking to the streets and the parks to smoke gigantic joints when the clock strikes 4:20 p.m.

The legacy of the psychedelic 1960s does not shine very brightly when it comes to the very essence of this era – the use of illicit, mind-altering drugs. Some of these hippies, now turning grandparents, still indulge, but fear of stigma, born of the state's construction of deviancy, forces many of these mature, responsible users to take a vow of silence about their indulgences. Regardless of whether the baby boomer remains a drug user, the fact remains that there are very few boomers who speak out against a policy they flouted in their youth. And by counselling their children to abstain, they become the very hypocrites they rebelled against when they were once full of life. Regrettably, the key to any progressive drug-law reform lies in the hands of all the middle-aged and elderly drug users who once extolled the virtues of mind-manifesting drugs and now quietly acquiesce in the state's construction of their past, and perhaps present, choices as those of deviant degenerates.

NOTES

1 Jarrett Rudy, 'Unmaking Manly Smokes: Church, State, Governance, and the First Anti-Smoking Campaigns in Montreal, 1892–1914,' in this volume.

2 Greg Marquis, 'From Beverage to Drug: Alcohol and Other Drugs in 1960s and 1970s Canada,' in this volume.

3 See, for example, Bernard Aaronson and Humphry Osmond, *Psychedelics* (New York: Doubleday 1970).

4 United Nations Office on Drugs and Crime, *2008 World Drug Report*, 111.

5 United Nations Office on Drugs and Crime, *2007 World Drug Report*; CBC News, 'The Drug Trade,' 6 July 2007, http://www.cbc.ca/news/background/drugs/users/html (accessed 14 August 2008).

6 *Medical Marihuana Access Regulations*, SOR/2001–227.

7 E. Abel, *Marijuana, The First 12,000 years* (New York: Plenum Press 1980).

8 M. Tjepkema, 'Use of Cannabis and Other Illicit Drugs,' *Health Reports*, 15, no. 4 (2004): 43–7.

9 Emily Murphy, *The Black Candle* (Toronto: Coles, 1922/1973), 332.

10 *Toronto Star*, 2 February 1938.

11 M. Wente, 'Not the Groovy 60s: Today's Cannabis Is Harder and Meaner,' *Globe and Mail*, 26 June 2007, A17.

12 Canada, House of Commons, *Policy for the New Millennium: Working Together to Redefine Canada's Drug Strategy*, Report of the Special Committee on Non-Medical Use of Drugs (Ottawa: Public Works and Government Services 2002); Canada, Senate, *Cannabis: Our Position for a Canadian Public Policy*, Report of the Senate Special Committee on Illegal Drugs (Ottawa: Public Works and Government Services 2002).

13 Of course, there still remains a heated debate regarding the health risks. However, the Senate Committee (note 12), the House of Commons Committee (note 12), and the Caine/Malmo-Levine and Clay cases (note 14) all concluded that marijuana is relatively harmless. In a brief afterword of this nature, I do not intend to provide complete citations for this 'controversial' proposition; however, I would commend the reader to commence his/her inquiries by reading L. Zimmer and J. Morgan, *Marijuana Myths, Marijuana Facts: A Review of the Scientific Evidence* (New York: Mirror Image Printing & Graphics 1997).

14 Angus Reid Strategies, *Drugs a National Problem – Canadians Would Mix Grit & Tory Policies* (2007); Angus Reid Strategies, *Canadians Support Some of the Federal Government's Policies, Express Concern about a National Drug Abuse Problem* (2007); Angus Reid Strategies, *Canadian Majority Would Legalize Marijuana* (2008). In terms of public-opinion polls from the 1970s and

1980s, the Supreme Court of Canada in *R. v. Clay* (2003, 179 C.C.C. [3d] 540 [S.C.C.]), *R. v. Malmo-Levine,* and *R. v. Caine* ([2003] 3 SCR 571) remarked on the consistency of a majority of Canadians in supporting law reform, whether by decriminalization or legalization.

15 *Ottawa Citizen,* 'Life's A Risky Business: Health and Accident Statistics,' 8 August 1997.

16 See *R. v. Malmo-Levine; R. v. Caine.* In fact, the evidence before the Court clearly demonstrated that less than 2 per cent of cannabis users are chronic, but the Court held that the evidence demonstrates that up to 5 per cent of users are chronic.

17 *R. v. Clay; R. v. Malmo-Levine; R. v. Caine.*

18 Janine Benedet, 'Hierarchies of Harm in Canadian Criminal Law: The Marijuana Trilogy and the Forcible "Correction" of Children' (2004) 24 Sup. Ct. L. Rev. (2d) 217; Paul Burstein, 'What's the Harm in Having a "Harm Principle" Enshrined in Section 7 of the Charter?' (2004) 24 S.C.L.R. (2d) 159; Alan Young, 'Fundamental Justice and Political Power: A Personal Reflection on Twenty Years in the Trenches' (2002), 16 S.C.L.R. (2d) 122.

19 *R. v. Butler* (1992), 70 C.C.C. (3d) 129 (S.C.C.) at para. 23.

20 *R. v. Clay* (2000) 146 C.C.C. (3d) 276 (Ont. C.A.); *R. v. Caine; R. v. Malmo-Levine* (2000) 145 C.C.C. (3d) 225 (B.C.C.A.); *R. v. Murdock* (2003), 176 C.C.C. (3d) 232 (Ont. C.A.).

21 George P. Fletcher, 'The Nature and Function of Criminal Theory' (2000) 88 Cal. L. Rev. 687 at 700.

22 Government of Canada, *The Criminal Law in Canadian Society* (Ottawa, 1982); Law Reform Commission of Canada, *Our Criminal Law* (Ottawa, 1976); Canadian Committee on Corrections, *Toward Unity: Criminal Justice and Corrections* (1969).

23 Fletcher, 'Nature and Function,' 698.

24 T. Szasz, *Cermonial Chemistry: The Ritual Persecution of Drugs, Addicts, and Pushers* (New York: Anchor Press/Doubleday 1974), 19.

25 R. Siegel, *Intoxication: Life in Pursuit of Artificial Paradise* (New York: E.P. Dutton 1989).

Contributors

Line Beauchesne is a doctor of political science, specializing in security and governance, and full professor in the Department of Criminology, University of Ottawa. Line Beauchesne is the author of many briefs and articles as well as a number of books on state policy and prevention of drug abuse, including: *Les drogues: légalisation et promotion de la santé* (Bayard Canada 2006); *Les drogues: les coûts caches de la prohibition* (Bayard Canada 2004); *Drogues, mythes et dependance, en parler aux enfants* (Bayard Canada 2005); *Les sports et la drogue* (with Éric Giguère) (Éditions du Méridien 1994); and *Légaliser les drogues pour mieux en prévenir les abus* (Éditions du Méridien 1991). She was the co-founder and first chair of MAGE (Mouvement pour des alternatives à la guerre à la drogue), a member of GREPO (Groupe de recherche sur la production de l'ordre), and a founding member of the Canadian Foundation for Drug Policy, as well as being, for many years, a member of the board of AITQ (Association des Intervenants en toxicomanies du Québec) and a member of CACTUS (needle-exchange service).

Catherine Carstairs is an associate professor of history at the University of Guelph. She is the author of *Jailed for Possession: Illegal Drug Use, Regulation and Power in Canada, 1920–1961* (University of Toronto Press 2006). She has published articles on water fluoridation in the *Canadian Historical Review* (2008) and *The Journal of Canadian Studies* (2010), on 'Roots Nationalism' in *Histoire Sociale/Social History* (2006), on international drug control in the *Drug and Alcohol Review* (2005), and on doping in sport in *Addiction Research & Theory* (2003). She is currently working on a book on the history of water fluoridation and on biographies of two American health-food writers.

Sharon Anne Cook is professor of educational history at the University of Ottawa in the Faculty of Education. She directs the Educational Research Unit, *Making History: Narratives and Collective Memory in Education/Faire de l'histoire: Récits et mémoires collectives en éducation*. Among its several aims is the acquisition and collecting of archival sources from educational sites throughout the Outaouais Region by using oral history. She is the author or editor of eight books in education and history as well as about fifty scholarly and professional articles and chapters, and her research interests extend to issues of pedagogy, especially related to teaching peace and development education, history, citizenship and health, equity and gender, and the intersections of the history of women, education, and addictions through visual culture. Her latest book is *Sex, Lies and Cigarettes: Canadian Women, Smoking and Visual Culture, 1880–2000* (McGill-Queen's University Press, forthcoming.)

Erika Dyck is an associate professor and Tier 2 Canada Research Chair in History of Medicine at the University of Saskatchewan. In 2005 she received a PhD in history from McMaster University, preceded by an MA from the University of Saskatchewan (2000) and a BA from Dalhousie University (1997). From 2005 to 2008 she was cross-appointed to the departments of history and classics in the Faculty of Arts and the Division of Studies in Medical Education in the Faculty of Medicine and Dentistry, as co-director of the History of Medicine Program. In 2008 she published *Psychedelic Psychiatry: LSD from Clinic to Campus* (Johns Hopkins University Press).

Kyle Grayson (PhD, York University) is a lecturer in international politics at Newcastle University, United Kingdom. Previously, he was a post-doctoral fellow of the Canadian Consortium on Human Security and associate director of the York University Centre for International and Security Studies. He has also been a visiting professor at l'Institut d'Etudes Politiques (Paris) and the University of Tromso (Norway). His first book, *Chasing Dragons: Security, Identity, and Illicit Drugs in Canada*, was published by the University of Toronto Press in 2008. Other work has appeared in *Canadian Foreign Policy, Security Dialogue, International Journal*, the *Cambridge Review of International Affairs*, and *Politics* (with Matt Davies and Simon Philpott). He is currently working on a manuscript that explores the ways that assassination has been problematized across a range of strategic, political, cultural, and legal discourses. His blog is available at www.chasingdragons.org.

Dan Malleck is an associate professor in the Department of Community Health Sciences at Brock University, where he teaches the history of medicine. He is also the editor-in-chief of the *Social History of Alcohol and Drugs: An Interdisciplinary Journal*, published by the Alcohol and Drugs History Society. His academic and personal life is heavily invested in issues related to alcohol and drug control in Canada.

Greg Marquis is a professor of history at the University of New Brunswick, Saint John. He is a graduate of St Francis Xavier University (BA Hon. 1980), the University of New Brunswick (MA 1982), and Queen's University (PhD 1987). His research interests include criminal justice history, urban history, popular culture, and the history of alcohol and drugs. At present he is working on a book on the history of alcohol control in Canada from Confederation until free trade.

Marcel Martel is an associate professor and holder of the Avie Bennett Historical Chair in Canadian History at York University. A specialist of twentieth-century Canada, he has published on nationalism, public policy, and counterculture. His recent publications include *Not This Time: Canadians, Public Policy and the Marijuana Question 1961–1975* (University of Toronto Press 2006); '"They Smell Bad, Have Diseases, and Are Lazy": RCMP Officers Reporting on Hippies in the Late Sixties,' *Canadian Historical Review*, 90, no. 2 (2009): 215–45; and, with Martin Pâquet, *Langue et politique au Canada et au Québec* (Boréal 2010)

Edgar-André Montigny obtained a PhD in Canadian history from the University of Ottawa in 1994, his dissertation focusing on the impact of social policy on Canadian families. In addition to a number of articles, he has published *Foisted upon the Government: State Responsibilities, Family Obligations, and the Care of the Dependent Aged in Late-Nineteenth-Century Ontario* (McGill-Queen's University Press 1997); and he has co-edited (with Lori Chambers) two collections, *Family Matters: Papers in Post-Confederation Family History* (Canadian Scholars' Press 1998) and *Ontario since Confederation* (University of Toronto Press 2000). He was also assistant editor and contributor to *Ontario Courtroom Procedure* (LexisNexis 2007 and 2009). Called to the Ontario bar in 2004, he is currently a staff lawyer with ARCH Disability Law Centre and is active on a number of committees of the Canadian and Ontario bar associations.

Dawn Moore is an assistant professor in the Department of Law, Carleton University. She is currently working on a three-year SSHRC-funded project examining the experiences of women in Drug Treatment Courts across the country. Her chapter in this collection builds on her earlier work on the rise of addiction treatment in the criminal justice system. In her teaching she draws on feminism, queer theory, risk, governmentality, political economy, and post-colonial theory to help students better understand the justice system. She is the author of *Criminal Artefacts: Governing, Drugs and Users* (University of British Columbia Press 2007). Dr Moore is managing editor of the *Canadian Journal of Law and Society/ Revue Canadienne du Droit et Société*.

Jarrett Rudy is an associate professor in the History Department at McGill University and director of McGill's Quebec Studies Program. He is the author of *The Freedom to Smoke: Tobacco Consumption and Identity* (McGill-Queen's University Press 2005), a co-editor of *Quebec Questions: Quebec Studies for the Twenty-First Century* (Oxford University Press of Canada 2010), and a member of the Montreal History Group.

Alan Young is an associate professor of law at Osgoode Hall Law School in Toronto, Ontario. He also maintains a small practice specializing in criminal law and procedure, largely devoted to challenging state authority to criminalize consensual activity. He has brought constitutional challenges to gambling, obscenity, bawdy-house, and drug laws and for ten years has provided free legal services for people whose alternative lifestyles have brought them into conflict with the law, including the 'bondage bungalow' dominatrix. Between 1998 and 2000 he played an integral part in compelling the federal government to take action to recognize the medicinal value of marijuana. In 1997 he co-founded the Innocence Project at Osgoode Hall Law School, which provides legal assistance for individuals who claim to have been wrongfully convicted and imprisoned. He is the author of *Justice Defiled: Perverts, Potheads, Serial Killers and Lawyers* (Key Porter 2003).

Index